Meriwether Lewis, William Clark, Paul Allen

History of the Expedition

Under the command of Captains Lewis and Clark, to the sources of Missouri,

thence across the Rocky Mountains, and down the river Columbia to the Pacific

Ocean. Vol. 2

Meriwether Lewis, William Clark, Paul Allen

History of the Expedition
Under the command of Captains Lewis and Clark, to the sources of Missouri, thence across the Rocky Mountains, and down the river Columbia to the Pacific Ocean. Vol. 2

ISBN/EAN: 9783337191443

Printed in Europe, USA, Canada, Australia, Japan

Cover: Foto ©Andreas Hilbeck / pixelio.de

More available books at **www.hansebooks.com**

HISTORY

OF

THE EXPEDITION

UNDER THE COMMAND OF
CAPTAINS LEWIS AND CLARKE,

TO

THE SOURCES OF THE MISSOURI, THENCE ACROSS THE ROCKY
MOUNTAINS, AND DOWN THE RIVER COLUMBIA TO THE
PACIFIC OCEAN : PERFORMED DURING THE
YEARS 1804, 1805, 1806,

BY ORDER OF THE

GOVERNMENT OF THE UNITED STATES.

PREPARED FOR THE PRESS

BY PAUL ALLEN, ESQ.

REVISED, AND ABRIDGED BY THE OMISSION OF UMIMPORTANT DE-
TAILS, WITH AN INTRODUCTION AND NOTES,

BY ARCHIBALD M'VICKAR.

IN TWO VOLUMES.

VOL. II

NEW YORK:

HARPER & BROTHERS, PUBLISHERS,
FRANKLIN SQUARE.

1868.

CONTENTS

OF

THE SECOND VOLUME.

CHAPTER IV.

CHAPTER V.

CHAPTER VI.

CHAPTER VII.

CHAPTER VIII.

CHAPTER IX.

CHAPTER X.

CHAPTER XI.

CHAPTER XV.

CHAPTER XVI.

CHAPTER XVII.

CHAPTER XVIII.

II.—B

CHAPTER XIX.

APPENDIX.

PLATES.

UP THE MISSOURI.

CHAPTER I.

The Party, after procuring Horses from the Shoshonees, proceed on their Journey through the Mountains.—Difficulties and Dangers of the Route.—Council held with another Band of the Shoshonees, of whom some Account is given.—They are reduced to the Necessity of killing their Horses for food.—Captain Clarke, with a small Party, precedes the main Body in quest of Provisions, and is hospitably received by the Pierced-Nose Indians.—Arrival of the main Body among this Tribe, with whom a Council is held.—They resolve to perform the Remainder of their Journey in Canoes.—Sickness among the Party.—They descend the Kooskooskee to its Junction with Lewis River, after passing several dangerous Rapids.—Brief Description of the Manners and Dress of the Pierced-Nose Indians.

" August 27. We were now occupied in determining on our route and in procuring horses from the Indians. The old guide who had been sent on by Captain Clarke now affirmed, through our interpreter, what he had already asserted of a road up Berry Creek, which would lead to Indian establishments on another branch of the Columbia: his reports were, however, contradicted by all the Shoshonees. This representation we ascribed to a wish on their part to keep us with them during the winter, as well for the protection we might afford them against their enemies, as for the purpose of consuming our mer-

chandise among them ; and as the old man promised to conduct us himself, the route indicated by him
seemed to be the most eligible. We were able to
procure some horses, though not enough for all our
purposes. This traffic, and our councils with the
Indians, consumed the remainder of the day.

" August 28. The purchase of horses was resumed,
and our stock raised to twenty-two. Having now
crossed more than once the country which separates
the head-waters of the Missouri from those of the
Columbia, we can designate the easiest and most ex-
peditious route for a portage. It is as follows :

" From the forks of the river, north 60 degrees
west, five miles, to the point of a hill on the right ;
then south 80 degrees west, ten miles, to a spot
where the creek is ten yards wide, and the highlands
approach within two hundred yards ; southwest five
miles, to a narrow part of the bottom ; then turning
south 70 degrees west, two miles, to a creek on the
right ; thence south 80 degrees west, three miles, to
a rocky point opposite to a thicket of pines on the
left ; thence west three miles, to the gap where is
the fountain of the Missouri ; on leaving this fountain, south 80 degrees west, six miles, across the dividing ridge to a run from the right, passing several
small streams north 80 degrees west, four miles,
over hilly ground to the east fork of Lewis's River,
which is here forty yards wide.*

---

* Since the time of Lewis and Clarke, a far more practicable
route has been discovered across the mountains, farther south,
by ascending the Platte River instead of the Missouri.
Mr. Parker, who left Council Bluffs with a party of the American Fur Company in 1835, and crossed the Rocky Mountains
by this southern route, says : " The passage through these
mountains is in a valley so gradual in the ascent and descent,
that I should not have known that we were passing them, had
it not been that, as we advanced, the atmosphere gradually be
came cooler ; and at length we found perpetual snows upon our
right hand and upon our left, elevated many thousand feet above
us, in some places ten thousand. The highest part of these

"August 29. Captain Clarke joined us this morning, and we continued bargaining for horses. The late misfortunes of the Shoshonees have made the price higher than common, so that one horse cost us a pistol, one hundred balls, some powder, and a knife ; another was purchased with a musket ; and in this way we finally obtained twenty-nine. The animals are young and vigorous, but very poor, and most of them have sore backs, in consequence of the roughness of the Shoshonee saddle. We are therefore afraid of burdening them too heavily, and are anxious to obtain one, at least, for each man, to carry the baggage or the man himself, or in the last resource to serve as food ; but with all our exertions we are unable to provide all our men with horses. We have, however, been fortunate in obtaining for the last three days a sufficient supply of flesh, our hunters having killed two or three deer every day.

"August 30. The weather was fine, and, having now made all our purchases, we loaded our horses and prepared to start. The greater part of the band, also, who had delayed their journey on our account, were ready to depart. We now took our leave of the Shoshonees, who set out on their visit to the Missouri at the same time that we, accompanied by the old guide, his four sons, and another Indian, began the descent of the river, along the same road which Captain Clarke had previously followed."

Before night they accomplished a distance of

mountains is found by measurement to be eighteen thousand feet above the level of the sea. This valley was not discovered until a few years since. Mr. Hunt and his party more than twenty years ago went near it, but did not find it, though in search of some favourable passage. It varies in width from five to twenty miles ; and, following its course, the distance through the mountains is about eighty miles, or four days' journey. Though there are some elevations and depressions in this valley, yet, comparatively speaking, it is level. *There would be no difficulty in the way of constructing a railroad from the Atlantic to the Pacific Ocean.*"—*Parker's Journal*, p. 72.

twelve miles. The following day they found the valleys and prairies in different places on fire, as a signal to collect the different bands of Shoshonees and Flatheads, preparatory to their migration to the Missouri. On reaching Tower Creek, they diverged from the former route taken by Captain Clarke, and followed for four miles the course of Berry Creek. On the 1st of September, quitting Berry Creek, they turned to the northwest, and, after travelling eighteen miles across a hilly country, they arrived at Fish Creek, a considerable stream flowing into the Columbia; and, after going up this creek four miles, they encamped. The next morning all the Indians left them except the old guide. In continuing to ascend Fish Creek, at the distance of seven and a half miles they found it divided into two branches, and the road they had been following turning to the east, and leading, as their guide informed them, to the Missouri.

"We were therefore," proceeds the narrative, "left without any track; but, as no time was to be lost, we began to cut our road up the west branch of the creek. This we effected with much difficulty. The thickets of trees and brush through which we were obliged to cut our way required great labour: the road itself was over the steep and rocky sides of the hills, where the horses could not move without danger of slipping down, while their feet were bruised by the rocks and stumps of trees. Accustomed as these animals were to this kind of travelling, they suffered severely: several of them fell some distance down the sides of the hills, some turned over with the baggage, one was crippled, and two gave out, exhausted with fatigue. After crossing the creek several times, we at length made five miles with great fatigue and labour, and encamped on the left bank, in some stony, low ground." * * *

"September 3. The horses were very stiff and weary. We sent back two men for the load of the horse which had been crippled yesterday, and which we had been forced to leave two miles behind.   On their return we set out at eight o'clock, and proceeded up the creek, making a passage through the brush and timber along its borders.   The country generally is well supplied with pine, and in the low grounds is a great abundance of fir-trees and under-brush.   The mountains are high and rugged, and those to the east of us covered with snow.   With all our precautions, the horses were very much injured in passing over the ridges and steep points of the hills, and, to add to the difficulty, at the distance of eleven miles the high mountains closed upon the creek, so that we were obliged to leave it to the right, and abruptly cross the mountain.   The ascent was here so steep that several of the horses slipped and hurt themselves ; but at last we succeeded in getting across, and encamped on a small branch of Fish Creek.   We had now made fourteen miles, in a direction nearly north from the river." * * * " At dusk it commenced snowing, and continued till the ground was covered to the depth of two inches, when it changed into a sleet.   We here met with a serious misfortune, the last of our thermometers being broken by accident.   After making a scanty supper on a little corn and a few pheasants killed in the course of the day, we laid down to sleep, and the next morning,

" September 4, found everything frozen, and the ground covered with snow.   We were obliged to wait some time, in order to thaw the covers of the baggage, after which we began our journey at eight o'clock.   We crossed a high mountain, which forms the dividing ridge between the waters of the creek we had been ascending, and those running to the north and west.   We had not gone more than six miles over the snow, when we reached the head of a stream from the right, which directed its course more to the west ; and, descending the steep sides of the hills along its border, at the distance of three miles found a small branch coming in from the east. We saw several of the argalia, but they were too shy to be killed, and we therefore made our dinner from a deer shot by one of the hunters. Then we pursued the course of the stream for three miles, till it emptied itself into a river from the east. In the wide valley at their junction we discovered a large encampment of Indians; and on reaching them, and alighting from our horses, we were received with great cordiality. A council was immediately assembled, white robes were thrown over our shoulders, and the pipe of peace was introduced. After this ceremony, as it was too late to go any farther, we encamped, and continued smoking and conversing with the chiefs till a late hour. The next morning,

"September 5, we assembled the chiefs and warriors, and informed them who we were, and the purpose for which we had visited their country. All this was, however, conveyed to them through so many different languages, that it was not comprehended without difficulty. We therefore proceeded to the more intelligible language of presents, and made four chiefs by giving a medal and a small quantity of tobacco to each. We received in turn from the principal chief a present consisting of the skins of a *blaireau* (badger), an otter, and two ante lopes, and were treated by the women to some dried roots and berries. We then began to traffic for horses, and succeeded in exchanging seven and purchasing eleven, for which we gave a few articles of merchandise.

" This encampment consists of thirty-three tents, in which were about four hundred souls, among whom eighty were men. They are called Ootla shoots, and represent themselves as one band of a nation called Tushepaws, a numerous people of four hundred and fifty tents, residing on the head-waters of the Missouri and Columbia Rivers, and some of them lower down the latter river. In person these Indians are stout, and their complexion lighter than that common among Indians. The hair of the men is worn in queues of otter skin, falling in front over the shoulders. A shirt of dressed skin covers the body to the knee, and over this is worn occasionally a robe. To these are added leggins and moccasins. The women suffer their hair to fall in disorder over the face and shoulders, and their chief article of covering is a long shirt of skin, reaching down to the ankles, and tied round the waist. In other respects, as also in the few ornaments which they possess, their appearance is similar to that of the Shoshonees : there is, however, a difference between the languages of these two people, which is still farther increased by the very extraordinary pronunciation of the Ootlashoots. Their words have all a remarkably guttural sound, and there is nothing which seems to represent the tone of their speaking more exactly than the clucking of a fowl or the noise of a parrot. This peculiarity renders their voices scarcely audible, except at a short distance ; and, when many of them are talking, forms a strange confusion of sounds. The common conversation that we overheard consisted of low, guttural sounds, occasionally broken by a low word or two, after which it would relapse, and could scarcely be dis-tinguished. They seemed kind and friendly, and willingly shared with us berries and roots, which formed their sole stock of provisions. Their only wealth is their horses, which are very fine, and so numerous that this party had with them at least five hundred.

" September 6. We spent the morning with the Ootlashoots, from whom we purchased two more horses, and obtained a vocabulary of their language. They set off about two o'clock to join the different bands who were collecting at the Three Forks of the Missouri, and we ourselves proceeded at the same time. Taking a direction north 30° west, we crossed, within the distance of a mile and a half, a small river from the right, and a creek coming in from the north. The river is the main stream, and when it reaches the end of the valley where the mountains close in upon it, it is joined by the stream on which we encamped last evening, as well as by the creek just mentioned. To the river thus formed we gave the name of Clarke, he being the first white man who had ever visited its waters. At the end of five miles on this course we crossed the valley, and reached the top of a mountain covered with pine : this we descended along the steep sides and ravines for a mile and a half, when we came to a spot on the river where the Ootlashoots had encamped a few days before. We then followed the course of the stream, which is from twenty-five to thirty yards wide, shallow and stony, and the low grounds on its borders narrow. Within the distance of three and a half miles we crossed it several times; and, after passing a run on each side, encamped on its right bank, having made ten miles during the afternoon. The horses were turned out to graze ; but those we had lately bought were secured and watched, lest they should escape, or be stolen by their former owners. Our stock of flour was now exhausted, and we had but little corn ; and, as our hunters had killed nothing except two pheasants, our supper consisted chiefly of berries."

The two following days they continued to follow the course of the river, being fortunate in procuring game, and encountering no particular difficulty. They were not a little annoyed, however, by the prickly pear, which, says the journalist, "grows here in clusters, is of an oval form, about the size of a pigeon's egg, and its thorns are so strong and bearded, that, when it penetrates our feet, it brings away the pear itself." Several horses were seen, which appeared to be in a wild state. They passed a small stream falling into the river, to which, from its having several channels, they gave the name of Scattering Creek.

"September 9. We resumed our journey," continues the narrative, "through the valley, and, leaving the road on our right, crossed Scattering Creek, and halted, at the distance of twelve miles, on a small run from the east, where we breakfasted on the remains of yesterday's hunt. We here took a meridian altitude, which gave the latitude of 46° 41' 38"; after which we proceeded on, and at the distance of four miles passed over to the left bank of the river, where we found a large road through the valley. At this place is a handsome stream of very clear water, a hundred yards wide, with low banks, and a bed formed entirely of gravel: it has every appearance of being navigable; but, as it contains no salmon, we presume there must be some fall below which obstructs their passage. Our guide could not inform us where this river discharged its waters. He said that, as far as he knew its course, it ran along the mountains to the north, and that not far from our present position it was joined by another stream nearly as large as itself, rising in the mountains to the east, near the Missouri, and flowing through an extensive valley or open prairie. Through this prairie was the great Indian road to the waters of the Missouri; and so direct was the route, that in four days' journey from this place we might reach the Missouri about thirty miles above what we called the Gates of the Rocky Mountains, or the spot where the valley of that river widens into an extensive plain on entering the chain of mountains. At ten miles from our camp was a small creek falling in from the eastward; five miles below which we halted, on a large stream, which empties itself on the west side of the river. It is a fine, bold stream of clear water, about twenty yards wide, and we

called it Traveller's-rest Creek; for, as our guide
told us that we should here leave the river, we determined to stop for the purpose of taking celestial
observations and collecting some food, as the country through which we were to pass had no game for
a great distance." * * *

"September 10. The morning being fair, all the
hunters were sent out, and the rest of the party employed in repairing their clothes: two of them were
despatched to the junction of the river from the east,
along which the Indians go to the Missouri, and
which is about seven miles below Traveller's-rest
Creek." * * *

"Towards evening one of the hunters returned
with three Indians, whom he had met in his excursion
up Traveller's-rest Creek.   As soon as they saw him
they prepared to attack him with arrows; but he pa-
cified them by laying down his gun, and, advancing
towards them, soon persuaded them to come to the
camp.   Our Shoshonee guide could not speak the
language of these people; but, by the universal language of signs and gesticulations, which is perfectly
intelligible among the Indians, he found that they
were three Tushepaw Flatheads, in pursuit of two
men, supposed to be Shoshonees. who had stolen
twenty-three of their horses.   We gave them some
boiled venison and a few presents, such as a fish-hook,
a steel to strike fire, and a little powder; but they
seemed best pleased with a piece of riband which we
tied in the hair of each of them.   They were in such
haste, however, lest their horses should be carried
off, that two of them set off after sunset in quest of
the robbers; but the third was persuaded to remain
with us, and to conduct us to his relations.   These,
he said, were numerous, and resided on the Columbia, in the plain below the mountains.   From that
place, he added, the river was navigable to the ocean.
that some of his kinsmen had been there last fall, and
seen an old white man, who resided there by himself,

and who gave them some handkerchiefs like those we have. The distance from this place was five sleeps, or days' journeys. When our hunters had all joined us, we found our provisions consisted of four deer, a beaver, and three grouse. The observation of to-day gave 46° 48′ 28″ as the latitude of Traveller's-rest Creek."

They were detained the whole of the next morning to recover some of their horses which had strayed away, so that they advanced but seven miles during the remainder of the day. The Indian became impatient to return home, and left them.

"September 12. We proceeded," continues the Journal, "at seven o'clock, and soon passed a stream falling in on the right, near which was an old Indian camp, with a bath or sweating-house covered with earth. At two miles' distance we ascended a high bank, and thence passed through a hilly and thickly-timbered country for nine miles, when we came to the forks of the creek, where the road branches up each fork. We followed the western route; and, finding that the creek made a considerable bend at the distance of four miles, crossed a high mountain in order to avoid the circuit. The road had been very bad during the first part of the day; but the passage over the mountain, which was eight miles across, was exceedingly trying to the horses, as we were obliged to go over steep, stony sides of hills, and along hollows and ravines, rendered still more troublesome by the fallen timber, chiefly pine, spruce-pine, and fir. We at length reached the creek, having made twenty-three miles on a route so difficult that some of the party did not join us before ten o'clock. We found the accounts of scantiness of game but too true, as we were not able to procure any during the whole of yesterday, and to-day we killed only a single pheasant. Along the road we observed many of the pine-trees peeled off, which is done by the Indians to procure the inner bark for food in the spring.

"September 13. Two of the horses strayed away during the night, and one of them being Captain Lewis's, he remained with four men to seek for them, while we proceeded up the creek. At the distance of two miles we came to several springs, issuing from large rocks of a coarse, hard grit, and nearly boiling hot. They seem to be much frequented, as there are several paths made by elk, deer, and other animals, and near one of them there is a hole or Indian bath, besides roads leading in different directions. These embarrassed our guide, who, making a mistake, took us three miles out of the proper course, over an exceedingly bad route. We then fell into the right road, and proceeded on very well, when, having made five miles, we stopped to refresh the horses. Captain Lewis here joined us; but, not having been able to find his horse, two men were sent back to continue the search."

They advanced till the evening, and encamped on a stream to which they gave the name of Glade Creek.

Starting early the next morning, they advanced along the right bank of Glade Creek, and at the distance of six miles found it joined by another of equal size, coming from the right. "Here," says the Journal, "we passed over to the left side of the creek, and began the ascent of a very high and steep mountain, nine miles across. On reaching the other side, we found a large branch from the left, which seems to rise in the Snowy Mountains to the south and southeast." * * * "The mountains we crossed to-day were much more difficult than those of yesterday : the last was particularly fatiguing, being steep and stony, broken by fallen timber, and thickly overgrown by pine, spruce, fir, hacmatack, and tamarac. Although we had made only seventeen miles, we were all very weary. Our whole stock of animal food was now exhausted, and we therefore killed a colt, on which we made a hearty sup-

per. From this incident we called the last creek
we had passed from the south Colt-killed Creek.
The river itself is eighty yards wide, with a swift
current and a stony channel. Its Indian name is
Kooskooskee.

"September 15. At an early hour we proceeded
along the right side of the Kooskooskee, over steep,
rocky points of land, till at the distance of four
miles we reached an old Indian fishing-place. The
road here turned to the right of the river, and began
to ascend a mountain; but the wind and the fire had
prostrated or scorched almost all the timber on the
south side, and the ascents were so steep that we
were forced to wind in every direction round the
high knobs, which constantly impeded our progress.
Several of the horses lost their foothold and slipped: one of them, which was loaded with a desk
and small trunk, rolled over and over for forty yards,
till his fall was stopped by a tree. The desk was
broken, but the poor animal escaped without much
injury. After clambering in this way for four miles,
we came to a high, snowy part of the mountain,
where was a spring of water, at which we halted
two hours to refresh our horses.

"On leaving the spring the road continued as bad
as it was below, and the timber more abundant. At
four miles we reached the top of the mountain, and,
foreseeing no chance of meeting with water, we encamped on the northern side, near an old bank of
snow three feet deep. Some of this we melted,
and supped on the remains of the colt killed yesterday. Our only game to-day was two pheasants;
and the horses, on which we calculated as a last resource, began to fail us, for two of them were so
poor and worn out with fatigue that we were obliged to leave them behind. All around us were high,
rugged mountains, among which was a lofty range
from southeast to northwest, whose tops were without timber, and in some places covered with snow.

The night was cloudy and very cold, and three hours before daybreak,

"September 16, it began to snow, and continued all day, so that by evening it was six or eight inches deep. This covered the track so completely that we were obliged constantly to halt and examine, lest we should lose our way. In many places we had nothing to guide us except the branches of the trees, which, being low, have been rubbed by the burdens of the Indian horses. The road was, like that of yesterday, along steep hillsides obstructed with fallen timber, and having a growth of eight different species of pine, standing so thick that the snow fell from them as we passed, and kept us continually wet to the skin, and so cold that we were anxious lest our feet should be frozen, as we had only thin moccasins to defend them.

"At noon we halted to let the horses feed on some long grass on the north side of the mountain, and endeavoured, by making fires, to keep ourselves warm. As soon as the horses were refreshed, Captain Clarke went ahead with one man, and at the distance of six miles reached a stream from the right, and prepared fires by the time of our arrival at dusk." * * * " We were all very wet, cold, and hungry : although before setting out this morning we had seen four deer, we could not procure any of them, and were obliged to kill a second colt for our supper."

The two following days they encountered similar difficulties from the ruggedness of the country and the absence of game, so that they were obliged to kill another colt for their subsistence. On the evening of the 18th they encamped, after a fatiguing day's journey of eighteen miles. " We now," continues the Journal, " melted some snow, and supped on a little portable soup, a few canisters of which, with about twenty pounds of bears' oil, are our only remaining means of subsistence. Our guns are scarcely of any service, for there is no living creature in these mountains, except a few small pheasants, a small species of gray squirrel, and a blue bird of the vulture kind, about the size of a turtle-dove or jay, and even these are difficult to shoot."

Captain Clarke, meanwhile, had proceeded in advance of the party, with six hunters, for the purpose of procuring game. In this, however, they were wholly unsuccessful; and, without anything to eat, they encamped in the evening on the banks of a stream, to which they gave the appropriate name of Hungry Creek.

"September 19. Captain Clarke proceeded up the creek, along which the road was more steep and stony than any he had yet passed. At six miles' distance he reached a small plain, in which he fortunately found a horse, on which he breakfasted, and hung the rest on a tree for the party in the rear. Two miles beyond this he left the creek and crossed three high mountains, rendered almost impassable from the steepness of the ascent and the quantity of fallen timber. After clambering over these ridges and mountains, and passing some branches of Hungry Creek, he came to a large creek running westward. This he followed for four miles, then turned to the right down the mountain, till he came to a small creek to the left. Here he halted, having made twenty-two miles on his course, south 80 degrees west, though the winding route over the mountains almost doubled the distance. On descending the last mountain, the heat became much more sensible, after the extreme cold he had experienced for several days past."

The main party advanced eighteen miles over mountains and along narrow, dangerous paths, and encamped for the night on a branch of Hungry Creek. They killed no game, and their only refreshment during the day was a little portable soup. From fatigue and want of food they were becoming much enfeebled, and dysentery began to prevail.

II.—C

" September 20. Captain Clarke went on through a country as rugged as before, till, on passing a low mountain, at the distance of four miles he came to the forks of a large creek. Down this he proceeded on a course south 60 degrees west for two miles, then turning to the right, continued over a dividing ridge, where were the heads of several little streams, and at twelve miles' distance descended the last of the Rocky Mountains, and reached the level country. A beautiful open plain, partially supplied with pine, now presented itself. After proceeding five miles, he discovered three Indian boys, who, on observing the party, ran off and hid themselves in the grass. Captain Clarke immediately alighted, and, giving his horse and gun to one of the men, went after the boys. He soon relieved their apprehensions, and sent them forward to the village, about a mile off, with presents of small pieces of riband. Soon after they reached home a man came out to meet the party, but with great caution: he conducted them to a large tent in the village, and all the inhabitants gathered round to view with a mixture of fear and pleasure the wonderful strangers. The conductor now informed Captain Clarke, by signs, that the spacious tent he was in was the residence of the great chief, who had set out three days ago, with all the warriors, to attack some of their enemies towards the southwest; that he would not return before fifteen or eighteen days, and that in the mean time there were only a few men left to guard the women and children. They now set before them a small piece of buffalo meat, some dried salmon, berries, and several kinds of roots. Among these last was one which was round, much like an onion in appearance, and sweet to the taste; its name is *quamash*, and it is eaten either in its natural state, boiled into a kind of soup, or made into a cake, when it is called *pasheco*. After their long abstinence this was a sumptuous treat. They returned the kindness of the people by a few small presents, and then went on, in company with one of the chiefs, to a second village in the same plain, at the distance of two miles. Here they were treated with great kindness, and passed the night. The hunters were sent out, but, though they saw some tracks of deer, were unable to procure anything."

Captain Lewis, with the main party, had proceeded about two miles, when they fortunately found the remainder of the horse left by Captain Clarke and also a note signifying his intention to descend into the plains to the southwest in search of provisions. One of their horses, with a valuable load, was missing, and two men were sent to find him. Their general course was south 25° west, through a dense forest of large pine, and they advanced fifteen miles before encamping.

"On descending the heights of the mountains," continues the Journal, "the soil becomes gradually more fertile, and the land through which we passed this evening is of an excellent quality. It has a dark gray soil, though very broken, and with large masses of gray freestone above the ground in many places. Among the vegetable productions we distinguished the alder, honeysuckle, and whortleberry, common in the United States ; also a species of honeysuckle known only west of the Rocky Mountains, which rises to the height of about four feet, and bears a white berry. There is likewise a plant resembling the chokecherry, which grows in thick clumps eight or ten feet high, and bears a black berry with a single stone, of a sweetish taste. The *arbor vitæ*, too, is very common, and grows to a great size, being from two to six feet in diameter.

"September 21. The free use of food, to which he had for some time not been accustomed, made Captain Clarke very sick. He therefore sent out all the hunters, and remained himself at the village, as well on account of his illness as for the pur-

pose of avoiding suspicion, and collecting information from the Indians as to the route.

"The two villages consisted of about thirty double
tents, and the inhabitants called themselves Chopunnish, or Pierced-Nose. The chief drew a chart of
the river, and explained that a greater chief than
himself, who governed these villages, and whose
name was Twisted Hair, was now fishing at the distance of half a day's ride down the river. His chart
made the Kooskooskee fork a little below his camp,
with a second fork farther on, and a large branch
flowing in on each side, below which the river passed the mountains : here was a great fall of water,
near which lived white people, from whom were procured the white beads and brass ornaments worn
by the women.

"A chief of another band made a visit this morning, and smoked with Captain Clarke. The hunters
returning without having been able to kill anything,
Captain Clarke purchased as much dried salmon,
roots, and berries as he could with the few articles
he chanced to have in his pockets, and having sent
them by one of the men and a hired Indian back to
Captain Lewis, he went on towards the camp of
Twisted Hair. It was four o'clock before he set
out, and the night soon came on ; but, meeting an
Indian coming from the river, they engaged him,
with the present of a neckcloth, to guide them to that
chief. They proceeded twelve miles through the
plain before they reached the river hills, which are
very high and steep. The whole valley, from these
hills to the Rocky Mountains, is a beautiful level
country, with a rich soil, covered with grass : there
is, however, but little timber, and the country is
badly watered. The plain is so much lower than
the surrounding hills, or so much sheltered by them,
that the weather was quite warm, while the cold
of the mountains was extreme. From the top of
the river hills they proceeded down for three miles.

till they reached the water side between eleven and twelve o'clock at night. Here they found a small camp of five squaws and three children, the chief himself being encamped, with two others, on a small island in the river. The guide called to him, and he soon came over: Captain Clarke gave him a medal, and they smoked together till one o'clock."

The main party proceeded on without anything worthy of note occurring. During the day they were so fortunate as to kill a few pheasants and a prairie wolf.

" September 22. Captain Clarke passed over to the island in company with Twisted Hair, who seemed to be cheerful and sincere in his conduct. The river at this place was about one hundred and sixty yards wide, but interrupted by shoals, and the low grounds on its borders were narrow. The hunters brought in three deer; after which Captain Clarke left his party, and, accompanied by Twisted Hair and his son, rode back to the village, where he arrived about sunset: they then walked up together to the second village, where we had just arrived.

" We had intended to set out early; but one of the men having neglected to hobble his horse, he strayed away, and we were obliged to wait till nearly twelve o'clock. We then proceeded on a western course for two and a half miles, when we met the hunters sent by Captain Clarke from the village, seven and a half miles distant, with provisions. This supply was most seasonable, as we had tasted nothing since last night; and the fish, roots, and berries, in addition to a crow which we killed on the route, completely satisfied our hunger. After this refreshment we proceeded in much better spirits, and at a few miles were overtaken by the two men who had been sent back after the lost horse on the 20th." * * *

" As we approached the village, most of the women, though apprized of our being expected, fled with

their children into the neighbouring woods. The
men, however, received us without any apprehen-
sion, and gave us a plentiful supply of provisions.
The plains were now crowded with Indians, who
had come to see the persons of the whites, and the
strange things they had brought with them; but, as
our guide was a perfect stranger to their language,
we could converse by signs only. Our inquiries
were chiefly directed to the character of the country, the courses of the rivers, and the Indian villages, in regard to all which we received more or less
information; and, as their accounts varied but little
from each other, we were induced to place confidence in them. Twisted Hair drew a chart of the
river on a white elkskin; according to which, the
Kooskooskee Forks were a few miles from this
place: two days' journey towards the south was
another and larger fork, on which the Shoshonee or
Snake Indians fished; five days' journey lower down
was a large river from the northwest, into which
Clarke's River empties itself; and from the mouth
of that river to the falls was five days' journey farther. On all the forks, as well as on the main river,
great numbers of Indians resided, and at the falls
were establishments of whites. This was the story
of Twisted Hair.

"September 23. The chiefs and warriors were all
assembled this morning, and we explained to them
from whence we came, the objects of our visiting
them, and our pacific intentions towards all the Indians. This, being conveyed by signs, might not
have been perfectly comprehended, but appeared to
give entire satisfaction. We now gave a medal to
two of the chiefs, a shirt to Twisted Hair, in addition to the medal he had already received, and a flag
and handkerchief for the grand chief on his return.
To these were added a knife, a handkerchief, and a
small piece of tobacco for each chief. The Indians
did not give us any provisions gratuitously. We

therefore purchased a quantity of fish, berries (chiefly red haws), and roots, and in the afternoon went on to the second village. Twisted Hair here introduced us into his own tent (which consisted, however, of nothing more than pine-bushes and bark), and gave us some dried salmon boiled. We continued our purchases, and obtained as much provision as our horses could carry, in their present weak condition, as far as the river. The men exchanged a few old canisters for dressed elkskins, of which they made shirts. Great crowds of the natives were round us all night, but we did not miss anything except a knife, and a few other articles stolen from a shotpouch the day before.

"September 24. We sent back Colter in search of the horses lost in the mountains; and, having collected the rest, set out at ten o'clock along the same route already passed by Captain Clarke towards the river. All round the village the women were busily employed in gathering and dressing the *pasheco* root, of which large quantities were heaped up in piles over the plain. We now felt severely the consequences of eating heartily after our late privations: Captain Lewis and two of the men were taken very ill last evening, and to-day he could scarcely sit on his horse, while others were obliged to be put on their horses, and some, from extreme weakness and pain, were forced to lie down by the side of the road for a considerable time. At sunset we reached the island where the hunters had been left on the 22d. They had been unsuccessful, having killed only two deer since that time, and two of them were very ill. A little below this island was a larger one, on which we encamped, and administered Rush's pills to the sick.

"September 25. The weather was very hot and oppressive to the party, most of whom were now complaining of sickness. Our situation, indeed, rendered it necessary to husband our remaining

strength, and it was determined to proceed down the
river in canoes : Captain Clarke therefore set out
with Twisted Hair and two young men in quest of
timber for their construction.   As he went down the
river, at the distance of a mile he crossed a creek
from the right, which, from the rocks that obstructed
its passage, he called Rockdam River.   The hills
along the river were high and steep, the low grounds
narrow, and the navigation was embarrassed by two
rapids.   At the distance of two miles farther he
reached two nearly equal forks of the stream, one
of which flowed in from the north.   At this place
he rested for an hour, and cooked a few salmon
which one of the Indians had struck with a gig.
Here, too, he was joined by some Indians in two
canoes from below.   These canoes were long,
steady, and loaded with the furniture and provisions
of two families.   He now crossed the south fork,
and returned to the camp on the south side, the
greater part of the way through a narrow pine bottom, in which was found much fine timber suitable
for canoes.   One of the Indian boats, with two men,
set out at the same time ; and such was their dexterity in managing the pole, that they reached camp
within fifteen minutes after him, although they had
to drag the canoe over three rapids.   He found Captain Lewis and several of the men still very sick,
and distributed to such as were in need of it salts
and tartar emetic.

"September 26.   Having resolved to go down to
some spot calculated for building canoes, we set out
early this morning, proceeded five miles, and encamped on a piece of low ground opposite the forks
of the river; but so weak were the men, that several were taken sick in coming down, the weather
being oppressively hot.   Two chiefs, with their families, followed us, and encamped, with a great number of horses, near us ; and soon after our arrival
we were joined by two Indians, who had come down

the north fork on a raft. We purchased some fresh salmon ; and, having distributed axes, and portioned off the labour of the party,

"September 27, at an early hour began our preparations for constructing five canoes. But few of the men, however, were able to work, and of these several were soon taken ill, as the day proved very hot. The hunters, too, returned without any game, and seriously indisposed, so that nearly the whole party were now sick. We procured some fresh salmon ; and Colter, who at this time returned with one of the horses, brought half a deer, which was very nourishing to the invalids. Several Indians from a camp below came up to see us."

From this time to the 5th of October, all the men capable of labour were employed in preparing the canoes. The health of the party gradually recruited, though they still suffered severely from want of food ; and, as the hunters had but little success in procuring game, they were obliged on the 2d to kill one of their horses. Indians from different quarters frequently visited them, but all that could be obtained from them was a little fish and some dried roots.

"October 5. The canoes being nearly finished," says the Journal, "it became necessary to dispose of our horses. They were therefore collected, to the number of thirty-eight, and, after being branded and marked, were delivered to three Indians, the two brothers and the son of a chief who had promised to accompany us down the river. To each of these men we gave a knife and some small articles, and they agreed to take care of the horses till our return. The hunters, with all their diligence, were unable to kill anything ; the hills being high and rugged, and the woods too dry to hunt deer, which was the only game in the country. We therefore continued to eat dried fish and roots, which were purchased of the squaws with small presents, but chiefly white beads, of which they are extravagantly fond. Some

of these roots seemed to possess very active prop-
erties; for, after supping on them this evening, we
were swelled to such a degree as to be scarcely able
to breathe for several hours. Towards night we
launched two canoes, which proved to be very good.

" October 6. The morning was cool, and the wind
easterly. The general course of the winds seems
to be nearly the same as we observed on the east
side of the mountains. While on the head-waters
of the Missouri, we had every morning a cool wind
from the west. At this place a cool breeze springs
up during the latter part of the night, or near daybreak, and continues till seven or eight o'clock, when
it subsides, and the other part of the day is warm.
Captain Lewis was now not so well as he had been,
and Captain Clarke was also taken ill. We had all
our saddles buried in a *cache* near the river, about
half a mile below, and deposited at the same time a
canister of powder and a bag of balls. The time
which could be spared from our labours on the canoes was devoted to some astronomical observations.
The latitude of our camp, as deduced from the mean
of two observations, was found to be 46° 34′ 56.3″
north.

" October 7. This morning all the canoes were
put in the water and loaded, the oars fixed, and every
preparation made for setting out; but when we were
all ready, the two chiefs who had promised to accompany us were not to be found, and at the same
time we missed a pipe tomahawk: we therefore proceeded without them. Below the forks the river is
called the Kooskooskee, and is a clear, rapid stream,
with a number of shoals and difficult places. For
some miles the hills were steep, and the low grounds
narrow; but then succeeded an open country, with
a few trees scattered along the river. At the distance of nine miles was a small creek on the left.
We passed in the course of the day ten rapids; in
descending one of which, one of the canoes struck a

rock and sprung aleak. We, however, continued foi nineteen miles, and encamped on the left side of the river, opposite to the mouth of a small run. Here the canoe was unloaded and repaired, and two lead canisters of powder were deposited. Several camps of Indians were on the sides of the river, but we had little intercourse with any of them.

"October 8. We set out at nine o'clock. At eight and a half miles we passed an island, and four and a half miles lower a second, opposite a small creek on the left side of the river. Five miles farther was another island on the left; and a mile and a half beyond, a fourth. At a short distance from this was a large creek coming from the right, to which we gave the name of Colter's Creek, from Colter, one of our men. We had proceeded from this creek about a mile and a half, and were passing the last of fifteen rapids, having gone over the other fourteen safely, when one of the canoes struck, and, a hole being made in her side, she immediately filled. The men, several of whom could not swim, clung to her till one of the other boats could be unloaded, and with the assistance of an Indian canoe they were all brought to shore. All the goods were so much wet that we were obliged to halt for the night, and spread them out to dry. While all this was doing it was necessary to place two sentinels over the merchandise, for we have found that these Indians, though kind and disposed to give us every aid during our distress, cannot resist the temptation of pilfering small articles. We passed, during our route of twenty miles, several encampments of Indians on the islands and near the rapids, which places are chosen as most convenient for taking salmon. At one of these camps we found the two chiefs who had left us after promising to descend the river with us: they, however, willingly came on board after we had gone through the ceremony of smoking.

" October 9. The morning, as usual, was cool ; but, as the weather was cloudy, our merchandise dried but slowly. The boat, though much injured, was repaired by ten o'clock so as to be perfectly fit for service: still we were obliged to remain through the day, for the articles to be sufficiently dry to be reloaded. The time we employed in purchasing fish for the voyage and in conversing with the Indians. In the afternoon we were surprised at hearing that our old Shoshonee guide and his son had left us, and been seen running up the river several miles above. As he had never given any notice of his intention, nor even received his pay for conducting us, we could not imagine the cause of his desertion, nor did he ever come back to explain his conduct. We requested the chief to send a horseman after him, to ask him to return and receive what we owed him. From this, however, he dissuaded us; saying very frankly, that his nation, the Chopunnish, would take from the old man any presents he might have on passing their camp.

"The Indians came about our encampment at night, and were very gay and good-humoured with the men. Among other exhibitions was that of a squaw, who appeared to be crazy: she sang in a wild, incoherent manner, and would offer to the spectators all the little articles she possessed, scarifying herself in a horrid manner if any one refused her presents. She seemed to be an object of pity among the Indians, who suffered her to do as she pleased, without any interruption.

"October 10. A fine morning. We loaded the canoes and set off at seven o'clock. At the distance of two and a half miles we had passed three islands, the last of which was opposite to a small stream on the right. Within the next three and a half miles was another island, and a creek on the left, with wide low grounds, containing willow and cottonwood trees, and on which were three tents of Indians. Two miles lower was the head of a large island, and six and a half miles beyond it we halted at an encampment of eight lodges on the left, in order to examine a rapid before us. We had already passed eight, some of them difficult; but this was worse than any of those, being strewed with rocks, and very hazard- ous: we purchased here some roots, and dined with the Indians. Among them was a man from the falls, who says that he has seen white people at that place, and is very desirous of going down with us: an offer, however, which we declined. Just above this camp we had passed a tent, near which was an Indian bath- ing himself in a small pond or hole of water, warmed by throwing in hot stones. After finishing our meal, we descended the rapid with no injury except to one of our boats, which ran against a rock, but in the course of an hour was got off, with only a small split in her side. This rapid, from its appearance and diffi- culty, we named Rugged Rapid. We went on over five others of a less dangerous character, and at the distance of five miles reached a large fork of the river from the south; and, after having gone twenty miles, halted below the junction on the right bank. Our arrival soon attracted the attention of the Indians, who flocked in all directions to see us. In the even ing, the Indian from the falls, whom we had seen at Rugged Rapid, joined us with his son, in a small ca- noe, and insisted on accompanying us to the falls. Being again reduced to fish and roots, we made an experiment to vary our food by purchasing a few dogs, and, after having been accustomed to horse-flesh, felt no disrelish to this new dish. The Chopunnish have great numbers of dogs, which they employ for do- mestic purposes, but never eat them; and our using the flesh of that animal soon brought us into ridicule as dog-eaters.

" The country at the junction of the two rivers is an open plain on all sides, broken towards the left by a distant ridge of high land, thinly covered with timber. This is the only body of timber which the country contains, for at the forks there is not a tree

to be seen ; and in almost the whole descent of sixty
miles down the Kooskooskee from its forks, there are
very few. This southern branch is, in fact, the main
stream of Lewis's River, on which we encamped when
among the Shoshonees. The Indians inform us that
it is navigable for sixty miles ; that not far from its
mouth it receives a branch from the south; and a
second and larger branch two days' march up, nearly
parallel to the first Chopunnish villages we met near
the mountains. This branch is called Pawnashte,
and is the residence of a chief who, according to
their expression, has more horses than he can count.
The river has many rapids, near which are numerous fishing camps, there being ten establishments of
this kind before reaching the first southern branch :
one on that stream, five between that and the Pawnashte, one on that river, and two above it; besides
which, there are many other Indian settlements on
the more distant waters of the river. All these Indians belong to the Chopunnish nation, and live in
tents of an oblong form, covered with flat roofs.

" At its mouth Lewis's River is about two hundred and fifty yards wide, and its water is of a green-
ish-blue colour. The Kooskooskee, whose waters
are clear as crystal, is one hundred and fifty yards
in width, and after the union the breadth is increased
to three hundred yards : at the point of union is an
Indian cabin, and in Lewis's River a small island.

" The men of the Chopunnish, or Pierced-Nose
nation, residing on the Kooskooskee and Lewis Rivers, are in person stout, portly, and well-looking;
the women are small, with good features, and are
generally handsome, though the complexion of both
sexes is darker than that of the Tushepaws. In
dress they resemble that nation, being fond of displaying their ornaments. Buffalo or elk skin robes,
decorated with beads, sea-shells, chiefly mother-of-
pearl, attached to an otter-skin collar, falling in front
in two queues ; feathers, paints of different kinds

principally white, green, and light blue, all of which they find in their own country—these are the chief ornaments they use.   In the winter they wear a short shirt of dressed skins, long painted leggins and moccasins, and a plait of twisted grass round the neck.

" The dress of the women is more simple, consisting of a long shirt of argalia or ibex skin, reaching down to the ankles, and without any girdle : to the bottom of it are tied little pieces of brass, shells, and other small articles, but the top is not at all ornamented.   The dress of the females is, indeed, more modest, and more studiously so than any we have observed, while the other sex are heedless of the indelicacy of exposure.

" The Chopunnish have very few amusements, their life being painful and laborious, and all their exertions being necessary to earn even a precarious subsistence.   During the summer and autumn they are busily occupied in fishing for salmon, and collecting their winter store of roots.   In the winter they hunt the deer on snow-shoes over the plains, and towards spring cross the mountains to the Missouri, for the purpose of trafficking for buffalo robes. The inconveniences of this comfortless life are increased by frequent encounters with their enemies from the west, who drive them over the mountains with the loss of their horses, and sometimes the lives of many of the nation.   Though originally the same people, their dialect varies very perceptibly from that of the Tushepaws.   Their treatment to us differed much from the kind and disinterested services of the Shoshonees : they are, indeed, selfish and avaricious, parting very reluctantly with every article of food or clothing ; and, while they expect a recompense for every service, however small, do not concern themselves about reciprocating any favours we may show them.

" They are generally healthy, the only disorders

we have remarked among them being of a scrofulous kind ; and for these, as well as for the amuse
ment of those who are in good health, hot and cold
bathing is very frequently used.

" The soil of these prairies is a light yellow clay :
it is barren, and produces little more than a bearded grass about three inches high, and the prickly
pear, of which we here found three species. The
first is of the broad-leafed kind, common to the Missouri ; the second has a leaf of a globular form, and
is also frequent in the upper parts of the Missouri,
particularly in the country along the river after it
enters the Rocky Mountains. The third is peculiar
to this country, and is much more troublesome than
either of the others. It consists of small, thick leaves
of a circular form, which grow from the margin of
each other, as in the broad-leafed pear of the Missouri. These leaves are armed with a great number
of thorns, which are very strong, and appear to be
barbed ; and, as the leaf itself is very slightly attached to the stem, as soon as one of the thorns
touches the moccasin, it adheres, and brings with it
the leaf, accompanied by a re-enforcement of other
thorns."

CHAPTER II.

Departure of the Party.—Descriptior of an Indian Sweating-bath and Burial-place.—Dangerous Rapids.—Visits from the Indians, who manifest a pacific Disposition.—Description of the Sokulk Tribe.—Their Dress, and Manner of building Houses.—Their pacific Character.—Their Habits of Living.—Their Mode of boiling Salmon.—Vast Quantities of Salmon among the Sokulks.—Council held with this Tribe.—The Terror and Consternation excited by Captain Clarke.—Some Account of the Pishquitpaws.—Their Mode of burying the Dead.

" October 11, 1805. This morning the wind was from the east, and the weather cloudy. We set out early, and at the distance of a mile and a half reached a point of rocks in a bend of the river towards the left, near to which was an old Indian house, and a meadow on the opposite bank. Here the hills came down towards the water, and, with the rocks which have fallen from their sides, formed a rapid, over which we were obliged to drag the canoes. A mile and a half farther we passed two Indian lodges in a bend towards the right, and at six miles from our camp of last evening reached the mouth of a brook on the left. Just above this stream we stopped for breakfast, at a large encampment of Indians on the same side. We soon began to trade with them for a stock of provisions, and were so fortunate as to purchase seven dogs and all the fish they could spare. While this traffic was going on, we observed a vapour-bath or sweating-house of a different form from any used on the frontiers of the United States or among the Rocky Mountains : it was a hollow square of six or eight feet deep, formed against the river-bank by damming up with mud the other three sides, and covering the top completely, except an aperture about two feet wide.

II.—D

The bathers descend by this hole, taking with them a number of heated stones and jugs of water ; and after seating themselves round the room, throw the water on the stones till the steam becomes of a temperature sufficiently high for their purpose. The baths of the Indians in the Rocky Mountains are of different sizes, the most common being made of mud and sticks, like an oven; but the mode of raising the steam is exactly the same. Among both these nations it is very uncommon for a man to bathe alone ; he is generally accompanied by one, and sometimes several of his acquaintances. Indeed, it is so essentially a social amusement, that to decline going in the bath when invited by a friend is one of the highest indignities which can be offered. The Indians on the frontiers generally use a bath that will accommodate only one person, and which is formed of a wicker-work of willows, about four feet high, arched at the top, and covered with skins In this the bather sits, till by means of the steam from the heated stones he has perspired sufficiently. These baths are almost universally in the neighbour- hood of running water, into which the Indians plunge immediately on coming out from them ; and sometimes they return again, and subject themselves to a second perspiration. This practice is, howev- er, less frequent among the nations on our borders than those to the westward. The bath is employed either for pleasure or health, and is used indiscrim- inately for all kinds of diseases.

" Shortly after leaving our encampment we passed two rapids, and at the distance of four and a half miles reached one which was much more ˙difficult. Three miles beyond this there were three huts of Indians on the right, where we stopped and obtain- ed, in exchange for a few trifles, some *pasheco* roots, five dogs, and a small quantity of dried fish. We made our dinner of part of each of these articles, and then proceeded on without any obstruction till after we had gone twelve and a half miles, when we came to a stony island on the right side of the river, opposite to which was a rapid, and a second at its lower point. About three and a half miles beyond this island was a small brook, emptying itself into a bend on the right, where we stopped at two Indian huts, which we found inhabited. Here we met two Indians belonging to a nation residing at the mouth of this river. We had made thirty-one miles to-day, although the weather was warm, and the current obstructed by nine different rapids, more or less difficult to pass. All these rapids are fishing-places, greatly resorted to in the season; and as we passed we observed near them slabs and pieces of split timber raised from the ground, and some entire houses, vacant at present, but which will be occupied as soon as the Indians return from the plains on both sides of the river, where our chief informs us they are now hunting the antelope. Near each of the houses is a small collection of graves, the burial-places of those who frequent these establishments. The dead are wrapped in robes of skins, and deposited in graves, which are covered over with earth, and marked or secured by little pickets or pieces of wood stuck promiscuously in and around them. The country on both sides, after mounting a steep ascent of about two hundred feet, becomes an open, level, and fertile plain, which is, however, as well as the borders of the river itself, entirely destitute of any kind of timber; and the chief growth we observed consisted of a few low blackberries." * * *

They continued to descend the river, and from the 12th to the 15th proceeded about sixty-three miles. On their way they passed several rapids, one of which was particularly dangerous, and two miles in length. They got over it safely, however, by the aid of their Indian pilots, but were less fortunate the next day; one of their canoes being driven sideways against a rock, so that she filled with water, and they

were obliged to unload her to dry the baggage she
had on board. Unfortunately, their roots and other
provisions were in this boat, and were entirely spoiled. The only game they procured was a few geese
and ducks. They passed two considerable streams
on the 13th, the first of which they called Kimooenim
Creek, and the other Drewyer's River. Having part-
ly dried their baggage, they set out again late in the
day on the 15th, intending to complete the drying at
the mouth of the river, where they proposed stopping
to take some celestial observations, and which they
supposed could not be far distant.

"For the first four miles," proceeds the Journal,
"we passed three islands, at the lower points of
which were the same number of rapids, besides a
fourth at a distance from them. In the next ten miles
we passed eight islands and three more rapids, and
reached a point of rocks on the left. These islands
were of various sizes, and were all composed of
round stone and sand : the rapids were in many places difficult and dangerous to pass. The country
now became lower than before, the ground near the
river not being higher than ninety or a hundred feet,
and extending back into a waving plain. Soon after
leaving this point of rocks we entered a narrow channel, formed by the projecting cliffs of the bank, which
rise nearly perpendicular from the water. The river
is not, however, rapid, but gentle and smooth the
whole length of its confinement, which continues for
three miles, when it falls, or rather widens, into a
kind of basin nearly round, and without any perceptible current. After passing through this basin we
were joined by the three Indians who had piloted us
through the rapids since we left the forks, and who,
in company with our two chiefs, had gone before us.
They had halted here to warn us of a dangerous rapid
which begins at the lower point of the basin. As the
day was too far spent to attempt it, we determined
to examine it before descending, and therefore en-

camped near an island at its head, and studied particularly all its narrow and difficult parts. The spot
where we landed was an old fishing establishment,
of which there yet remained the timbers of a house,
carefully raised on scaffolds to protect them against
the spring freshet. Not being able to procure any
other fuel, and the night being cold, we were a second time obliged to use the property of the Indians,
who still remain in the plains hunting the antelope.
Our progress had been but twenty miles, in consequence of the difficulty of passing the rapids; and
our game consisted of only two teal.

"October 16. Having fully examined the rapids,
which we found even more difficult than the report
of the Indians had induced us to believe, we set out
early, and, putting our Indian guide in front, our
smallest canoe next, and the rest in succession, began the descent. The passage proved to be very
disagreeable, as there was a continuation of shoals,
extending from bank to bank, for the distance of
three miles, the channel being narrow and crooked,
and obstructed by large rocks in every direction, so
as to require great dexterity to avoid being dashed
against them. We got through, however, with no
injury to any of the boats except the hindmost, which
ran on a rock; but, by the assistance of the other
boats and of the Indians, who were very alert, she
escaped, though the baggage on board of her was
wet. Within three miles we passed three small islands, on one of which were the parts of a house, put
on scaffolds as usual, and soon after came to another
rapid at the lower extremity of three small islands;
and to a second, again, at the distance of a mile and a
half below them. At six miles from the great rapid
we reached a point of rocks at a rapid opposite to the
upper part of a small island on the left: three miles
farther there was another rapid; and two miles beyond this, a very bad one, or, rather, a fall of the river.
This last proved, on examination, to be so difficult,

that we thought it imprudent to attempt it, and therefore unloaded the canoes, and made a portage of three
quarters of a mile. This rapid, which is of about the
same length, is much broken by rocks and shoals,
and has a small island in it, on the right side.

" After completing the transportation we halted
for dinner, and while we were eating were visited
by five Indians, who had come up the river on foot
in great haste. We received them kindly, smoked
with them, and gave them a piece of tobacco to smoke
with their tribe; on receiving which they set out to
return, and continued running as fast as they could
while they remained in sight. Their curiosity had
been excited by the accounts of our two chiefs, who
had gone on ahead, to apprize the tribes of our approach, and of our friendly dispositions towards
them. After dinner we reloaded the canoes and proceeded. We soon passed a rapid opposite to the upper point of a sandy island on the left, which has a
smaller island near it. At three miles there was a
gravelly bar in the river ; and four miles beyond this,
the Kimooenim River empties itself into the Columbia, having an island at its mouth, just below a small
rapid. We halted above the point of junction, on the
Kimooenim, to confer with the Indians, who had collected in great numbers to receive us. On landing
we were met by our two chiefs, to whose good offices
we were indebted for this reception, and also by the
two Indians who had passed us a few days since on
horseback ; one of them appearing to be a man of influence, as he harangued the assembly on our arrival.
After smoking with the Indians, we formed a camp at
the point where the two rivers unite, near which we
found some driftwood : we were also supplied by our
two old chiefs with the stalks of willows and some
small bushes for fuel. Scarcely had we fixed our
quarters and got the fires prepared, when a chief
came from the Indian camp about a fourth of a mile
up the Columbia, at the head of nearly two hundred

men. They formed a regular procession, keeping time to the music, or, rather, noise of their drums, which they accompanied with their voices; and as they advanced, they ranged themselves in a semicircle around us, and continued singing for some time. We then smoked with them all, and communicated, as well as we could by signs, our friendly intentions towards every nation, and our joy at finding ourselves surrounded by our children. After this we proceeded to distribute presents among them, giving the principal chief a large medal, a shirt, and a handkerchief; to the second chief, a medal of a smaller size ; and to a third, who had come down from some of the upper villages, a small medal and a handkerchief. This ceremony being concluded, they left us ; but in the course of the afternoon several of them returned, and remained with us till a late hour. After they had dispersed, we proceeded to purchase provisions, and were enabled to collect seven dogs, to which some of the Indians added small presents of fish, and one of them gave us twenty pounds of fat dried horse-flesh.

"October 17. The day being fair, we were occupied in taking the necessary observations for determining our longitude, and we obtained a meridian altitude, from which it appeared that we were in latitude 46° 15' 13.9". We also measured the two rivers by angles, and found that at the junction the Columbia was nine hundred and sixty yards wide, and Lewis's River five hundred and seventy-five ; but, soon after they unite, the former widens to the breadth of from one to three miles, including the islands. From the point of confluence the country is a continued plain, low near the water, and rising gradually from it ; the only elevation to be seen being a range of high country running from the northeast towards the southwest, where it joins a chain of mountains from the southwest, and on the opposite side is about two miles from the Columbia.

There is throughout this plain not a single tree, nor scarcely any shrubs, except a few willow bushes; and even of smaller plants there is not much more than the prickly pear, which is in great abundance, and even more thorny and troublesome than any we had yet seen. In the mean time the principal chief came down, with several of his warriors, and smoked with us. We were also visited by several men and women, who offered dogs and dried fish for sale; but as the fish was out of season, being at present abundant in the river, we contented ourselves with purchasing the dogs. The nation among whom we now are call themselves Sokulks; and with them are united a few of another nation, who reside on a western branch, emptying itself into the Columbia a few miles above the mouth of the latter river, and whose name is Chimnapum.

"The languages of these two nations, of both of which we obtained a vocabulary, differ but little from each other or from that of the Chopunnish, who inhabit the Kooskooskee and Lewis Rivers. In their dress and general appearance, also, they much resemble that nation; the men wearing a robe of deer or antelope skin, under which a few of them have a short leathern shirt. The most striking difference is among the females, the Sokulk women being more inclined to corpulency than any we have yet seen. Their stature is low, their faces are broad, and their heads flattened in such a manner that the forehead is in a straight line from the nose to the crown of the head. Their eyes are of a dirty sable, their hair is coarse and black, and braided without ornament of any kind. Instead of wearing, as do the Chopunnish, long leathern shirts highly decorated with beads and shells, the Sokulk women have no other covering but a truss or piece of leather tied round the hips, and drawn tight between the legs. The ornaments usually worn by both sexes are large blue or white beads, either pendant from their ears.

ɔr round the neck, wrists, and arms : they have likewise bracelets of brass, copper, and horn, and some
trinkets of shells, fish-bones, and curious feathers.
The houses of the Sokulks are made of large mats
of rushes, and are generally of a square or oblong
form, varying in length from fifteen to sixty feet, and
supported in the inside by poles or forks about six
feet high.   The top is covered with mats, leaving a
space of twelve or fifteen inches the whole length
of the house, for the purpose of admitting the light
and suffering the smoke to escape.   The roof is
nearly flat, which seems to indicate that rains are
not common in this open country ; and the house is
not divided into apartments, the fire being in the middle of the enclosure, and immediately under the hole
in the roof.   The interior is ornamented with their
nets, gigs, and other fishing-tackle, as well as the
bow of each inmate, and a large quiver of arrows,
which are headed with flint.

" The Sokulks seem to be of a mild and peaceable
disposition, and live in a state of comparative happi-
ness.   The men, like those on the Kimooenim, are
said to content themselves with a single wife, with
whom the husband, we observe, shares the labours
of procuring subsistence much more than is common
among savages.   What may be considered an une-
quivocal proof of their good disposition, is the great
respect which is shown to old age.   Among other
marks of it, we noticed in one of the houses an old
woman perfectly blind, and who, we were told, had
lived more than a hundred winters.   In this state of
decrepitude, she occupied the best position in the
house, seemed to be treated with great kindness,
and whatever she said was listened to with much
attention.   They are by no means obtrusive ; and as
their fisheries supply them with a competent, if not
an abundant subsistence, although they receive
thankfully whatever we choose to give, they do not
importune us by begging.   Fish is, indeed, their chief
II.—E

food, to which they add roots, and occasionally the flesh of the antelope, which, as they have only bows and arrows, must be very scanty. This diet may be the immediate or remote cause of the principal disorder prevailing among them, as well as among the Flatheads on the Kooskooskee and Lewis Rivers With all these Indians soreness of the eyes is very common, and it is so aggravated by neglect that many are deprived of one of their eyes, and some have lost entirely the use of both. This dreadful disorder may also, we think, be imputed, in part, to the reflection of the sun from the waters, where they are constantly fishing in the spring, summer, and autumn, and during the rest of the year from the snow, in a country where there is no object to relieve the sight. Among the Sokulks, too, and, indeed, among all the tribes whose chief subsistence is fish, we have observed that bad teeth are very general; some have the teeth, particularly those of the upper jaw, worn down to the gums; and many of both sexes, and even of middle age, have lost them entirely. This decay of the teeth is a circumstance very unusual among the Indians, either on the mountains or plains, and seems peculiar to those of the Columbia. We cannot avoid regarding as one cause of it the manner in which they eat their food. The roots are swallowed as they are dug from the ground, frequently nearly covered with a gritty sand; and so little idea have they that this is offensive, that all the roots they bring to us for sale are in the same condition. Another and important cause may be their great use of dried salmon, the bad effects of which are most probably increased by their mode of cooking it, which is simply to warm it, and then eat the skin, scales, and flesh, without any farther preparation. The Sokulks possess but few horses, the greater part of their labours being performed in canoes. Their amusements are similar to those of the Missouri Indians.

" In the course of the day, Captain Clarke, in a small canoe with two men, ascended the Columbia. At the distance of five miles he passed an island in the middle of the river, at the head of which was a small but not dangerous rapid. On the left bank, opposite to this island, was a fishing-place consisting of three mat houses. Here were great quantities of salmon drying on scaffolds ; and, indeed, from the mouth of the river upward, he saw immense numbers of dead salmon strewed along the shore, or floating on the surface of the water, which is so clear that the fish may be seen swimming at the depth of fifteen or twenty feet. The Indians, who had collected on the banks to observe him, now joined him in eighteen canoes, and accompanied him up the river. A mile above the rapids he came to the lower point of an island, where the course of the stream, which had been from its mouth north 83° west, now became due west. He proceeded in that direction, until, observing three houses of mats at a short distance, he landed to visit them. On entering one of these houses, he found it crowded with men, women, and children, who immediately provided a mat for him to sit on, and one of the party undertook to prepare something to eat. He began by bringing in a piece of pine wood that had drifted down the river, which he split into small pieces with a wedge made of elkhorn, by means of a mallet of stone curiously carved. The pieces of wood were then laid on the fire, and several round stones placed upon them. One of the squaws now brought a bucket of water, in which was a large salmon about half dried, and, as the stones became heated, they were put into the bucket till the salmon was sufficiently boiled for use. It was then taken out, put on a platter of rushes neatly made, and laid before Captain Clarke, while another was boiled for each of his men. During these preparations he smoked with such about him as would accept of tobacco,

though very few would do it, smoking not being
general among them, and chiefly used as a matter
of form in great ceremonies. After eating the fish,
which was of an excellent flavour, Captain Clarke
again set out, and at the distance of four miles from
the last island came to the lower point of another,
near the left shore, where he halted at two large
mat houses. Here, as at the three houses below,
the inhabitants were occupied in splitting and drying
salmon. The multitudes of this fish, indeed, are almost inconceivable. The water is so clear, as we
have already remarked, that they can readily be
seen at the depth of fifteen or twenty feet; but at
this season they float down the stream, and are
drifted ashore in such quantities that the Indians
have only to collect, split, and dry them on the scaffolds. Where they procure the timber of which
these scaffolds are composed, he could not learn;
and, as there are nothing but willow bushes to be
seen for a great distance from this place, it renders
very probable, what the Indians assured him by
signs, that they often use dried fish as fuel for the
common occasions of cooking. From this island
they showed him the entrance of a western branch
of the Columbia, called the Tapteal, which, as far as
could be seen, bears nearly west, and empties itself
about eight miles above into the Columbia, the general course of which is northwest. Towards the
southwest a range of high land runs parallel to the
river, at the distance of two miles on the left, while
on the right side the country is low, and covered
with the prickly pear, and a weed or plant two or
three feet high, resembling the whin. To the eastward is a range of mountains about fifty or sixty
miles distant, bearing north and south ; but neither
in the low grounds nor in the high lands is any timber to be seen. The evening coming on, he determined not to proceed farther than the island, and
therefore returned to camp, accompanied by three

canoes containing twenty Indians. In the course of his excursion he shot several grouse and ducks, and received some presents of fish, for which he gave in return small pieces of riband. He also killed a prairie-cock, a bird of the pheasant kind, but about the size of a small turkey. It measured from the beak to the end of the toe two feet six inches and three quarters ; from the extremities of the wings three feet six inches ; and the feathers of the tail were thirteen inches long. This bird we have seen nowhere except on this river. Its chief food is the grasshopper, and the seed of a wild plant which is peculiar to this river and the upper parts of the Missouri.

"The men availed themselves of this day's rest to mend their clothes, dress skins, and put their arms in order: an object always of primary concern, but particularly at a moment when we were surrounded by so many strangers.

"October 18. We were visited this morning by several canoes of Indians, who joined those already with us, and formed a numerous council. We informed them, as we had done all the other Indian nations, of our friendship for them, and of our desire to promote peace among all our red children in this country. This was conveyed by signs through our two chiefs, and seemed to be perfectly understood. We then made a second chief, and gave to all the chiefs a string of wampum, in remembrance of what we had said. While the conference was going on, four men came in a canoe from a large encampment on an island about eight miles below, but, after staying a few minutes, returned without saying a word to us. We now procured from the principal chief and one of the Cuimnapum nation a sketch of the Columbia, and some account of the tribes of his nation living along its banks and those of the Tapteal. They drew it with a piece of coal on a

robe, and, as we afterward transferred it to paper, it
exhibited a valuable specimen of Indian delineation.

"Having completed the purposes of our stay, we
now began to lay in our stores, and as it was not the
season for dried fish, purchased forty dogs, for which
we gave small articles, such as bells, thimbles, knit-
ting-needles, brass wire, and a few beads: an exchange with which they all seemed perfectly satisfied.   These dogs, with six prairie-cocks killed
this morning, formed a plentiful supply for the present.   We here left our guide, and the two young
men who had accompanied him ; two of the three
not being willing to go any farther, and the third being of no use, as he was not acquainted with the
river below.   We therefore took no Indians but our
two chiefs, and resumed our journey in the presence
of many of the Sokulks, who came to witness our
departure.   The morning was cool and fair, and the
wind from the southeast."

Soon after starting they passed the mouth of
Lewis's River, and as they continued to descend,
saw different fishing establishments on the shore.
Having proceeded twenty miles, they encamped for
the night, and soon after landing were informed by
their two chiefs that the largest of these establishments belonged to the most important chief in that
part of the country.   On receiving this intelligence,
the two chiefs were despatched to invite the great
chief to spend the night at the encampment.   He
accordingly came, accompanied by twenty men,
bringing a basket of mashed berries, which he presented to the strangers, but established a separate
camp at some distance from them.

"October 19. The great chief," continues the
narrative, "with two of his inferior chiefs, and a
third belonging to a band on the river below, made
us a visit at a very early hour.   The first of these,
called Yellepit, was a handsome, well-proportioned
man, about five feet eight inches high, and thirty-five

years of age, with a bold and dignified countenance: the rest had nothing remarkable in their appearance. We smoked with them, and, after making a speech, gave a medal, a handkerchief, and a string of wampum to Yellepit, and a string of wampum only to the inferior chiefs. He requested us to remain till the middle of the day, that all his nation might come and see us; but we excused ourselves by telling him that on our return we would spend two or three days with him. This conference detained us till nine o'clock, by which time great numbers of the Indians had come down to visit us."

As they descended they passed an island where were several Indian houses, the occupants of which were, as usual, employed in drying fish, and seemed to be much alarmed at the approach of the party. They proceeded on, and at the distance of about twelve miles from the point they had left in the morning, they came to a very dangerous rapid, which, however, they succeeded in passing safely, though with great fatigue and difficulty. "In order," proceeds the Journal, "to lighten the boats, Captain Clarke, with the two chiefs, the interpreter and his wife, had walked across the low grounds on the left to the foot of the rapids. On the way he ascended a cliff about two hundred feet above the water, from which he saw that the country on both sides of the river, immediately from its cliffs, was low, and spread itself into a level plain, extending for a great distance in every direction. To the west, at the distance of about one hundred and fifty miles, was a very high mountain covered with snow; and, from its direction and appearance, he supposed it to be Mount St. Helen's, laid down by Vancouver as visible from the mouth of the Columbia: there was also another mountain of a conical form, whose top was covered with snow, in a south-west direction.

"As Captain Clarke arrived at the lower end of

the rapid before any, except one of the small canoes, he sat down on a rock to wait for them, and, seeing a crane fly across the river, shot it, and it fell near him. Several Indians had been before this passing on the opposite side towards the rapids, and some who were then nearly in front of him, being either alarmed at his appearance or the report of the gun, fled to their houses. Captain Clarke was afraid that these people had not yet heard that the white men were coming, and therefore, in order to allay their uneasiness before the rest of the party should arrive, he got into the small canoe with three men, rowed over towards the houses, and, while crossing, shot a duck, which fell into the water. As he approached no person was to be seen except three men in the plains, and they, too, fled as he came near the shore. He landed in front of five houses close to each other, but no one appeared, and the doors, which were of mat, were closed. He went towards one of them with a pipe in his hand, and, pushing aside the mat, entered the lodge, where he found thirty-two persons, chiefly men and women, with a few children, all in the greatest consternation; some hanging down their heads, others crying and wringing their hands. He went up to them, and shook hands with each one in the most friendly manner; but their apprehensions, which had for a moment subsided, revived on his taking out a burning-glass, as there was no roof to the house, and lighting his pipe: he then offered it to several of the men, and distributed among the women and children some small trinkets which he had with him, and gradually restored a degree of tranquillity among them. Leaving this house, and directing each of his men to visit a house, he entered a second. Here he found the inmates more terrified than those in the first; but he succeeded in pacifying them, and afterward went into the other houses, where the men had been equally successful. Retiring from

the houses, he seated himself on a rock, and beckoned to some of the men to come and smoke with
him; but none of them ventured to join him till the
canoes arrived with the two chiefs, who immediately explained our pacific intention towards them.
Soon after the interpreter's wife landed, and her
presence dissipated all doubts of our being well-dis-
posed, since in this country no woman ever accom-
panies a war party : they therefore all came out,
and seemed perfectly reconciled ; nor could we, indeed, blame them for their terrors, which were perfectly natural. They told the two chiefs that they
knew we were not men, for they had seen us fall
from the clouds. In fact, unperceived by them,
Captain Clarke had shot the white crane, which they
had seen fall just before he appeared to their eyes :
the duck which he had killed also fell close by him ;
and as there were some clouds flying over at the moment, they connected the fall of the birds with his
sudden appearance, and believed that he had himself
actually dropped from the clouds ; considering the
noise of the rifle, which they had never heard before, the sound announcing so extraordinary an
event. This belief was strengthened, when, on entering the room, he brought down fire from the
heavens by means of his burning-glass. We soon
convinced them, however, that we were merely
mortals; and after one of our chiefs had explained
our history and objects, we all smoked together in
great harmony. These people do not speak precisely the same language as the Indians farther up,
but understand them in conversation. In a short
time we were joined by many of the inhabitants
from below, several of them on horseback, and all
pleased to see us, and to exchange their fish and berries for a few trinkets.

"We remained here till after dinner, and then proceeded. At half a mile the hilly country on the right
side of the river ceased ; at eleven miles we found

a small rapid ; and a mile farther we came to a
small island on the left, where there were some
willows. In going this distance from the five lodges
we passed twenty more, dispersed along the river
at different points of the valley on the right ; but, as
the inhabitants were now apprized of our coming,
they showed no signs of alarm. On leaving the isl-
and we proceeded three miles farther, through a
country which was low on both sides of the river,
and encamped under some willow-trees on the left,
having made thirty-six miles. Immediately opposite to us was an island close to the left shore, and
another in the middle of the river, on which were
twenty-four houses of Indians, all engaged in drying
fish. We had scarcely landed before about a hundred of them came over in their boats to visit us,
bringing with them a present of some wood, which
was very acceptable. We received them in as kind
a manner as we could, smoked with all of them, and
gave the principal chief a string of wampum ; but
the highest satisfaction they derived from the music
of two of our violins, with which they seemed much
delighted : they remained all night at our fires.

  " This tribe is a branch of the nation called Pishquitpaws, and can raise about three hundred and
fifty men. In their dress they resemble the Indians
near the Forks of the Columbia, except that their
robes are smaller, and do not reach lower than the
waist ; indeed, three fourths of them have scarcely
anything that can be called a robe. The dress of
the females is equally scanty, for they wear only a
small piece of a robe, which covers their shoulders
and neck, and reaches down the back to the waist,
where it is attached by a piece of leather tied tight
round the body : their cheek-bones are high, their
heads flattened, and their persons in general adorned
with scarcely any ornaments. Both sexes were
employed in curing fish, of which they had great
quantities on their scaffolds.

" October 20. The morning was cool, the wind from the southwest. Our appearance had excited the curiosity of the neighbourhood so much, that before we set out about two hundred Indians had collected to see us ; and, as we were desirous of securing their friendship, we remained to smoke and confer with them till breakfast. We then took our repast, which consisted wholly of dog's flesh, and proceeded. We passed three vacant houses near our camp, and at six miles reached the head of a rapid, on descending which we soon came to another very difficult and dangerous : it is formed by a chain of large black rocks stretching from the right side of the river, and, with several small islands on the left, nearly choking the channel. To this we gave the name of Pelican Rapid, from seeing a number of pelicans and black cormorants about it. Just below it was a small island near the right shore, where were four houses, the occupants of which were busy in drying fish. At sixteen miles from our camp we reached a bend to the left, opposite a large island, and at one o'clock halted for dinner, on the lower point of an island on the right side of the channel. Close to this was a larger island on the same side, and near the left bank a small one, a little below. We landed near some Indian huts, and counted on this cluster of three islands seventeen of them, filled with inhabitants resembling in every respect those higher up ; and, like them, they were busy in preparing fish. We purchased of them some dried fish, which were not good, and a few berries, on which we dined, and then walked to the head of the island, for the purpose of examining a vault which we had observed in coming along.

" This place, in which the dead were deposited, was a building about sixty feet long and twelve feet wide, and was formed by fixing in the ground poles, with forks, six feet high, across which a long pole was extended the whole length of the structure. Against this ridge-pole were placed broad boards and pieces of canoes in a slanting direction, so as to form a shed. It stood east and west, and neither of the extremities was closed. On entering the western end we observed a number of bodies wrapped carefully in leathern robes, arranged in rows on boards, and covered with a mat. This was the part destined for those recently deceased; while a little farther on there were bones half decayed and scattered about, and in the centre of the building there was a large pile of them heaped promiscuously on each other. At the eastern extremity was a mat, on which were placed twenty-one sculls, in a circular form: the mode of interment being, first, to wrap the body in robes, and as it decays the bones are thrown into a heap, and the sculls placed together. From the different boards and pieces of canoes which formed the vault, there were suspended on the inside fishing-nets, baskets, wooden bowls, robes, skins, trenchers, and trinkets of various kinds, obviously intended as offerings of affection to deceased relatives. On the outside of the burial-place were the skeletons of several horses, and great quantities of their bones in the neighbourhood, which induced us to believe that these animals were most probably sacrificed at the funeral rites of their masters."

After leaving this place the country became more hilly, and they encamped in the evening, having made forty-two miles. They killed several ducks and two speckled gulls.

CHAPTER III.

The Party in their Descent still visited by the Indians.—Le-
page's River.—Towahnahiooks River.—Indian Mode of stack
ing Fish, and preparing them for Market.—Description of the
Great Falls.—Description of an Indian Canoe.—Alarm excited
by an anticipated Attack from the Eheltoots.—Dangerous
Rapid, called by the Indians The Falls.—Account of the In-
dian Houses in the Neighbourhood.—Another frightful Rapid.
—Some Account of the Chilluckittequaw Indians.—Captain
Clarke examines the Great Rapids.—Description of an Indian
Burial-place.—The Rapids passed in Safety.

" OCTOBER 21. The morning was cool, and the wind
from the southwest. At five and a half miles we
passed a small island, and one and a half farther another in the middle of the river, with some rapid water near its head, and opposite to its lower extremity
were eight cabins of Indians. We landed near them
for breakfast; but such was the scarcity of wood,
that the last evening we had not been able to collect
anything except dry willows, and of these not more
than barely sufficient to cook our supper : this morning we could not find enough even to prepare our
breakfast. The Indians received us with great kindness, and examined everything they saw with much
attention. In their appearance and employments,
as well as in their language, they did not differ from
those higher up the river. Their dress, too, was
nearly the same ; that of the men consisting of no-
:hing but a short robe of deer or goat skin, and the
women wearing only a piece of dressed skin, falling
from the neck so as to cover the front of the body
as low as the waist ; a bandage tied round the body,
and passing between the legs ; and over this a short
robe of deer and antelope skin was occasionally

thrown.   Here we saw two blankets of scarlet and
one of blue cloth, and also a sailor's round jacket;
but we could obtain only a few pounded roots and
some fish, for which, of course, we paid.   Among
other things we observed some acorns, the fruit of
the white oak.   These they use as food, either raw
or roasted; and on inquiry, they informed us that they
were procured from the Indians who live near the
Great Falls.   This place they designated by a name
very commonly applied to it by the Indians, and
highly expressive, the word Timm, which they pro-
nounce so as to make it perfectly represent the
sound of a distant cataract."*

They found the river obstructed by rocks and frequent rapids, and towards the close of the day it became   much   narrower.   Passing a considerable
stream coming in from the southeast, to which they
gave the name of Lepage's River, about seven miles
below they encamped near some Indian huts to
spend the night.

" The inhabitants of these huts," says the journalist, "stated to us that they were the relations of the
Indians living at the Great Falls.   They appeared
to be of the same nation with those we had seen
above, resembling them, indeed, in everything, except that their language, though essentially the same,
has some words different.   They have all pierced
noses ; and the men, when in full dress, wear a long
tapering piece of shell or bead put through the nose.
These people did not, however, receive us with as
much   cordiality as we had been accustomed to.
They were poor, but we were able to purchase from
them some wood to make a fire, of which, however,
they had but little, and which they said they brought
from the Great Falls.   The hills in this neighbour-

* The Indians, according to Parker, call the Falls of the
Columbia " Tum-Tum."   They use the same expression for the
beating of the heart.

hood are high and rugged, and a few scattered trees, either small pine or scrubby white oak, were occasionally seen on them. From the last rapids we observed a conical mountain towards the southwest, which the Indians said was not far to the left of the Great Falls; and from its vicinity to that place, we called it the Timm, or Falls Mountain. The country through which we passed is furnished with several fine springs, which rise either high up the sides of the hills, or else in the river meadows, and discharge themselves into the Columbia. We could not help remarking that the fishing establishments of the Indians, both on the Columbia and the waters of Lewis's River, are almost universally on the right bank. On inquiry, we were led to believe that the reason of this may be found in their fear of the Snake Indians; between whom and themselves, considering the warlike temper of that people, and the peaceful habits of the river tribes, it is very natural that the latter should be anxious to interpose so good a barrier. These Indians are described as residing on a great river to the south, and as always at war with the people of this neighbourhood. One of our chiefs pointed out to-day a spot on the left, where, not many years ago, a great battle had been fought, in which numbers of both nations were killed."

The following day they passed an island four miles in length, and about midway of it a large river appearing to come from the southeast, two hundred yards wide at its mouth, and increasing the volume of the Columbia one fourth. The Indians called it the Towahnahiooks. Six miles below this, near some Indian huts, they came to the commencement of the Great Falls. "Here," continues the Journal, "we halted, and immediately on landing walked down, accompanied by an old Indian from the huts, to examine the falls, in order to ascertain on which side we could make a portage most easily.

We soon discovered that the nearest route was on
the right side, and therefore dropped down to the
head of the rapid, unloaded the canoes, and took all
the baggage over by land to the foot of it.   The distance is twelve hundred yards.   On setting out, we
crossed a solid rock about one third of the whole
distance ; then reached a space of two hundred yards
wide, which forms a hollow, where the loose sand
from the low grounds has been driven by the winds,
and is steep and loose, and therefore difficult to
pass ; the rest of the route was over firm and solid
ground.   The labour of crossing would have been
very great, if the Indians had not assisted us in carrying some of the heavy articles on their horses ;
but for this service they repaid themselves so adroit-
ly, that, on reaching the foot of the rapids, we found
it necessary to form a camp in a position which
would secure us from their pilfering, which we
dreaded much more than their hostility.   Near our
camp were five large huts, the occupants being engaged in drying fish and preparing it for market.

" Their manner of doing this is, first, opening the
fish and exposing it to the sun on scaffolds.   When
it is sufficiently dried, it is pounded between two
stones till it is completely pulverized, and is then
placed in a basket about two feet long and one in
diameter, neatly made of grass and rushes, and lined
with the skin of a salmon stretched and dried for the
purpose.   Here it is pressed down as hard as possible, and the top covered with the skins of fish, which
are secured by cords through the holes of the basket.   The baskets are then put in some dry situation, the corded part upward, seven being usually
placed as closely as they can be together, and five
on the top of them.   The whole is then wrapped up
in mats, and made fast by cords, over which other
mats are thrown.   Twelve of these baskets, each of
which contains from ninety to a hundred pounds,
form a stack, which is now left till it is sent to mar-

ket. Fish thus prepared is kept sound and sweet for several years, and great quantities of it, they told us, were sent to the Indians living below the falls, whence it found its way to the whites who visited the mouth of the Columbia. We observed, both near the lodges and on the rocks in the river, great numbers of stacks of these pounded fish.

" Besides fish, these people supplied us with filberts and berries, and we purchased a dog for supper; but it was with much difficulty that we were able to buy wood enough to cook it. In the course of the day we were visited by many Indians, from whom we learned that the principal chiefs of the bands residing in this neighbourhood were now hunting in the mountains towards the southwest. On that side of the river none of the tribes have any permanent habitations ; and on inquiry, we were confirmed in our belief that it was from the fear of being attacked by the Snake Indians, with whom they are constantly at war. This nation they represent as being very numerous, and residing in a great number of villages on the Towahnahiooks, where they live principally on salmon. That river, they add, is not obstructed by rapids above its mouth, but becomes large, and reaches to a considerable distance ; the first villages of the Snake Indians being twelve days' journey, on a course about southeast from this place.

" October 23. Having ascertained from the Indians, and by our own examination, the best mode of bringing down the canoes, it was concluded, as the river was divided into several narrow channels by rocks and islands, to follow the route adopted by the Indians themselves. This labour Captain Clarke commenced in the morning, and, after crossing to the other side of the river, hauled the canoes over a point of land, so as to avoid a perpendicular fall of seventy feet. At the distance of four hundred and fifty-seven yards we reached the water, and em-

II.—F

barked at a place where a long, rocky island com-
presses the channel within the space of a hundred
and fifty yards, so as to form nearly a semicircle.
On leaving this rocky island the channel is somewhat wider, but a second and much larger island of
hard black rock still divides it from the main stream,
while on the left shore it is closely bordered by perpendicular cliffs.   Having descended in this way for
a mile, we reached a pitch of the river, which, being
divided by two large rocks, descends with great rapidity down a fall eight feet in height.   As the boats
could not be navigated down this steep descent, we
were obliged to land, and let them down as slowly
as possible by strong ropes of elkskin, which we had
prepared for the purpose.   They all passed in safety
except one, which, being loosed by the breaking of
the ropes, was driven down with all the force of the
current, but afterward recovered by the Indians below.   With this rapid ends the first pitch of the
Great Falls, which are not so remarkable in point
of height as for the singular manner in which the
rocks divide its channel.   From the marks everywhere perceivable at these falls, it is obvious that, in
the high floods in the spring, the water below the
falls rises nearly to a level with that above.   Of this
rise, occasioned by obstructions we had not yet seen,
the salmon must avail themselves to pass up the
river, and in such multitudes that that fish is almost
the only one caught in great abundance above the
falls : below these, however, we observed the salmon trout, and the heads of a smaller species of trout,
which are in great numbers, and which they are now
burying, to be used for winter food.   A hole being
dug, the sides and bottom are lined with straw, over
which skins are laid ; and on these the fish, after
being well dried, is placed, covered with other skins,
and the hole closed with a layer of earth twelve or
fifteen inches deep.

    " About three o'clock we reached the lower camp;

but our joy at having accomplished this object was somewhat diminished by the persecution of a new acquaintance. On reaching the upper point of the portage, we found that the Indians had been encamped there not long since, and had left behind them multitudes of fleas. These sagacious tormentors were so well pleased to exchange the straw and fish skins in which they had been living for a more comfortable residence, that we were soon covered with them ; and during the portage the men were obliged to strip to the skin, in order to brush them from their bodies. They were not, however, so easily dislodged from our clothes, and accompanied us in great numbers to our camp.

" We saw no game except a sea-otter, which was shot in the narrow channel as we were coming down, but we could not get it. Having, therefore, scarcely any provisions, we purchased eight small fat dogs : a food to which we were compelled to have recourse, as the Indians were very unwilling to sell us any of their good fish, which they reserved for the market below. Fortunately, however, habit had completely overcome the repugnance which we felt at first at eating this animal, and the dog, if not a favourite dish, was always an acceptable one. The meridian altitude of to-day gave 45° 42' 57.3" north as the latitude of our camp.

" On the beach, near the Indian huts, we observed two canoes of a different shape and size from any which we had hitherto seen. One of these we got by giving our smallest canoe, a hatchet, and a few trinkets to the owner, who said he had obtained it from a white man below the falls in exchange for a horse. These canoes were very beautifully made : wide in the middle, and tapering towards each end, with curious figures carved on the bow. They were thin, but, being strengthened by crossbars about an inch in diameter, tied with strong pieces of bark through holes in the sides, were able to bear very heavy burdens, and seemed calculated to live in the roughest water.

" A great number of Indians both from above and below the falls visited us this day, and towards evening we were informed by one of the chiefs who had accompanied us, that he had overheard that the Indians below intended to attack us as we went down the river ; but, being at all times ready for an attempt of that sort, we were not under any particular apprehensions at this intelligence : we therefore merely examined our arms, and increased the ammunition to one hundred rounds. Our chiefs, who had not the same motives of confidence, were by no means so much at their ease ; and when at night they saw the Indians leave us earlier than usual, their suspicions of an intended attack were confirmed, and they were very much alarmed. The next morning,

" October 24, the Indians, approached us with apparent caution, and behaved with more than usual reserve. Our two chiefs, by whom these circumstances were not unobserved, now told us that they wished to return home; that they could no longer be of any service to us, as they could not understand the language of the people below the falls; that these people formed a different nation from their own ; that the two people had been at war with each other; and as the Indians had expressed a resolution to attack us, they would certainly kill them. We endeavoured to quiet their fears, and requested them to stay two nights longer, in which time we would see the Indians below, and make a peace between the two nations. They replied that they were anxious to return, to look after their horses. We, however, insisted on their remaining with us, not only in the hope of bringing about an accommodation between them and their enemies, but because they might be able to detect any hostile designs against us, and also assist us in passing the next falls, which were not far off, and represented as very difficult : they at length consent-

ed to our proposal. About nine o'clock we proceeded, and on leaving our camp near the lower fall,
found the river about four hundred yards wide, with
a current more rapid than usual, though with no perceptible descent. At the distance of two and a half
miles it widened into a large bend or basin on the
right, at the beginning of which were three Indian
huts. At the extremity of this basin stood a high
black rock, which, rising perpendicularly from the
right shore, seemed to run wholly across the river :
so totally, indeed, did it appear to stop the passage,
that we could not see where the water escaped, except that the current was seemingly drawn with more
than usual velocity to the left of the rock, where was
heard a great roaring. We landed at the huts of the
Indians, who went with us to the top of the rock,
from which we had a view of all the difficulties of the
channel. We were now no longer at a loss to account for the rising of the river at the falls ; for this
tremendous rock was seen stretching across the
river, to meet the high hills on the left shore, leaving
a channel of only forty-five yards wide, through
which the whole body of the Columbia pressed its
way. The water, thus forced into so narrow a passage, was thrown into whirls, and swelled and boiled
in every part with the wildest agitation. But the
alternative of carrying the boats over this high rock
was almost impossible in our present situation ; and
as the chief danger seemed to be, not from any obstructions in the channel, but from the great waves
and whirlpools, we resolved to attempt the passage,
in the hope of being able, by dexterous steering, to
descend in safety. This we undertook, and with
great care were able to get through, to the astonishment of the Indians in the huts we had just passed,
who now collected to see us from the top of the rock.
The channel continued thus confined for the space
of about half a mile, when the rock ceased. We
passed a single Indian hut at the foot of it, where the

river again enlarged itself to the width of two hundred yards, and at the distance of a mile and a half stopped to view a very bad rapid, formed by the rocky islands which divided the channel, and the lower and larger of which was in the middle of the river. The appearance of this place was so unpromising, that we unloaded all the most valuable articles, such as guns, ammunition, our papers, &c., and sent them by land, with such of the men as could not swim, to the extremity of the rapid. We then descended with the canoes, two at a time, and though they took in some water, we all passed down safely; after which we made two miles, and stopped in a deep bend of the river towards the right, and encamped a little above a large village of twenty-one houses. Here we landed, and as it was late before all the canoes joined us, we were obliged to remain, the difficulties of the navigation having permitted us to make only six miles. This village was situated at the extremity of a deep bend towards the right, and immediately above a ledge of high rocks, twenty feet above the marks of the highest flood, but broken in several places so as to form channels, which were then dry, extending nearly across the river: this forms the second fall, or the place, most probably, which the Indians mean by the word Timm. While the canoes were coming up, Captain Clarke walked down with two men to examine these channels. On the rocks here the Indians are accustomed to dry fish; and as the season for that purpose was now over, the poles which they use were tied up very securely in bundles, and placed on the scaffolds. The stock of dried and pounded fish was so abundant, that he counted one hundred and seven heaps, making more than ten thousand pounds of that provision. After examining the narrows as well as the lateness of the hour would permit, he returned to the village through a rocky, open country, infested with polecats. This village, the residence of a tribe called the Echeloots, consisted of houses scattered promiscuously over an elevated situation, near a mound more than thirty feet above the common level, with some remains of houses on it, and having every appearance of being artificial.

" The houses, which were the first wooden buildings we had seen since leaving the Illinois country, were nearly equal in size, and exhibited a very singular appearance. A large hole, twenty feet wide and thirty in length, was dug to the depth of six feet ; the sides of which were lined with split pieces of timber rising just above the surface of the ground, and smoothed to the same width by burning, or by being shaved with small iron axes. These timbers were secured in their erect position by a pole stretched along the side of the building near the eaves, and supported on a strong post fixed at each corner. The timbers at the gable ends rose gradually higher, the middle pieces being the broadest. At the top of these was a sort of semicircle, made to receive a ridge-pole the whole length of the house, propped by an additional post in the middle, and forming the top of the roof. From this ridge-pole to the eaves of the house were placed a number of small poles or rafters, secured at each end by fibres of the cedar. On these poles, which were connected by small transverse bars of wood, was laid a covering of white cedar, or *arbor vitæ*, kept on by strands of cedar fibres ; but a small space along the whole length of the ridge-pole was left uncovered, for the purpose of light, and of permitting the smoke to pass out. The roof, thus formed, had a descent about equal to that common among us, and near the eaves it was perforated with a number of small holes, made, most probably, for the discharge of arrows in case of an attack. The only entrance was by a small door at the gable end, cut out of the middle piece of timber, twenty-nine and a half inches high, fourteen inches broad, and reaching only eighteen inches above the earth. Before this hole was hung a mat, and on pushing it aside and crawling through, the descent was by a small ladder, made in the form of those used among us. One half of the inside was used as a place of deposite for their dried fish, in which there were large quantities stored away, and which, with a few baskets of berries, formed the provisions for the family ; the other half, adjoining the door, was for the accommodation of the family. On each side were arranged, near the walls, small beds of mats, placed on little scaffolds or bedsteads raised from eighteen inches to three feet from the ground, and in the middle of the vacant space was the fire, or sometimes two or three fires, where, as, indeed, is usually the case, the house contained three families.

"The inhabitants received us with much kindness, invited us to their houses, and in the evening, after our camp had been formed, came in great numbers to see us, accompanied by a principal chief and several warriors of the nation below the Great Narrows. We made use of this opportunity to attempt a reconciliation between them and our two chiefs, and to put an end to the war which had disturbed the two nations. On representing to the chiefs the evils which the war inflicted on them, and the wants and privations to which it subjected them, they soon became disposed to be reconciled with each other, and we had some reason to believe in the sincerity of their mutual promises, that the war should no longer be continued, and that in future they would live in peace with each other. On concluding this negotiation, we proceeded to invest the chief with the insignia of command—a medal and some small articles of clothing ; after which the violin was produced, and our men danced, to the great delight of the Indians.

" October 25. We walked down with several of the Indians to view the part of the narrows which they represented as most dangerous, and found it very difficult; and, as the portage was impracticable with our large canoes, we concluded to carry our most valuable articles by land, and then hazard the passage. We therefore returned to the village, and, having sent some of the party, with our best stores, to make a portage, and placed others on the rocks, to assist, by means of ropes, the canoes that might meet with any difficulty, we began the descent, in the presence of a great number of Indians who had collected to witness the exploit. The channel for three miles is worn through a hard. rough, black rock, from fifty to one hundred yards wide, in which the water swells and boils in a tremendous manner. The first three canoes escaped very well; the fourth, however, nearly filled with water; and the fifth passed through with taking in only a small quantity of water. At half a mile we had got through the worst part, and, having reloaded our canoes, went on very well for the remaining two and a half miles, except that one of the boats was nearly lost by running against a rock. At the end of this channel, in which the Indians told us they caught as many salmon as they wished, we reached a deep basin or bend of the river towards the right, near the entrance of which were two rocks. We crossed the basin, which has a quiet and gentle current, and at the distance of a mile from its commencement, and a little below where the river resumes its channel, reached a rock which divides it. At this place we met our old chiefs, who, when we began the portage, had walked down to a village below, to smoke a pipe of friendship on the renewal of peace. Just after our meeting we saw a chief of the village above, with a party who had been out hunting, and were then crossing the river with their horses on their way home. We landed to smoke with this chief, whom we found to be a bold-looking man, of a pleasing appearance, about fifty years of age, and dressed in a war-jacket, cap, leggins, and moccasins. We presented him with a medal and other small articles, and he gave us some meat, of which he had been able to procure but little ; for on his route he met with a war-party of Indians from the Towahnahiooks, between whom he had a battle. We here smoked a parting pipe with our two faithful friends, the chiefs who had accompanied us from the heads of the river, and who had now each bought a horse, intending to go home by land. On leaving this rock the current of the river is gentle, but its bed is strewed with a great number of rocks for several miles, when it becomes a beautiful, still stream, about half a mile wide. At five miles from the large bend we came to the mouth of a creek twenty yards in breadth, heading in a range of mountains which run S.S.W. and S.W. for a long distance, and discharging a considerable quantity of water : it is called by the Indians Quenett. We halted below it, under a high point of rocks on the left, and formed a camp on their top to take some celestial observations." * * * "From this rock, the pinnacle of the round mountain covered with snow, which we had seen a short distance below the Forks of the Columbia, and called the Falls or Timm Mountain, was south 43° west, and about thirty-seven miles distant." * * *

" Both above and below the narrows, as well as in them, we had seen a great number of sea-otter, and in the evening a deer was killed, and numerous traces of that animal were observed near the camp." * * *

" October 26. The morning was fine, and we sent six men to hunt, and to collect rosin to pitch the canoes, which, by being frequently hauled over the rocks, had become very leaky. They were also drawn up to dry, and on examination it was found that many of the articles on board of them had become spoiled by being repeatedly wet. We were

occupied with the observations necessary to determine our longitude, and with conferences with the
Indians, many of whom came on horseback to the
opposite shore in the fore part of the day, and showed some anxiety to cross over to us ; we did not, however, think it expedient to send for them, but towards
evening two chiefs, with fifteen men, came over
in a small canoe. They proved to be the two principal chiefs of the tribes at and above the Falls, and
had been absent on a hunting excursion as we passed their residence : each of them, on arriving, made
us a present of deer's flesh, and of small white cakes
made of roots. Being anxious to ingratiate ourselves with them so as to ensure a friendly reception
on our return, we treated them with all the kindness
we could show. We accordingly acknowledged the
chiefs, giving a medal of the small size, a red silk
handkerchief, an armband, a knife, and a piece of
paint to each, and small presents to others of the
party, with half a deer. These attentions were not
lost on them, for they appeared very well pleased.
At night a fire was made in the middle of our camp,
and as the Indians sat round it, our men danced to
the music of the violin, which so delighted them
that several resolved to remain with us through the
night : the rest crossed the river. All the tribes in
this neighbourhood were at war with the Snake Indians, whom they described as living on the Towahnahiooks, and whose nearest town was, they said,
four days' march from this place, and in a direction
nearly southwest." * * *

"October 27. The two chiefs who remained with
us were joined by seven Indians, who came in a canoe from below. To these men we were very particular in our attentions, smoking and eating with
them ; but some of them being tempted, by the sight
of our goods that were exposed to dry, to take lib-
erties with them, we were under the necessity of
putting an immediate check to it, and this displeas-

ed them so much that they returned down the river in a very ill humour. The two chiefs, however, remained with us till the evening, when they crossed the river to their party.

" Before they went we obtained from them a vocabulary of the Echeloot, their native language; and, on comparison, were surprised at its difference from the Eneeshur tongue. In fact, although the Echeloots, who live at the Great Narrows, are not more than six miles from the Eneeshurs, who reside at and above the Great Falls, the two people are separated by a broad distinction of language. The Eneeshurs are understood by all the tribes on the Columbia above the Falls; but at that place they meet with the unintelligible language of the Echeloots, which descends the river from thence a considerable distance. Yet this may, after all, be only a difference of dialect, and not a radical difference, since in both languages many words are the same; and the identity cannot be accounted for by supposing that their neighbourhood has interwoven them into their daily conversation, since the same words are equally familiar among all the Flathead bands we have passed. The strange clucking or guttural noise which first struck us, is common to all these tribes. They also flatten the heads of their children in nearly the same manner; but we now begin to observe that the heads of the males, as well as of the other sex, are subjected to this operation; whereas, among the mountains, the custom is confined almost entirely to the females." * * *

" October 28. The morning was cool and windy. Having dried our goods, we were about setting out, when three canoes came from above to visit us, and two others from below for the same purpose. Among the Indians in these last was one who wore his hair in a queue, and had on a round hat and a sailor's jacket, which he said he had obtained from the people below the Great Rapids, who bought them from the whites."

This interview being over, the party again started to descend the river, and after proceeding four miles, landed near a small Indian settlement of eight houses. " On entering one of them," says the Journal, " we saw a British musket, a cutlass, and several brass tea-kettles, which they seemed to prize very highly. There were also figures of men, birds, and different animals, cut and painted on the boards which form the sides of the room ; and though the workmanship of these uncouth figures was very rough, they were as highly esteemed by the Indians as the finest frescoes of more civilized people. This tribe is called the Chilluckittequaw, and their language, although somewhat different from that of the Echeloots, has many of the same words, and is sufficiently intelligible to the neighbouring Indians. We obtained from them a vocabulary ; and, after buying five small dogs, some dried berries, and a white bread or cake made of roots, left them." * * *

The wind was so high, however, that after proceeding a mile they were obliged to land, and stop for the day. " We had not been long on shore," proceeds the narrative, " before a canoe, with a man, his wife, and two children, came from below, through the high waves, with a few roots to sell ; and soon after we were visited by many Indians from the village above, with whom we smoked and conversed. The canoes used by these people were, like those already described, built of white cedar or pine, very light, wide in the middle, and tapering towards the ends, the bow being raised, and ornamented with carvings of the heads of animals. As the canoe is their chief vehicle for transportation, the Indians have acquired great dexterity in its management, and guide it safely over the highest waves. They have, among their utensils, bowls and baskets very neatly made of bark and grass, in which they boil their provisions." * * *

" October 29. The morning was cloudy, and the

wind from the west; but, as it had abated its violence, we set out at daylight. At the distance of
four miles we passed a creek on the right, one mile
below which was a village of seven houses on the
same side. This was the residence of the principal
chief of the Chilluckittequaw nation, who we found
was the same between whom and our two chiefs
we had made a peace at the Echeloot village. He
received us very kindly, and set before us pounded
fish, filberts, nuts, the berries of the *sacacommis*,
and white bread made of roots. We gave, in return, a bracelet of riband to each of the women of
the house, with which they were very much pleased. The chief had several articles, such as scarlet
and blue cloth, a sword, a jacket, and a hat, which
must have been procured from the whites, and on
one side of the room were two wide, split boards,
placed together so as to make space for a rude figure of a man cut and painted on them. On pointing
to this, and asking him what it meant, he said something, of which all that we understood was 'good,'
and then stepped up to the painting, and took out
his bow and quiver, which, with some other warlike
instruments, were kept behind it. He then directed
his wife to hand him his medicine-bag, from which
he drew out fourteen forefingers, which he told us
had belonged to the same number of his enemies,
whom he had killed in fighting with the nations to
the southeast, in which direction he pointed; allu-
ding, no doubt, to the Snake Indians, the common
enemy of the tribes on the Columbia. This bag is
usually about two feet in length, and contains roots,
pounded dirt, &c., which only the Indians know how
to appreciate. It is suspended in the middle of the
lodge; and it is considered as a species of sacrilege
for any one but the owner to touch it. It is an object of religious fear; and, from its supposed sanc-
tity, is the chief place for depositing their medals
and more valuable articles. They have likewise

small bags, which they preserve in their great medicine-bag, from whence they are taken, and worn
around their waists and necks as amulets against
any real or imaginary evils. This was the first
time we had been apprized that the Indians ever
carried from the field any other trophy than the
scalp. These fingers were shown with great exul-
tation; and, after an harangue, which we were left
to presume was in praise of his exploits, the chief
carefully replaced them among the valuable contents
of his red medicine-bag. The inhabitants of this
village being part of the same nation with those of
the village we had passed above, the language of the
two was the same, and their houses were of similar
form and materials, and calculated to contain about
thirty souls. They were unusually hospitable and
good-humoured, so that we gave to the place the
name of the Friendly village. We breakfasted here;
and after purchasing twelve dogs, four sacks of fish,
and a few dried berries, proceeded on our journey.
The hills as we passed were high, with steep, rocky
sides, with pine and white oak, and an undergrowth
of shrubs scattered over them."

Four miles farther on they passed the mouth of a
small river on the right, which they called Cataract
River; and twelve miles beyond this, another stream
on the left, to which they gave the name of Labieshe,
after one of the party. Here were the first houses
which they had noticed on the right side of the Columbia. They landed for the night at three Indian huts
on the right bank, after having made thirty-two
miles.

"On our first arrival," says the Journal, "the inhabitants seemed surprised, but not alarmed, at our
appearance; and we soon became intimate by means
of smoking, and, what was ever a favourite amusement with the Indians, the music of the violin. They
gave us fruit, some roots, and root-bread, and we
purchased from them three dogs. The houses of

these people were similar to those of the Indians above, and their language the same. Their dress also, consisting of robes made of the skin of the wolf, deer, elk, and wild-cat, was nearly after the same fashion. Their hair was worn in plaits down each shoulder, and round their neck was a strip of skin, with the tail of the animal hanging over the breast. Like the Indians above, they were fond of otter skins, and gave a great price for them. We here saw the skin of a mountain sheep, which they said lived among the rocks in the mountains. It was covered with white hair; the wool was long, thick, and coarse, with long, coarse hair on the top of the neck, and on the back resembling somewhat the bristles of a goat. Immediately behind the village was a pond, in which were great numbers of small swan."

The Columbia was here about three fourths of a mile wide, with a gentle current, though occasionally obstructed by rocks. In proceeding the following day they passed a river on the right, sixty yards in width, which, after one of their men, they called Crusatte's River. About two and a half miles below this they came to a rapid, which is called the Great Shoot of the river, where they found it necessary to terminate their voyage for the day. It became necessary to explore the country to ascertain the best route for a portage, and Captain Clarke started for this purpose, soon after landing. The night obliging him to return after he had proceeded about three miles, he resumed his examination the next morning.

"At the extremity of a basin," says the narrative, "in which was situated the island where we were encamped, several rocks and rocky islands were scattered along the bed of the river. The rocks on each side had fallen down from the mountains, the one on the left being high, and the hill on the right, which was lower, having bodily slid into the river, so that the current was here compressed within a space of one hun-

dred and fifty yards. Within this narrow limit it runs
for the distance of four hundred yards with great rapidity, swelling over the rocks with a fall of about
twenty feet. It then widens to two hundred paces,
and the current for a short distance becomes gentle;
but a mile and a half farther on, opposite to an old
Indian village, it is obstructed by a very bad rapid,
where the waves are unusually high, the river being
confined between large rocks, many of which are at
the surface of the water."

Following the same route he had taken the day
before, two and a half miles below the shoot he struck
the river at a point where the Indians commence
their portage round the rapids. From this place he
sent one of his men up the stream, to ascertain if it
were practicable to bring down the canoes by water;
while with the other he proceeded farther down
(the rapids extending as far as he could see), when
at the distance of a mile and a half, in the midst of a
dense wood, he came to an ancient burial-place: "it
consisted," says the journalist, "of eight vaults,
formed of pine or cedar boards closely connected,
each about eight feet square and six in height: the
top was covered with boards sloping a little, so as to
carry off the rain. Their direction was east and
west; the door being on the eastern side, partially
stopped with wide boards, and decorated with rude
pictures of men and animals. On entering, we found
in some of them four dead bodies, carefully wrapped
in skins tied with cords of grass and bark, and lying
on a mat in an east and west direction: the others
contained only bones, which were in some of them
piled to the height of four feet. On the tops of the
vaults, and on poles attached to them, were hung
brass kettles and frying-pans with holes in their bottoms, baskets, bowls, sea-shells, skins, pieces of
cloth, hair, bags of trinkets and small bones, the
offerings of friendship or affection, which a pious
veneration had preserved from the ferocity of war,

II.—G

and the more dangerous temptations of individual selfishness. The whole of the walls, as well as the door, were ornamented with strange figures cut and painted on them; and, besides these, there were several wooden images of men, some of them so old and decayed as to have almost lost their shape, all placed against the sides of the vaults. Neither these images, nor those in the houses we had lately visited, appeared to be at all the objects of adoration. In this place they were most probably intended for resemblances of the deceased; and those we had observed in the houses occupied the most conspicuous part, but were treated more like ornaments than objects of worship. Near the vaults that were standing were the remains of others, completely rotted and covered with moss; and as they were formed of the most durable pine and cedar timber, it would appear that this retired spot had long been a depository for the dead."

After proceeding down the river somewhat farther, and carefully examining the country, Captain Clarke returned to the encampment.

"We had an opportunity to-day," says the Journal, "of witnessing the hardihood of the Indians of the neighbouring village. One of our men shot a goose, which fell into the river, and was floating rapidly towards the Great Shoot, when an Indian plunged in after it. The entire mass of the waters of the Columbia, rushing onward to descend the narrow channel, hurried the bird along with great rapidity. The Indian followed it fearlessly to within one hundred and fifty feet of the rocks, where he would inevitably have been dashed to pieces; when, seizing his prey, he turned round and swam to the shore with the utmost composure. We very willingly relinquished our right to the game in favour of one who had thus saved it at the imminent hazard of his life: he immediately set to work and picked off about half the feathers, and then, without opening it, ran a stick through it, and carried it off to roast."

The next day, November 1, following the example of some Indians who preceded them, they transported their baggage and small canoe by land to the foot of the shoot ; and the four large canoes they managed to slide along on poles extended from one rock to another, occasionally availing themselves of small streams at the side of the river.   They now re-embarked on board the boats, and, making their way with no little difficulty through other less formidable rapids, at the distance of seven miles from the head of the Great Shoot they landed for the night.

"The meridian altitude of to-day," proceeds the Journal, "gave us the latitude of 45° 44′ 3″.   As we passed a village of four houses, we stopped to visit them.   They were similar to those already described, but larger, from thirty-five to fifty feet long. and thirty feet wide, being sunk in the ground about six feet, and raised the same height above.   Their beds were raised about four feet and a half above the floor, and the ascent to them was by a newly-painted ladder, with which every family is provided, and under them were stored their dried fish, while the space between the part of the beds on which they lay and the wall of the house was occupied by the nuts, roots, berries, and other provisions, spread on mats.   The fireplace was about eight feet long and six feet wide, sunk a foot below the floor, and secured by a frame, with mats placed around for the family to sit on.   In all of the houses were images of men of different shapes, placed as ornaments in the parts where they would be most seen.   The inhabitants gave us nuts, berries, and some dried fish to eat ; and we purchased, among other articles, a hat made after their own taste, and such as they wear, without a brim.   They asked high prices for all that they sold, observing that the whites below paid dear for whatever they carried to them. We could not learn precisely the nature of the trade carried on by the Indians with the inhabitants below. But, as their knowledge of the whites seemed to be very imperfect, and the only articles which they took to market, such as pounded fish, bear-grass, and roots, could not be objects of much foreign traffic, their intercourse appeared to be an intermediate trade with the natives near the mouth of the Columbia ; from whom they obtained, in exchange for their fish, roots, and bear-grass, blue and white beads, copper tea-kettles, brass armbands, some scarlet and blue robes, and a few articles of second-hand European clothing. But their great object is to obtain beads : an article which holds the first place in their ideas of value, and to procure which they will sacrifice their last garment and last mouthful of food. Independently of their fondness for them as an ornament, these beads are employed as a medium of trade, by which they obtain from the Indians still higher up the river, robes, skins, root-bread, bear-grass, &c. These, in turn, make use of them to procure from the Indians in the Rocky Mountains bear-grass, *pacheco*, roots, robes, &c.

" These Indians were rather below the common size, with high cheek-bones, their noses pierced, and, when in full dress, were ornamented with a tapering piece of white shell or wampum about two inches long. Their eyes were exceedingly sore and weak, many of them having only a single eye, and some were perfectly blind. Their teeth had prematurely decayed, and in many instances were altogether worn away. Their general health, however, seemed to be good, the only disorder we remarked among them being tumours in different parts of the body. The women were small, and homely in their appearance ; their legs much swelled, and their knees remarkably large ; deformities which are no doubt owing to the manner in which they sit on their hams

They go nearly naked, having only a piece of leather tied round the breast, falling thence nearly as low as the waist, with a small robe about three feet square, and a piece of leather tied between the legs. Their hair was suffered to hang loose in every direction ; and in their persons, as well as in their cookery, they were filthy to a most disgusting degree. We here observed that the women universally have their heads flattened; and in many of the villages we have recently seen the female children undergo the operation."

CHAPTER IV.

First Appearance of Tide-water in the Columbia River.—The Quicksand River.—Some Account of the Skilloot Indians.— The Party pass the Coweliske River.—Some Account of the Wahkiacum Indians.—Arrival on the Borders of the Pacific. —Disagreeable and Critical Situation of the Party when first encamped.—Their Distress from incessant Torrents of Rain. —Exposed for thirty Days to this drenching Deluge, during which Time their Provisions are spoiled, and most of their few Articles of Merchandise destroyed.—Distress of the Party. —Adventure of Shannon, and his Danger from the Wahkiacums.—Difficulty of finding a Place suitable for a permanent Encampment.—Visited by several Indians of different Tribes, on whom Medals were bestowed.

" November 2. We now examined the rapid below more particularly, and the danger appearing to be too great for the loaded canoes, all those who could not swim were sent with the baggage by land. The canoes then passed safely down, and were reloaded. At the foot of the rapid we took a meridian altitude, and found our latitude to be 59° 45′ 45″."

This rapid forms the last of the descents of the Columbia ; and immediately below it the river wi-

dens, and tide-water commences. Shortly after starting they passed an island three miles in length and to
which, from that plant being seen on it in great abundance, they gave the name of Strawberry Island. Directly beyond were three small islands, and in the
meadow to the right, at some distance from the hills
in the background was a single perpendicular rock,
which they judged to be not less than eight hundred feet high, and four hundred yards at the base,
which they called Beacon Rock. A little farther on
they found the river a mile in breadth, and double this
breadth four miles beyond. After making twenty-
nine miles from the foot of the Great Shoot, they halted for the night at a point where the river was two
and a half miles wide. The character of the country
they had passed through during the day was very different from that they had lately been accustomed to,
the hills being thickly covered with timber, chiefly of
the pine species. The tide rose at their encampment
about nine inches, and they saw great numbers
of water-fowl, such as swan, geese, ducks of various kinds, gulls, &c.

The next day, November 3d, they set off in company with some Indians who had joined them the
evening before. At the distance of three miles they
passed a river on the left, to which, from the quantity of sand it bears along with it, they gave the name
of Quicksand River. So great, indeed, was the
quantity it had discharged into the Columbia, that
that river was compressed to the width of half a mile,
and the whole force of the current thrown against
the right shore. Opposite to this was a large creek,
which they called Seal River. The mountain which
they had supposed to be the Mount Hood of Vancouver, now bore S. 85° E., about forty-seven miles
distant. About three miles farther on they passed the
lower mouth of Quicksand River, opposite to which
was another large creek, and near it the head of an
island three miles and a half in extent; and half a

mile beyond it was another island, which they called Diamond Island, opposite to which they encamped, having made but thirteen miles' distance. Here
they met with some Indians ascending the river, who
stated that they had seen three vessels at its mouth.

"Below Quicksand River," says the Journal, "the
country is low, rich, and thickly wooded on each
side of the Columbia; the islands have less timber,
and on them are numerous ponds, near which were
vast quantities of fowl, such as swan, geese, brant,
cranes, storks, white gulls, cormorants, and plover.
The river is wide, and contains a great number of
sea-otters. In the evening the hunters brought in
game for a sumptuous supper."

In continuing their descent the next day, they
found Diamond Island to be six miles in length and
three broad; and near its termination were two other islands. "Just below the last of these," proceeds
the narrative, "we landed on the left bank of the river, at a village of twenty-five houses, all of which were
thatched with straw, and built of bark except one,
which was about fifty feet long, and constructed of
boards, in the form of those higher up the river, from
which it differed, however, in being completely above
ground, and covered with broad, split boards. This
village contained about two hundred men of the
Skilloot nation, who seemed well provided with canoes, of which there were at least fifty-two, and
some of them very large, drawn up in front of the
village. On landing, we found an Indian from above,
who had left us this morning, and who now invited
us into a lodge of which he appeared to be part owner. Here he treated us with a root, round in shape,
and about the size of a small Irish potato, which they
call *wappatoo*: it is the common arrow-head or *sag
ittifolia* so much cultivated by the Chinese, and, when
roasted in the embers till it becomes soft, has an
agreeable taste, and is a very good substitute for
bread. After purchasing some of this root we re-

sumed our journey, and at seven miles' distance came
to the head of a large island near the left bank.   On
the right shore was a fine open prairie for about a
mile, back of which the country rises, and is well supplied with timber, such as white oak, pine of different
kinds, wild crab, and several species of undergrowth,
while along the borders of the river there were only
a few cottonwood and ash trees.   In this prairie
were also signs of deer and elk.

" When we landed for dinner a number of Indians
came down, for the purpose, as we supposed, of pay-
ing us a friendly visit, as they had put on their finest
dresses.   In addition to their usual covering, they
had scarlet and blue blankets, sailors' jackets and
trowsers, shirts, and hats.   They had all of them
either war-axes, spears, and bows and arrows, or
muskets and pistols, with tin powder-flasks.   We
smoked with them, and endeavoured to show them
every attention, but soon found them very assuming
and disagreeable companions.   While we were eating, they stole the pipe with which they were smoking, and a greatcoat of one of the men.   We immediately searched them all, and found the coat stuffed
under the root of a tree near where they were sitting; but the pipe we could not recover.   Finding us
discontented with them, and determined not to suffer
any imposition, they showed their displeasure in the
only way they dared, by returning in ill humour to
their village.   We then proceeded, and soon met
two canoes, with twelve men of the same Skilloot
nation, who were on their way from below.   The
larger of the canoes was ornamented with the figures of a bear in the bow and a man in the stern,
both nearly as large as life, both made of painted
wood, and very neatly fastened to the boat.   In the
same canoe were two Indians gaudily dressed, and
with round hats.   This circumstance induced us to
give the name of Image Canoe to the large island,
the lower end of which we were now passing, at the

distance of nine miles from its head. We had seen
two smaller islands to the right, and three more near
its lower extremity." * * * "The river was now
about a mile and a half in width, with a gentle current, and the bottoms extensive and low, but not subject to be overflowed. Three miles below Image-
Canoe Island we came to four large houses on the
left side ; here we had a full view of the mountain
which we had first seen from the Muscleshell Rapid
on the 19th of October, and which we now found to
be, in fact, the Mount St. Helen of Vancouver. It
bore north 25° east, about ninety miles distant, rose
in the form of a sugar-loaf to a very great height,
and was covered with snow. A mile lower we passed a single house on the left, and another on the
right. The Indians had now learned so much of us
that their curiosity was without any mixture of fear,
and their visits became very frequent and troublesome. We therefore continued on till after night, in
hopes of getting rid of them ; but, after passing a
village on each side, which, on account of the lateness of the hour, we could only see indistinctly, we
found there was no escaping from their importunities.
We accordingly landed at the distance of seven
miles below Image-Canoe Island, and encamped near
a single house on the right, having made during the
day twenty-nine miles.

"The Skilloots that we passed to-day speak a
language somewhat different from that of the Echeloots or Chilluckittequaws near the long narrows.
Their dress, however, is similar, except that the
Skilloots possess more articles procured from the
white traders ; and there is this farther difference
between them, that the Skilloots, both males and females, have the head flattened. Their principal food
is fish, *wappatoo* roots, and some elk and deer, in killing which with arrows they seem to be very expert;
for during the short time we remained at the village,
three deer were brought in. We also observed there
a tame *blaireau*.

II.—H

" As soon as we landed we were visited by two ca
noes loaded with Indians, from whom we purchased
a few roots.   The grounds along the river continued
low and rich, and among the shrubs were large
quantities of vines resembling the raspberry.   On
the right, the low grounds were terminated, at the
distance of five miles, by a range of high hills covered with tall timber, and running southeast and
northwest.   The game, as usual, was very abundant ; and, among other birds, we observed some
white geese, with a part of their wings black."

Early the next morning they resumed their voyage, passing several islands. in the course of the
day, the river alternately widening and contracting,
and the hills sometimes retiring from, and at others
approaching, its banks,.   They stopped for the night
at the distance of thirty-two miles from their last
encampment.   " Before landing," proceeds the Journal, " we met two canoes, the largest of which had
at the bow the image of a bear, and that of a man
on the stern : there were twenty-six Indians on
board, but they proceeded upward, and we were left,
for the first time since we reached the waters of the
Columbia, without any of the natives with us during the night.   Besides other game, we killed a
grouse much larger than the common kind, and observed along the shore a number of striped snakes.
The river is here deep, and about a mile and a half
in width.   Here, too, the ridge of low mountains,
running northwest and southeast, crosses the river,
and forms the western boundary of the plain through
which we had just passed.   This great plain or valley begins above the mouth of Quicksand River, and
is about sixty miles long in a straight line, while on
the right and left it extends to a great distance : it
is a fertile and delightful country, shaded by thick
groves of tall timber, and watered by small ponds
on both sides of the river.   The soil is rich, and capable of any species of culture ; but in the present

condition of the Indians, its chief production is the *wappatoo* root, which grows spontaneously and exclusively in this region. Sheltered as it is on both sides, the temperature is much milder than that of the surrounding country; for even at this season of the year we observed but very little appearance of frost. It is inhabited by numerous tribes of Indians, who either reside in it permanently, or visit its waters in quest of fish and *wappatoo* roots. We gave it the name of the Columbia Valley.

" November 6. The morning was cool and rainy. We proceeded at an early hour, between high hills on both sides of the river, till at the distance of four miles we came to two tents of Indians in a small plain on the left, where the hills on the right recede a few miles, and a long narrow island stretches along the right shore. Behind this island is the mouth of a large river, a hundred and fifty yards wide, called by the Indians Coweliske. We halted on the island for dinner, but the redwood and green briers were so interwoven with the pine, alder, ash, a species of beech, and other trees, that the woods formed a thicket which our hunters could not penetrate. Below the mouth of the Coweliske a very remarkable knob rises from the water's edge to the height of eighty feet, being two hundred paces round the base ; and as it is in a low part of the island, and at some distance from the high grounds, its appearance is very singular. On setting out after dinner we overtook two canoes going down to trade. One of the Indians, who spoke a few words of English, mentioned that the principal person who traded with them was a Mr. Haley ; and he showed us a bow of iron, and several other things, which he said he had given him. Nine miles below Coweliske River is a creek on the same side ; and between them three smaller islands, one on the left shore, the other about the middle of the river, and a third near the lower end of the long narrow island, and

opposite a high cliff of black rocks on the left, sixteen miles from our last night's encampment. Here
we were overtaken by some Indians from the two
tents we had passed in the morning, from whom we
purchased *wappatoo* roots, salmon, trout, and two
beaver-skins, for which last we gave five small fish-
hooks."

Here the mountains, which had been high and rugged on the left, retired from the river, as had the
hills on the right, since leaving the Coweliske, and
a beautiful plain was spread out before them. They
met with several islands on their way, and having,
at the distance of five miles, come to the termination
of the plain, they proceeded for eight miles through
a hilly country, and encamped for the night after
having made twenty-nine miles.

" November 7. The morning," proceeds the narrative, " was rainy, and the fog so thick that we
could not see across the river. We observed, however, opposite to our camp, the upper point of an isl-
and, between which and the steep hills on the right
we proceeded for five miles. Three miles lower
was the beginning of an island, separated from the
right shore by a narrow channel: down this we proceeded, under the direction of some Indians whom
we had just met going up the river, and who returned in order to show us their village. It consisted
of four houses only, situated on this channel, behind
several marshy islands formed by two small creeks.
On our arrival they gave us some fish, and we afterward purchased *wappatoo* roots, fish, three dogs, and
two otter-skins, for which we gave fish-hooks chiefly, that being an article which they are very anxious
to obtain.

" These people seemed to be of a different nation
from those we had just passed : they were low in
stature, ill-shaped, and all had their heads flattened
They called themselves Wahkiacum, and their language differed from that of the tribes above, with

whom they trade for *wappatoo* roots. The houses, too, were built in a different style, being raised entirely above ground, with the eaves about five feet high, and the door at the corner. Near the end opposite to the door was a single fireplace, round which were the beds, raised four feet from the floor of earth : over the fire were hung fresh fish, and when dried they are stowed away with the *wappatoo* roots under the beds. The dress of the men was like that of the people above ; but the women were clad in a peculiar manner, the robe not reaching lower than the hip, and the body being covered in cold weather by a sort of corset of fur, curiously plaited, and reaching from the arms to the hip : added to this was a sort of petticoat, or, rather, tissue of white cedar bark, bruised or broken into small strands, and woven into a girdle by several cords of the same material. Being tied round the middle, these strands hang down as low as the knee in front, and to the middle of the leg behind : sometimes the tissue consists of strings of silk-grass, twisted and knotted at the end.

"After remaining with them about an hour, we proceeded down the channel with an Indian dressed in a sailor's jacket for our pilot ; and, on reaching the main channel, were visited by some Indians, who have a temporary residence on a marshy island in the middle of the river, where there are great numbers of water-fowl. Here the mountainous country again approaches the river on the left, and a higher mountain is perceived towards the south-west. At a distance of twenty miles from our camp, we halted at a village of Wahkiacums, consisting of seven ill-looking houses, built in the same form with those above, and situated at the foot of the high hills on the right, behind two small marshy islands. We merely stopped to purchase some food and two beaver skins, and then proceeded. Opposite to these islands the hills on the left retire, and the river widens into a kind of bay, crowded with low islands, subject to be overflowed occasionally by the tide. We had not gone far from this village when, the fog suddenly clearing away, we were at last presented with the glorious sight of the ocean— that ocean, the object of all our labours, the reward of all our anxieties. This animating sight exhilarated the spirits of all the party, who were still more delighted on hearing the distant roar of the breakers. We went on with great cheerfulness along the high, mountainous country which bordered the right bank : the shore, however, was so bold and rocky, that we could not, until at a distance of fourteen miles from the last village, find any spot fit for an encampment. Having made during the day thirty-four miles, we now spread our mats on the ground, and passed the night in the rain. Here we were joined by our small canoe, which had been separated from us during the fog this morning. Two Indians from the last village also accompanied us to the camp; but, having detected them in stealing a knife, they were sent off.

"November 8. It rained this morning ; and, having changed our clothing, which had been wet by yesterday's rain, we set out at nine o'clock. Immediately opposite our camp was a rock, at the distance of a mile in the river, about twenty feet in diameter and fifty in height, and towards the southwest some high mountains, one of which was covered with snow at the top. We proceeded past several low islands in the bend or bay of the river to the left, which was here five or six miles wide. On the right side we passed an old village, and then, at the distance of three miles, entered an inlet or niche, about six miles across, and making a deep bend of nearly five miles into the hills on the right shore, where it receives the waters of several creeks. We coasted along this inlet, which, from its little depth, we called Shallow Bay, and at the bottom of it stopped to dine, near the remains of an old village, from which, however, we kept at a cautious distance, as, like all these places, it was occupied by a plentiful stock of fleas. At this place we observed a number of fowl, among which we killed a goose, and two ducks exactly resembling in appearance and flavour the canvass-back duck of the Susquehanna. After dinner we took advantage of the returning tide to go on about three miles to a point on the right, eight miles distant from our camp; but here the waves ran so high, and dashed about our canoes so much, that several of the men became seasick. It was therefore judged imprudent to proceed in the present state of the weather, and we landed at the point. Our situation here was extremely uncomfortable : the high hills jutted in so closely that there was not room for us to lie level, nor to secure our baggage from the tide, and the water of the river was too salt to be used ; but the waves increasing so much that we could not move from the spot with safety, we fixed ourselves on the beach left by the ebb-tide, and, raising the baggage on poles, passed a disagreeable night, the rain during the day having wet us completely, as, indeed, we had been for some days past.

"November 9. Fortunately, the tide did not rise as high as our camp during the night ; but, being accompanied by high winds from the south, the canoes, which we could not place beyond its reach, were filled with water, and saved with much difficulty : our position was exceedingly disagreeable ; but, as it was impossible to move from it, we waited for a change of weather. It rained, however, during the whole day, and at two o'clock in the afternoon the flood-tide came in, accompanied by a high wind from the south, which at about four o'clock shifted to the southwest, and blew almost a gale directly from the sea. Immense waves now broke over the place where we were, and large trees, some of them five or six feet through, which had been lodged on the

point, drifted over our camp, so that the utmost vi
gilance of every man could scarcely save the canoes
from being crushed to pieces. We remained in the
water, and were drenched with rain during the rest
of the day, our only sustenance being some dried
fish and the rain-water which we caught. Yet,
though wet and cold, and some of them sick from
using salt-water, the men were cheerful, and full of
anxiety to see more of the ocean. The rain continued all night, and the following morning,

"November 10, the wind lulling, and the waves
not being so high, we loaded our canoes and proceeded. The mountains on the right are here high,
covered with timber, chiefly pine, and descend with
a bold and rocky shore to the water. We went
through a deep niche and several inlets on the right,
while on the opposite side was a large bay, above
which the hills are close on the river. At the distance of ten miles the wind rose from the northwest, and the waves became so high that we were
forced to return two miles for a place where we
could unload with safety. Here we landed at the
mouth of a small run, and, having placed our baggage on a pile of drifted logs, waited until low water.
The river then appearing more calm, we started
again ; but, after going a mile, found the waves too
turbulent for our canoes, and were obliged to put to
shore. Here we landed the baggage, and, having
placed it on a rock above the reach of the tide, encamped on some drift logs, which formed the only
place where we could lie, the hills rising steep over
our heads to the height of five hundred feet. All
our baggage, as well as ourselves, was thoroughly
wet with the rain, which did not cease during the
day : it continued, indeed, violently through the
night, in the course of which the tide reached the
logs on which we lay, and set them afloat.

" November 11. The wind was still high from the
southwest, and drove the waves against the shore

with great fury : the rain, too, fell in torrents, and not only drenched us to the skin, but loosened the stones on the hill sides, so that they came rolling down upon us. In this comfortless condition we remained all day, wet and cold, and with nothing but dried fish to satisfy our hunger; the canoes at the mercy of the waves at one place, the baggage in another, and the men scattered on floating logs, or sheltering themselves in the crevices of the rocks and hill sides. A hunter was despatched in the hope of finding some game ; but the hills were so steep, and so covered with undergrowth and fallen timber, that he could not proceed, and was forced to return. About twelve o'clock we were visited by five Indians in a canoe. They came from the opposite side of the river, above where we were, and their language much resembled that of the Wahkiacums : they called themselves Cathlamahs. In person they were small, ill made, and badly clothed ; though one of them had on a sailor's jacket and pantaloons, which, as he explained by signs, he had received from the whites below the point. We purchased from them thirteen red charr, a fish which we found very excellent. After some time they went on board their boat, and crossed the river, which is here five miles wide, through a very heavy sea.

" November 12. About three o'clock a tremendous gale of wind arose, accompanied with lightning, thunder, and hail: at six it lightened up for a short time, but a violent rain soon began, and lasted through the day. During the storm, one of our boats, secured by being sunk with great quantities of stone, got loose, but, drifting against a rock, was recovered without having received much injury. Our situation now became much more dangerous, for the waves were driven with fury against the rocks and trees, which till now had afforded us refuge : we therefore took advantage of the low tide, and moved about half a mile round a point to a small brook, which we had not observed before on account of the thick bushes and driftwood which concealed its mouth.   Here we were more safe, but still cold and wet ; our clothes and bedding rotten as well as wet, our baggage at a distance, and the canoes, our only means of escape from this place, at the mercy of the waves.   Still, we continued to enjoy good health, and even had the luxury of feasting on some salmon and three salmon trout which we caught in the brook.   Three of the men attempted to go round a point in our small Indian canoe, but the high waves rendered her quite unmanageable, these boats requiring the seamanship of the natives to make them live in so rough a sea.

"November 13.   During the night we had short intervals of fair weather, but it began to rain in the morning, and continued through the day.   In order to obtain a view of the country below, Captain Clarke followed the course of the brook, and with much fatigue, and after walking three miles, ascended the first spur of the mountains.   The whole lower country he found covered with almost impenetrable thickets of small pine, with which is mixed a species of plant resembling arrow-wood, twelve or fifteen feet high, with a thorny stem, almost interwoven with each other, and scattered among the fern and fallen timber: there is also a red berry, somewhat like the Solomon's seal, which is called by the natives *solme*, and used as an article of diet.   This thick growth rendered travelling almost impossible, and it was rendered still more fatiguing by the abruptness of the mountain, which was so steep as to oblige him to draw himself up by means of the bushes.   The timber on the hills is chiefly of a large, tall species of pine, many of the trees eight or ten feet in diameter at the stump, and rising sometimes more than one hundred feet in height.   The hail which fell two nights before was still to be seen on the mountains : there was no game, and no marks of any, except some old tracks of elk. The cloudy weather prevented his seeing to any distance, and he therefore returned to camp, and sent three men in the Indian canoe to try if they could double the point, and find some safer harbour for our boats. At every flood-tide the sea broke in great swells against the rocks, and drifted the trees against our establishment, so as to render it very insecure.

"November 14. It had rained without intermission during the night, and continued to through the day : the wind, too, was very high, and one of our canoes much injured by being driven against the rocks. Five Indians from below came to us in a canoe, and three of them landed, and informed us that they had seen the men sent down yesterday. Fortunately, at this moment one of the men arrived, and told us that these very Indians had stolen his gig and basket: we therefore ordered the two women, who remained in the canoe, to restore them ; but this they refused to do till we threatened to shoot them, when they gave back the articles, and we commanded them to leave us. They were of the Wahkiacum nation. The man now informed us that they had gone round the point as far as the high sea would suffer them in the canoe, and then landed ; that in the night he had separated from his companions, who had proceeded farther down ; and that, at no great distance from where we were, was a beautiful sand beach and a good harbour. Captain Lewis determined to examine more minutely the lower part of the bay, and, embarking in one of the large canoes, was put on shore at the point, whence he proceeded by land with four men, and the canoe returned nearly filled with water.

"November 15. It continued raining all night, but in the morning the weather became calm and fair. We began, therefore, to prepare for setting out ; but before we were ready, a high wind sprang up from the southeast, and obliged us to remain. The sun

shone until one o'clock, and we were thus enabled
to dry our bedding and examine our baggage. The
rain, which had continued for the last ten days without any interval of more than two hours, had completely wet all our merchandise, spoiled some of our
fish, destroyed the robes, and rotted nearly one half
of our few remaining articles of clothing, particularly the leather dresses. About three o'clock the wind
fell, and we instantly loaded the canoes, and left the
miserable spot to which we had been confined the
last six days. On turning the point we came to the
sand beach, through which runs a small stream from
the hills, at the mouth of which was an ancient village
of thirty-six houses, without any inhabitants at the
time except fleas. Here we met Shannon, who had
been sent back to us by Captain Lewis. The day
Shannon left us in the canoe, he and Willard proceeded on till they met a party of twenty Indians,
who, not having heard of us, did not know who they
were ; but they behaved with great civility—so great,
indeed, and seemed so anxious that our men should
accompany them towards the sea, that their suspicions were excited, and they declined going. The
Indians, however, would not leave them ; and the
men, becoming confirmed in their suspicions, and
fearful, if they went into the woods to sleep, that
they would be cut to pieces in the night, thought it
best to remain with the Indians : they therefore made
a fire, and after talking with them to a late hour, laid
down with their rifles under their heads. When
they awoke they found that the Indians had stolen
and concealed their arms ; and having demanded
them in vain, Shannon seized a club, and was about
assaulting one of the Indians whom he suspected to
be the thief, when another of them began to load his
fowling-piece with the intention of shooting him.
He therefore stopped, and explained to them by
signs, that if they did not give up the guns, a large
party would come down the river before the sun rose

to a certain height, and put every one of them to death. Fortunately, Captain Lewis and his party appeared at this very time, and the terrified Indians immediately brought the guns, and five of them came in with Shannon. To these men we declared that, if ever any of their nation stole anything from us, he should be instantly shot. They resided to the north of this place, and spoke a language different from that of the people higher up the river. It was now apparent that the sea was at all times too rough for us to proceed farther down the bay by water: we therefore landed, and, having chosen the best spot we could, made our camp of boards from the old village. We were now comfortably situated; and, being visited by four Wahkiacums with *wappatoo* roots, were enabled to make an agreeable addition to our food.

"November 16. The morning was clear and pleasant. We therefore put out all our baggage to dry, and sent several of the party to hunt. Our camp was in full view of the ocean, on the bay laid down by Vancouver, which we distinguished by the name of Haley's Bay, from a trader who visits the Indians here, and is a great favourite among them. The meridian altitude of this day gave 46° 19′ 11.7″ as our latitude. The wind was strong from the southwest, and the waves very high, yet the Indians were passing up and down the bay in canoes, and several of them encamped near us. We smoked with them, but, after our recent experience of their thievish disposition, treated them with caution." * * *

'The hunters brought in two deer, a crane, some geese and ducks, and several brant, three of which were white, except a part of the wing, which was black, and they were much larger than the gray brant.

"November 17. A fair, cool morning, and easterly wind. The tide rises at this place eight feet six inches.

"About one o'clock Captain Lewis returned, after

having coasted down Haley's Bay to Cape Disappointment, and some distance to the north, along the seacoast.   He was followed by several Chinnooks, among whom were the principal chief and his fam ily.   They made us a present of a boiled root very much like the common liquorice in taste and size, called *culwhamo;* and in return we gave them articles of double its value.   We now learned, however, the danger of accepting anything from them, since nothing given in payment, even though ten times more valuable, would satisfy them.   We were chiefly occupied in hunting, and were able to procure three deer, four brant, and two ducks; and also saw some signs of elk.   Captain Clarke now prepared for an excursion down the bay, and accordingly started,

"November 18, at daylight, accompanied by eleven men.   He proceeded along the beach one mile to a point of rocks about forty feet high, where the hills retired, leaving a wide beach, and a number of ponds covered with water-fowl, between which and the mountain was a narrow bottom covered with alder and small balsam trees.   Seven miles from the rocks was the entrance of a creek, or rather drain from the ponds and hills, where was a cabin of Chinnooks.   The cabin contained some children and four women.   They were taken across the creek in a canoe by two squaws, to each of whom they gave a fish-hook, and then, coasting along the bay, passed at two miles the low bluff of a small hill, below which were the ruins of some old huts, and close to it the remains of a whale.   The country was low, open, and marshy, interspersed with some high pine and with a thick undergrowth.   Five miles from the creek they came to a stream, forty yards wide at low water, which they called Chinnook River.   The hills up this river and towards the bay were not high, but very thickly covered with large pine of several species."

Proceeding along the shore, they came to a deep bend, appearing to afford a good harbour, and here the natives told them that European vessels usually anchored. About two miles farther on they reached Cape Disappointment, "an elevated circular knob," says the Journal, "rising with a steep ascent one hundred and fifty or one hundred and sixty feet above the water, formed like the whole shore of the bay, as well as of the seacoast, and covered with thick timber on the inner side, but open and grassy on the exposure next the sea. From this cape a high point of land bears south 20° west, about twenty-five miles distant. In the range between these two eminences is the opposite point of the bay, a very low ground, which has been variously called Cape Rond by La Perouse, and Point Adams by Vancouver. The water, for a great distance off the mouth of the river, appears very shallow, and within the mouth, nearest to Point Adams, is a large sand-bar, almost covered at high tide." * * *

"November 19. In the evening it began to rain, and continued till eleven o'clock. Two hunters were sent out in the morning to kill something for breakfast, and the rest of the party, after drying their blankets, soon followed. At three miles they overtook the hunters, and breakfasted on a small deer which they had been fortunate enough to kill. This, like all those that we saw on this coast, was much darker than our common deer. Their bodies, too, are deeper, their legs shorter, and their eyes larger. The branches of the horns are similar, but the upper part of the tail is black, from the root to the end, and they do not leap, but jump like a sheep frightened." * * *

Continuing along five miles farther, they reached a point of high land, below which a sandy point extended in a direction north 19° west, to another high point twenty miles distant. To this they gave the name of Point Lewis. They proceeded four miles farther along the sandy beach to a small pine-tree, on which Captain Clarke marked his name, with the year and day, and then set out to return to the camp, where they arrived the following day, having met a large number of Chinnooks coming from it.

"November 21. The morning was cloudy, and from noon till night it rained. The wind, too, was high from the southeast, and the sea so rough that the water reached our camp. Most of the Chinnooks returned home, but we were visited in the course of the day by people of different bands in the neighbourhood, among whom were the Chiltz, a nation residing on the seacoast near Point Lewis, and the Clatsops, who live immediately opposite, on the south side of the Columbia. A chief from the grand rapid also came to see us, and we gave him a medal. To each of our visiters we made a present of a small piece of riband, and purchased some cranberries, and some articles of their manufacture, such as mats and household furniture, for all which we paid high prices." * * *

CHAPTER V.

Extravagant Passion of the Natives for blue Beads.—The Party in Search of a suitable Place for Winter-quarters.—Suffering from the Deluges of Rain.—Visits of the Indians.—Return of Captain Lewis, who reported that he had found a suitable Place for Wintering.—Captain Clarke goes with a Party to find a Place suitable for the Manufacture of Salt.—He is hospitably entertained by the Clatsops.—This Tribe addicted to Gambling.—Sickness of some of the Party, occasioned by the incessant Rains.—They form, notwithstanding, a permanent Encampment for their Winter-quarters.

"November 22. It rained during the whole night, and about daylight a tremendous gale of wind rose from the S.S.E., and continued through the day with great violence. The sea ran so high that the water came into our camp, which the rain prevents us from leaving. We purchased from the old squaw, for armbands and rings, a few *wappatoo* roots, on which we subsisted. They are nearly equal in flavour to the Irish potato, and afford a very good substitute for bread. The bad weather drove several Indians to our camp, but they were still under the terrors of the threat which we made on first seeing them, and behaved with the greatest decency.

"November 23. The rain continued through the night, and the morning was calm and cloudy. The hunters were sent out, and killed three deer, four brant, and three ducks. Towards evening seven Clatsops came over in a canoe, with two skins of the sea-otter. To this article they attached an extravagant value; and their demands for it were so high, that we were fearful it would too much reduce our small stock of merchandise, on which we had to depend for subsistence on our return, to venture on purchasing it. To ascertain, however, their ideas as to the value of different objects, we offered for one of these skins a watch, a handkerchief, an American dollar, and a bunch of red beads ; but neither the curious mechanism of the watch, nor even the red beads, could tempt the owner : he refused the offer, but asked for *tiacomoshack*, or chief beads, the most common sort of coarse blue-coloured beds, the article beyond all price in their estimation. Of these blue beads we had but few, and therefore reserved them for more necessitous circumstances."

* * * " Having now examined the coast, it became necessary to decide on the spot for our winter-quarters. The people of the country subsisted chiefly on dried fish and roots ; but of these there did not seem to be a sufficient quantity for our support, even were we able to purchase them ; and the extravagant prices, as well as our small stock of merchandise, forbade us to depend on that resource. We

II.—I

had therefore to rely for subsistence on our arms, and to be guided in the choice of our residence by the abundance of game which any particular spot might offer. The Indians said that the deer were most numerous some distance above, on the river, but that the country on the opposite side of the bay was better supplied with elk, an animal much larger, and more easily killed than the deer, with a skin better fitted for clothing, and the meat of which is more nutritive during the winter, when they are both poor. The climate, too, was obviously much milder here than above the first range of mountains, for the Indians were thinly clad, and said they had little snow : indeed, since our arrival the weather had been very warm, and sometimes disagreeably so : and dressed, as we were, altogether in leather, the cold would be very unpleasant, if not injurious. The neighbourhood of the sea was moreover recommended by the facility it afforded of supplying ourselves with salt, and the chance of meeting some of the trading vessels, who were expected in about three months, and from whom we might procure a fresh supply of trinkets for our route homeward. These considerations induced us to determine on visiting the opposite side of the bay, and if there was an appearance of much game, to establish ourselves there for the winter."

Having come to this determination, they proceeded, as soon as the weather would permit, to put it into execution. On the 26th they crossed the river, and landed three miles below a point, to which they gave the name of Point Samuel. They proceeded along the shore as far as they could this day, and the next morning " we came," says the journalist, " to a very remarkable knob of land, projecting about a mile and a half towards Shallow Bay, and about four miles round, while the neck of land which connects it to the main shore is not more than fifty yards wide. We went round this projection, which we named Point William ; but the waves then became so high that we could not venture any farther, and therefore landed on a beautiful shore of pebbles of various colours, and encamped near an old Indian hut on the isthmus." * * * " It had rained hard during the whole day, continued all the night, and in the morning,

" November 28, began more violently, attended with a high wind from the southwest. It was now impossible to proceed on so rough a sea. We therefore sent several men to hunt, and the rest of us remained during the day in a situation the most cheerless and uncomfortable. On this little neck of land we were exposed with a little miserable covering, which did not deserve the name of a shelter, to the violence of the winds ; all our bedding and stores, as well as our bodies, being completely wet, our clothes rotting with constant exposure, and having no food except the dried fish obtained from the falls, to which we were again reduced. The hunters all returned hungry and drenched with rain, having seen neither deer nor elk, and the swan and brant were too shy to be approached. At noon the wind shifted to the northwest, and blew with such tremendous fury that many trees were thrown down near us."* * *

The rain continued through the next day, but the weather cleared on the morning of the 30th, and the day was spent in drying their baggage, and in endeavouring to procure some game. Captain Lewis, with five men, proceeded in the Indian canoe down to a small bay below, in the hope of finding elk. " Several of the men," proceeds the narrative, " complained of disorders in their bowels, which could be ascribed only to their diet of pounded fish mixed with salt-water ; and they are therefore directed to use for that purpose the fresh water above the point. The hunters had seen three elk, but could not obtain any of them. They, however, brought in three hawks, and a few black ducks, of a species common in the United States, living in large flocks, and feeding on grass : they are distinguished by a sharp white beak, toes separated, and having no craw. Besides these wild-fowl, there were in this neighbourhood a large kind of buzzard with white wings, the gray and the bald eagle, the large red-tailed hawk, the blue magpie, and great numbers of ravens and crows. We observed, however, but few small birds : the one which most attracted our attention was a small brown bird, which seemed to frequent logs and the roots of trees. Of other animals there was a great abundance. We saw great numbers of snakes, lizards, worms, and spiders, as well as small bugs, flies, and other insects of various kinds. The vegetable productions were also numerous. The hills along the coast are high and steep, and the general covering is a growth of lofty pines of different species, some of which rise more than two hundred feet, and are from ten to twelve feet in diameter near the root. Besides these trees, we observed on the point a species of ash, the alder, the laurel, one species of the wild crab, and several kinds of underbrush, among which the rosebush was conspicuous." * * *

It rained almost incessantly the three following days, and sickness began to prevail among the men to such an extent, from eating little else than pounded fish, that they redoubled their efforts to procure a supply of game. Fortunately, on the 2d of December, one of the hunters succeeded in killing an elk, of which animal numerous traces were now seen. "This," says the journalist, "was the first elk we had killed on the west side of the Rocky Mountains; and condemned, as we had been for so long a time, to dried fish, it proved a most nourishing food. After eating the marrow of the shank bones, the squaw chopped them fine, and by boiling extracted a pint of grease, superior to the tallow itself of the animal.

A canoe of eight Indians, who were carrying down *wappatoo* roots to trade with the Clatsops, stopped at our camp. We bought of them a few roots for some small fish-hooks, and they left us; when, accustomed as we had been to the sight, we could not but view with admiration the wonderful dexterity with which they guided their canoes through such boisterous seas; for though the waves were so high that, before they had gone half a mile, the canoe was at times out of sight, they proceeded with the utmost calmness and security. Two of the hunters who set out yesterday had lost their way, and did not return till this evening : they had seen in their ramble numerous signs of elk, and had killed six, which they had skinned and left at a great distance.

" December 4. A party was sent in the morning to carry the elk killed yesterday to a bay some distance below, to which place, if the weather permitted, we had determined to remove our camp in the evening; but the rain, which had continued during the night, lasted all the day, and was accompanied by so high a wind from the southeast and south that we dared not risk our canoes on the water. It was high water at eleven o'clock, when the tide rose two feet higher than common. We passed the day around our fires ; and as we were so situated that the smoke would not immediately leave the camp, we were very much incommoded by it. No news had yet been received from Captain Lewis, and we began to have much uneasiness for his safety."

The next day, however, Captain Lewis returned to the encampment with the gratifying intelligence that he had discovered a river at no great distance below, where there were abundance of elk, and a favourable position for their winter-quarters. He had also killed six elk and five deer, and left two of his men to guard them. Continued bad weather prevented their removing until the 7th, when a favourable change enabled them to proceed. " But the tide," says the

Journal, " was against us, and the waves very high, so that we were obliged to go on slowly and cautiously. We at length turned a point, and found ourselves in a deep bay : here we landed for breakfast, and were joined by the party sent out three days ago to look for the six elk. They had lost their way for a day and a half, and when they at last reached the place, found the elk so much spoiled that they brought away nothing but the skins of four of them. After breakfast we coasted round the bay, which is about four miles across, and receives, besides several small creeks, two rivers, called by the Indians, the one Kilhowanakel, the other Netul. We named it Meriwether's Bay, from the Christian name of Captain Lewis, who was, no doubt, the first white man who had surveyed it. The wind was high from the northeast, and in the middle of the day it rained for two hours, and then cleared off. On reaching the south side of the bay we ascended the Netul three miles, to the first point of high land on its western bank, and formed our camp in a thick grove of lofty pines, about two hundred yards from the water, and thirty feet above the level of the high tides."

Having determined on this spot for their winter encampment, Captain Clarke set out the next day with five men in order to find a favourable place for making salt. After pursuing a southwesterly course for some time across a ridge covered with heavy pine timber, they passed some swampy ground, and then an open prairie, and crossed on a raft a considerable creek running towards Point Adams. "At this place," says the Journal, "they discovered a large herd of elk, and after pursuing them for three miles over swamps and small ponds, killed one of them. The agility with which the animals crossed the swamps and bogs seemed almost incredible. As our men followed their track, the ground for a whole acre would shake under their tread, and sometimes they sunk to their hips without finding bottom. Over the surface of these bogs is a species of moss, among which are great numbers of cranberries, and here and there are small, steep knobs of earth, thickly covered with pine and laurel. On one of these they halted for the night."

It had rained all the night, and the next morning, sending three of his men to hunt the elk, Captain Clarke proceeded with the other two to accomplish the object he had in view. After a short time he came to a creek too deep to be forded, and, following it for some distance, found that he was between the creek he had crossed yesterday and another branch of it. He returned, therefore, to the point where he had crossed with the raft, and about a mile below it met with three Indians.

"They were loaded," says the Journal, "with fresh salmon, which they had taken with a gig, and were now returning to their village on the seacoast, where they invited him to accompany them. He agreed, and they brought out a canoe hid on the banks of the creek. In this they passed over the branch which he had crossed on the raft, and then carried their canoe a quarter of a mile to the other fork, which they also crossed, and then continued down to the mouth of the stream. At this place it makes a great bend and is seventy yards wide: just above, to the south, was the village.

"They crossed over, and found that it consisted of three houses, inhabited by twelve families of Clatsops. They were situated on the south side of a hill, and sunk about four feet deep into the ground; the walls, roof, and gable-ends being formed of split pine boards: the descent was through a small door, down a ladder. There were two fires in the middle of the room, and the beds were disposed round the walls, two or three feet high, so as to leave room under them for their bags, baskets, and household articles. The floor itself was covered with mats. Captain Clarke was received with much hospitality.

As soon as he entered clean mats were spread, and fish, berries, and roots were set before him on small neat platters made of rushes. After he had eaten, the men of the other houses came and smoked with him. They all appeared much cleanlier in their persons and diet than Indians generally are, and frequently washed their hands and faces, a ceremony by no means frequent elsewhere. While he was conversing with them, a flock of brant lighted on the water, and with a small rifle he shot one of them at a great distance. They immediately jumped in and brought it on shore, very much astonished at the shot, which contributed to increase their respect.

" Towards evening it began to rain and blow very violently from the southwest, and Captain Clarke therefore determined to remain during the night. When they thought sufficient time had elapsed for his appetite to return, an old woman presented him, in a bowl made of light-coloured horn, with a kind of sirup, pleasant to the taste, and made from a species of berry common in this country, about the size of a cherry, and called by the Indians *shelwel :* of these berries a bread was also prepared, which, being boiled with roots, formed a kind of soup, which was served in neat wooden trenchers ; and these, with some cockles, constituted his repast. The men of the village now collected and began to gamble. Their principal game was one in which one of the company was banker, and played against all the rest. He had a piece of bone about the size of a large bean, and, having agreed with some individual as to the value of the stake, passed the bone from one hand to the other with great dexterity, singing, at the same time, to divert the attention of his adversary ; and then, holding it in one of his hands, his antagonist was challenged to guess in which of them it was, losing or winning as he pointed to the right or wrong hand. To this game they abandoned themselves with great ardour ; sometimes everything they possess is sacrificed to it, and this evening several of the Indians lost all the beads which they had with them. It lasted for three hours, when Captain Clarke appearing disposed to sleep, the man who had been most attentive, and whose name was Cuskalah, spread two new mats near the fire, and ordering his wife to retire to her bed, the rest of the company dispersed at the same time. Captain Clarke then laid down, but the violence with which the fleas attacked him was far from leaving his rest undisturbed, and he rose early.

" December 10. The morning was cloudy, with some rain. Captain Clarke walked to the seacoast, and observed the Indians walking up and down the creek, and examining the shore. He was at a loss to understand their object till one of them came to him, and explained that they were in search of any fish which might have been thrown on shore and left by the tide, adding in English, ' sturgeon is very good.' There is, indeed, every reason to believe that these Clatsops depend for their subsistence, during the winter, chiefly on the fish thus casually thrown on the coast. After amusing himself for some time on the beach, he returned towards the village, and shot on his way two brant. As he came near the village, one of the Indians asked him to shoot a duck about thirty steps distant : he did so, and, having accidentally shot off its head, the bird was brought to the village, when all the Indians came round in astonishment. They examined the duck, the musket, and the very small bullets, which were a hundred to the pound, and then exclaimed, *Clouch musque, wakct, commatax musquet : Good musket ; do not understand this kind of musket.* They now placed before him their best roots, fish, and sirup, after which he attempted to purchase a sea-otter skin with some red beads which he happened to have about him ; but they declined trading, as they valued none except blue or white beads. He therefore bought nothing but a little berry-bread and a few roots, in exchange for fish-hooks, and then set out to return by the same route he had come. He was accompanied by Cuskalah and his brother as far as the third creek, and then proceeded to the camp through a heavy rain. The whole party had been occupied during his absence in cutting down trees to make huts, and in hunting."

The next day, notwithstanding it rained without any intermission, and a considerable number of the party were ill, they kept busily at work in putting up their winter-cabins.

" December 12. We continued to work in the rain at our houses. In the evening there arrived two canoes of Clatsops, among whom was a principal chief called Comowool. We gave him a medal, and treated his companions with great attention; after which we began to bargain for a small sea-otter skin, some *wappatoo* roots, and another species of root called *shanataque*. We readily perceived that they were close dealers, stickled much for trifles, and never closed a bargain until they thought they had the advantage. The *wappatoo* is dear, as they themselves are obliged to give a high price for it to the Indians above. Blue beads are the articles most in request ; the white occupy the next place in their estimation; but they do not value much those of any other colour. We succeeded at last in purchasing their whole cargo for a few fish-hooks and a small sack of Indian tobacco which we had received from the Shoshonees."

From the 13th to the 21st, although it rained almost incessantly, with occasional hail, sleet, and snow, they continued to labour diligently on their houses, and were tolerably successful in procuring game. On the last-mentioned day they were visited by three Indians in a canoe, with mats, roots, and *sacacommis* berries. " These people proceeded with a dexterity and finesse in their bargains," says the

Journal, " which, if they had not learned them from their foreign visiters, might show how nearly allied is the cunning of savages to the little arts of civilized traffic. They began by asking double or treble the value of what they had to sell, and lowered their demands in proportion to the greater or less degree of ardour or knowledge of the purchaser, who, with all his management, was not able to procure the article for less than its real value, which they perfectly understood. Our chief medium of trade consisted of blue and white beads, files with which they sharpen their tools, fish-hooks, and tobacco; but of all these articles, blue beads and tobacco were the most esteemed."

Owing to the constant and long-continued rains, sickness was increasing among the party, and much of their elk-meat was spoiled by the warmth of the weather.

" December 23. It continued raining the whole day, with no variation, except occasional thunder and hail. Two canoes of Clatsops came to us with various articles for sale : we bought three mats and bags neatly made of flags and rushes, and also the skin of a panther seven feet long, including the tail. For all these we gave six small fish-hooks, a worn-out file, and some pounded fish, which had become so soft and mouldy by exposure that we could not use it : it was, however, highly prized by the Indians. Although a very portable and convenient food, the mode of curing it seems to be known, or at least practised, only by the Indians near the Great Falls, and, coming from such a distance, has an additional value in the eyes of these people, who are anxious to possess something less precarious than their ordinary food. Among these Clatsops was a second chief, to whom we gave a medal, and sent some pounded fish to Cuskalah, who could not come to see us on account of sickness. The next day, however,

"December 24, he came in a canoe with his young brother and two squaws. Having treated Captain Clarke so kindly at his village, we were pleased to see him, and he gave us two mats and a parcel of roots. These we accepted, as it would have been offensive to decline them ; but afterward two files were demanded in return for the presents, and, not being able to spare those articles, we restored the mats and roots, at which Cuskalah was a little displeased." * * * " Our whole stock of meat being now completely spoiled, our pounded fish became again our chief dependance. It had rained constantly all day, but we still continued working, and at last moved into our huts.

" December 25. We were awakened at daylight by a discharge of firearms, which was followed by a song from the men as a compliment to us on the return of Christmas, which we have always been accustomed to observe as a day of rejoicing. After breakfast we divided our remaining stock of tobacco, which amounted to twelve carrots, into two parts, one of which we distributed among such of the party as made use of it, making a present of a handkerchief to the others. The remainder of the day was passed in good spirits, though there was nothing in our situation to excite much gayety. The rain confined us to the house, and our only luxuries in honour of the season were some poor elk-meat, so much spoiled that we ate it through mere necessity, a few roots, and some mouldy pounded fish.

" December 26. The rain continued, accompanied by thunder, and a high wind from the southeast. We were therefore still obliged to remain in our huts, and endeavoured to dry our wet articles before the fire. The fleas, which annoyed us near the portage of the Great Falls, had so completely taken possession of our clothes, that we were obliged to have a regular search every day through our blankets, as a necessary preliminary to sleeping at night. These insects, indeed, are so numerous that they are almost a calamity to the Indians of this country. When they have once obtained the mastery of any house, it is impossible to expel them; and the Indians have frequently other houses, to which they resort when the fleas have rendered their longer residence in one intolerable: yet, in spite of these precautions, every Indian is constantly attended by multitudes of them, and no one came into our houses without leaving behind him swarms of these tormenting creatures.

"December 27. The rain did not cease last night, nor the greater part of the day. In the evening we were visited by Comowool, the chief, and four men of the Clatsop nation, who brought a very timely supply of roots and berries. Among these was one called *culhomo*, resembling liquorice in size and taste, which they roast like a potato; there was also the *shanataque*, a root of which they are very fond. It is of a black colour, sweet to the taste, and is prepared for eating in a kiln, as the Indians up the Columbia dry the *pasheco*. These, as well as the *shelwel* berries, they value highly, but were perfectly satisfied with the return we made them, consisting of a small piece of sheepskin for the chief to wear round his head, a pair of earbobs for his son, a small piece of brass, and a little riband." * * *

It rained, as usual, the following day. They sent five men with a large kettle to the seaside, which was about seven miles off, for the purpose of manufacturing salt. "On the 29th," proceeds the Journal, "we were employed all day in picketing the encampment; and in the evening a young Wahkiacum chief, with four men and two women, arrived with some dressed elkskin and *wappatoo* for sale. We purchased about a bushel and a half of those roots for some red beads, small pieces of brass wire, and old check. The chief, too, made us a present of half a bushel more, for which we gave him a medal, and a piece of riband to tie round his hat. These roots were extremely grateful, as our meat had be come spoiled, and we were desirous of purchasing the remainder ; but the chief would not dispose of any more, as he was on his way to trade with the Clatsops. They remained with us, however, till the next day,

"December 30, when they were joined by four more of their countrymen from the Wahkiacum village. These last began by offering us some roots ; but, as we had learned that they always expect three or four times as much in return as the real value of the articles they give, and are not satisfied even with that, we declined such dangerous presents. Towards evening the hunters brought in four elk ; and, after so long a course of abstinence and miserable diet, we had a most sumptuous supper of elk's tongues and marrow. Besides this agreeable repast, the state of the weather had been quite exhilarating. It rained during the night, but in the morning, though the high wind continued, we enjoyed the fairest and most pleasant weather we had had since our arrival ; the sun shining at intervals, with only three showers in the course of the day. By sunset we had completed our fortification ; and we now announced to the Indians that every day at that hour the gates would be closed, when they must leave the place, and not enter it till sunrise. The Wahkiacums, who had remained with us, and who were very forward in their deportment, complied very reluctantly with this order ; and, being excluded from our houses, formed a camp near us.

"December 31. As if it were impossible to have twenty-four hours of pleasant weather, the sky last evening clouded, and the rain began and continued through the day. In the morning there came down two canoes, one from the Wahkiacum village, and the other contained three men and a squaw of the

Skilloot nation. They brought *wappatoo* and *shana-taque* roots, dried fish, mats made of flags and rush-es, dressed elkskins, and tobacco, for which, particu-larly the skins, they asked a very extravagant price. We purchased some *wappatoo* and a little tobac-co, very much like that we had seen among the Shoshonees, put up in small, neat bags made of rush-es. These we obtained in exchange for a few arti-cles, among which fish-hooks were the most esteem-ed. One of the Skilloots brought a gun which want-ed some repair, and, having put it in order, we re-ceived from him a present of about a peck of *wap-patoo*; we then gave him a piece of sheepskin and blue cloth to cover the lock, and he very thankfully offered a farther present of roots. There is, in fact, an obvious superiority in these Skilloots over the Wahkiacums, who are intrusive, thievish, and im-pertinent. Our new regulations, however, and the appearance of the sentinel, have improved the beha-. viour of all our Indian visiters. They left the fort before sunset, even without being ordered.

" Besides the fleas, we observed a number of oth-er insects in motion. Snakes were yet to be seen; and snails without covers were common." * * *

" January 1, 1806. We were awaked at an early hour by the discharge of a volley of small arms, to salute the new year. This was the only mode of commemorating the day which our situation permit-ted; for, though we had reason to be gayer than we were at Christmas, our only dainties were boiled elk and *wappatoo*, enlivened by draughts of pure water. We were visited by a few Clatsops, who came by water, bringing roots and berries for sale. Among this nation we observed a man about twenty-five years old, of a much lighter complexion than the In-dians generally: his face was even freckled, and his hair long, and of a colour inclining to red. He was in habits and manners perfectly Indian; but, though he did not speak a word of English, he seemed to understand more than the others of his party; and, as we could obtain no account of his origin, we concluded that one of his parents, at least, must have been white." * * *

" January 2. The hunters brought in two elk, and we obtained from the traps another. This animal, as well as the beaver and the raccoon, are in plenty near the seacoast, and along the small creeks and rivers as high as the Grand Rapids, and in this coun try have an extremely good fur.

" The birds most common were the large as well as the small or whistling swan, the sandhill crane, the large and small goose, cormorants, brown and white brant, mallard, and the canvass-back, with several other species of ducks. There were also a small crow, the blue-crested corvus, and the smaller corvus with a white breast, the little brown wren, a large brown sparrow, the bald eagle, and the beautiful buzzard of the Columbia. All these birds continued with us, though they were not in such numbers as on our first arrival in this neighbourhood.

" January 3. At eleven o'clock we were visited by our neighbour the tia, or chief Comowool, who was also called Coone, with six Clatsops. Besides roots and berries, they brought for sale three dogs and some fresh blubber. Having been so long accustomed to the flesh of dogs, the greater part of us had acquired a fondness for it; and our original aversion for it was overcome by reflecting that, while we subsisted on that food, we were fatter, stronger, and, in general, enjoyed better health than at any period since leaving the buffalo country eastward of the mountains. The blubber, which is esteemed by the Indians an excellent food, had been obtained, they told us, from their neighbours the Killamucks, a nation who live on the seacoast to the southeast, and near one of whose villages a whale had recently been thrown and foundered." * * *

On the 5th, two of the men who had been sent to

make salt returned to the encampment with about a gallon of that article, which proved to be of good quality, and furnished a very grateful addition to their food. They also brought some blubber of the whale, which had been obtained by the Indians from one of those fish that had floated ashore. " The appearance of this whale," says the narrative, " seemed to be a matter of importance to all the neighbouring Indians ; and as we might be able to procure some of it for ourselves, or at least purchase blubber from the Indians, a small parcel of merchandise was prepared, and a party of the men got in readiness to set out in the morning. As soon as this was made known, Chaboneau and his wife requested that they might be permitted to accompany the party. The poor woman stated very earnestly that she had travelled a long way with us to behold the great water, yet she had never been down to the coast ; and, now that this monstrous fish was also to be seen, it seemed hard that she should not be permitted to see either the ocean or the whale. So reasonable a request could not be denied; they were therefore suffered to go with Captain Clarke.

" January 6. After an early breakfast, he set out with twelve men in two canoes. He proceeded down the Netul into Meriwether Bay, intending to go to the Clatsop town, and there procure a guide through the creeks, which there was reason to believe communicated not only with the bay, but with a small river running towards the sea, near which our salt-makers were encamped." A high wind springing up, however, from the northwest, and obliging them to put into a small creek, he determined to attempt the passage without any guide. After proceeding up this creek three miles, they left their canoes, and followed an Indian path for some distance, when, arriving at the creek they had formerly passed on a raft, they crossed it, and, having killed an elk for their supper, encamped for the night.

II.—K

CHAPTER VI.

Captain Clarke continues his Route in Quest of the Whale.—
Passes Clatsop River.—Perilous Nature of the Journey.—
Grandeur of the Scenery.—Indian Mode of extracting Whale
oil.—The Life of one of Captain Clarke's Party preserved by
the Kindness of an Indian Woman.—Short Account of the
Chinnooks, Clatsops, Killamucks, and Lucktons.—Manner of
Sepulture among the Chinnooks, Clatsops, &c.—Their Weap-
ons of War and Hunting.—Their Mode of building Houses.—
Their Manufactures and Cookery.— Their Canoes.— Great
Dexterity in managing them.

THEY started again early the next morning, and
after encountering some difficulties, came to the
seashore, which they followed for five miles, when
they reached the encampment of their salt-makers.
" Here," proceeds the narrative, " we persuaded a
young Indian, by the present of a file and a promise
of some other articles, to guide us to the spot where
the whale lay.   He led us for two and a half miles
over round slippery stones at the foot of a high hill
projecting into the sea, and then suddenly stopping,
and uttering the word *peshack*, or bad, explained by
signs that we could no longer follow the coast, but
must cross the mountain.   This promised to be a
most laborious undertaking, for the side was nearly
perpendicular, and the top lost in clouds.   He, however, followed an Indian path, which wound about
as much as possible, but still the ascent was so
steep that at one place we drew ourselves up for
about a hundred feet by means of bushes and roots.
At length, after two hours' labour, we reached the
top of the mountain, whence we looked down with
astonishment on the prodigious height of ten or
twelve hundred feet which we had ascended.   Immediately below us, in the face of this precipice,

was a stratum of white earth, used, as our guide informed us, as a paint by the neighbouring Indians. It obviously contains argil, and resembles the earth of which the French porcelain is made; but whether it contains either silex or magnesia, or, if so, in what proportions, we could not determine. We were here met by fourteen Indians with oil and blubber, the spoils of the whale, which they were carrying in very heavy loads over this rough mountain. On leaving them, we proceeded over a bad road till night, when we encamped on a small run : we were all much fatigued, but the weather was pleasant, and, for the first time since our arrival here, an entire day had been passed without rain.

" January 8. We set out early, and proceeded along the top of the mountain, the highest point of which is an open spot facing the ocean. It is situated about thirty miles southeast of Cape Disappointment, and projects nearly two and a half miles into the sea. Here one of the most delightful views in nature presented itself. Immediately in front was the ocean, breaking with fury on the coast, from the rocks of Cape Disappointment as far as the eye could discern to the northwest, and against the high lands and irregular piles of rock which diversify the shore to the southeast. To this boisterous scene, the Columbia, with its tributary waters, widening into bays as it approaches the ocean, and studded on both sides with the Chinnook and Clatsop villages, formed a charming contrast; while immediately beneath our feet were stretched rich prairies, enlivened by three beautiful streams, which conducted the eye to small lakes at the foot of the hills. We stopped to enjoy the romantic prospect from this place, which we distinguished by the name of Clarke's Point of View, and then followed our guide down the mountain. The descent was steep and dangerous : in many places the hillsides, which are formed principally of yellow clay, had been washed

by the late rains, and were now slipping into the
sea in large masses of from fifty to a hundred
acres. In other parts the path crossed the rugged
perpendicular rocks which overhang the sea, into
which a single false step would have precipitated us.
This mountain is covered with a very thick growth
of timber, chiefly pine and fir; some of which, near
Clarke's Point of View, perfectly sound and solid,
rose to the height of two hundred and ten feet, and
were from eight to twelve in diameter. Intermixed
is the white cedar, or *arbor vitæ*, and a small quantity of black alder, two or three feet thick, and sixty
or seventy in height. At length we reached a single
house, the remains of an old Killamuck village, situated among some rocks, in a bay immediately on
the coast. We then continued for two miles along
the sand beach, and after crossing a creek eighty
yards in width, near which were five cabins, reached
the place where the waves had thrown the whale on
shore. The animal had been landed between two
Killamuck villages; and such had been the industry
of the natives, that there now remained nothing
more than the skeleton, which we found to be one
hundred and five feet in length. Captain Clarke
then returned to the village of five huts on the creek,
to which he gave the name of Ecola, or Whale
Creek. The Indians were all busied in boiling the
blubber in a large, square trough of wood, by means
of heated stones, and preserving the oil thus extracted in bladders and the entrails of the whale. The
refuse of the blubber, which still contained a portion
of oil, was hung up in large flitches, and when wanted for use is warmed on a wooden spit before the
fire, and eaten either alone or dipped in oil, or with
the roots of the rush and *shanataque*. The Killamucks, though they had great quantities of it, parted
with it reluctantly, and at such high prices that our
whole stock of merchandise was exhausted in the
purchase of about three hundred pounds of blubber

and a few gallons of oil. With this we set out to
return; and, having crossed Ecola Creek, encamped
on its bank, where there was abundance of fine timber. We were soon joined by the men of the village, with whom we smoked, and who gave us all
the information they possessed relative to their
country.

" These Killamucks are part of a much larger nation of the same name, and reside chiefly in four
villages, each at the entrance of a different creek,
and all falling into a bay on the southwest coast;
that at which we now were being the most northern,
and at the distance of about forty-five miles southeast of Point Adams. The rest of the nation are
scattered along the coast, and on the banks of a river, which, as it was marked in their delineations, we
called Killamuck's River, emptying itself in the same
direction. During the salmon season they catch
great quantities of that fish in the small creeks, and
when these fail, their chief resource is the sturgeon
and other fish stranded along the coast. The elk
are very numerous in the mountains, but they cannot
procure many of them with their arrows; and their
principal communication with strangers is by means
of the Killamuck River, up which they pass to the
Shocatilcum, or Columbia, to trade for *wappatoo*
roots. In their dress, appearance, and, indeed, everything else, they differ very little from the Chinnooks, Clatsops, and other nations in the neighbourhood : the chief difference we have observed is in
their manner of burying the dead, the bodies being
deposited in an oblong box of plank, which is placed
in an open canoe, lying on the ground, with a paddle and other small articles of the deceased by his
side.

" While smoking with the Indians, Captain Clarke
was startled about ten o'clock by a loud, shrill cry
from the opposite village, on hearing which all the
natives immediately started up to cross the creek,

and the guide informed him that some one had been killed. On examination, one of our men was discovered to be absent, and a guard was despatched, who met him crossing the creek in great haste. An Indian belonging to another band, and who happened to be with the Killamucks that evening, had treated him with much kindness, and walked arm in arm with him to a tent, where our man found a Chinnook squaw who was 'an old acquaintance. From the conversation and manner of the stranger, this woman discovered that his object was to murder the white man for the sake of the few articles on his person; and when he rose and pressed our man to go to another tent, where they would find something better to eat, she held M'Neal by the blanket. Not knowing her object, he freed himself from her, and was going on with his pretended friend, when she ran out and gave a shriek which brought the men of the village over, and the stranger ran off before M'Neal knew what had occasioned the alarm.

"January 9. The morning was fine, the wind from the northeast. Having divided our stock of blubber, we began at sunrise to retrace our steps, in order to reach Fort Clatsop, at the distance of thirty-five miles. We met several parties of Indians on their way to trade for blubber and oil with the Killamucks (our route lay across the same mountains which we had already passed) : we also overtook a party returning from the village, and could not but regard with astonishment the heavy loads which the women carry along these fatiguing and dangerous paths. As one of them was descending a steep part of the mountain, her load slipped from her back, and she stood holding it by a strap with one hand, and with the other supporting herself by a bush : Captain Clarke being near her, undertook to replace the load, and found it almost as much as he could lift, and above one hundred pounds in weight. Loaded as they were, they kept pace with us till we reached he salt-makers' tents, where we passed the night, while they continued their route."

The party the next day proceeded to the point where they had left their canoes, and reached the encampment late in the evening. "This morning," proceeds the Journal (January 10), "there came to the fort twelve Indians in a large canoe : they were of the Cathlamah nation, our nearest neighbours above, on the south side of the river. Their tia or chief, whose name was Shahawacap, having been absent on a hunting excursion as we passed his village, had never yet seen us, and we therefore showed him all the honours which our reduced finances would permit. We invested him with a small medal, and received a present of Indian tobacco and a basket of *wappatoo* in return, for which we gave him a small piece of our tobacco and thread for a fishing-net. They had brought dried salmon, *wappatoo*, dogs, and mats made of rushes and flags; but we purchased only some dogs and *wappatoo*. These Cathlamahs speak the same language as the Chinnooks and Clatsops, whom they also resemble in dress and manners."

Their Indian canoe drifted away during the night, and, although they made diligent search for her, the men sent out were unable to find her.

"January 12. Our meat," continues the Journal, " was now becoming scarce, and we therefore determined to jerk it, and issue it in small quantities, instead of dividing it among the four messes, and leaving to each the care of its own provisions : a plan by which much was lost, in consequence of the improvidence of the men. Two hunters had been despatched in the morning, and one of them, Drewyer, had before evening killed seven elk. We should, indeed, have been scarcely able to subsist but for the exertions of this excellent hunter. The game was scarce, and nothing was now to be seen except elk, which almost all the men found it very difficult to shoot; but Drewyer, who was the son of a Canadian Frenchman and an Indian woman, had passed his life in the woods, and united, in a wonderful degree, the dexterous aim of the frontier huntsman with the intuitive sagacity of the Indian in pursuing the faintest tracks through the forest. All our men, however, had become so expert with the rifle, that we were never under serious apprehensions as to food, since, whenever there was game of any kind, we were almost certain of procuring it." * * *

" January 13. From all that we had seen and learned of the Chinnooks, we were induced to estimate the nation at about twenty-eight houses and four hundred souls. They reside chiefly along the banks of a river, to which we gave the same name ; and which, running parallel to the seacoast, waters a low country with many stagnant ponds, and then empties itself into Haley's Bay. The wild-fowl of these ponds, and the elk and deer of the neighbourhood, furnish them with occasional luxuries ; but their chief subsistence is derived from the salmon and other fish which are caught in the small streams by means of nets and gigs, or thrown on shore by the violence of the tide. To these are added some roots, such as the wild liquorice, which is the most common, the *shanataque*, and the *wappatoo*, brought down the river by the traders.

" The men are low in stature, rather ugly, and ill made ; their legs being small and crooked, their feet large, and their heads, like those of the women, flattened in a most disgusting manner. These deformities are in part concealed by robes made of sea-otter, deer, elk, beaver or fox skins. They also employ in their dress robes of the skin of a cat peculiar to this country, and of another animal of the same size, which is light and durable, and sold at a high price by the Indians who bring it from above. In addition to these are worn blankets, wrappers of red, blue, or spotted cloth, and some old sailors' clothes, which are very highly prized. The greater part of the men have guns, with powder and ball.

"The women have in general handsome faces, but are low and disproportioned, with small feet and large legs, occasioned, probably, by strands of beads, or various strings, drawn so tight above the ankles as to prevent the circulation of the blood. Their dress, like that of the Wahkiacums, consists of a short robe and a tissue of cedar bark. Their hair hangs loosely down the shoulders and back; and their ears, neck, and wrists are ornamented with blue beads. Another decoration, which is very highly prized, consists of figures made by puncturing the arms or legs; and on the arms of one of the squaws we observed the name of J. Bowman, executed in the same way. In language, habits, and in almost every other particular, they resemble the Clatsops, Cathlamahs, and, indeed, all the people near the mouth of the Columbia, though they appeared to be inferior to their neighbours in honesty as well as spirit. No ill treatment or indignity on our part seemed to excite any feeling except fear: nor, although better provided than their neighbours with arms, have they enterprise enough either to use them advantageously against the animals of the forest, or offensively against the tribes near them, who owe their safety more to the timidity than the forbearance of the Chinnooks. We had heard instances of pilfering while we were among them, and therefore gave a general order excluding them from our encampment, so that whenever an Indian wished to visit us, he began by calling out ' No Chinnook.' It is not improbable that this first impression may have left a prejudice against them, since, when we were among the Clatsops and other tribes at the mouth of the Columbia, they had less opportunity of stealing, if they were so disposed."

The next day they were so fortunate as to recover their missing canoe, and took precautions to pre-

II.—L

vent any future accident of the kind. The Journal proceeds to give a more particular account of the Clatsops and Killamucks, from such knowledge as could be obtained in relation to them, either from the Indians or by personal observation. ·

* * * " The first nation to the south are the Clatsops, who reside on the southern side of the bay and along the seacoast, on both sides of Point Adams. They were represented as the remains of a much larger nation ; but about four years ago, a disorder, to which till then they were strangers, but which seems, from their description, to have been the smallpox, destroyed four chiefs and several hundred of the nation. These were deposited in canoes, a few miles below us in the bay, and the survivers do not number more than fourteen houses and about two hundred souls. Next to them, along the southeast coast, is a much larger nation, the Killamucks, who number fifty houses and a thousand souls. Their first establishment consists of the four huts at the mouth of Ecola Creek, thirty-five miles from Point Adams, and two miles below are a few more huts ; but the principal town is situated twenty miles lower, at the entrance of a creek called Nielee, into the bay which we designated by the name of Killamuck Bay. Into the same bay empties a second creek, five miles farther, where is a Killamuck village called Kilherhurst ; at two miles a third creek, and a town called Kilherner ; and at the same distance a town called Chishuck, at the mouth of Killamuck River. Towerquotton and Chucklin are the names of two other towns, situated on creeks which empty into the bottom of the bay, the last of which is seventy miles from Point Adams. The Killamuck River is about one hundred yards wide, and very rapid, but, having no perpendicular fall, is the great avenue for trade. There are two small villages of Killamucks settled above its mouth, and the whole trading part of the tribe

ascend it, till by a short portage they carry their canoes over to the Columbian Valley, and descend the Multnomah to Wappatoo Island. Here they purchase roots, which they carry down the Chockalilum or Columbia ; and, after trafficking with the tribes on its banks for the various articles which they require, either return up the Columbia, or cross over through the country of the Clatsops. This trade, however, is obviously little more than a loose and irregular barter, on a very small scale ; for the materials for commerce are so extremely scanty and precarious, that the stranding of a whale is an important commercial incident, which interests all the adjoining country. The Killamucks have little that is peculiar, either in character or manners, and resemble in almost every particular the Clatsops and Chinnooks."* * * *

" The Chinnooks, Clatsops, and most of the adjoining nations deposite their dead in canoes. For this purpose a scaffold is erected, by fixing perpendicularly in the ground four long pieces of split timber. These are placed two by two, just wide enough apart to admit the canoe, and sufficiently long to support its two extremities. The boards are connected by a bar of wood run through them at the height of six feet, on which is placed a small canoe, containing the body of the deceased carefully wrapped in a robe of dressed skins, with a paddle and other articles that had belonged to him by his side. Over this canoe is placed one of a larger size, reversed, with its gunwale resting on the crossbars, so as to cover the body completely. One or more large mats of rushes or flags are then rolled round both the canoes, and the whole is secured by cords, usually made of the bark of the white cedar. On these crossbars are hung different articles of cloth-

---

* Farther details in regard to the names, residence, numbers, &c., of the different tribes along the coast, on both sides of the Columbia, will be found in the Appendix.

ng, or culinary utensils. The method practised by the Killamucks differs somewhat from this, the body being deposited in an oblong box of plank, which, with the paddle and other articles, is placed in a canoe resting on the ground. With the religious opinions of these people we became but little acquainted, since we understood their language too imperfectly to converse on a subject so abstruse; but it is obvious, from the different articles which they place by their dead, that they believe in a future state of existence."

* * * " The implements used in hunting by the Clatsops, Chinnooks, and other neighbouring nations, are the gun, bow and arrow, deadfall, pits, snares, and spears or gigs. The guns are generally old American or British muskets, repaired for this trade ; and, although there are some good pieces among them, they are constantly out of order, as the Indians have not been sufficiently accustomed to arms to understand the management of them. Their powder is kept in the small japanned tin flasks in which the traders sell it ; and when ball or shot fails them, they make use of gravel, or pieces of metal from their pots, without being sensible of the injury done to their guns. These arms are reserved for hunting elk, and the few deer and bear in the neighbourhood ; but, as they have no rifles, they are not very successful hunters. The most common weapon is the bow and arrow, with which every man is provided, even though he may carry a gun, and which is used in every kind of hunting. The bow is extremely neat, and, being very thin and flat, possesses great elasticity. It is made of the heart of the white cedar, about two feet and a half in length, and two inches wide in the centre, whence it tapers to the width of half an inch at the extremities ; and the back is covered with the sinews of elk, fastened on by means of a glue made from the sturgeon. The string is formed of the same sinews. The arrow

generally consists of two parts : the first is about twenty inches long, and formed of light white pine, with the feather at one end, and at the other a circular hole, which receives the second part, formed of some harder wood, about five inches long, and secured in its place by means of sinews. The barb is either of stone, or of iron or copper; and when of the latter, the angle is more obtuse than any we have seen. If, as sometimes happens, the arrow is formed of a single piece, the whole is of a firmer and heavier wood; but the kind just described is preferred, since much of the game consisting of wildfowl on the ponds, it is desirable that their arrows should be of a material to float when they fall into the water. These arrows are kept in a quiver made of elk or young bear skin, opening, not at the ends, like the common quivers, but at the sides, which for those who hunt in canoes is much more convenient. These weapons are not very powerful, however, for many of the elk we killed had been wounded with them ; and although the barb, with the small end of the arrow, remained, the flesh had closed, and the animal suffered no permanent injury. The deadfalls and snares are used in taking the wolf, raccoon, and fox, of which there are, however, but few in this country. The spear or gig employed in the pursuit of the sea-otter (which they call *spuck*), the common otter, and beaver, consists of two points of barbs, and is like those already described as common among the Indians on the upper part of the Columbia. The pits are chiefly for the elk, and are therefore usually large cubes, twelve or fourteen feet in depth, and are made by the side of a fallen tree lying across some path frequented by the animal. They are covered with slender boughs and moss, and the elk either sinks into the pit as he approaches the tree, or in leaping over the tree falls into it on the other side." * * *

" In fishing, the Clatsops, Chinnooks, and other

nations near this place employ the common straight net, the scoop or dip net with a long handle, the gig, and the hook and line. The first is of different lengths and depths, and is employed in taking salmon, charr, and trout in the deep inlets among the marshy grounds and at the mouths of deep creeks. The scoop-net is used for small fish in the spring and summer season; and in both kinds the net is formed of silk-grass, or of the bark of white cedar. The gig is employed at all seasons, and for all kinds of fish they can take with it; so, too, is the hook and line, the latter being made of the same material as the net, and their hooks being generally brought by the traders; though, before the whites came, they made their hooks out of two small pieces of bone, resembling the European hook, but with a much more acute angle where the two pieces were joined." * * *

" The houses in this neighbourhood are all large wooden buildings, varying in length from twenty to sixty feet, and from fourteen to twenty in width. They are constructed in the following manner: two or more posts of split timber, according to the number of partitions, are sunk in the ground, above which they rise to the height of from fourteen to eighteen feet. They are hollowed at the top so as to receive the ends of a round beam or pole stretching from one to the other, and forming the upper point of the roof for the whole extent of the building. On each side of this range is placed another, which forms the eaves of the house, and is about five feet high; but as the building is often sunk to the depth of four or five feet, the eaves come very near the surface of the earth. Smaller pieces of timber are now extended by pairs, in the form of rafters, from the lower to the upper beam, where they are attached at both ends with cords of cedar bark. On these rafters two or three ranges of small poles are placed horizontally, and secured in the

same way with strings of cedar bark. The sides
are now formed with a range of wide boards, sunk
a small distance into the ground, with the upper
ends projecting above the poles at the eaves, to
which they are secured by a beam running along outside parallel with the eave-poles, and tied by cords
of cedar bark passing through holes made in the
boards at certain distances. The gable ends and
partitions are formed in the same way, being fastened by beams on the outside parallel to the rafters.
The roof is then covered with a double range of
thin boards, except an aperture of two or three feet
in the centre for the smoke to pass through. The
entrance is by a small hole cut out of the boards,
and just large enough to admit the body. Only the
very largest houses are divided by partitions ; for,
though three or more families reside in the same
room, there is quite space enough for all of them.
In the centre of each room is a space six or eight
feet square, sunk to the depth of twelve inches below the rest of the floor, and enclosed by four pieces of square timber. Here they make the fire, for
which pine bark is generally preferred. Around
this fireplace mats are spread, which serve as seats
during the day, and very frequently as beds at night ;
there is, however, a more permanent bed, made by
fixing in two, or sometimes three sides of the room,
posts reaching from the roof down to the ground,
and at the distance of four feet from the wall. From
these posts to the wall itself one or two ranges of
boards are placed, so as to form shelves, on which
they either sleep, or stow their various articles of
merchandise. The uncured fish is hung in the smoke
of their fires, as is also the flesh of the elk, when
they are fortunate enough to procure any, which is
but rarely the case."

  * * * "The hats of the Clatsops are made of cedar and bear-grass, interwoven together in the form
of a European hat, with a small brim of about two

inches, and a high crown widening upward. They are light, ornamented with various colours and figures, and, being nearly water-proof, are much more durable than either chip or straw hats. These hats form a small article of traffic with the whites, and the manufacture is one of the best specimens of Indian industry. They are, however, very dexterous in making a variety of domestic utensils, among which are bowls, spoons, skewers, spits, and baskets. The bowl or trough is of different shapes, round, semicircular, in the form of a canoe, or cubic, and generally dug out of a single piece of wood, the larger vessels having holes in the sides by way of handle, and all being executed with great neatness. In these vessels they boil their food by throwing hot stones into the water, and extract oil from different animals in the same way. Spoons are not very abundant, nor is there anything remarkable in their shape, except that they are large, with the bowl broad. Meat is roasted on one end of a sharp skewer, placed erect before the fire, with the other fixed in the ground. The spit for fish is split at the top into two parts, between which the fish is placed, cut open, and its sides extended by means of small splinters. The usual plate is a small mat of rushes or flags, on which everything is served. The instrument with which they dig up roots is a strong stick, about three feet and a half long, sharpened and a little curved at the lower end, while the upper is inserted into a handle, standing transversely, and made of part of an elk or buck's horn. But the most curious workmanship is that of the basket. It is formed of cedar bark and bear-grass, so closely interwoven that it is water-tight, without the aid either of gum or resin. The form is generally conic, or, rather, that of the segment of a cone, of which the smaller end is the bottom of the basket; and being made of all sizes, from that of the smallest cup to the capacity of five or six gallons, they an-

swer the double purpose of a covering for the head
and to contain water. Some of them are highly ornamented with strands of bear-grass, woven into
figures of various colours, which require great labour ; yet they are made very expeditiously, and
sold for a trifle. It is for the construction of these
baskets that the bear-grass forms an article of considerable traffic. It grows only near the snowy region of the high mountains, and the blade, which is
two feet long, and about three eighths of an inch
wide, is smooth, strong, and pliant ; the young blades
particularly, from their not being exposed to the sun
and air, have an appearance of great neatness, and
are generally preferred. Other baskets, and also
bags, not water-proof, are made of cedar bark, silk-
grass, rushes, flags, and common coarse sedge, for
the use of families. In the manufactures, as well
as in the ordinary work of the house, the instrument
most in use is a knife, or rather dagger. The handle of it is small, and has a strong loop of twine for
the thumb, to prevent its being wrested from the
hand. At each end is a blade, double edged and
pointed ; the longer from nine to ten inches, the
shorter from four to five. This knife is carried
about habitually in the hand, sometimes exposed,
but mostly under the robe."

* * * " The industry of the Indians is not confined to household articles : the greatest effort of
their skill is in the construction of their canoes. In
a country, indeed, where so much of the intercourse
between the different tribes is carried on by water,
their ingenuity would naturally be directed to the
improvement of their canoes, which would gradually advance from a mere safe conveyance to something tasteful and elegant. We have, accordingly,
seen canoes of various forms, from the simple boats
near the mountains, to the highly-decorated ones,
because more used, near the mouth of the Columbia. Below the Grand Cataract there are four kinds

of canoes. The first and smallest is about fifteen feet long, and calculated for one or two persons : it is, indeed, by no means remarkable in its structure, and is chiefly employed by the Cathlamahs and Wahkiacums among the marshy islands. The second is from twenty to thirty-five feet long, about two and a half or three feet in the beam, and two feet in the hold. It is chiefly remarkable in having the bowsprit, which rises to some height above the bow, formed by tapering graduallly from the sides into a sharp point. Canoes of this shape are common to all the nations below the Grand Rapids.

" But the canoes most used by the Columbia Indians, from the Chilluckittequaws inclusive to the ocean, are from thirty to thirty-five feet long. The bow, which looks more like the stern of our boats, is higher than the other end, and is ornamented with a sort of comb, an inch in thickness, cut out of the same log which forms the canoe, and extending from nine to eleven inches from the bowsprit to the bottom of the boat. The stern is neatly rounded off, and gradually ascends to a point. This canoe is very light and convenient ; for, though it will contain ten or twelve persons, it may be carried with great ease by four.

" The fourth and largest kind of canoe we did not meet till we reached tide-water, near the Grand Rapids below, where they are found among all the nations, especially the Killamucks and others residing on the seacoast. They are upward of fifty feet long, and will carry from eight to ten thousand pounds' weight, or from twenty to thirty persons. Like all the canoes we have mentioned, they are cut out of a single trunk of a tree, which is generally white cedar, though the fir is sometimes used. The sides are secured by cross-bars or round sticks two or three inches in thickness, which are inserted through holes made just below the gunwale, and made fast with cords. The upper edge of the gun-

wale itself is about five eighths of an inch thick and
four or five in breadth, and folds outward, so as to
form a kind of rim, which prevents the water from
beating into the boat. The bow and stern are about
the same height, and each provided with a comb,
reaching to the bottom of the boat. At each end
also are pedestals, formed of the same solid piece,
on which are placed strange grotesque figures of
men or animals, rising sometimes to the height of
five feet, and composed of small pieces of wood,
firmly united, with great ingenuity, by inlaying and
mortising, without a spike of any kind. The paddle
is usually from four feet and a half to five feet in
length, the handle being thick for one third of its
length, when it widens, and is hollowed and thinned
on each side of the centre, which forms a sort of rib.
When they embark, one Indian sits in the stern, and
steers with a paddle, the others kneel in pairs in the
bottom of the canoe, and, sitting on their heels, paddle over the gunwale next to them. In this way
they ride with perfect safety the highest waves, and
venture without the least concern in seas where
other boats or seamen could not live an instant.
They sit quietly, with no other movement but that
required in paddling, except a large wave chances to
throw the boat on her side, and to the eye of a spec-
tator she seems lost, when the man to windward
steadies her by throwing his body towards the upper side, and sinking his paddle deep into the wave,
appearing to catch the water and force it under the
boat, while the same stroke pushes her on with
great velocity. In the management of these canoes, the women are equally as expert as the men;
for in the smaller boats, which contain four oarsmen, the helm is generally given to a female. As
soon as they land, the canoe is generally drawn on
shore, unless she is very heavily laden; but at night
the load is universally taken out, and the canoe
hauled up

" Our admiration of their skill in these curious constructions was increased by observing the very inadequate implements which they use.   These Indians possess very few axes, and the only tool they employ, from felling the tree to the delicate workmanship of the images, is a chisel made of an old file, about an inch or an inch and a half in width. Even of this, too, they have not learned the proper management ; for the chisel is sometimes fixed in a large block of wood, and, being held in the right hand, the block is pushed with the left, without the aid of a mallet.   But under all these disadvantages, their canoes, which one would suppose to be the work of years, are made in a few weeks.   A canoe, however, is very highly prized, being in traffic an article of the greatest value except a wife, and of equal value with her ; so that a lover generally gives a canoe to the father in exchange for his daughter."

Nothing special occurred from the 14th to the 20th.   As they had a supply of salt, they used it in curing the meat brought in by the hunters ; and the season for their return being near at hand, they were busily employed in preparing clothes, &c., for the journey.

CHAPTER VII.

ʀarther Account of the Clatsops, Killamucks, and Chinnooks ; also of the Cathlamahs.—Their Custom of Flattening the Forehead.—Their Dress and Ornaments described.—Their Diseases.—The common Opinion that the Treatment of their Women is the Standard by which the Virtues of the Indians may be known, combated, and disproved by Examples. — The Respect entertained by these Indians for old Age, compared with the different Conduct of those who subsist by the Chase.—Their Mode of Government.—Their Ignorance of ardent Spirits, and their Fondness for Gambling.—Their Dexterity in Traffic.—In what Articles their Traffic consists.— Their extraordinary Fondness for blue Beads, which form their circulating Medium.   .

" The Killamucks," continues the Journal, " and the Clatsops, Chinnooks, and Cathlamahs, the four neighbouring nations with whom we had most intercourse, have a general resemblance in person, dress, and manners. They are commonly of a diminutive stature, badly shaped, and their appearance is by no means prepossessing. They have broad, thick, flat feet, thick ankles, and crooked legs : the last of which deformities is to be ascribed, in part, as we have already observed, to the universal practice of squatting, or sitting on the calves of their legs and on their heels, and also to the tight bandages ʻof beads and strings worn round the ankles by the women, which prevent the circulation of the blood, and render the legs of the females, in particular, ill shaped and swollen. The complexion is the usual copper-coloured brown of the North American tribes, though it is rather lighter than that of the Indians on the Missouri and the frontiers of the United States. The mouth is wide, and the lips are thick : the nose is of a moderate size, fleshy, wide at the extremities, with large nostrils, and generally low between the eyes, though there are rare instances of high aquiline noses ; the eyes are generally black, though we occasionally saw them of a dark yellowish-brown, with a black pupil. But the most distinguishing part of their physiognomy is the peculiar flatness and width of their forehead : a peculiarity which they owe to one of those customs by which nature is sacrificed to fantastic ideas of beauty. The practice, indeed, of flattening the head by artificial pressure during infancy, prevails among all the nations we have seen west of the Rocky Mountains ; whereas to the east of that barrier the fashion is so perfectly unknown, that there the western Indians, with the exception of the Alliatan or Snake nation, are designated by the common name of Flatheads. This singular usage, which it would scarcely seem possible that nature should suggest to remote nations, might perhaps incline us to believe in the common and not very ancient origin of all the western tribes. Such an opinion would well accord with the fact that, while on the lower parts of the Columbia both sexes are universally flatheads, the custom diminishes in receding eastward from the common centre of the practice, till among the remoter tribes near the mountains nature recovers her rights, and the exhausted folly is confined to a few females. This opinion, however, is corrected or weakened by considering that the flattening of the head is not, in fact, peculiar to that part of the continent, since it was among the first objects which struck the attention of Columbus.

" But, wherever it may have begun, the practice is now universal among these nations. Soon after the birth of her child, the mother, anxious to procure for her infant the recommendation of a broad forehead, places it in the compressing machine, where it is kept for ten or twelve months, though the females remain longer than the boys. The operation is so gradual that it is not attended with pain; but the impression is deep and permanent. The heads of the children, when they are released from the bandage, are not more than two inches thick about the upper edge of the forehead, and still thinner above; nor, with all her efforts, can nature ever restore their proper shape, the heads of grown persons being often in a straight line from the nose to the top of the forehead.

" The hair of both sexes is parted at the top of the head, and thence falls loosely behind the ears, over the back and shoulders. They use combs, of which they are very fond; but contrive, without the aid of them, to keep their hair in very good order. The dress of the men consists of a small robe, reaching to the middle of the thigh, tied by a string across the breast, with its corners hanging loosely over their arms. These robes are, in general, composed of the skins of a small animal which we supposed to be the brown mungo. They have, besides, those made of the tiger, cat, deer, panther, bear, and elk skin, which last is principally used in war parties. Sometimes they have a blanket, woven with the fingers from the wool of their native sheep. Occasionally a mat is thrown over them to keep off the rain; but they have no article of clothing during winter or summer excepting this robe, so that every part of the body but the head and shoulders is exposed to view. They are very fond of the dress of the whites, whom they call *pashisheooks*, or clothmen; and, whenever they can procure any of our clothes, wear them in our manner: the only article, indeed, used by the whites, which we have not seen among them, is the shoe.

" The robe of the women is like that worn by the men, except that it does not reach below the waist. Those most esteemed are made of strips of sea-otter skin, which, being twisted, are interwoven with silk-grass or the bark of the white cedar in such a

manner that the fur appears equally on both sides,
so as to form a soft and warm covering. The skin
of the raccoon or beaver is also employed in the same
way; though, on other occasions, these skins are
simply dressed in the hair, and worn without farther
preparation. The garment which covers the body
from the waist as low as the knee before and the
thigh behind, is the tissue already described, and is
made either of the bruised bark of white cedar,
twisted cords of silk-grass, or of flags and rushes.
Neither leggins nor moccasins are ever used, the
mildness of the climate not requiring them as a security from the weather, and their being so much in
the water rendering them an encumbrance. The
only covering for the head is a hat made of bear-
grass and the bark of cedar, interwoven in a conic
form, with a knob of the same shape at the top. It
has no brim, but is held on the head by a string passing under the chin, and tied to a small rim inside of
the hat. The colours are generally black and white
only, and these are made into squares, triangles, and
sometimes rude figures of canoes and seamen har-
pooning whales. This is all the usual dress of the
females; but if the weather be unusually severe,
they add a vest formed of skins like the robe, and
tied behind, without any shoulder-straps to keep it
up." * * *

" Sometimes, though not often, they mark their
skins by puncturing and introducing some coloured
matter: this ornament is chiefly· confined to the
women, who thus imprint on their legs and arms
circular or parallel dots. On the arm of one of the
squaws, as has been before mentioned, we read the
name of ' J. Bowman,' probably a trader who has
visited the mouth of the Columbia. The favourite
decoration, however, of both sexes, consists of the
common coarse blue or white beads, which are folded very tightly round their wrists and ankles, to the
width of three or four inches, and worn in large loose

rolls round the neck, or as earrings, or hanging from the nose, which last mode is peculiar to the men. There is also a species of wampum very much in use, which seems to be worn in its natural form, without any preparation. It is in the shape of a cone, somewhat curved, about the size of a raven's quill at the base, and tapering to a point, its whole length being from one to two and a half inches, white, smooth, hard, and thin. A small thread is passed through it, and the wampum is either suspended from the nose, or passed through the cartilage horizontally, forming a ring from which other ornaments hang. Wampum is employed in the same way as beads, but more especially as a decoration for the noses of the men, who also use collars made of bears' claws, while the women and children wear those of elk's tusks, and both sexes are adorned with bracelets of copper, iron, or brass, in various forms." * * *

" The Clatsops, and other nations at the mouth of the Columbia, visited us with great freedom, and we endeavoured to cultivate their friendship, as well for the purposes of obtaining information, as to leave behind us impressions favourable to our country. Having acquired much of their language, we were enabled, with the aid of gestures, to hold conversations with great ease. We found them inquisitive and loquacious, with understandings by no means deficient in acuteness, and with very retentive memories; and, though fond of feasts, and generally cheerful, they are never gay. Everything they observe excites their attention and inquiry ; but, having been accustomed to see the whites, nothing appeared to astonish them more than the air-gun. To all our questions they answered with great intelligence, and the conversation rarely slackened, as there was a constant discussion of the events, trade, politics, &c., in the small but active circle of the Killamucks, Clatsops, Cathlamahs, Wahkiacums, and Chinnooks." * * *

II.—M

"The treatment of their women is often considered as the standard by which the moral qualities
of savages are to be estimated. Our own observation, however, induced us to think that the condition
of the female in savage life has no necessary relation to the virtues of the men, but is regulated wholly
by their capacity to be useful. The Indians who
treat their females most mildly, and pay most deference to their opinions, are by no means the most
distinguished for their virtues; nor is this deference
attended by any increase of attachment. On the
other hand, the tribes among whom the women are
very much debased, possess the loftiest sense of
honour, the greatest liberality, and all the good qualities of which their situation demands the exercise.
Where the women can aid in procuring food for the
tribe, they are treated with more equality, and their
importance is proportioned to the share which they
take in that labour; while in countries where subsistence is chiefly procured by the exertions of the
men, the women are considered and treated as burdens. Thus, among the Clatsops and Chinnooks,
who live upon fish and roots, which the women are
equally expert with the men in procuring, the former
have a rank and influence very rarely found among
Indians. Here the females are permitted to speak
freely before the men, whom, indeed, they sometimes address in a tone of authority. On many sub-
jects their judgment and opinions are respected, and
in matters of trade their advice is generally asked
and followed. The labours of the family are shared
almost equally. The men collect wood and attend
to the fires, assist in cleaning the fish, make the
houses, canoes, and wooden utensils; and, whenever
strangers are to be entertained, or a great feast prepared, the meats are cooked and served up by them.
The peculiar province of the female is to gather
roots, and to manufacture the various articles which
are formed of rushes, flags, cedar bark, and bear-

grass ; but the management of the canoes, and many
of the occupations, which elsewhere devolve wholly
on the female, are here common to both sexes.

" The observation in regard to the treatment of
females applies with equal force to that of old men.
Among tribes who subsist by hunting, the labours
of the chase and the wandering existence to which
that occupation condemns them, necessarily throw
the burden of procuring provisions on the active
young men. As soon, therefore, as a man is no.
longer able to pursue the chase, he begins to with-
draw something from the precarious supplies of the
tribe.   Still, however, his counsels may compensate
his want of activity ; but in the next stage of infirm-
ity, when he can no longer travel from camp to
camp, as the tribe roams about for food, he is found
to be a heavy burden.   In this situation the aged are
abandoned among the Sioux, the Assiniboins, and
the hunting tribes on the Missouri.   As they are setting out for some new excursion, where the old man
is unable to follow, his children or nearest connex-
ions place before him a piece of meat and some water, and telling him that he has lived long enough,
that it is now time for him to go home to his relations, who can take better care of him than his
friends on earth, leave him, without remorse, to perish when his little supply is exhausted.   The same
custom is said to prevail among the Minnetarees,
Ahnahawas, and Ricaras, when they are encumbered by old men on their hunting excursions.   Yet in
their villages we saw no want of kindness to the
aged : on the contrary, probably because in villages
the means of more abundant subsistence renders
such cruelty unnecessary, old people appeared to be
treated with attention, and some of their feasts, particularly the buffalo dances, are intended chiefly for
the entertainment of the aged and infirm.

" The dispositions of these people seem mild and
inoffensive, and their behaviour to us was uniformly

the most friendly. They are addicted to begging, and to pilfering small articles when it can be done without danger of detection, but do not rob wantonly, nor to any large amount: some of them having purloined some of the meat which our hunters had been obliged to leave in the woods, they voluntarily brought some dogs a few days after, by way of compensation. Our numbers, and great superiority in the use of firearms, enabled us always to command; and such was the friendly deportment of these people, that the men were accustomed to treat them with the greatest confidence. It was therefore with difficulty that we could impress on our men a conviction of the necessity of being always on our guard, since we were perfectly acquainted with the treacherous character of Indians generally. We were always prepared for an attack, and uniformly excluded all considerable parties of the natives from the fort.

"Their large houses usually contain several families, consisting of the parents, their children, their sons and daughters-in-law, and grandchildren, among whom the provisions are all in common, and whose harmony is scarcely ever interrupted by disputes. Although polygamy is permitted by their customs, very few have more than a single wife; and she is brought immediately after the marriage into the husband's family, where she resides until increasing numbers oblige them to seek another house. In this state the old man is not considered as the head of the family, since the active duties, as well as principal responsibility, fall on some of the younger members. As these families gradually expand into bands, tribes, or nations, the paternal authority is represented by the chief of each association. This chieftain, however, is not hereditary; his ability to be of service to his tribe, and the popularity which follows it, being at once the foundation and measure of his authority, the exercise of which does not extend beyond a reprimard for some improper action.

"The harmony of their private life is indeed secured by their ignorance of spirituous liquors, the earliest and most dreadful present which civilization has bestowed on the other natives of the Continent. Although they have had so much intercourse with the whites, they do not appear to possess any knowledge of those dangerous luxuries: at least, they never inquired of us after them, which they probably would have done if they had ever been introduced among them. Indeed, we did not observe any liquor of an intoxicating quality used among these or any Indians west of the Rocky Mountains, the universal beverage being pure water. They, however, sometimes almost intoxicate themselves with tobacco, of which they are excessively fond; and the pleasure of which they prolong as much as possible, by retaining vast quantities of the smoke at a time, till, after circulating through the lungs and stomach, it issues in volumes from the mouth and nostrils. But the most inveterate vice of all these people is an attachment to games of hazard, which they pursue with a strange and ruinous avidity. Their games are of two kinds. In the first, of which we have already given some account, one of the company assumes the office of banker, and plays against the rest. He takes a small stone, about the size of a bean, which he shifts from one hand to the other with great dexterity, repeating, at the same time, a song adapted to the game, and which serves to divert the attention of the company, till, having agreed on the stake, he holds out his hands, and his antagonist wins or loses as he succeeds or fails in guessing in which hand the stone is. After the banker has lost his money, or whenever he is tired, the stone is transferred to another, who in turn challenges the company. The other play is something like that of ninepins: the two pins are placed on the floor, at about the distance of a foot from each other, and a small hole is made behind them. The players then go about ten feet from the hole, into which they try to roll, between the pins, a small piece resembling the men used at draughts. If they succeed in getting it into the hole, they win the stake; if the piece passes between the pins, but does not go into the hole, nothing is won or lost; but the wager is wholly lost if the piece rolls outside of the pins. Entire days are wasted at these games, which are often continued through the night round the blaze of their fires, till the last article of clothing, and even the last blue bead, is won from the desperate adventurer.

"In traffic they are acute and intelligent, displaying a dexterity and finesse that would scarcely be expected. They begin by asking double or treble its value for their merchandise, and lower their demands in proportion to the ardour or indifference of the purchaser: and if he expresses any anxiety, the smallest article, even a handful of roots, will furnish a whole morning's negotiation. Being naturally suspicious, they, of course, conceive that you are pursuing the same system. They therefore invariably refuse the first offer, however high, fearful that they or the other party may have mistaken the value of the merchandise, and cautiously wait for a larger offer. In this way, after rejecting the most extravagant prices, which we had offered merely for experiment, they would afterward importune us for a tenth part of what they had before refused. In this respect they differ from almost all Indians, who will generally exchange, in a thoughtless moment, the most valuable article they possess for any bawble which happens to please their fancy.

" These habits of cunning or prudence have been formed or increased by their being largely engaged in the traffic of the Columbia : of this trade, however, the chief mart is at the Falls, where all the neighbouring nations assemble. The inhabitants of the plains on the Columbia, after having passed the winter near the mountains, come down as soon as the snow has left the valleys, and are occupied in collecting and drying roots till about the month of May. They then crowd to the river, and, fixing themselves on its north side, to avoid the incursions of the Snake Indians, continue fishing till about the first of September, when the salmon are no longer fit for use. Then they bury their fish, and return to the plains, where they remain gathering *quamash* till the snow obliges them to desist, when they come back to the Columbia, and, taking their store of fish, retire to the foot of the mountains and along the creeks which supply timber for their houses, and pass the winter in hunting deer or elk, which, with the aid of their fish, enables them to subsist till the spring, on the arrival of which they resume the same circle of employments. During their residence on the rivers, from May to September, or, rather, before they begin the regular fishery, they go down to the Falls, carrying with them skins, mats, silk-grass, rushes, and root-bread. They are here met by the Chopunnish and other tribes of the Rocky Mountains, who descend the Kooskooskee and Lewis Rivers for the purpose of selling bear-grass, horses, *quamash*, and the few skins they may have obtained by hunting, or in exchange for horses with the Tushepaws.

"At the Falls they find the Chilluckittequaws, Eneeshurs, Echeloots, and Skilloots, which last serve as intermediate traders or carriers between the inhabitants above and below the Falls. These tribes prepare pounded fish for market, and the nations below bring *wappatoo* roots, the fish of the seacoast, berries, and such trinkets and small articles as they have procured from the whites.

"The trade then begins. The Chopunnish and other Indians of the Rocky Mountains exchange the articles which they have brought for *wappatoo*, pounded fish, and beads. The Indians of the plains, being their own fishermen, take only *wappatoo*, horses, beads, and other articles procured from the Europeans. The Indians, however, from Lewis's River to the Falls, consume for food or fuel all the fish which they take ; so that the whole stock for sale is prepared by the nations between the Towahniahiooks and the Falls, and amounts, as nearly as we could estimate, to about thirty thousand pounds, chiefly salmon, beyond the quantity which they use themselves, or barter with the more eastern Indians This is now carried down the river by the Indians at the Falls, and is consumed among the nations at the mouth of the Columbia, who, in return, give the fish of the seacoast, and the articles which they obtain from the whites. The neighbouring tribes catch large quantities of salmon and dry them, but they do not understand the art of drying and pounding it in the manner practised at the Falls, and, being very fond of it, are forced to purchase it at high prices. This article, indeed, and the *wappatoo*, form the principal objects of trade with the people of our immediate vicinity. The traffic is wholly carried on by water; and there are not even any roads or paths through the country, except across the portages which connect the creeks.

" But that which chiefly gives animation to this trade is the visits of the whites. They arrive generally about the month of April, and either return in October, or remain till that time ; during which period, having no establishment on shore, they anchor on the north side of the bay, at the place already described, which is a spacious and commodious harbour, perfectly secure from all except the south and southeast winds; and, as they leave it before winter, they do not suffer from these, which are the most usual and violent at that season. This situation is also recommended by its neighbourhood to fresh water, wood, and excellent timber for repairs. Here they are immediately visited by the tribes along the coast, by the Cathlamahs, and, lastly, by the Skilloots, that numerous and active peo-

ple who skirt the river between the marshy islands
and the Grand Rapids, as well as the Coweliskee,
and who carry down the fish prepared by their immediate neighbours, the Chilluckittequaws, Eneeshurs, and Echeeloots, residing from the Grand Rapids to the Falls, and also the articles which they
have themselves procured in barter at the market in
May. The principal articles of traffic now concen-
trated at the mouth of the Columbia consist of dressed and undressed skins of the elk, sea-otter, common otter, beaver, common fox, spuck, and tiger-
cat; besides articles of less importance, as a small
quantity of dried or pounded salmon, biscuit made
of the *chappelell* root, and some of the manufactures of the neighbourhood. In return they receive
guns (principally old British or American muskets),
powder, ball and shot, copper and brass kettles,
brass teakettles and coffee-pots, blankets, coarse
scarlet and blue cloth, plates and strips of sheet
copper and brass, large brass wire, knives, tobacco,
fish-hooks, buttons, and a considerable quantity of
sailors' hats, trowsers, coats, and shirts. But, as we
have had occasion to remark more than once, the
objects most desired are the common cheap blue or
white beads, of from about fifty to seventy to the
pennyweight, which are strung on strands a fathom
long, and sold by the yard, or the length of both
arms. Of these, blue beads, which are called *tia
commashuck*, or chief beads, hold the first rank in
their estimation; the most inferior kind being more
highly prized than the finest wampum, and offering
a temptation so strong as to induce them to part
with their most valuable effects. Indeed, if the example of civilized life did not completely vindicate
their predilection, we might wonder at their infatu-
ated fondness for a bawble in itself so worthless.
Yet these beads are perhaps quite as reasonable
objects of passionate desire as the precious metals,
since they are at once beautiful ornaments for the

person, and furnish the chief medium of trade among the nations on the Columbia.

" These strangers, who visit the Columbia for the purpose of trade or hunting, must be either English or Americans. The Indians informed us that they spoke the same language as we did ; and, indeed, the few words which they have learned from the sailors, such as musket, powder, shot, knife, file, heave the lead, and other phrases, sufficiently show this." * * *

" The nations near the mouth of the Columbia enjoy great tranquillity, none of them being engaged in war. Not long since, however, some of the tribes were at war on the coast to the southwest, in which the Killamucks took several prisoners. These, as far as we could perceive, were treated very kindly, and, though nominally slaves, they had been adopted into the families of their masters, the young ones being placed on the same footing with their children.

" The month of February and the greater part of March were passed much in the same manner. Every day, parties as large as we could spare from our other occupations were sent out to hunt, and we were thus enabled to command some days' provision in advance. This consisted chiefly of deer and elk meat : the first was very lean, and by no means as good as that of the elk, which, though it had been poor, was getting better : it was, indeed, our chief dependance. At this season of the year the animals are in much better order in the prairies near the point, where they feed on grass and rushes, considerable quantities of which remain green, than in the woody country up the Netul. There they subsist on whortleberry bushes and fern, but chiefly on an evergreen called *shallun*, resembling the laurel, which abounds through all the timbered lands, particularly along the broken sides of hills. Towards the latter end of February, however, they left the prairies near Point Adams, and reti 'ed back to the hills ; but, fortunately, at the same time the sturgeon and anchovies began to appear, and afforded us a delicious variety of food. The party on the seacoast continued to supply us with salt." * * *

" The neighbouring tribes still visited us for the purpose of trading, or to smoke with us. On the 21st, a Chinnook chief, whom we had not before seen, came over with twenty-five of his men. His name was Taheum : a man about fifty years of age, of a larger stature and better carriage, than most of his nation. We received him with the usual cere- monies, gave the party something to eat, smoked very freely with them all, and presented the chief with a small medal. They seemed well satisfied with their treatment ; but, though we were willing to show the chief every civility, we could not dispense with our rule of not suffering a large number of stran- gers to sleep in the fort. They therefore left us at sunset. On the 24th, Comowool, who was by far the most friendly and decent savage we had seen in this neighbourhood, came with a large party of Clatsops, bringing, among other articles, sturgeon, and a small fish which had just begun to make its appearance in the Columbia."

As the elk were now less plentiful, they subsisted on fish whenever they could take them, or their lim- ited means would procure them from the Indians. There were a considerable number of invalids in the party, the principal complaint being a sort of influ- enza, which they ascribed to the nature of the cli- mate.

CHAPTER VIII.

Difficulty of procuring the Means of Subsistence.—They determine to start on their Journey to the Mountains.—They leave
with the Indians a written Memorandum, giving an Account
of their having penetrated to the Pacific by the way of the
Missouri and Columbia, and across the Rocky Mountains.—
The Party commence their Return.—Dexterity of the Cathlamah Indians in Carving.—The Coweliskee River.—Hospitality of the Natives.—Instance of the extreme Voracity of the
Vulture.—The Party are visited by many strange Indians, all
of whom are kind and hospitable.—Scarcity of Game, and
Embarrassments on that Account.—Captain Clarke discovers
a Tribe not seen in the Descent down the Columbia.—Partic-
ular Description of the Multnomah Village and River.—Mount
Jefferson.— Captain Clarke's Account of the Neerchokio
Tribe, and of their Architecture.— Their Sufferings from
Smallpox.

" Many reasons," continues the Journal, " had determined us to remain at Fort Clatsop till the 1st of
April. Besides the want of fuel in the plains on the
Columbia, and the impracticability of passing the
mountains before the beginning of June, we were
anxious to see some of the foreign traders, from
whom, by means of our ample letters of credit, we
might recruit our exhausted stores of merchandise.
About the middle of March, however, we became
seriously alarmed for the want of food: the elk, our
chief dependance, had at length deserted their usual
haunts in our neighbourhood, and retreated to the
mountains. We were too poor to purchase other
food from the Indians, so that we were sometimes
reduced, notwithstanding all the exertions of our
hunters, to a single day's provision in advance.
The men, too, whom the constant rains and confinement had rendered unhealthy, might, we hoped, be
benefited by quitting the coast, and resuming the ex-

ercise of travelling. We determined, therefore, to leave Fort Clatsop, ascend the river slowly, spend the remainder of March in the woody country, where we hoped to find subsistence, and in this way reach the plains about the first of April, before which time it would be fruitless to attempt crossing them ; and for this purpose we now began our preparations.

" During the winter we had been very industrious in dressing skins, so that we had now a sufficient quantity of clothing, besides between three and four hundred pairs of moccasins. But the whole stock of goods on which we were to depend, both for the purchase of horses and of food, during the long tour of nearly four thousand miles, was so much diminished that it might all be tied in two handkerchiefs We had, in fact, nothing but six blue robes, one of scarlet, a coat and hat of the United States artillery uniform, five robes made of our large flag, and a few old clothes trimmed with riband. We therefore felt that our chief dependance must be on our guns, which, fortunately, were all in good order, as we had taken the precaution of bringing a number of extra locks, and one of our men proved to be an excellent artist in that way. The powder had been secured in leaden canisters, and though on many occasions they had been under water, it had remained perfectly dry, and we now found ourselves in possession of one hundred and forty pounds of powder, and twice that weight of lead, a stock quite sufficient for the route homeward.

" After much trafficking, we at last succeeded in purchasing a canoe for a uniform coat and half a carrot of tobacco, and took another from the Clatsops, by way of reprisal for some elk which they had stolen from us in the winter. We were now ready to leave, but the rain prevented us for several days from caulking the canoes, and we were forced to wait for calm weather before we could attempt to pass Point William. In the mean time we were visited by many of our neighbours, for the purpose of taking leave of us. The Clatsop Comowool had been the most friendly and hospitable of all the Indians in this quarter: we therefore gave him a certificate of the kindness and attention which we had received from him, and added a more substantial proof of our gratitude—the gift of all our houses and furniture. To the Chinnook chief Delashelwilt we gave a certificate of the same kind ; and distributed among the natives several papers (one of which we also posted up in the fort), to the following effect :

" The object of this is, that through the medium of some civilized person who may see the same, it may be made known to the world that the party, consisting of the persons whose names are hereunto annexed, and who were sent out by the government of the United States to explore the interior of the continent of North America, did cross the same by the way of the Missouri and Columbia Rivers, to the discharge of the latter into the Pacific Ocean, where they arrived on the 14th day of November, 1805, and departed the 23d day of March, 1806, on their return to the United States, by the same route by which they had come out.'* On the back of some of these

* By a singular casualty this note fell into the possession of Captain Hill, who, while on the coast of the Pacific, procured it from the natives. This note was taken by him to Canton, from whence it was brought to the United States. The following is an extract of a letter from a gentleman at Canton to his friend in Philadelphia :

Extract of a letter from —— to —— in Philadelphia.

Canton, January, 1807.

I wrote you last by the Governor Strong, Cleveland, for Boston ; the present is by the brig Lydia, Hill, of the same place.

Captain Hill, while on the coast, met some Indian natives near the mouth of the Columbia River, who delivered to him a *paper*, of which I enclose you a copy. It had been committed to their charge by Captains Clarke and Lewis, who had penetrated papers we sketched the connexion of the upper branches of the Missouri and Columbia Rivers, with our route, and the track which we intended to follow on our return." * * *

" The rains and wind still confined us to the fort ; but at last our provisions were reduced to a single day's stock, and it became absolutely necessary to remove : we therefore sent a few hunters ahead, and stopped the rents in the boats as well as we could with mud.

" March 23. The canoes were loaded, and at one o'clock in the afternoon we took a final leave of Fort Clatsop. The wind was still high, but we must have remained without provisions, and we hoped to be able to double Point William. We had scarcely left the fort, when we met Delashelwilt and a party of twenty Chinnooks, who, understanding that we had been trying to procure a canoe, had brought one for sale. Being, however, already supplied, we left them, and, after getting out of Meriwether's Bay, began to coast along the south side of the river. We doubled Point William without any accident, and at six o'clock reached, at the distance of sixteen miles from Fort Clatsop, the mouth of a small creek, where we found our hunters." * * *

Starting immediately after breakfast the next morning, at one o'clock they reached the Cathlamah village, opposite to the Seal Islands, and which has been already mentioned. " These people," says the Journal, " seem to be more fond of carving in wood

to the Pacific Ocean. The original is a rough draught with a pen of their outward route, and that which they intended returning by. Just below the junction of Madison's River they found an immense fall of *three hundred and sixty-two* feet perpendicular. This, I believe, exceeds in magnitude any other known. From the natives Captain Hill learned that they were all in good health and spirits ; had met many difficulties on their progress from various tribes of Indians, but had found them about the sources of the Missouri very friendly, as were those on Colum bia River and the coast.—*Note of the original Editor.*

than their neighbours, and have various specimens of their workmanship about their houses. The broad piece supporting the roof and the board through which the doors are cut are the objects on which they chiefly display their ingenuity, being ornamented with curious figures, sometimes representing persons in a sitting posture supporting a burden. On resuming our route among the Seal Islands we mistook our way, which an Indian observing, he pursued us and put us in the right channel. Soon, however, he somewhat embarrassed us by claiming the canoe we had taken from the Clatsops, and which he declared to be his property. We had found it among the Clatsops, and seized it, as has been already stated, by way of reprisal for a theft committed by that nation ; but, being unwilling to do an act of injustice to this Indian, and having no time to discuss the question of right, we compromised the matter with him for an elkskin, with which he returned perfectly satisfied." * * * After making a distance of fifteen miles, they encamped opposite to the lower village of the Wahkiacums.

The two following days they ascended the river about thirty-three miles, meeting with different parties of the Clatsops and Cathlamahs, from whom they obtained a small supply of fish, while their hunters succeeded in killing a goose and three eagles.

"March 27. We set out early," continues the Journal, "and were soon joined by some Skilloots with fish and roots for sale. At ten o'clock we stopped to breakfast at two houses of the same nation, where we found our hunters, who had not returned to camp last night, but had killed nothing. The inhabitants seemed very kind and hospitable. They gave almost the whole party as much as they could eat of dried anchovies, *wappatoo*, sturgeon, *quamash*, and a small white tuberous root, two inches long, and as thick as a man's finger, which when

eaten raw, is crisp, milky, and of an agreeable flavour. They also urged us to remain with them all
the day, and hunt elk and deer, which they said were
abundant in the neighbourhood; but, as the weather
would not permit us to dry and pitch our canoes, we
declined their invitation, and proceeded. At the distance of two miles we passed the entrance of Coweliskee River. This stream discharges itself on the
north side of the Columbia, about three miles above
a remarkably high rocky knoll, the south side of
which it washes in passing, and which is separated from the northern hills by a wide bottom several
miles in extent. The Coweliskee is one hundred
and fifty yards wide, deep and navigable, as the Indians assert, for a considerable distance, and most
probably waters the country west and north of the
range of mountains which cross the Columbia between the Great Falls and Rapids. On the lower
side of this river, a few miles from its entrance into
the Columbia, is the principal village of the Skilloots, a numerous people, differing, however, neither
in language, dress, nor manners from the Clatsops,
Chinnooks, and other nations at the mouth of the
Columbia. With the Chinnooks they have lately
been at war, and, though hostilities have ceased,
they have not yet resumed their usual intercourse,
so that the Skilloots do not go down as far as the
sea, nor do the Chinnooks come higher up than the
Seal Islands, the trade between them being carried
on by the Clatsops, Cathlamahs, and Wahkiacums,
their mutual friends. On this same river, above the
Skilloots, resides a nation called Hullooetell, of
whom we learned nothing except that they were
numerous." * * * They halted late in the evening,
after making twenty miles, having been enabled to
purchase of the natives a plentiful supply of fish and
roots at a very moderate price.

The next day they set out as usual, but after proceeding five miles they landed on Deer Island, where,
Il.—N

the weather becoming fair, they concluded to remain, for the purpose of drying their baggage and pitching their boats. " Our hunters," proceeds the Journal, " brought in three deer, a goose, some ducks, an eagle, and a tiger-cat ; but such is the extreme voracity of the vultures, that they had devoured in the space of a few hours four of the deer killed in the morning ; and one of our men declared that they had, besides, dragged a large buck about thirty yards, skinned it, and broke the back-bone. We were visited during the day by a large canoe with ten Indians of the Quathlapotle nation, who reside about seventeen miles farther up.

" March 29. At an early hour we proceeded along the side of Deer Island, and halted for breakfast at the upper end of it, where is properly the commencement of the great Columbian Valley. We were joined here by three men of the Towahnahiook nation, with whom we proceeded, till at the distance of fourteen miles from our camp of last evening we reached a large inlet or arm of the river, about three hundred yards wide, up which they went to their villages. A short distance above this inlet, a considerable river empties itself on the north side of the Columbia ; its name is Chawahnahiooks. It is about one hundred and fifty yards wide, and discharges a large body of water, though the Indians assured us that at a short distance above its mouth the navigation is obstructed by falls and rapids. Three miles beyond the inlet is an island near the north shore of the river, behind the lower end of which was a village of Quathlapotles, where we landed about three o'clock. This village consisted of fourteen large wooden houses. The people received us very kindly, and voluntarily spread before us anchovies and *wappatoo ;* but, as soon as we had finished enjoying their hospitality, if it deserves that name, they began to ask for presents. They were, however, perfectly satisfied with the trifling articles which we distributed among them, and equally pleased with our purchasing some *wappatoo*, twelve dogs, and two sea-otter skins. We also gave to the chief a small medal, which he soon transferred to his wife. After remaining some time we embarked, and, coasting along this island, which, after the nation, we called Quathlapotle Island, encamped for the night in a small prairie on the north side of the Columbia, having made by estimate nineteen miles. The river was rising fast. In the course of the day we saw great numbers of geese, ducks, and large and small swans, which last were very abundant in the ponds where the *wappatoo* grew, as they feed much on that root. We also observed the crested kingfisher, and the large and small blackbird; and in the evening heard, without seeing, the large hooting-owl. Frogs, which we did not find in the wet marshes near the entrance of the Columbia, were now croaking in the swamps and marshes, with precisely the same note as in the United States. Garter-snakes appeared in vast numbers, and were seen in the prairies in large bundles of forty or fifty entwined round each other. Among the moss on the rocks we observed a species of small wild onions, growing so closely together as to form a perfect turf, and equal in flavour to the chives of our gardens, which they resemble in appearance also.

" March 30. Soon after our departure we were met by three Clanaminanums, one of whom we recognised as our companion yesterday. He pressed us very much to visit his countrymen on the inlet, but we had no time to make the circuit, and parted. We had not proceeded far before a party of Claxtars and Cathlacumups passed us in two canoes, on their way down the river; and soon after we were met by several other canoes, filled with Indians of different tribes on each side of the river. We also passed several fishing camps on Wappatoo Island, and then halted for breakfast on the north side of the river, near our camp of the 4th of November. Here we

were visited by several canoes from two villages on
Wappatoo Island: the first, about two miles farther
up, was called Clahnaquah; the other, a mile above
it, Multnomah.   After higgling much in the manner
of those on the seacoast, these Indians gave us a
sturgeon, with some *wappatoo* and *pashequaw*, in exchange for a few small fish-hooks.   As we proceeded
we were joined by other Indians, and on coming opposite to the Clahnaquah village, we were shown
another village, about two miles from the river on
the northeast side, and behind a pond running parallel with it.   Here they said the tribe called Shotos
resided.   About four o'clock the Indians all left us.
Their chief object in accompanying us appeared to
have been to gratify their curiosity; but, though they
behaved in the most friendly manner, most of them
were furnished with their instruments of war.   About
sunset we reached a beautiful prairie, opposite to the
middle of what we had called Image-Canoe Island;
and, having made twenty-three miles, encamped for
the night." * * *

The next day they proceeded twenty-five miles,
passing a considerable stream from the north, which
they called Seal River, and encamped opposite to
the upper entrance of Quicksand River.   The latter
stream they ascertained, from the accounts of the
Indians and by their own examination, to be much
less extensive than they had supposed in passing it
on their way down.   They remained here till the
6th of April, for the purpose of collecting a stock of
provisions.   Several parties of Indians were met descending the river in quest of food.   "They told us,"
says the Journal, "that they lived at the Great Rapids; but that the scarcity of provisions there had
induced them to come down, in the hopes of finding
subsistence in the more fertile valley.   All the peo
ple living at the Rapids, as well as the nations above
them, were in much distress for want of food, having
consumed their winter store of dried fish, and not

expecting the return of the salmon before the next full moon, which would be on the 2d of May: this information was not a little embarrassing. From the Falls to the Chopunnish nation, the plains afforded neither deer, elk, nor antelope for our subsistence. The horses were very poor at this season, and the dogs must be in the same condition, if their food, the dried fish, had failed. Still, it was obviously inexpedient for us to wait for the return of the salmon, since in that case we might not reach the Missouri before the ice would prevent our navigating it. We might, besides, hazard the loss of our horses, as the Chopunnish, with whom we had left them, would cross the mountains as early as possible, or about the beginning of May, and take our horses with them, or suffer them to disperse, in either of which cases the passage of the mountains will be almost impracticable. We therefore, after much deliberation, decided to remain where we were till we could collect meat enough to last us till we should reach the Chopunnish nation, and to obtain canoes from the natives as we ascended, either in exchange for our pirogues, or by purchasing them with skins and merchandise. These canoes, again, we might exchange for horses with the natives of the plains, till we should obtain enough to travel altogether by land. On reaching the southeast branch of the Columbia, four or five men could be sent on to the Chopunnish to have our horses in readiness; and thus we should have a stock of horses sufficient both to transport our baggage and supply us with food, as we now perceived that they would form our only certain dependance for subsistence.

"The hunters returned from the opposite side of the river with some deer and elk, which were abundant there, as were also the tracks of the black bear, while on the north side we could kill nothing.

"In the course of our dealings to-day we purchased a canoe from an Indian for six fathoms of wampum beads. He seemed perfectly satisfied, and went away; but returned soon after, cancelled the bargain, and, giving back the wampum, requested us to restore the canoe. To this we consented, as we knew that this method of trading was very common, and deemed perfectly fair.

" April 2. Being now determined to collect as much game as possible, two parties, consisting of nine men, were sent over the river to hunt, and three were ordered to range the country on the side where we were, while the rest were employed in cutting up and scaffolding the meat which had been already brought in. About eight o'clock several canoes arrived with visiters, and among the rest were two young men who were pointed out as Cushooks. They said that their nation resided at the falls of a large river, which emptied itself into the south side of the Columbia a few miles above us; and they drew a map of the country with a coal, on a mat. In order to satisfy himself as to the truth of this information, Captain Clarke persuaded one of the young Cushooks, by a present of a burning-glass, to accompany him to the river, in search of which he immediately set out with a canoe and seven of our men. After his departure other canoes arrived, bringing families of women and children, who confirmed the accounts of scarcity above. One of these families, consisting of ten or twelve persons, encamped near us, and behaved perfectly well. The hunters on our side of the river returned with the skins only of two deer, the animals themselves being too lean for use.

" April 3. A considerable number of Indians crowded about us to-day, many of them from the upper part of the river. These poor wretches gave a dismal account of the scarcity prevailing there; which, indeed, their appearance sufficiently proved, for they seemed almost starved, and greedily picked the bones and refuse meat thrown away by us.

"In the evening Captain Clarke returned from his excursion. On setting out yesterday at half past eleven o'clock, he directed his course along the south side of the river, where, at the distance of eight miles, he passed a village of the Nechacohee tribe, belonging to the Eloot nation. The village itself was small, and, being situated behind Diamond Island, was concealed from our view, as we had passed both times along the northern shore. He proceeded onward till three o'clock, when he landed near a single house, the only remains of a village of twenty-four straw huts. Along the shore were great numbers of small canoes for receiving *wappatoo*, having been left here by the Shahalas, who visit the place annually. The present inmates of the house were part of the Neerchokioo tribe of the same nation. On entering one of the apartments of the house, Captain Clarke offered several articles to the Indians in exchange for *wappatoo;* but they appeared sullen and ill humoured, and refused to give him any. He therefore sat down by the fire opposite to the men, and, drawing a portfire match from his pocket, threw a small piece of it into the flames; at the same time he took out his pocket compass, and by means of a magnet which happened to be in his ink-horn, made the needle turn round very briskly. The match immediately took fire and burned violently, on which the Indians, terrified at this strange exhibition, brought a quantity of *wappatoo* and laid it at his feet, begging him to put out the bad fire; while an old woman continued to speak with great vehemence, as if praying, and imploring protection. After receiving the roots, Captain Clarke put up the compass, and, as the match went out of itself, tranquillity was restored, though the women and children still sought refuge in their beds and behind the men. He now paid them for what he had used, and, after lighting his pipe and smoking with them, continued down the river. He found that what we had

called Image-Canoe Island consisted of three islands,
the one in the middle concealing the opening between the other two in such a way as to present to
us on the opposite side of the river the appearance
of a single island.   At the lower point of the third,
and thirteen miles below the last village, he entered
the mouth of a large river, which was concealed by
three small islands at its mouth from those who descend or ascend the Columbia.   This river, which
the Indians call Multnomah, from a nation of the
same name residing near it on Wappatoo Island, enters the Columbia one hundred and forty miles from
the mouth of the latter river, of which it may justly be
considered as forming one fourth, though it had now
fallen eighteen inches below its greatest annual
height.   From its entrance Mount Regnier bears
nearly north, and Mount St. Helen north, with a very
high humped mountain a little to the east of it, which
seems to lie in the same chain with the conic-point-
ed mountains before mentioned.   Mount Hood bore
due east, and Captain Clarke now discovered to the
southeast a mountain which we had not yet seen,
and to which he gave the name of Mount Jefferson.
Like Mount St. Helen, its figure is a regular cone,
covered with snow, and it is probably of equal height
with that mountain, though, being more distant, so
large a portion of it did not appear above the range
of mountains which lie between these and the point
where they were.   Soon after entering the Multnomah he was met by an old Indian descending the
river alone in a canoe.   After some conversation
with him, the pilot informed Captain Clarke that
this old man belonged to the Clackamos nation, who
reside on a river forty miles up the Multnomah.
The current of this latter river is as gentle as that
of the Columbia, its surface is smooth and even, and
it appears to possess water enough for the largest
ship, since, on sounding with a line of five fathoms,
he could find no bottom for at least one third of the

width of the stream. At the distance of seven miles he passed a sluice or opening on the right, eighty yards wide, which separates Wappatoo Island from the continent by emptying itself into the inlet below. Three miles farther up he reached a large wooden house on the east side, where he intended to sleep; but on entering the rooms he found such swarms of fleas, that he preferred lying on the ground near by. The guide informed him that this house was the temporary residence of the Nemal-quinner tribe of the Cushook nation, who reside just below the falls of the Multnomah, but come down here occasionally to collect *wappatoo:* it was thirty feet long and forty deep, built of broad boards, and covered with the bark of white cedar, the floor being on a level with the surface of the earth, and the arrangement of the interior like that of the houses near the seacoast. The former inhabitants had left their canoes, mats, bladders, train oil, baskets, bowls, and trenchers lying about the house at the mercy of every visiter; a proof, indeed, of their respect for the property of each other, though we had had very conclusive evidence that the property of white men was not deemed equally sacred. The guide inform-ed him farther, that at a small distance above there were two *bayous*, on which were a number of small houses belonging to the Cushooks, but that they had then all gone up to the falls of the Multnomah for the purpose of fishing.

" Early the next morning Captain Clarke proceeded up the river, which during the night had fallen about five inches. At the distance of two miles he came to the centre of a bend under the high lands on the right side, from which its course, as far as could be discerned, was to the east of southeast. At this place the Multnomah is five hundred yards wide, and for half that distance across a cord of five fathoms would not reach the bottom. It appears to be washing away its banks, and has more sand-bars

II.—O

and willow-points than the Columbia. Its regular, gentle current, the depth, smoothness, and uniformity with which it rolls its vast body of water, proves that its supplies are at once distant and steady; nor judging from its appearance and course, is it rash to believe that the Multnomah and its tributary streams water the vast extent of country between the western mountains and those of the seacoast, as far, perhaps, as the Gulf of California. At about eleven o'clock he again reached the house of the Neerchokioos, in which he now found eight families ; but they were all so much alarmed at his presence, notwithstanding his visit yesterday, that he remained a very few minutes only. Soon after setting out he met five canoes, filled with the same number of families, belonging to the Shahala nation. They were descending the river in search of food, and seemed very desirous of coming alongside the boat; but, as there were twenty-one of them, and the guide said that these Shahalas, as well as their relations at the house we had just left, were all mischievous, bad men, they were not suffered to approach.

"At three o'clock he halted for an hour at the Nechecolce house, where his guide resided. This large building was two hundred and twenty-six feet in front, entirely above ground, and might be considered as a single house, since the whole was under one roof : otherwise it appeared more like a range of buildings, as it was divided into seven distinct apartments, each thirty feet square, by means of broad poles set on end, and reaching from the floor to the roof. The apartments were separated from each other by a passage or alley four feet wide, extending through the whole depth of the house, and the only entrance to them was from these alleys, through a small hole about twenty-two inches wide, and not more than three feet high. The roof was formed of rafters and round poles laid on them longitudinally ; the whole being covered with a dou

ble row of the bark of the white cedar, extending
from the top eighteen inches over the eaves, and secured as well as kept smooth by splinters of dried
fir inserted through it at regular distances. In this
manner the roof was made light, strong, and durable. Near this house were the remains of several
other large buildings, sunk in the ground, and constructed like those we had seen at the Great Narrows of the Columbia, belonging to the Eloots, with
whom these people claim affinity. In manners and
dress these Nechecolees differ but little from the
Quathlapotles, and others of this neighbourhood; but
their language is the same used by the Eloots, and
though it has some words in common with the dia ·
lects spoken here, yet its whole structure is obvi
ously different. The men, too, are of larger stature,
and both sexes better formed than among the nations below; and the females are distinguished by
wearing larger and longer robes (which are generally of deerskin dressed in the hair) than those of
the neighbouring tribes. In the house there were
several old people of both sexes, who were treated
with much respect, and still seemed healthy, though
most of them were perfectly blind. On inquiring
the cause of the decline of their village, an old man,
the father of the guide, and a person of some distinction, brought forward a woman very much pit-
ted with the smallpox, and said that, when a girl, she
was very near dying with the disorder which had
left those marks, and that all the inhabitants of the
houses now in ruins had fallen victims to the same
disease. From the apparent age of the woman
then, connected with what it was at the time of her
illness, Captain Clarke judged that this sickness
must have been about thirty years before, or about
the period we had supposed that the smallpox probably prevailed on the seacoast.

  " He then entered into a long conversation in regard to the adjacent country and its inhabitants, the

old man replying to his questions with great intelligence ; and at the close he drew with his finger in the dust a sketch of the Multnomah, and of Wappatoo Island. This Captain Clarke copied and preserved. He then purchased five dogs, and, taking leave of the Nechecolee village, returned to camp."

CHAPTER IX.

Description of Wappatoo Island, and of the Mode in which the Natives gather the Wappatoo Root.—Character of the Soil and its Productions.—Numerous Tribes residing in its Vicinity.—Probability that they were all of the Multnomah Tribe originally, inferred from Similarity of Dress, Manners, Language, &c.—Description of their Dress, Weapons of War, and Mode of burying the Dead.—Description of another Village, called the Wahclellah Village.—Their Mode of Architecture. —Extraordinary Height of Beacon Rock.—Unfriendly Character of the Indians at that Place.—The Party, alarmed for their Safety, resolve to inflict summary Vengeance, in case the Wahclellah Tribe persist in their Outrages and Insults.— Interview with the Chief of that Tribe, and Confidence resto red.—Difficulty of drawing the Canoes over the Rapids.— Visited by a Party of the Yehugh Tribe.—Brief Notice of the Weocksockwillackum Tribe.—Curious Phenomenon observed in the Columbia, from the Rapids to the Chilluckittequaws

" APRIL 4. The hunters were still out in every direction. Those from the opposite side of the river returned with a bear and some venison; but the flesh of six deer and an elk which they had killed was so meager and unfit for use that they had left it in the woods. Two other deer were brought in ; but, as the game was all poor, we despatched a large party to some low grounds on the south, six miles above us, to hunt there until our arrival. As usual, many Indians came to our camp, some of them descending the river with their families, and others from below, with no object except to gratify their curiosity.

" The visit of Captain Clarke to the Multnomahs, and information obtained from other sources, now enabled us to give some account of the neighbouring countries and nations. The most important spot is Wappatoo Island, a large tract lying between the Multnomah and an arm of the Columbia, which we called Wappatoo Inlet, and separated from the main land by a sluice eighty yards wide, which at the distance of seven miles up the Multnomah connects that river with the inlet. The island thus formed is about twenty miles long, and varies in breadth from five to ten miles. The land is high, and extremely fertile ; and on most parts is covered with a heavy growth of cottonwood, ash, the large-leafed ash, and sweet willow, the black alder common on the coast having now disappeared. But the chief wealth of this island is found in the numerous ponds in the interior, which abound with the common arrowhead (*sagittaria sagittifolia*), to the root of which is attached a bulb growing beneath it in the mud. This bulb, to which the Indians give the name of *wappatoo*, is their great article of food, and almost the staple article of commerce on the Columbia. It is never out of season ; so that at all times of the year the valley is frequented by the neighbouring Indians, who come to gather it. It is collected chiefly by the women, who employ for the purpose canoes from ten to fourteen feet in length, about two feet wide, nine inches deep, and tapering from the middle. They are sufficient to contain a single person and several bushels of roots, yet so very light that a woman can carry them with ease. She takes one of these canoes into a pond where the water is as high as the breast, and by means of her toes separates this bulb from the root, which, on being freed from the mud, rises immediately to the surface of the water, and is thrown into the canoe. In this

manner these patient females will remain in the water for several hours, even in the depth of winter.
This plant is found throughout the whole extent of
the valley in which we then were, but does not grow
on the Columbia farther east.

" This valley is bounded on the west by the mountainous country bordering the coast, from which it
extends eastward thirty miles in a direct line, to the
range of mountains crossing the Columbia above
the Great Falls: its length from north to south we
were unable to determine, but we believed it to extend in this direction a great distance.   It is, in fact,
the only desirable situation for a settlement on the
western side of the Rocky Mountains; and, being
naturally fertile, would, if properly cultivated, afford
subsistence for forty or fifty thousand souls.   The
high lands are generally of a dark rich loam, not
much encumbered with stones, and, though waving,
by no means too steep for cultivation: a few miles
from the river they widen, at least on the north side,
into rich, extensive prairies.   The timber on them
is abundant, and consists almost exclusively of the
several species of fir already described, some of the
trees growing to a great height.   We measured a
fallen tree of that species, and found that, including
the stump of about six feet, it was three hundred
and eighteen feet in length, though its diameter was
only three feet.   The dogwood is also abundant on
the uplands: it differs from that of the United States
in having a much smoother bark, and in being much
larger, the trunk attaining a diameter of nearly two
feet.   There is some white cedar of a large size,
but no pine of any kind.   In the bottom lands are
the cottonwood, ash, large-leafed ash, and sweet
willow; interspersed with which are the *pashequaw,*
shanataque, and compound fern, of which the natives
use the roots.   The red flowering currant abounds
on the uplands, while along the river bottoms grow
luxuriantly the water-cress, strawberry, cinquefoil

narrow dock, sandrush, and the flowering pea.
There is also a species of the bear's-claw, but the
large-leafed thorn had disappeared, nor did we see
any longer the whortleberry, the *shallun*, nor any of
the other evergreen shrubs bearing berries, except a
species the leaf of which has a prickly margin.

" Among the animals we observed the martin,
small geese, the small speckled woodpecker with a
white back, the blue-crested corvus, ravens, crows,
eagles, vultures, and hawks. The mellow bug and
long-legged spider, as well as the butterfly, blowing-
fly, and tick, had already made their appearance ; but
none of these are different from insects of the same
sort in the United States. The moschetoes, too, had
resumed their visits, but were not yet troublesome.

" The nations who inhabit this fertile neighbourhood are very numerous. The Wappatoo Inlet,
three hundred yards wide, extends for ten or twelve
miles to the south, as far as the hills, near which it
receives the waters of a small creek; whose sources
are not far from those of the Killamuck River. On
that creek reside the Clackstar nation, a numerous people of twelve hundred souls, who subsist on
fish and *wappatoo*, and trade, by means of the Killamuck River, with the nation of that name on the
seacoast. Lower down the inlet, towards the Columbia, is the tribe called Cathlacumup. On the
sluice which connects the inlet with the Multnomah
are the Cathlanahquiah and Cathlacomatup tribes ;
and on Wappatoo Island the Clannahminamuns and
Clahnaquahs. Immediately opposite, near the Towahnahiooks, are the Quathlapotles, and higher up, on
the side of the Columbia, the Shotos. All these
tribes, as well as the Cathlahaws, who live somewhat lower on the river, and have an old village on
Deer Island, may be considered as parts of the great
Multnomah nation, which has its principal residence
on Wappatoo Island, near the mouth of the large
river to which they give their name. Forty miles

above its junction with the Columbia, this river receives the waters of the Clackamos, a river which
may be traced through a woody and fertile country
to its sources in Mount Jefferson, almost to the foot
of which it is navigable for canoes. A nation of the
same name resides in eleven villages along its borders: they live chiefly on fish and roots, which
abound in the Clackamos and along its banks, though
they sometimes descend to the Columbia to gather
wappatoo, where they cannot be distinguished in
dress, manners, or language from the tribes of the
Multnomahs. Two days' journey from the Columbia, or about twenty miles beyond the entrance of
the Clackamos, are the Falls of the Multnomah. At
this place reside the Cushooks and Chahcowahs,
two tribes that are attracted there by the fish, and
by the convenience of trading across the mountains,
and down the Killamuck River, with the Killamucks,
from whom they procure train oil. These falls are
occasioned by a high range of mountains, beyond
which the country stretches into a vast level plain
wholly destitute of timber. As far as the Indians
with whom we conversed had ever penetrated that
country, it seems to be inhabited by a nation called
Calahpoewah, a very numerous people, whose villages, nearly forty in number, are scattered along
each side of the Multnomah, which furnishes them
with their chief subsistence, viz., fish, and the roots
along its banks.

" All the tribes in the neighbourhood of Wappatoo
Island we considered as Multnomahs; not because
they are in any degree subordinate to that nation,
but they all seem to regard it as being the most powerful. There was no distinguished chief except the
one at the head of the Multnomahs; and they are,
moreover, allied by similarity of dress and manners,
and of houses and language, which, much more than
the feeble restraints of Indian government, contribute to make one people. These circumstances sep-

arate them also from the nations lower down the river. The Clatsops, Chinnooks, Wahkiacums, and Cathlamahs understand each other perfectly : their language varies, however, in some respects from that of the Skilloots; but, on reaching the Multnomah Indians, we found that, although many words were the same, while a great number differed only in the mode of accenting them from those employed by the Indians near the mouth of the Columbia, yet there was, in fact, a very sensible distinction. The natives of the valley are of larger stature, and rather better shaped than those on the seacoast: their appearance, too, is generally healthy, though they are afflicted with the common disease of the Columbia, soreness of the eyes." * * *

" The dress of the men does not differ from that used below ; they are chiefly distinguished by a passion for large brass buttons, which they will fix on a sailor's jacket, whenever they are so fortunate as to obtain one, without the slightest regard to arrangement. The women, also, wear the short robe already described; but their hair is most commonly braided into two tresses, falling over each ear in front of the body ; and instead of the tissue of bark, they employ a piece of leather in the shape of a pocket handkerchief, tied round the loins." * * *

" The houses are generally on a level with the ground, though some are sunk to the depth of two or three feet, and, like those near the coast, are adorned, or rather disfigured, with carvings or paintings on the posts, doors, and beds. They have no peculiar weapon except a kind of broadsword made of iron, from three to four feet long, the blade about four inches wide, and very thin and sharp at both its edges, as well as at the point. They have also bludgeons of wood of the same form ; and both kinds generally hang at the head of their beds : these are formidable weapons. Like the natives of the seacoast, they are also very fond of cold, hot, and vapour baths, which are used at all seasons, for the purpose of health as well as pleasure.

" The mode of burying the dead in canoes is not practised by the natives here. The place of deposite is a vault formed of boards, slanting like the roof of a house, from a pole supported by two forks. Under this the dead are placed horizontally on boards, on the surface of the earth, and carefully covered with mats. The bodies are here laid to the height of three or four upon each other, and the different articles which were most esteemed by the deceased are placed by their side ; their canoes themselves being sometimes taken to pieces to strengthen the vault.

" All these people trade in anchovies and sturgeon, but chiefly in *wappatoo ;* to obtain which, the inhabitants both above and below come at all seasons, the latter bringing, in turn, beads, cloth, and various other articles procured from the Europeans.

" April 5. We dried our meat as well as the cloudy weather would permit. In the course of the chase yesterday, one of our men who had killed the bear found the den of another with three cubs in it. He returned to it to-day in hope of finding the dam, but, being disappointed in this, he brought the cubs ; and on this occasion Drewyer, our most experienced huntsman, assured us that he had never known a single instance where a female bear had been once disturbed by the hunter and obliged to leave her young, that she returned to them again. The young bears we sold for *wappatoo* to some of the numerous Indians who visited us in parties during the day, and who behaved very well. Having prepared our stock of dried meat, we set out the next morning." * * *

They proceeded, however, but a few miles the next day, as they were obliged to wait and collect their hunters ; nor did they start again the two following days, being employed in drying some additional meat that was brought in on the 7th, and on the 8th the weather would not permit their leaving.

" April 9. The wind having moderated, we reloaded the canoes, and set out by seven o'clock. We
stopped to take up two of our hunters who had left
us yesterday, but had been unsuccessful in the chase,
and then proceeded to the Wahclellah village, situated on the north side of the river, about a mile below Beacon Rock. During the whole of the route
from our camp we passed along under high, steep,
and rocky sides of mountains, which here close in on
each side of the river, forming stupendous precipices
covered with fir and white cedar. Down these
heights descend the most beautiful cascades, one of
which, formed by a large creek, falls over a perpendicular rock three hundred feet above the water,
while other smaller streams precipitate themselves
from a still greater elevation, and, partially evapora-
ting in a mist, collect again, and make a second descent before they reach the bottom of the rocks.
We stopped to breakfast at this village; and here
we found the tomahawk which had been stolen from
us on the 4th of last November. They assured us
that they had bought it of the Indians below ; but, as
the latter had already informed us that the Wahclellahs had such an article which they had stolen,
we made no difficulty about retaking our property."
* * * " After purchasing, with much difficulty, a few
dogs and some *wappatoo* from the Wahclellahs, we
left them at two o'clock, and, passing along the Beacon Rock, reached in two hours the Clahclellah village.
    " This rock, which we now observed more accu-
rately than we had done in our descent, stands on
the north side of the river, insulated from the hills.
The northern side has a partial growth of fir or pine.
To the south it rises in an unbroken precipice to the
height of seven hundred feet, where it terminates in
a sharp point, and may be seen at the distance of
twenty miles below. This rock may be considered
as the point where tide-water commences : though

the influence of the tide is perceptible here in autumn only, at which time the river is low. What
the precise difference is at those seasons, we could
not determine ; but, on examining a rock which we
had lately passed, and comparing its appearance
with what we had observed last November, we
judged the flood of this spring to be twelve feet
above the height of the river at that time. From
Beacon Rock as low down as the marshy islands,
the general width of the river is from one to two
miles, though in many places it is greater. On
landing at the village of the Clahclellahs, we found
them busy in erecting their huts, which seemed to
be of a temporary kind only, so that most probably
they do not remain longer than the salmon season.
Like their countrymen whom we had just left, these
people were sulky·and ill humoured, and so much
on the alert to pilfer that we were obliged to keep
them at a distance from our baggage. As our large
canoes could not ascend the rapids on the north
side, we passed to the opposite shore, and entered
the narrow channel which separates it from Brant
Island. The weather was very cold and rainy, and
the wind so high that we were afraid to attempt the
rapids the same evening, and therefore, finding a
safe harbour, we encamped for the night." * * *

"April 10. Early in the morning we dropped down
the channel to the lower end of Brant Island, and
then drew our boats up the rapid. At the distance
of a quarter of a mile we crossed over to a village
of Clahclellahs, consisting of six houses, on the opposite side. The river is here about four hundred
yards wide, and the current so rapid that, although
we employed five oars for each canoe, we were
borne down a considerable distance. While we
were at breakfast, one of the Indians offered us
two sheepskins for sale, one of which was the skin
of a full-grown animal, and was as large as that of a
common deer ; the second was smaller, and the skin

of the head, with the horns on it, had been made into a cap, and was highly prized by the owner. He, however, sold the cap to us for a knife, and the rest of the skin for those of two elk; but, observing our anxiety to purchase the other skin, they would not accept the same price for it, and, as we hoped to procure more in the neighbourhood, we would not offer a greater. The horns of the animal were black, smooth, and erect, and rise from the middle of the forehead, a little above the eyes, in a cylindrical form, to the height of four inches, where they are pointed. The Clahclellahs informed us that these sheep were very abundant on the heights and among the cliffs of the adjacent mountains, and that these two had been lately killed out of a herd of thirty-six, at no great distance from the village. We were soon joined by our hunters, with three black-tailed fallow deer, and, having purchased a few white salmon, proceeded on our route. The south side of the river is impassable, and the rapidity of the current, as well as the large rocks along the shore, renders the navigation of even the north side extremely difficult. During the greater part of the day it was necessary to draw them along the shore; and, as we had only a single towrope that was strong enough, we were obliged to bring them one after the other. In this tedious and laborious manner we at length reached the portage on the. north side, and carried our baggage to the top of a hill about two hundred paces distant, where we encamped for the night. The canoes were drawn on shore and secured, but one of them having got loose, drifted down to the last village, the inhabitants of which brought her back to us, an instance of honesty which we rewarded with a present of two knives. It rained all night, and the next morning,

"April 11, so that the tents and the skins which covered the baggage were wet. We therefore determined to take the canoes over the portage first, in hopes that by the afternoon the rain would cease, and we might carry our baggage across without injury. The work was immediately begun by almost the whole party, who in the course of the day dragged four of the canoes to the head of the rapids with great difficulty and labour, A guard, consisting of one sick man and three who had been lamed by accidents, remained with Captain Lewis to protect the baggage. This precaution was absolutely necessary to save it from the depredations of the Wahclellahs, who, we discovered, were great thieves, notwithstanding their apparent honesty in restoring our boat: indeed, so arrogant and intrusive did they become, that nothing but our numbers, we were convinced, preserved us from attack. They crowded about us while we were taking up the boats, and one of them had the insolence to throw stones down the bank at two of our men. ·We now found it necessary to depart from our uniformly mild and pacific course of conduct. On returning to the head of the portage, a large number of them met our men, and seemed very ill disposed. Shields had stopped to purchase a dog, and, being separated from the rest of the party, two Indians pushed him out of the road, and attempted to take the dog from him. He had no weapon but a long knife, with which he immediately attacked them both, hoping to despatch them before they had time to draw their arrows; but, as soon as they saw his design, they fled into the woods. Soon afterward we were told by an Indian who spoke Clatsop, which language we had learned during the winter, that the Wahclellahs had carried off Captain Lewis's dog to their village below. Three men, well armed, were instantly sent in pursuit of them, with orders to fire if there was the slightest resistance or hesitation. At the distance of two miles they came within sight of the thieves, who, finding themselves pursued, left the dog and made off. We now ordered all the Indians out of our camp, and signified to ᴖ em that, if any one of them stole our baggage or insulted our men, he would be instantly shot; a resolution which we were determined to enforce, as it was now our only means of safety. We were visited during the day by a chief of the Clahclellahs, who seemed mortified at the treatment we had received, and told us that the persons at the head of these outrages were two very bad men who belonged to the Wahclellahs, but that the nation itself did not by any means wish to displease us. This chief seemed very well disposed, and we had every reason to believe was much respected by the neighbouring Indians. We therefore gave him a small medal, and showed him all the attention in our power, with which he appeared to be very much gratified ; and we trusted that his interposition would prevent the necessity of our resorting to force against his countrymen.

" Many Indians from the villages above passed us in the course of the day, on their return from trading with the natives of the valley, and among others we recognised an Eloot, who, with ten or twelve of his nation, were on their way home to the Long Narrows of the Columbia. These people do not, as we are compelled to do, drag their canoes up the rapids, but leave them at the head as they descend, and, carrying their goods across the portage, hire or borrow others from the people below. When the traffic is over, they return to the foot of the rapids, where they leave these boats, and resume their own at the head of the portage. The labour of carrying the goods across is equally shared by the men and women ; and we were struck by the contrast between the decent conduct of all the natives from above, and the profligacy and ill manners of the Wahclellahs. About three quarters of a mile below our camp was a burial-ground, which seemed common to the Wahclellahs, Clahclellahs, and Yehhuhs. It consisted of eight sepulchres on the north bank of the river."

In dragging their remaining pirogue up the rapids the next day, they unfortunately lost her, but succeeded in transporting all their baggage to the head of the portage by five o'clock in the afternoon; and the weather being cold and rainy, they concluded to remain there during the night. "The portage," says the Journal, "was two thousand eight hundred yards, along a narrow road, at all times rough, and then rendered slippery by the rain. About half way was an old village, which the Clahclellah chief informed us was the occasional residence of his tribe. These houses were uncommonly large; one of them measuring one hundred and sixty by forty feet, the frames being constructed in the usual manner, except that they were double, so as to appear like one house within another. The floors were on a level with the ground, and the roofs had been taken down, and sunk in a pond behind the village. We now found that our firmness the day before had made the Indians much more respectful: they did not crowd about us in such numbers, and behaved with much more propriety.

"Among those who visited us here were about twenty of the Yehhuhs, a tribe of Shahalas, whom we had found on the north side of the river, immediately above the rapids, but who had now emigrated to the opposite shore, where they generally take salmon. Like their relations, the Wahclellahs, they had taken their houses with them, so that only one was now standing where the old village was." * * *

"There is but little difference in appearance between the Yehhuhs, Wahclellahs, Clahclellahs, and Neerchokioos, who compose the Shahala nation. On comparing the vocabulary of the Wahclellahs with that of the Chinnooks, we found that the names for numbers were precisely the same, though the other parts of the language were essentially different. The women of all these tribes braid their hair, pierce the nose, and some of them have lines of dots reaching from the ankle as high as the middle of the leg. These Yehhuhs behaved with great propriety, and condemned the treatment we had received from the Wahclellahs. We purchased from one of them the skin of a sheep killed near this place, for which we gave in exchange the skins of a deer and an elk. These animals, he told us, usually frequent the rocky parts of the mountains, where they are found in great numbers. The bighorn is also an inhabitant of these mountains, and the natives have several robes made of their skins." * * *

In ascending the river the next day, they found that their boats were too heavily laden, in consequence of the loss of their pirogue ;. but they succeeded in purchasing two additional canoes at a Yehhuh village, the inhabitants of which were very friendly. They advanced about six miles beyond Cruzatte's River, where they encamped, and, being joined by all their hunters the next morning, resumed their journey. "At one o'clock," continues the Journal, "we halted for dinner at a large village, situated in a narrow bottom just above the entrance of Canoe Creek. The houses were detached from each other so as to occupy an extent of several miles, though only twenty in number. Those which were inhabited were on the surface of the ground, and built in the same shape as those near the Rapids ; but there were others not occupied, which were completely under ground. They were sunk about eight feet deep, and covered with strong timbers, and several feet of earth in a conical form. On descending by means of a ladder through a hole at the top, which answered the double purpose of a door and a chimney, we found that the house consisted of a single room, nearly circular, and about sixteen feet in diameter.

"The inhabitants, who called themselves Weock-

II.—P

sockwillacums, differed but little from those near the Rapids, the chief distinction in dress being a few leggins and moccasins resembling those worn by the Chopunnish. These people had ten or twelve very good horses, which were the first we had seen since leaving this neighbourhood in the preceding autumn. The country below is, indeed, of such a nature as to prevent the use of this animal, except in the Columbia Valley, and there they would be of no great service, as the inhabitants reside chiefly on the river side, and the country is too thickly wooded to suffer them to hunt on horseback. Most of these horses, they informed us, had been taken in a warlike excursion lately made against the Towahnahiooks, a part of the Snake nation living on the upper part of the Multnomah, to the southeast of this place. Their language is the same with that of the Chilluckittequaws. They seemed inclined to be very civil, and gave us in traffic some roots, *chappelell*, filberts, dried berries, and five dogs.

"After dinner we proceeded, and, passing at the distance of six miles high cliffs on the left, encamped at the mouth of a small run on the same side. A little above us was a village, consisting of about one hundred fighting men, of a tribe called Smackshops, many of whom passed the evening with us. They did not differ in any respect from the inhabitants of the village below." * * *

Soon after starting the next morning they came to Sepulchre Rock. "This rock," says the Journal, "stands near the middle of the river, and contains about two acres of ground above high water. Over this surface are scattered thirteen vaults, constructed like those below the Rapids, and some of them more than half filled with dead bodies. After satisfying our curiosity with these venerable remains we returned to the northern shore, and proceeded to a village at the distance of four miles. On landing, we found that the inhabitants belonged to the same

nation as those we had just left, and as they had
horses, we made an attempt to purchase some of
them ; but, with all our dexterity in exhibiting our
wares, we could not succeed, as we had none of the
only article which they seemed desirous of procuring, a sort of war-hatchet called by the Northwest
traders an eye-dog. We therefore purchased two
dogs, and, taking leave of these Weocksockwilla-
cums, proceeded to another of their villages, just
below the entrance of Cataract River. Here, too,
we tried in vain to purchase horses ; nor did we
meet with better success at the two villages of Chilluckittequaws, a few miles farther up the river. At
three in the afternoon we came to the mouth of
Quinette Creek, which we ascended a short distance,
and encamped for the night at the spot we had called Rock Fort. Here we were soon visited by some
of the people from the Great Narrows and Falls ;
and on our expressing a wish to purchase horses,
they agreed to meet us the next day on the north
side of the river, where they would open a trade.
They then returned to their villages to collect the
horses, and in the morning,

" April 16, Captain Clarke crossed with nine men,
and a large part of the merchandise, to purchase, if
it were possible, twelve horses to transport our baggage, and some pounded fish, as a reserve on the
passage across the Rocky Mountains. The rest of
the men were employed in hunting and preparing
saddles.

" From the Rapids to this place, and, indeed, as
far as the commencement of the Narrows, the Columbia is from half a mile to three quarters in width,
and possesses scarcely any current : its bed consists
principally of rock, except at the entrance of Labiche
River, which takes its rise in Mount Hood, from
which, like Quicksand River, it brings down vast
quantities of sand. Along the whole course of the
Columbia, from the Rapids to the Chilluckittequaws,

the trunks of many large pine-trees are seen standing erect in water, which was now thirty feet deep,
and is never less than ten. These trees could never
have grown in their present state, for they are all
very much rotted, and none of them vegetate ; so
that the only reasonable account which can be given
of this phenomena is, that at some period, which the
appearance of the trees induced us to fix within
twenty years, the rocks from the hill sides have obstructed the narrow pass at the Rapids, and caused
the river to spread through the woods. The mountains which border it as far as Sepulchre Rock are
high and broken, and its romantic views are occasionally enlivened by beautiful cascades rushing
from the heights, and forming a striking contrast
with the firs, cedars, and pines which darken their
sides. From Sepulchre Rock, where the low country begins, the long-leafed pine is the almost exclu-
sive growth of timber ; but our camp was the last
spot where a single tree is to be seen on the wide
plain, spreading beyond it to the foot of the Rocky
Mountains. This plain is, however, covered with a
rich verdure of grass and herbs, some inches in
height, which forms a delightful and exhilarating
prospect, after being confined to the mountains and
thick forests on the seacoast. The climate, too,
though we were only on the border of the plain, was
very different here from what we had lately experienced : the air was drier and more pure, and the
ground as free from moisture as if there had been
no rain for the last ten days. Around this place
were many esculent plants used by the Indians,
among which was a currant now in bloom, with a
yellow blossom, like that of the yellow currant of
the Missouri, from which, however, it differs specif
ically. There was also a species of hyacinth grow
ing in the plains, which presented at this time a
pretty flower of a pale blue colour, the bulb of which
is boiled, or baked, or dried in the sun, and eaten by

the Indians. The bulb of the present year was white, flat in shape, and not quite solid: it overlaid and pressed closely that of the last year, which, though much thinner and withered, was equally wide, and sent forth from its sides a number of small radicles." * * *

" Captain Clarke, meanwhile, had been unsuccessfully endeavouring to purchase horses; but the Indians promised to trade with him if he would go up to the Skilloot village, above the Long Narrows. He therefore sent over to us for more merchandise, and then accompanied them in the evening to that place, where he passed the night.

"April 17. Captain Clarke sent to inform us that he was still unable to purchase any horses, but intended going as far as the Eneeshur village, whence he would return to meet us the next day at the Skilloot village. In the evening, the principal chief of the Chilluckittequaws came to see us, accompanied by twelve of his nation, and, hearing that we wanted horses, promised to meet us at the Narrows with some for sale."

CHAPTER X.

Captain Clarke procures four Horses for the Transportation of the Baggage.—Some farther Account of the Skilloot Tribe.—Their Joy at the first Appearance of Salmon in the Columbia.—Their thievish Propensities.—The Party arrive at the Village of the Eneeshurs, where the Natives are found alike un friendly.—The Party now provided with Horses.—Prevented from the Exercise of Hostility against this nation by a friendly Adjustment.—The Scarcity of Timber so great that they are compelled to buy Wood to cook their Provisions.—Arrive at the Wahhowpum Village.—Dance of the Natives.—Having obtained their Complement of Horses, the Party proceed by Land.—Arrive at the Pishquitpah Village, and some Account of that People.—Frank and hospitable Conduct of the Wollawollahs.—Their Mode of Dancing described.—Their Mode of making Fish-wears.—Their amiable Character.

SETTING out early on the morning of the 18th, at the distance of nine miles they reached the Skilloot village, at the foot of the Long Narrows. Here they found Captain Clarke, who had succeeded in purchasing four horses, though at double the price that had been paid the Shoshonees. Owing to the great quantity of water in the river, the passage of the Long Narrows was wholly impracticable for boats, so that they cut up their two pirogues to be used for fuel.

"April 19. All the party," proceeds the Journal, "were employed in carrying the merchandise over the portage. This we accomplished with the aid of our four horses by three o'clock in the afternoon, when we formed our camp a little above the Skilloot settlement. Since we left them in the autumn they had removed their village a few hundred yards lower down the river, and exchanged the cellars in which we then found them for more pleasant dwellings on the surface of the ground. These were formed by sticks covered with mats and straw, and so large that each was the residence of several families." * *

" The whole village was filled with rejoicing at having caught a salmon, which was considered as the harbinger of vast quantities that would arrive in a few days. In the belief that it would hasten their coming, the Indians, according to their custom, dressed the fish and cut it into small pieces, one of which was given to each child in the village; and in the good humour excited by this occurrence, they parted, though reluctantly, with four other horses, for which we gave them two kettles, reserving only a single small one for a mess of eight men. Unluckily, however, we lost one of the horses by the negligence of the person to whose charge he was committed." * * *

" April 20. As it was so much for our interest to preserve the good-will of these people, we passed over several small thefts which they had committed ; but this morning we learned that six tomahawks and a knife had been stolen during the night. We addressed ourselves to the chief, who seemed angry with his people, and made an harangue to them, but we did not recover the articles, and soon afterward two of our spoons were missing. We therefore ordered them all from our camp, threatening to beat severely any one detected in purloining. This harshness irritated them so much that they left us in ill humour, and we therefore kept on our guard against any insult. Besides this knavery, their faithlessness was intolerable : frequently, after receiving goods in exchange for a horse, they would return in a few hours and insist on revoking the bargain, or that they should receive some additional value. We discovered, too, that the horse missed yesterday had been gambled away by the fellow from whom we had purchased him to a man of a different nation, who had carried him off. We succeeded in buying two more horses, two dogs, and

some *chappelell*, and also exchanged a couple of elkskins for a gun belonging to the chief." * * * " One
of the canoes, for which the Indians would give us
very little, was cut up for fuel; two others, together
with some elkskins and pieces of old iron, we bar-
tered for beads, and the remaining two small ones
were despatched early next morning,

" April 21, with all the baggage which could not
be carried on horseback. We had intended setting
out at the same time, but one of our horses broke
loose during the night, and we were under the necessity of sending several men in search of him. In
the mean time, the Indians, who were always on the
alert, stole a tomahawk, which we could not recover, though several of them were searched; and another fellow was detected in carrying off a piece of
iron, and kicked out of camp; upon which Captain
Lewis, addressing them, told them he was not afraid
to fight them, for, if he chose, he could easily put
them all to death, and burn their village, but that he
did not wish to treat them ill if they kept from stealing; and that, although, if he could discover who had
the tomahawks, he would take away their horses, yet
he would rather lose the property altogether than
take the horse of an innocent man. The chiefs
were present at this harangue, hung their heads, and
made no reply.

" At ten o'clock the men returned with the horse,
and soon after an Indian, who had promised to go
with us as far as the Chopunnish, came with two
horses, one of which he politely offered to assist in
carrying our baggage. We therefore loaded nine
horses, and, giving the tenth to Bratton, who was
still too sick to walk, at about ten o'clock left the
village of these disagreeable people. At one o'clock
we arrived at the village of the Eneeshurs, where
we found Captain Clarke, who had been altogether
unsuccessful in his attempts to purchase horses, the
Eneeshurs being quite as unfriendly as the Skilloots.

Fortunately, however, the fellow who had sold us a horse, and afterward lost him in gambling, belonged to this village, and we insisted on having the kettle and knife which had been given to him for his horse, or that he should furnish us with one of equal value. He preferred the latter, and brought us a very good horse. Being joined here by the canoes and baggage, we halted half a mile above the town, and dined on the flesh of dogs, after which we proceeded about four miles farther, and encamped at a village of Eneeshurs, consisting of nine mat huts, a little below the mouth of the Towahnahiooks. We obtained from these people a couple of dogs and a small quantity of fuel, for which we were obliged to give a higher price than usual. We also bought a horse, with his back so much injured that he could scarcely be of much service to us; but the price was only some trifling articles, which in the United States would not cost above a dollar and a quarter. The dress, manners, and language of the Eneeshurs differ in no respect from those of the Skilloots. Like them, too, they are inhospitable and parsimonious, faithless to their engagements, and in the midst of poverty and filth retained a degree of pride and arrogance which rendered our numbers our only protection against insult, pillage, and even murder. We were, however, assured by our Chopunnish guide, who appeared to be a very sincere, honest Indian, that the nations above would treat us with much greater hospitality.

" April 22. Two of our horses broke loose in the night, and strayed to some distance, so that we were not able to retake them and begin our march before seven o'clock. We had just reached the top of a hill near the village, when the load of one of the horses turned, and the animal, taking fright at a robe which still adhered to him, ran furiously towards the village : just as he came there the robe fell, and an Indian hid it in his hut. Two men went

back after the horse, which they soon caught, but
the robe was still missing, and the Indians denied
having seen it. These repeated acts of knavery
had quite exhausted our patience, and Captain Lewis
therefore set out for the village, determined to make
them deliver up the robe, or to burn their houses to
the ground. This disagreeable retaliation was, how
ever, rendered unnecessary, for on his way he met
one of our men, who had found the robe in one of
the huts, hid behind some baggage. We resumed
our route, and soon after halted on a hill, from the
top of which we had a commanding view of the
range of mountains in which Mount Hood stands,
and which continued south as far as the eye could
reach, their summits being covered with snow.
Mount Hood itself bore south 30° west, and the
snowy summit of Mount Jefferson south 10° west.
Towards the south, and at no great distance, we
discerned some woody country, and opposite to this
point of view is the mouth of the Towahnahiooks."
* * * " From this place we proceeded with our baggage in the centre, escorted both before and behind
by such of the men as had not the care of the horses,
and, having crossed a plain eight miles in extent,
reached a village of the Eneeshurs, consisting of
six houses. Here we bought some dogs, on which
we dined near the village, and, having purchased another horse, went up the river four miles farther, to
another Eneeshur village of seven mat houses." * * *
Being informed by their guide .that they would not
be able to reach the next village the same evening,
they concluded to halt where they were. Here
they purchased a horse and some dogs ; but such
was the scarcity of fuel, that they were obliged to
buy what was required to cook their supper.

The party were detained for a considerable time
the next morning in consequence of two of their
horses having strayed during the night. One they
recovered, but the other they could not find, and

were obliged to start without him. "After marching twelve miles," says the Journal, "we came to a village near the Rock Rapid, at the mouth of a large creek which we had not observed in descending. It consisted of twelve temporary huts of mats, and was inhabited by a tribe called Wahhowpum, who speak a language very similar to that of the Chopunnish, whom they resemble also in dress, both sexes being clad in robes and shirts, as well as leggins and moccasins. These people seemed much pleased to see us, and readily gave us four dogs, and some *chappelell* and wood, in exchange for a few small articles, such as pewter buttons, strips of tin, iron, and brass, and some twisted wire, which we had previously prepared for our journey across the plains. They, as well as others of the same tribe, living in five huts a little below, were waiting the return of the salmon. We also found a Chopunnish returning home with his family and a dozen young horses, some of which he wanted us to hire ; but this we declined, as by doing so we should be obliged to maintain him and his family on the route. After arranging our camp, we assembled all the warriors, and, having smoked with them, the violins were produced, and some of the men danced. This civility was returned by the Indians with a kind of dance that we had not before seen. The spectators formed a circle about the dancers, who, with their robes drawn tightly round the shoulders, and divided into parties of five or six men, kept crossing in a line from one side of the circle to the other. Both the performers and spectators sang, and, after proceeding in this way for some time, the latter joined in, and the whole concluded with a promiscuous dance and song. This being finished, the natives retired at our request, after promising to barter horses with us in the morning. The river was by no means so difficult of passage, nor obstructed by so many rapids, as it had been in the autumn, the water being sufficiently high to cover the rocks in its bed.

"April 24. We began early to look for our horses, but they were not collected before one o'clock. In the mean time we prepared saddles for three new horses which we had purchased from the Wahhowpums, and agreed to hire three more from the Chopunnish Indian, who was to accompany us with his family. The natives had also promised to take our canoes in exchange for horses; but, when they found that we were resolved on travelling by land, they refused giving us anything, in hopes that we would be forced to leave them. Disgusted at this conduct, we determined rather to cut them in pieces than suffer these people to possess them, and actually began to split them up, when they consented to give us several strands of beads for each canoe. We had now a sufficient number of horses to carry our baggage, and therefore proceeded wholly by land. At two o'clock we set out, and, passing between the hills and the northern shore of the river, had a difficult and fatiguing march over a road alternately sandy and rocky. At the distance of four miles we came to four huts of the Meteowwee tribe; two miles farther, to the same number of huts; and, after making twelve miles from our last night's camp, we halted at a larger village of five huts of Meteowwees." * * *

As they had passed along they met several parties of the natives, who were distant and reserved, and, though respectful, would hold no conversation with them. They found the nights cold, though it was warm in the day, and what rendered them exceedingly uncomfortable was the scarcity of wood.

"April 25. We collected our horses," continues the Journal, "and proceeded eleven miles to a large village of fifty-one mat houses, where we purchased some wood and a few dogs, on which we made our dinner. This village contained about seven hundred

persons, of a tribe called Pishquitpah, whose residence on the river is only during the spring and summer, the autumn and winter being passed in hunting
through the plains and along the borders of the
mountains. The greater part of them had been at
a distance from the river when we descended, and
never having seen white men before, they flocked
round us in great numbers ; but, although they were
exceedingly curious, they treated us with much respect, and were very urgent that we should spend
the night with them. Two principal chiefs were
pointed out by our Chopunnish companion, and being
acknowledged as such by the tribe, we invested each
of them with a small medal. We were also very
desirous of purchasing more horses ; but as our
stock of merchandise consisted of little more than
a dirk, a sword, and a few old clothes, the Indians
could not be induced to traffic with us. The Pishquitpahs are generally of good stature and proportions, and as the heads neither of the males nor females are so much flattened as those of the natives
lower down, their features are rather pleasant.
Their hair is braided in the manner practised by their
western neighbours ; but the generality of the men
are dressed in a large robe, under which is a shirt
reaching to the knees, where it is met by long leggins, and the feet are covered with moccasins : some,
however, wear only the truss and robe. As they
unite the occupations of hunting and fishing, both
sexes ride very dexterously ; their caparison being
a saddle or pad of dressed skin, stuffed with goat's
hair, from which wooden stirrups are suspended, and
a hair rope is tied at both ends to the under jaw of
the animal. The horses, however, though good,
suffer much, as do, in fact, all the Indian horses, from
sore backs.

" Finding them not disposed to barter with us, we
left the Pishquitpahs at four o'clock, accompanied
by eighteen or twenty of their young men on horse-

back. At the distance of four miles we passed, with out halting, five houses belonging to the Wollawol lahs; and five miles farther, observing as many willows as would enable us to make fires, we availed ourselves of the circumstance, and encamped near them.

"The country through which we passed resembled that of yesterday. The hills on both sides of the river are about two hundred and fifty feet high, generally abrupt and craggy, and in many places presenting a perpendicular face of black, solid rock. From the top of these hills the country extends itself in level plains to a very great distance, and though not so fertile as the land near the Falls, produces an abundant supply of low grass, which is an excellent food for horses. This grass must, indeed, be unusually nutritious, for even at this season of the year, after wintering on the dry grass of the plains, and being used with greater severity than is usual among the whites, many of the horses were perfectly fat, nor had we seen a single one that was really poor. In the course of the day we killed several rattlesnakes, like those of the United States, and saw many of the common as well as the horned lizard." * * *

As they advanced the next day the hills became low, and left an extensive plain on each side of the river. Having proceeded thirty-one miles, they halted for the night not far from some houses of the Wollawollahs. On the 27th they found the abrupt, rocky hills again approaching the river; and, after a march of twenty-four miles, they halted for dinner. "Soon after stopping," says the Journal, "we were joined by seven Wollawollahs, among whom we recognised a chief by the name of Yellept, who had visited us on the 19th of October, when we gave him a medal, with the promise of a larger one on our return. He appeared very much pleased at seeing us again, and invited us to remain at his village three or four days, during which he would supply us with the only food they had, and furnish us with horses for our journey. After the cold, inhospitable treatment we had lately received, this kind offer was peculiarly acceptable; and, having made a hasty meal, we accompanied him to his village, six miles above, situated on the edge of the low country, and about twelve miles below the mouth of Lewis's River. Immediately on our arrival, Yellept, who proved to be a man of much influence, not only in his own, but among the neighbouring nations, collected the inhabitants, and, after having made an harangue to them, the purport of which was to induce them to treat us hospitably, set them an example by bringing himself an armful of wood, and a platter containing three roasted mullets. They immediately complied with one part, at least, of the recommendation, by furnishing us with an abundance of the only sort of fuel they use, the stems of shrubs growing in the plains. We then purchased four dogs, on which we supped heartily, having been on short allowance for two days previously. When we were disposed to sleep, the Indians retired immediately on our requesting them to do so, and, indeed, uniformly conducted themselves with great propriety. These people live mostly on roots, which are very abundant in the plains, and catch a few salmon-trout; but they then seemed to be subsisting chiefly on a species of mullet, weighing from one to three pounds. They informed us that opposite to their village there was a route which led to the mouth of the Kooskooskee, on the south side of Lewis's River; that the road itself was good, and passed over a level country well supplied with water and grass; and that we should meet with plenty of deer and antelope. We knew that a road in that direction would shorten the distance at least eighty miles; and as the report of our guide was confirmed by Yellept and other Indians, we did not hesitate to adopt this route: they added, however, that there were no houses, nor permanent Indian residences on the road, and that it would therefore be prudent not to trust wholly to our guns, but to lay in a stock of provisions.

"April 28. Taking their advice, therefore, we this morning purchased ten dogs. While the trade for these was being conducted by our men, Yellept brought a fine white horse, and presented him to Captain Clarke, expressing at the same time a wish to have a kettle ; but, on being informed that we had already disposed of the last kettle we could spare, he said he would be content with any present we chose to make him in return. Captain Clarke thereupon gave him his sword, for which the chief had before expressed a desire, adding one hundred balls, some powder, and other small articles, with which he appeared perfectly satisfied. We were now anxious to depart, and requested Yellept to lend us canoes for the purpose of crossing the river; but he would not listen to any proposal of the kind. He wished us to remain for two or three days; but, at all events, would not consent to our going to-day, for he had already sent to invite his neighbours, the Chimnapoos, to come down in the evening and join his people in a dance for our amusement. We urged in vain that by setting out sooner we should the earlier return with the articles they desired : a day, he observed, would make but little difference. We at length suggested that, as there was then no wind, it was the best time to cross the river, and that we would merely take the horses over, and return to sleep at their village. To this he assented ; and we then crossed with the horses, and, having hoppled them, came back to their camp. Fortunately, there was among these Wollawollahs a prisoner belonging to a tribe of the Shoshonee or Snake Indians, residing to the south of the Multnomah, and visiting occasionally the heads of Wollawollah Creek

Our Shoshonee woman, Sacajaweah, though she belonged to a tribe near the Missouri, spoke the same
language as this prisoner ; and by their means we
were able to explain ourselves to the Indians, and
answer all their inquiries with respect to ourselves
and the object of our journey. Our conversation
inspired them with much confidence, and they soon
brought several sick persons, for whom they requested our assistance. We splintered the broken
arm of one, gave some relief to another whose knee
was contracted by rheumatism, and administered
what we thought would be beneficial for ulcers, and
eruptions of the skin on various parts of the body,
which are very common disorders among them.
But our most valuable medicine was eye-water,
which we distributed, and which, indeed, they very
much required ; for the complaints of the eyes, occasioned by living so much on the water, and aggravated by the fine sand of the plains, were universal among them.

" A little before sunset the Chimnapoos, amounting to one hundred men and a few women, came to
the village, and, joining the Wollawollahs, who were
about the same number of men, formed themselves
in a circle round our camp, and waited very patiently
till our men were disposed to dance, which they did
for about an hour, to the music of the violin. They
then requested the Indians to dance. With this
they readily complied ; and the whole assemblage,
amounting, with the women and children of the village, to several hundred, stood up, and sang and
danced at the same time. The exercise was not,
indeed, very violent nor very graceful ; for the greater part of them were formed into a solid column,
round a kind of hollow square, stood on the same
place, and merely jumped up at intervals, to keep
time to the music. Some, however, of the more active warriors entered the square and danced round
it sideways, and some of our men joined in with

II.— Q

them, to the great satisfaction of the Indians. The dance continued till ten o'clock. The next morning, " April 29, Yellept supplied us with two canoes, in which we crossed with all our baggage by eleven o'clock; but the horses having strayed to some distance, we could not collect them in time to reach any suitable place for encamping if we should then begin our journey, as night would overtake us before we came to any water. We therefore thought it advisable to encamp about a mile from the Co lumbia, at the mouth of the Wollawollah River. This is a handsome stream, about fifty yards wide, and four and a half feet in depth. Its waters, which are clear, roll over a bed composed principally of gravel, intermixed with some sand and mud; and, though the banks are low, they do not seem to be overflowed. It empties into the Columbia about twelve or fifteen miles from the entrance of Lewis's River, and just above a range of high hills crossing the former. Its sources, like those of the Towahnahiooks, Lapage, Youmalolam, and Wollawollah, are, as the Indians informed us, on the north side of a range of mountains which we saw to the east and southeast, and which, commencing to the south of Mount Hood, stretch in a northeastern direction to the neighbourhood of a southern branch of Lewis's River, at some distance from the Rocky Mountains. Two principal branches, however, of the Towahnahiooks, take their rise in Mount Jefferson and Mount Hood, which in fact appear to separate the waters of the Multnomah and Columbia. They were about sixty-five or seventy miles from this place, and, although covered with snow, did not seem high. To the south of these mountains, the Indian prisoner said there was a river running towards the northwest, as wide as the Columbia at this place, which was nearly a mile. This account might be exaggerated, but it served to show that the Multnomah was a very large river, and that, with the assistance of a southeastern branch of Lewis s River, passing round the eastern extremity of the chain of mountains in which Mounts Hood and Jefferson are so conspicuous, it might water the vast tract of country to the south, till its remote sources approached those of the Missouri and the Rio del Norte.

" Near our camp was a fish-wear, formed of two curtains of small willow switches, matted together with withes of the same plant, and extending across the river in two parallel lines, six feet asunder. These were supported by several parcels of poles, in the manner already described as in use among the Shoshonees, and were rolled up or let down at pleasure for a few feet, so as either to let the fish pass or to detain them. A seine of from fifteen to eighteen feet in length is dragged down the river by two persons, and the bottom drawn up against the curtain of willows. They also employ a smaller seine, like a scoop-net, one side of which is confined to a semicircular bow five feet long, and half the size of a man's arm, and the other side held by a strong rope, which, being tied at both ends to the bow, forms the chord to the semicircle : this is used by one person. But the only fish they could take at this time were mullet of from four to five pounds in weight, and which formed the chief subsistence of a village of twelve houses of Wollawollahs, a little below us on the Columbia, as well as of others on the opposite side of the river. In the course of the day we gave small medals to two inferior chiefs, each of whom made us a present of a fine horse. We were in a poor condition to make an adequate acknowledgment for this kindness, but gave them several articles, among which was a pistol, with some hundred rounds of ammunition. We had, indeed, been treated by these people with an unusual degree of kindness and civility. They seemed to have been successful in their hunting during the last

winter, for all of them, but particularly the women,
were much better clad than when we had seen them
before ; both sexes among the Wollawollahs, as well
as the Chimnapoos, being provided with good robes,
moccasins, long shirts, and leggins. Their ornaments were similar to those used below, the hair
being cut on the forehead, and queues falling over
the shoulders in front of the body : some have small
plaits at the earlocks, and others tie a bundle of the
docked foretop in front of the forehead." * * *

"April 30. We had now twenty-three horses, many
of them young and excellent animals, but the greater part had sore backs. The Indians are generally
cruel masters : they ride very hard, and their saddles being so badly constructed that it is almost impossible to avoid wounding the animal, they will
continue to ride the poor creatures after their backs
are scarified in the most shocking manner. At
eleven o'clock we left these honest, worthy people,
accompanied by our guide and the Chopunnish family, and directed our course north 50° east, across
an open, level sandy plain, unbroken except by
large banks of pure sand, which had drifted in many
parts to the height of fifteen or twenty feet. The
rest of the plain is poor in point of soil, but throughout there is generally a short grass interspersed with
aromatic shrubs, and a number of plants, the roots
of which supply the principal food of the natives.
Among these we observed a root something like the
sweet potato. At the distance of fourteen miles we
reached a branch of Wollawollah River, rising in the
same range of mountains, and emptying itself six
miles above the mouth of the latter. It is a bold,
deep stream, about ten yards wide, and seems to be
navigable for canoes. The hills along this creek
are generally abrupt and rocky, but the narrow bottom is very fertile, and both possess twenty times
as much timber as the Columbia itself: indeed, we
now find, for the first time since leaving Rock Fort,

an abundance of firewood. The growth consists of cottonwood, birch, the crimson haw, red and sweet willow, chokecherry, yellow currants, gooseberry, the honeysuckle with a white berry, rosebushes, sevenbark, and sumach, together with some corn-grass and rushes. The advantage of a comfortable fire induced us, as it was already night, to halt at this place.

" We were soon supplied by Drewyer with a bea-ver and an otter, of which we took only a part of the former, and gave the rest to the Indians. The otter is with them a favourite food, though much inferior, at least in our estimation, to the dog, which they will not eat. The flesh of the horse, too, is seldom eaten, and never except when absolute necessity compels them to eat it, as the only alternative to save them from dying with hunger. This fastidi-ousness does not seem, however, to proceed so much from any dislike to the food as from attachment to the animal itself, for many of them ate very heartily of the horseflesh which we gave them." * * *

After they had proceeded nine miles the next day, their Chopunnish Indian left them, taking an old, unbeaten road which led to the left. " At the dis-tance of three miles farther," continues the Journal, " the hills on the north side became lower, and the bottoms of the creek widened into a pleasant coun-try, two or three miles in extent. The timber, too, was now more abundant, and our guide told us that we should not want either wood or game from this place as far as the Kooskooskee. We had already seen several deer, of which we killed one, and ob-served great numbers of curlew, as well as some cranes, ducks, prairie larks, and several species of the sparrow common to the prairies. There is, in fact, very little difference in the general face of the country here from that of the plains on the Missou-ri, except that the latter are enlivened by vast herds of buffalo, elk, and other animals, which give it an additional interest. Over these wide bottoms we continued on a course north 75° east, till, at the distance of seventeen miles from where we had dined, and twenty-six from our last encampment, we halted for the night. We had scarcely encamped when three young men came up from the Wollawollah village, with a steel-trap which had inadvertently been left behind, and which they had come a whole day's journey in order to restore. This act of integrity was the more pleasing, because, though very rare among Indians, it corresponded perfectly with the general behaviour of the Wollawollahs, among whom we had lost carelessly several knives, which were always returned as soon as found. We may, indeed, justly affirm, that of all the Indians whom we had met since leaving the United States, the Wollawollahs were the most hospitable, honest, and sincere."

CHAPTER XI.

The Party pursue their Route towards the Kooskooskee.—They reach the Kinnooenim Creek.—Meet with an old Acquaintance, called the Bighorn Indian.—Arrive at the Mouth of the Kooskooskee.—Difficulty of purchasing Provisions from the Natives, and new Device of the Party to obtain them.—Chopun nish Style of Architecture.—Captain Clarke turns Physician, and performs several Experiments upon the Natives with Success.—Instance of their Honesty.—Distress of the Indians for want of Provisions during the Winter.—The Party finally meet Twisted Hair, to whom their Horses had been intrusted on their Journey down.—Quarrel between that Chief and another of his Nation, in regard to his Horses.—Causes of the Controversy stated at large.—The two Chiefs reconciled by the Interference of the Party, and the Horses restored.—Extraordinary Instance of Indian Hospitality towards Strangers.—Council held with the Chopunnish, and the Object of the Expedition explained.—The Party perform other medical Cures.—Answer of the Chopunnish to the Speech delivered at the Council, ratified by a singular Ceremony.—They promise faithfully to follow the Advice of their Visiters.

THEY followed the course of the creek the next day, and, after travelling nineteen miles, encamped for the night. The mountains to the southwest, at the distance of twenty-five miles, though not appearing to be very high, were still covered with snow. Pursuing a course north 25° east on the morning of the 3d, at the distance of twelve miles they reached the Kinnooenim Creek; and three miles beyond this, in a northeasterly direction, they came to a branch of this creek, which they followed for eleven miles, and "at that distance," says the Journal, we were agreeably surprised by the appearance of Weahkoonut, or the Indian whom we had called The Bighorn, from the circumstance of his wearing a horn of that animal suspended from his left arm. He had gone down with us last year along Lewis's River, and was highly serviceable in preparing the minds of the natives for our reception. He was, moreover, the first chief of a large band of Chopunnish ; and, hearing that we were on our return, he had come with ten of his warriors to meet us. He now turned back with us, and we continued up the bottoms of the creek for two miles, till the road began to leave it, and to cross the hill towards the plains. We therefore encamped for the night in a grove of cottonwood, after we had made a disagreeable journey of twenty-eight miles. During the greater part of the day the air had been keen and cold, and it alternately rained, hailed, and snowed ; but, though the wind blew with great violence, it was fortunately from the southwest, and on our backs. We had consumed at dinner the last of our dried meat, and nearly all that was left of the dogs ; so that we supped very scantily on the remainder, and had nothing for the next day. Weahkoonut, however, assured us that there was a house on the river at no great distance, where we could supply ourselves with provisions. We now missed our guide and the Wollawollahs, who had left us abruptly in the morning, and never returned.

"May 4. We were now nearer to the southwest mountains, which appeared to become lower as they advanced towards the northeast. We followed the road over the plains, north 60° east, for four miles to a ravine, where was the source of a small creek, down the hilly and rocky sides of which we proceeded for eight miles to its entrance into Lewis's River, about seven miles and a half above the mouth of the Kooskooskee. Near this place we found the house which Weahkoonut had mentioned, and where we now halted for breakfast. It contained six families, but so miserably poor that all we could obtain from them were two lean dogs and a few large cakes of half-prepared bread, made of a root resembling the sweet potato, of all which we contrived to form a kind of soup. The soil of the plain is good, but it has no timber. The range of southwestern mountains was about fifteen miles above us, but continued to become lower, and was still covered with snow to its base. After giving a passage to Lewis's River near their northeastern extremity, they terminate in a high level plain between that river and the Kooskooskee. The salmon not having yet called them to the rivers, the greater part of the Chopunnish were still dispersed in villages through this plain, for the purpose of collecting *quamash* and cow-weed, which grow here in great abundance, the soil being extremely fertile, and in many places covered with the long-leafed pine, the larch, and balsam-fir, which contribute to render it less dry than the open, unsheltered plains. After our repast we continued our route along the west side of the river, where, as well as on the opposite shore, the high hills approached it closely, till, at the distance of three miles, we halted near two houses. The inmates consisted of five families of Chopunnish, among whom were Tetoh or Sky, the younger of the two chiefs who accompanied us in the autumn to the Great Falls of the Columbia, and also our old pilot who had conducted us down to that river. They both advised us to cross here, and ascend the Kooskooskee on the northeast 'ide, this being the shortest and best route to the forks of that river, where we should find Twisted Hair, in whose charge we had left our horses, and to which place they promised to show us the way. We did not hesitate to accept their offer, and crossed over with the assistance of three canoes; but, as the night was coming on, we purchased a little wood and some roots of cow-weed, and encamped, though we had made only fifteen miles during the day. The evening proved cold and disagreeable, and the natives crowded round our fire in such

II.—R

numbers that we could scarcely cook or keep ourselves warm." * * *

" May 5. We collected our horses, and at seven o'clock set forward alone; for Weahkoonut, whose people resided above on the west side of Lewis's River, resumed his route homeward when we crossed to the huts. Our road was over the plains for four and a half miles to the entrance of the Kooskooskee. We then proceeded up that river, and at five miles reached a large mat house, but could not procure any provisions from the inhabitants ; however, on reaching another three miles beyond, we were surprised at the liberality of an Indian, who presented to Captain Clarke a very fine gray mare, for which all he requested was a vial of eyewater. Last autumn, while we were encamped at the mouth of the Chopunnish River, a man who complained of a pain in his knee and thigh was brought to us, in hopes of receiving some relief. To appearance he had recovered from his disorder, though he had not walked for some time ; but, that we might not disappoint them, Captain Clarke, with much ceremony, washed and rubbed his sore limb, and gave him some volatile liniment to continue the operation, which caused, or, more properly, perhaps, did not prevent, his complete cure. The man gratefully circulated our praises, and our fame as physicians was farther increased by the efficacy of some eye-water which we had given them at the same time. We were by no means dissatisfied at this new resource for obtaining subsistence, as the Indians would give us no provisions without merchandise, and our stock was now very much reduced. We cautiously abstained from giving them any but harmless medicines, and as we could not possibly do harm, our prescriptions, though unsanctioned by the faculty, might be useful, and were therefore entitled to some remuneration. Four miles beyond this we came to another large house, containing ten families, where we halted, and made our dinner on two dogs and a small quantity of roots, which we did not obtain without much difficulty. While we were eating, an Indian standing by, and looking with great derision at our eating dog's flesh, threw a poor half-starved puppy almost into Captain Lewis's plate, laughing heartily at the humour of it. Captain Lewis took up the animal, and flung it back with great force into the fellow's face, and, seizing his tomahawk, threatened to cut him down if he dared to repeat such insolence. He immediately withdrew, apparently much mortified, and we continued our dog repast very quietly. Here we met our old Chopunnish guide, with his family ; and soon afterward one of our horses, which had been separated from the others in the charge of Twisted Hair, and been in this neighbourhood for several weeks, was caught and restored to us.

" After dinner we proceeded to the entrance of Colter's Creek, at the distance of four miles, and, having made twenty and a half miles, encamped on the lower side of it. This creek rises not far from the Rocky Mountains, and, passing in the greater part of its course through a country well supplied with pine, discharges a large body of water. It is about twenty-five yards wide, with a pebbled bed and low banks. At a little distance from us were two Chopunnish houses, one of which contained eight families, and the other, much the largest we had yet seen, was inhabited by at least thirty. It was rather a kind of shed, built, like all the other houses, of straw and mats, with a roof one hundred and fifty-six feet long, and about fifteen wide, closed at the ends, and having a number of doors on each side. The vast interior was without partitions, but the fires of the different families were kindled in a row through the middle of the building, and about ten feet apart. This village was the residence of one of the principal chiefs of the nation, who was called Neeshnepahkeeook, or Cut Nose, from the cir-

cumstance of his nose having been cut by the stroke
of a lance in battle with the Snake Indians. We
gave him a small medal; but, though he was a great
chief, his influence among his own people did not
seem to be considerable, and his countenance possessed very little intelligence. We arrived very
hungry and weary, but could not purchase any pro
visions except a small quantity of the roots of the
cow-weed, and some bread made from them. They
had, however, heard of our medical skill, and made
many applications for assistance; but we refused to
do anything for them, unless they gave us either
some dog or horse flesh to eat. We had soon nearly
fifty patients. A chief brought his wife with an abscess in her back, and promised to furnish us with a
horse the next day if we would relieve her. Captain Clarke therefore opened the abscess, introduced a tent, and dressed it with basilicon. We
also prepared and distributed some doses of the flour
of sulphur and cream of tartar, with directions for
their use. For these we obtained several dogs; but
they were too poor to be eaten, and we therefore
postponed our medical operations till the morning.
In the mean time a number of Indians, besides the
residents of the village, gathered about us, or encamped in the woody bottom of the creek.

" In the evening we learned from a Snake Indian,
who happened to be at the place, that one of the old
men had been endeavouring to excite prejudices
against us by observing that he thought we were
bad men, and came there, most probably, for the
purpose of killing them. In order to remove such
suspicions, we made a speech, in which, by means
of the same Indian, we informed them of our country, and of the purposes of our visit. While we
were thus engaged, we were joined by Weahkoonut, who assisted us in effacing all unfavourable impressions from the minds of the Indians. The following morning

" May 6, our practice became more lucrative. The woman declared that she had slept better than she had before since her illness. She was therefore dressed a second time, and her husband, according to promise, brought us a horse, which we immediately killed. Besides this woman, we had crowds of applicants, chiefly afflicted with sore eyes ; and, after administering to them for several hours, found ourselves once more in possession of a plentiful meal ; for the inhabitants became more and more friendly, and one of them even gave us a horse for our prescriptions for his daughter, a little girl who was afflicted with the rheumatism. We moreover exchanged one of our horses with Weahkoonut by adding a small flag, obtaining an excellent sorrel horse.

" We found here three men of a nation called Skeetsomish, who reside at the falls of a large river emptying itself into the north side of the Columbia, and which takes its rise from a spacious lake in the mountains, at no great distance from these falls. We now designated this river by the name of Clarke's River, as we did not know its Indian name, and we were the first whites who had ever visited its principal branches ; for the Great Lake River, mentioned by Mr. Fidler, if at all connected with Clarke's River, must be a very inconsiderable branch. To the river, moreover, which we had before called Clarke's River, rising in the southwest mountains, we restored the name of Towahnahiooks, the appellation by which it is known to the Eneeshurs. In dress and appearance these Skeetsomish were not to be distinguished from the Chopunnish ; but their language was entirely different, a circumstance which we did not learn till their departure, when it was too late to obtain from them a vocabulary of it." * * *

They set out about two o'clock, accompanied by Weahkoonut, with ten or twelve men, and an Indian who called himself the brother of Twisted Hair ;

and after proceeding nine miles they halted, having lost the horse they had intended to kill, and, consequently, being obliged to lie down supperless for the night.

They started the next morning with the brother of Twisted Hair for their guide ; and after proceeding four miles, to a house containing six families, by his advice they crossed to the other side of the river, expecting to find game more plentiful near the mouth of the Chopunnish. "An Indian," says the narrative, "now brought two canisters of powder, which his dog," he stated, "had discovered under ground, in a bottom some miles above. We immediately knew them to be the same we had buried last autumn, and as he had kept them safely, and was honest enough to return them, we rewarded him—inadequately, to be sure, but as well as we could—with a steel for striking fire. We set out at three o'clock, and pursued a difficult and stony road for two miles, when we left the river, and ascended the hills on the right, which began to resemble mountains. But when we reached the heights we saw before us a beautiful level country, partially covered with the long-leafed pine, and supplied with an excellent herbage, the abundant productions of a dark, rich soil. In many parts of the plain the earth was thrown up into little mounds by some animal whose habits most resemble those of the salamander ; but, although these mounds were scattered all over the plains from the Mississippi to the Pacific, we had never been able to obtain a sight of the animal to which they owe their origin."

Coming to a deserted Indian settlement, on a small creek emptying into the Kooskooskee, they encamped there for the night. The spurs of the Rocky Mountains were covered with snow, which the Indians said was still deep, and that they would not be able to cross them before the 1st of June. They had seen some deer in the course of the day, and the tracks of many others.

" May 8. Most of the hunters set out at daylight. By eleven o'clock they all returned, with four deer, and a duck of an uncommon kind, which, with the remains of our horse, formed a stock of provisions such as we had not lately possessed. Not having our facilities of procuring subsistence with guns, the natives of this country must often suffer very severely. During the last winter they had been so much distressed for food, that they were obliged to boil and eat the moss growing on the pine-trees. At the same time they cut down nearly all the long-leafed pines (which we observed lying on the ground), for the purpose of collecting its seed, which resembles in size and shape that of the large sun-flower, and, when roasted or boiled, is nutritious, and not disagreeable to the taste. In the spring they peel this pine, and eat the inner bark ; and in the creek near us they take some trout by means of a falling trap, similar to those common in the United States. We gave Neeshnepahkeeook and his people some of our game and horseflesh, besides the entrails of the deer. They did not eat any of it perfectly raw, but the entrails had very little cooking. The Shoshonee was offended at not receiving as much venison as he wished, and refused to interpret ; but, as we took no notice of him, he became very officious in the course of a few hours, and made many advances to reinstate himself in our favour. The mother of Twisted Hair and Neeshnepahkeeook now drew a sketch, which we preserved, of all the waters west of the Rocky Mountains. They made the main southern branch of Lewis's River much more extensive than the other, and placed a great number of Shoshonee villages on its western side.

" Between three and four o'clock in the afternoon we set out, in company with Neeshnepahkeeook and other Indians, the brother of Twisted Hair having left us. Our route was up a high steep hill to a level plain, with little wood, over which we passed in a direction parallel to the river for four miles, when we met Twisted Hair and six of his people. To this chief we had confided our horses and part of our saddles the preceding autumn, and we therefore formed very unfavourable surmises on finding that he received us with much coldness. He soon began to speak to Neeshnepahkeeook in a very loud, angry tone, and was answered by him. We now discovered that there was a violent quarrel between these chiefs, on the subject, as we afterward understood, of our horses. But, as we could not learn the cause, and were desirous of terminating the dispute, we interposed, and told them that we should go on to the first water and halt. We therefore set out, followed by all the Indians, and, having reached, at two miles' distance, a small stream running to the right, we encamped, the two chiefs and their little bands forming separate camps at a distance from each other. They all appeared to be in very ill humour; and as we had already heard a report that the Indians had discovered and carried off our saddles, and that the horses were much scattered, we began to be uneasy lest there should be too much foundation for the rumour. We were therefore anxious to reconcile the two chiefs as soon as possible, and desired the Shoshonee to interpret for us while we attempted to mediate between them : but he peremptorily refused to speak a word. He observed that it was a quarrel between the two chiefs, and he had therefore no right to interfere ; nor could all our representations, that, in merely repeating what we said, he could not possibly be considered as meddling between them, induce him to take any part in it.

" Soon afterward Drewyer returned from hunting, and was sent to invite Twisted Hair to smoke with us. He accepted the invitation, and, as we were smoking over our fire, he informed us that, according to his promise on leaving us at the Falls of the Columbia, he collected our horses and took charge of them as soon as he reached home. But about this time Neeshnepahkeeook and Tunnachemootoolt, or Broken Arm, who, as we passed, had been on a war party against the Shoshonees on the south branch of Lewis's River, returned, and becoming jealous of him because the horses had been confided to his care, constantly sought to quarrel with him. At length, being an old man, and unwilling to live in a perpetual broil with these chiefs, he gave up the care of the horses to them, in consequence of which the animals had become very much scattered. The greater part of them were, however, still in the neighbourhood; some in the forks between the Chopunnish and Kooskooskee, and three or four at the village of Broken Arm, about half a day's march higher up the river. He added, that on the rise of the river in the spring, the earth had fallen from the door of the *cache*, and exposed the saddles, some of which had probably been lost; but that, as soon as he was acquainted with the situation of them, he had them buried in another deposite, where they now were. He promised that, if we would stay the next day at his house, a few miles distant, he would collect such of the horses as were in the neighbourhood, and send his young men for those in the forks, over the Kooskooskee. He moreover advised us to visit Broken Arm, who was a chief of great eminence, and he would himself guide us to his dwelling.

"We told him that we would follow his advice in every respect; that we had confided our horses to his care, and expected he would deliver them to us, on which we should cheerfully give him the two guns and the ammunition we had promised him. With this he seemed very much pleased, and declared he would use every exertion to restore the horses. We now sent for Neeshnepahkeeook, or Cut Nose, and, after smoking for some time, began by expressing to the two chiefs our regret at seeing a misunderstanding between them. Neeshnepahkeeook replied

that Twisted Hair was a bad old man, and wore two
faces; for, instead of taking care of our horses, he
had suffered his young men to hunt with them, so
that they had been very much injured, and it was
for this reason that Broken Arm and himself had for-
bidden him to use them. Twisted Hair made no reply to this speech, and we then told Neeshnepahkeeook of our arrangement for the next day. He
appeared to be very well satisfied, and said he would
himself go with us to Broken Arm, who expected to
see us, and had *two bad horses for us;* by which expression it was meant that he intended making us a
present of two valuable horses. That chief, he also
informed us, had been apprized of our want of provisions, and had sent four young men with a supply
for us; but that, having taken a different road, they
had missed us. After this interview we retired to
rest at a late hour, and in the morning,

"May 9, after sending out several hunters, we
proceeded through a rich, level country, similar to
that of the previous day, for six miles, when we
reached the house of Twisted Hair, situated near
some larch-trees and a few bushes of the balsam-
fir." * * * "Late in the afternoon Twisted Hair returned with about half the saddles we had left in the
autumn, and some powder and lead that had been
buried at the same place. Soon after the Indians
brought us twenty-one of our horses, the greater
part of which were in excellent order, though some
of them had not yet recovered from hard usage, and
three had sore backs. We were, however, very
glad to recover them in any condition. Several Indians came down from the village of Tunnachemootoolt, and passed the night with us. Cut Nose and
Twisted Hair seemed now to be perfectly reconciled,
for they both slept in the house of the latter. The
man who had imposed himself upon us as a brother
of Twisted Hair also came and renewed his advances:
but we found that he was an impertinent, proud

fellow, of no respectability in the nation, and we therefore felt no inclination to cultivate any intimacy with him. Our camp was in an open plain, and soon became very uncomfortable ; for the wind was high and cold, and the rain and hail, which began about seven o'clock, changed in about two hours to a heavy fall of snow, which continued till after six o'clock the next morning,

" May 10, when it ceased, after covering the ground eight inches deep, and leaving the air keen and frosty. We soon collected our horses, and, after a scanty breakfast of roots, set out on a course south 35° east. The road was very slippery, and the snow stuck to the horses' feet, and made them stumble very frequently. After going about sixteen miles we came to the hills on Commearp Creek, which were six hundred feet high, and their tops covered with snow, though in the lower parts, as well as along the bottom of the creek, there had been only rain, while it was snowing on the elevated plains. Descending these hills to the creek, at about four o'clock we reached the house of Tunnachemootoolt, where the flag which we had given him was displayed on a staff, and beneath which we were received with due form, and then conducted a short distance to a good spot for an encampment, on Commearp Creek. We next collected the men of consideration in the tribe, and, after smoking with them, explained how destitute we were of provisions. The chief then spoke to the people, and they immediately brought about two bushels of dried *quamash* roots, some cakes of the roots of cow-weed, and a dried salmon-trout. We thanked them for this supply, but observed at the same time that, not being accustomed to live on roots only, we feared that such diet might make our men sick, and proposed to exchange one of our good horses which was rather poor, for one that was fatter that we might kill The hospitable feelings of the chief were shocked at the idea of an exchange; and he at once replied that his people had an abundance of young horses, and that, if we were disposed to eat such food, we might have as many as we wanted. Accordingly, they soon brought us two fat young horses, asking for nothing in return: an act of liberal kindness much greater than any we had witnessed since crossing the Rocky Mountains, if it may not, indeed, be considered the only really hospitable treatment we had received in this part of the world. We killed one of the horses, and then telling the natives that we were fatigued and hungry, and that, as soon as we were refreshed, we would communicate freely with them, began to prepare our repast.

" During this time a principal chief, called Hohastillpilp, came from his village, about six miles distant, with a party of fifty men, for the purpose of visiting us. We invited him into our circle, and he alighted and smoked with us, while his retinue, with five elegant horses, continued mounted at a short distance. While this was going on, the chief had a large leathern tent spread for us, and desired that we would make it our home so long as we remained at his village. We removed there, and having made a fire, and cooked our supper of horseflesh and roots, collected all the distinguished men present, and spent the evening in making known who we were, what were the objects of our journey, and in answering their inquiries. To each of the chiefs Tunnachemootoolt and Hohastillpilp we gave a small medal, explaining their use and importance as honorary distinctions both among the whites and the red men. Our men were well pleased at once more having made a hearty meal. They had generally been in the habit of crowding into the houses of the Indians, to purchase provisions on the best terms they could; for the inhospitality of the country was such, that often, in the extreme of hunger, they were obliged to treat the natives with but little ceremony;

but this Twisted Hair had told us was very disagreeable. Finding that these people are so kind and
liberal, we ordered our men to treat them with the
greatest respect, and not to throng round their fires.
so that they now agree perfectly well together. Af
ter the council the Indians felt no disposition to re.
tire, and our tent was filled with them all night
The next morning,

" May 11, we arose early, and breakfasted again
on horseflesh. This village of Tunnachemootoolt
was, in fact, only a single house, one hundred and
fifty feet long, built after the Chopunnish fashion,
with sticks, straw, and dried grass. It contained
twenty-four fires, about double that number of families, and might muster, perhaps, one hundred fighting men. Their chief subsistence was roots; and
the noise made by the women in pounding them
gave one the idea of a nail-factory. Yet, notwithstanding so many families were crowded together,
we found the Chopunnish much more cleanly in
their persons and habitations than any people we
had met since leaving the Ottoes on the River Platte.
In the course of the morning, a chief named Yoompahkatim, a stout, good-looking man of about forty
years of age, who had lost his left eye, arrived from
his village on the south side of Lewis's River. We
gave him a small medal, and, finding that there were
now present the principal chiefs of the Chopunnish
nation, viz., Tunnachemootoolt, Broken Arm, Neeshnepahkeeook, Yoompahkatim, and Hohastillpilp,
whose rank was in the order they are mentioned,
we thought this a favourable moment to explain to
them the intentions of our government. We therefore collected the chiefs and warriors, and having
drawn a map of the relative situation of our country on a mat with a piece of coal, detailed the nature and power of the American nation, its desire to
preserve harmony between all its red brethren, and
its intention of establishing trading-houses for their

relief and support. It was not without difficulty, nor till nearly half the day had been spent, that we were able to convey all this information to the Chopunnish, much of which might have been lost or misapprehended in its translation into so many different languages; for, in the first place, we spoke in English to one of our men, who translated it into French to Chaboneau, who interpreted it to his wife in the Minnetaree tongue, while she then put it into Shoshonee, and the young Shoshonee prisoner explained it to the Chopunnish in their own dialect. At last, however, we succeeded in communicating the impression we wished, and then adjourned the council; after which we amused our hosts by showing them the wonders of the compass, the spyglass, the magnet, the watch, and the air-gun, each of which attracted its share of admiration. They said that after we left the Minnetarees last autumn, three young Chopunnish had gone over to that nation, the people of which had mentioned to them our visit, and the extraordinary articles we had with us, but that they had placed no confidence in it until now. Among other persons present was a youth, son of a Chopunnish chief of much consideration, killed not long since by the Minnetarees of Fort de Prairie. As soon as the council was over, he brought a very fine mare, with her colt, and begged us to accept them, as a proof that he intended to follow our advice, for he had opened his ears to it, and it had made his heart glad. We now resumed our medical labours, and had a number of patients afflicted with scrofula, rheumatism, and sore eyes, to all whom we administered very cheerfully as far as our skill and supplies of medicine would permit. We also visited a chief who had for three years past so completely lost the use of his limbs, that he lay like a corpse in whatever position he was placed; yet he ate heartily, digested his food well, had a regular pulse, and retained his flesh; in short, but that he was somewhat pale with lying so long out of the sun, he might have been mistaken for a man in perfect health. This disease did not seem to be common ; indeed, we saw only three cases of it among the Chopunnish, who alone are afflicted with it. The scrofulous disorders we may readily conjecture to originate in the long confinement to vegetable diet, which may also, perhaps, increase the soreness of the eyes; but this strange disorder baffled at once our curiosity and our skill. Our assistance was again demanded early the next morning,

"May 12, by a crowd of Indians, to whom we gave eye-water. Shortly after, the chiefs and warriors held a council among themselves, to decide on an answer to our speech, and the result was, as we were informed, that they had full confidence in what we had told them, and were resolved to follow our advice. This determination having been made, the principal chief, Tunnachemootoolt, took a quantity of flour of the roots of cow-weed, and going round to all the kettles and baskets in which his people were cooking, thickened the soup into a kind of mush. He then began an harangue, setting forth the result of the deliberations among the chiefs, and after exhorting them to unanimity, concluded with an invitation to all who acquiesced in the proceedings of the council to come and eat ; while those who were of a different mind were requested to show their dissent by not partaking of the feast. During this animated harangue, the women, who were probably uneasy at the prospect of forming this proposed new connexion with strangers, tore their hair, and wrung their hands with the greatest appearance of distress. But the concluding appeal of the orator effectually stopped the mouths of every malecontent, and the proceedings were ratified, and the mush devoured with the most zealous unanimity. The chiefs and warriors then came in a body to visit us as we were seated near our tent ; and at their

instance, two young men, one of whom was a son
of Tunnachemootoolt, and the other the youth whose
father had been killed by the Pahkees, presented tc
us each a fine horse. We invited the chiefs to be
seated, and gave every one of them a flag, a pound
of powder, and fifty balls, and a present of the same
kind to the young men from whom we had received
the horses. They then invited us into the tent, and
said that they now wished to answer what we had
told them yesterday, but that many of their people
were at that moment waiting in great pain for our
medical assistance. It was therefore agreed that
Captain Clarke, who was the favourite physician,
should visit the sick, while Captain Lewis held the
council; which was opened by an old man, the father of Hohastillpilp. He began by declaring that
the nation had listened with attention to our advice,
and had only one heart and one tongue in declaring
their determination to follow it. They knew well
the advantages of peace, for they valued the lives of
their young men too much to expose them to the
dangers of war; and their desire to live quietly with
their neighbours had induced them last summer to
send three warriors with a pipe to the Shoshonees,
in the plains of the Columbia south of Lewis's River. These ministers of peace had been killed by the
Shoshonees, against whom the nation immediately
took up arms. They had met them last winter and
killed forty-two men, with the loss of only three of
their own party; so that, having revenged their deceased brethren, they would no longer make war on
the Shoshonees, but receive them as friends. As to
going with us to the plains of the Missouri, they
would be very willing to do so; for, though the Blackfoot Indians and the Pahkees had shed much of their
blood, they still wished to live in peace with them.
But we had not yet seen either of these nations, and
it would therefore be unsafe for them to venture
till they were assured of not being attacked by them

Still, however, some of their young men should accompany us across the mountains, and if they could
effect a peace with their enemies, the whole nation
would go over to the Missouri in the course of the
next summer. On our proposal that one of their
chiefs should go with us to the country of the whites,
they had not yet decided, but would let us know before we left ; but that, at all events, the whites might
calculate on their attachment and their best services,
for, though poor, their hearts were good. The snow
was, however, still so deep on the mountains, that
we should perish in attempting the passage, but if
we waited till after the next full moon, the snows
would have melted sufficiently to enable our horses
to subsist on the grass.

"As soon as this speech was concluded, Captain
Lewis replied at some length : they appeared to be
highly gratified with what he said, and after smoking
the pipe, made us a present of another fat horse.
In turn, we gave Broken Arm a vial of eye-water,
with directions how to wash the eyes of those who
should apply for it ; and as we promised to fill it again
when it was exhausted, he seemed very much pleased with our liberality. To Twisted Hair, who had
last night collected six more horses, we gave a
gun, a hundred balls, and two pounds of powder,
and told him he should have the same quantity when
we received the remainder of our horses. In the
course of the day three more of them were brought
in, and a fresh exchange of small presents put the
Indians in excellent humour. On our expressing a
wish to cross the river, and form a camp in order to
hunt and fish till the snows had melted, they recommended a position a few miles distant, and promised
to furnish us the next day with a canoe to pass over.
We invited Twisted Hair to establish himself near our
camp, for he had several young sons, one of whom
we hoped to engage as a guide, and he promised to
do so. Having now settled all their affairs, the In-

II.—S

dians divided themselves into two parties, and began
to play the game of hiding a bone, already described
as common to all the natives of this country."

CHAPTER XII.

The Party encamp among the Chopunnish, and receive farther
Evidence of their Hospitality.—Indian Mode of boiling Bear's
Flesh.—Of decoying the Deer within Reach of their Arrows.
—Character of the Soil and Climate among the Rocky Mount
ains.—Varieties of Climate.—Character of the Natives.—
Their Dress and Ornaments.—Mode of burying the Dead.—
The Party administer medical Relief to the Natives.—One
of the Natives restored to the Use of his Limbs by Sweating, and the curious Process by which Perspiration was excited.—Another Proof of Chopunnish Hospitality.—Success
of their sweating Prescription on an Indian Chief.—Description of the Horned Lizard and a Variety of Insects.—Attachment of the Friends of a dying Indian to a Tomahawk which he
had stolen from the Party, and which they desired to bury with
the Body.—Description of the River Tommanamah.—The Indians return an Answer to a Proposition made by the Party.

THEY were disappointed in being furnished with a
canoe in season to cross the river the next day, but
passed over on the 14th, and formed their camp
where the Indians had recommended. " As soon as
we had encamped," says the Journal, " Tunnachemootoolt and Hohastillpilp, with about twelve of their
nation, came to the opposite side and began to sing,
this being the usual token of friendship on such occasions. We sent the canoe for them, and the two
chiefs came over with several of the party, among
whom were the two young men who had given us
the two horses in behalf of the nation. After smoking for some time, Hohastillpilp presented to Captain Lewis an elegant gray gelding which he had
brought for the purpose, and was perfectly satisfied at

receiving in return a handkerchief, two hundred balls, and four pounds of powder.

" The hunters killed some pheasants, two squirrels, and a male and a female bear, the first of which was large and fat, and of a bay colour; the second, meager, grizzly, and of a smaller size. They were of the species common to the upper part of the Missouri, and might well be termed the variegated bear, for they are found occasionally of a black grizzly brown or red colour. There is every reason to believe that they are of precisely the same species. Those of different colours are sometimes killed together, as in the case of these two, and as we had found the white and bay associated together on the Missouri : some nearly white were seen in this neighbourhood by the hunters. Indeed, it is not common to find any two bears of the same colour ; and if difference of colour were allowed to constitute a distinct species, the number would be increased to almost twenty. Soon after they killed a female bear with two cubs. The mother was black, with a considerable intermixture of white hairs, and a white spot on her breast. One of the cubs was jet black, and the other of a light reddish brown or bay colour. The fur of these variegated bears is much finer, longer, and more abundant than that of the common black bear ; but the most striking difference between them is, that the former are larger, have longer tusks, and longer as well as blunter claws ; that they prey more on other animals ; and that they lie neither so long nor so closely in winter-quarters, and never climb a tree, however closely pressed by the hunters. The variegated bear here, though specifically the same with those we met on the Missouri, are by no means so ferocious, probably because the scarcity of game and the habit of living on roots may have weaned them from attacking and devouring animals. Still, however, they are not so passive as the common black bear, which are also found here ; for they had fought with our hunters, though with less fury than those on the other side of the mountains.

" A large part of the meat we gave to the Indians, to whom it was a great luxury, as they scarcely taste flesh once in a month.   They immediately prepared a large fire of dried wood, on which were thrown a number of smooth stones from the river.   As soon as the fire went down and the stones were heated, they were laid close to each other in a level position, and covered with a quantity of pine branches, on which were placed flitches of the meat, and then boughs and flesh alternately for several courses, leaving a thick layer of pine on the top.   On this heap they then poured a small quantity of water, and covered the whole with earth to the depth of four inches.   After remaining in this state for about three hours, the meat was taken off, and was really more tender than that which we had boiled or roasted, though the strong flavour of the pine rendered it disagreeable to our palates.   This repast gave them much satisfaction; for, though they sometimes kill the black bear, they attack very reluctantly the fierce variegated bear; and never except when they can pursue him on horseback over the plains, and shoot him with arrows." * * *

" May 15. As we were compelled to pass some time in this neighbourhood, a number of hunters were sent in different directions, and the rest were employed in completing the camp.   We secured the baggage with a shelter of grass, and made a kind of bower of the under part of an old sail, the leathern tent being too rotten for use, while the men formed very comfortable huts in the shape of the awning of a wagon, by means of willow poles and grass. Tunnachemootoolt and his young men left us in the morning to go home, and soon after we were visited by a party of fourteen Indians on horseback, proceeding on a hunting excursion, armed with bows and arrows.   The chief game is the deer, and, whenever the ground will permit, they prefer hunting on horse-back; but in the woodlands, where this is impracticable, they make use of a decoy. This consists of the skin of the head and upper part of the neck of a deer, kept in its natural shape by a frame of small sticks in the inside. As soon as the hunter perceives a deer, he conceals himself, and with his hand moves the decoy so as to represent a real deer in the act of feeding, which is done so naturally that the game is enticed within reach of their arrows." * * *

The next day a horse which had strayed was brought back by one of the Indians, thus affording another instance of the honesty of these people. Their native guests all left them in the course of the day.

" May 17. It rained," continues the narrative, " during the greater part of the night, and our flimsy covering being insufficient for our protection, we lay in water the most of the time; and, what was more unlucky, our chronometer got wet. The rain continued with us nearly the whole day, while on the high plains the snow was falling, and lay two or three inches in depth. This weather confined us to our camp, and kept the Indians from us; so that for the first time since we had left the Narrows of the Columbia, a day was passed without being visited by them.

" The country along the Rocky Mountains, for several hundred miles in length and about fifty in width, is a high level plain; in all its parts extremely fertile, and in many places covered with a growth of tall long-leafed pine. This plain is chiefly interrupted near the streams of water, where the hills are steep and lofty; but the soil on them is good, being unencumbered by much stone, and possessing more timber than the level country. Under shelter of these hills, the bottom lands skirt the margins of the rivers, and though narrow and confined, are fertile and rarely inundated. Nearly the whole of this

widespread tract is covered with a profusion of
grass and plants, which were at this time as high as
the knee. Among these are a variety of esculent
plants and roots, gathered without much difficulty,
and yielding not only a nutritious, but a very agreeable food. The air is pure and dry, the climate quite
as mild, if not milder, than in the same parallels of
latitude in the Atlantic States, and must be equally
healthy; for all the disorders which we had witnessed might fairly be imputed more to the nature
of the diet of the inhabitants than to any peculiarity
of climate. This general observation is of course
to be qualified, since in the same tract of country
the degrees of the variation of heat and cold depend
much upon the influence of situation. Thus the
rains of the low grounds near our camp were snows
in the high plains; and while the sun shone with in-
tense heat in the confined bottoms, the plains had
a much colder air, and the vegetation was retarded
there at least fifteen days, while at the foot of the
mountains the snows were still many feet in depth;
so that within twenty miles of our camp we observed the rigours of winter cold, the cool air of spring,
and the oppressive heat of midsummer. On the
plains, however, where the snow had fallen, it seemed to do but little injury to the grass and other plants,
which, though apparently tender and susceptible,
were still blooming at the height of nearly eighteen
inches through their wintry mantle. In short, this
district affords many advantages to settlers; and, if
properly cultivated, would yield every object necessary for the subsistence and comfort of civilized
man.

"The Chopunnish are in general stout, well formed, and active: they have high, and many of them
aquiline noses, and the general appearance of the
face is cheerful and agreeable, though without any
indication of gayety and mirth. Like most of the
Indians, they extract their beards: there does not

appear to be any natural deficiency in this respect, for we observed several men, who, if they had adopted the practice of shaving, would have been as well supplied with beards as ourselves. The dress of both sexes resembles that of the Shoshonees, and consists of a long shirt reaching to the thigh, leggins as high as the waist, and moccasins and robes, all of which are formed of skins.

" Their ornaments are beads, shells, and pieces of brass attached to different parts of the dress, tied round the arms, neck, and wrists, or thrown over the shoulders ; and to these are added pearls and beads suspended from the ears, and a single shell of wampum through the nose. The headdress of the men is a *bandeau* of fox or otter skin, either with or without the fur, and sometimes an ornament is tied to a plait of hair falling from the crown of the head : that of the women is a cap without rim, formed of bear-grass and cedar bark ; while the hair itself of both sexes falls in two rows down the front of the body. Collars of bears' claws are also common. But the personal ornament most esteemed is a sort of breastplate, formed of a strip of otter-skin six inches wide, cut out of the whole length of the back of the animal, including the head : this being dressed with the hair on, a hole is made in the upper end for the head of the wearer to pass through, and the skin hangs down in front, with the tail reaching below the knee, and ornamented with pieces of pearl, red cloth, wampum, or, in short, any other fanciful decoration. Tippets, also, are occasionally worn. That of Hohastillpilp was formed of human scalps, and adorned with the thumbs and fingers of the enemies he had slain in battle.*

* And yet this chief belonged to a nation immediately after ward praised for their amiability. Such are the contradictions in the character of the wild, uncultivated, and ungoverned savage. This chief showed unbounded liberality, and the most hospitable attentions to the party.

"The Chopunnish are among the most amiable Indians we had seen. Their character is placid and gentle, rarely moved into passion, and not often enlivened by gayety. Their amusements consist in running races, and in shooting with arrows at a target, and they are addicted to the all-prevailing vice of gambling. They are much less taken with bawbles than the generality of Indians, and are chiefly anxious to obtain articles of utility, such as knives, tomahawks, kettles, blankets, and awls for making moccasins. They have also suffered so much from the superior equipment of their enemies, that they are very desirous of procuring arms and ammunition, which they are gradually acquiring; for the band of Tunnachemootoolt have already six guns, which they obtained from the Minnetarees.

"The Chopunnish bury their dead in sepulchres formed of boards, and in shape like the roof of a house. The bodies are rolled in skins, and laid one above another, separated only by a board. We have sometimes seen their dead deposited in wooden boxes, after being rolled in skins in the same manner. They sacrifice to the deceased their horses, canoes, and every other species of property, and numerous bones of horses may be seen lying round their sepulchres." * * *

"Among the reptiles common in this country is a species of lizard, which we called the horned lizard, about the size, and much resembling in figure the ordinary black lizard. Its belly is, however, broader, its tail shorter, and its action much slower than that of the common lizard. It crawls like the toad, and is of a brown colour variegated with yellowish brown spots : it is covered with minute shells, interspersed with little horny projections like prickles, on the upper part of the body. The belly and throat resemble that of the frog, and are of a light yellowish brown. The edges of the belly are regularly studded with these horny projections, which give to them a serrated appearance: the eye is small and of a dark colour. Above and behind the eyes are several bony projections, which, being armed at the extremities with a firm black substance, looking like horns sprouting from the head, induced us to call it the horned lizard. These animals are found in great abundance in the sandy parts of the plains, and after a shower of rain are seen basking in the sun, but for the greater part of the time they are concealed in holes. They are also seen in great numbers on the banks of the Missouri, and in the plains through which we passed above the Wollawollahs."

* * * " Most of the insects of the United States are common here, though there is neither the hornet, the wasp, nor the yellow-jacket, but an insect resembling the last of these, though much larger. They are very numerous, particularly in the Rocky Mountains and on the waters of the Columbia : the body and abdomen are yellow, with transverse circles of black, the head black, and the wings, which are four in number, are of a dark brown colour; their nests are built in the ground, and resemble that of the hornet, with an outer covering to the comb. These insects are very fierce, and sting severely, so that we found them exceedingly troublesome in frightening our horses as we passed the mountains. The silkworm is also found here, as well as the humble-bee, though the honey-bee is not."

From the 18th to the 23d nothing of special interest occurred. For several days they had almost constant rains, and the hunters had very little success in killing game, so that they were very scantily supplied with food. The salmon, however, were soon expected, as they had received accounts of their having made their appearance in Lewis's River.

"May 24. This proved the warmest day," says the Journal, "since our arrival. Besides administering medical relief to the Indians, we were now obliged to devote much of our time to the care of our own invalids. The child of Sacajawea was very unwell; and with one of the men we had ventured an experiment of a very bold character. He had been for some time sick, but had now recovered his flesh, ate heartily, and digested well, but had so great a weakness in the loins that he could not walk, nor even sit upright without extreme pain. After we had in vain exhausted the resources of our art, one of the hunters mentioned that he had known persons in a similar situation restored by violent sweats, and at the request of the patient we permitted the remedy to be applied. For this purpose, a hole about four feet deep and three in diameter was dug in the earth, and heated well by a large fire in the bottom of it. The fire was then taken out, and an arch formed over the hole by means of willow poles, and covered with several blankets, so as to form a perfect awning. The patient, being stripped naked, was seated under this on a bench, with a piece of board for his feet, while with a jug of water he sprinkled the bottom and sides of the hole, so as to keep up as hot a steam as he could bear. After remaining twenty minutes in this situation he was taken out, immediately plunged twice into cold water, and then brought back to the hole, where he was again subjected to the vapour bath. During all this time he drank copiously a strong infusion of horsemint, which was used as a substitute for the seneca root, which our informant said he had seen employed on these occasions, but of which there was none in this country. At the end of three quarters of an hour he was again withdrawn from the hole, carefully wrapped up, and suffered to cool gradually. The morning after this operation was performed he walked about, and was nearly free from pain.

" About eleven o'clock a canoe arrived with three Indians, one of whom was the poor creature who had lost the use of his limbs, and for whose recovery the natives seemed very anxious, as he was a chief of considerable rank among them. His situation, however, was beyond the reach of our skill. He complained of no pain in any particular limb, and we therefore thought his disorder could not be rheumatic ; and his limbs would have been more attenuated if his disease had been a paralytic affection." * * *

The two following days the hunters failed altogether in obtaining game, but purchased a few roots, which they brought in. The Indians still remained at the encampment with their sick chief, discovering the most affectionate anxiety for his cure, and continually soliciting that something farther might be done for him. The snows on the mountains were evidently disappearing, and on the 26th they were gladdened by the sight of a salmon in the river.

" May 27. The horse the Indians had given us some time ago had gone astray, but in our present dearth of provisions we searched for him and killed him. Observing that we were in want of food, Hohastillpilp told us that most of the horses which we saw running at large belonged to him or his people, and that, whenever we wished for meat, we might take one without any restraint. We had, indeed, more than once, occasion to admire the generosity of this Indian, whose conduct presented a model of what is due to strangers in distress. A party was sent to a village that had been discovered the day before, and returned with a large supply of bread and roots. Sergeant Ordway and two men were also despatched to Lewis's River, about half a day's ride to the south, where we expected to obtain salmon, which were said to be very abundant at that place. Three of our hunters returned with five deer." * * * " The Indians who attended the sick chief were so anxious to have the operation of sweating performed on him under our inspection, that we determined to gratify them by making the attempt. The hole was therefore enlarged, and the father of the chief, a very good-looking old man, went in with him, and held him in a proper position. This strong evidence of affection is directly opposite to the received opinion of the insensibility of savages ; nor were we less struck with the kindness and attentions shown to the sick man by those who were wholly unrelated to him, and which was the more remarkable, as his long illness of three years might be supposed to have exhausted their sympathy. We could not produce as complete a perspiration as we desired, and after he was taken out he complained of suffering considerable pain, which we relieved with a few drops of laudanum, and he then rested well. The next morning,

" May 28, he was able to use his arms, felt better than he had done for many months, and sat up during the greater part of the day." * * *

" May 29. The Indian chief was still rapidly recovering, and for the first time during the last twelve months had strength enough to wash his face. We had intended to repeat the sweating to-day, but as the weather was cloudy, with occasional rain, we deferred it. This operation, though violent, appears highly efficacious ; for our own man, on whom the experiment was first made, is recovering his strength very fast, and the restoration of the chief is wonderful. He continued to improve, and on the following day,

" May 30, after a very violent sweating, was able to move one of his legs and some of his toes, the fingers and arms being almost entirely restored to their former strength." * * *

" May 31. Two men visited the Indian village, where they purchased a dressed bearskin of a uniform pale reddish brown colour, which the Indians called *yackah*, in contradistinction to *hohhost*, or the white bear. This induced us to inquire more particularly into their opinions as to the several species of bears ; and we produced all the skins of that ani-

mal which we had purchased. The natives immediately classed the white, the deep and the pale grizzly red, the grizzly dark brown, in short, all those
with the extremities of the hair of a white or frosty
colour, without regard to the colour of the ground
of the fur, under the name of *hohhost*. They assured us that they were all of the same species
with the white bear; that they associated together,
had longer nails than the others, and never climbed
trees. On the other hand, the animals with black
skins, those which were black with a number of entire white hairs intermixed, or with a white breast,
the uniform bay, and the brown and light reddish
brown, they ranged under the class *yackah*, and said
they resembled each other in being smaller, in having shorter nails than the white bear, in climbing
trees, and being so little vicious that they could be
pursued with safety. This distinction of the Indians seemed to be well founded, and we were inclined to believe,

" First, that the white or grizzly bear of this neighbourhood form a distinct species, which, moreover,
are the same with those of the same colour on the
upper part of the Missouri, where the other species
is not found.

" Second, that the black and reddish brown, &c.,
are a second species, equally distinct from the white
bear of this country, and from the black bear on the
Atlantic and Pacific Oceans, which last two seem to
form only one species. The common black bear is
indeed unknown in this country; for the bear of
which we are speaking, though in most respects
similar, differs from it in having much finer, thicker,
and longer hair, with a greater proportion of fur
mixed with it, and also in having a variety of colours, while the common black bear has no intermixture or change of colour, but is of a uniform black.*

* Townsend, in his Catalogue of the Quadrupeds of this

"In the course of the day the natives brought us another of our original stock of horses, of which we had now recovered all except two; and those, we were informed, were taken back by our Shoshonee guide when he returned home. They amounted to sixty-five, most of them fine, strong, active animals, and in excellent order."

The next day, in crossing the river, they had the misfortune to lose all their remaining stock of merchandise. "We therefore," says the Journal, "created a new fund, by cutting off the buttons from our clothes, and preparing some eye-water and basilicon, to which were added a few vials and small tin boxes, in which we had once kept phosphorus. With these articles two men set out in the morning,

"June 2, to trade, and brought home three bushels of roots and some bread. In the mean time several hunters were sent out. The Indians informed us that there were great numbers of moose to the southeast of the east branch of Lewis's River, which they called the Tommanamah. We had lately heard, also, that some Indians, residing at a considerable distance, on the south side of the Kooskooskee, were in possession of two tomahawks, one of which had been left at our camp on Moscheto Creek, and the other had been stolen while we were with the Chopunnish in the autumn. This last we were anxious to obtain, in order to give it to the relations of our unfortunate companion, Sergeant Floyd, to whom it once belonged. We therefore sent Drewyer, with the two chiefs Neeshnepahkeeook and Hohastillpilp, to demand it. On their arrival, they found that the present possessor of it, who had purchased it of the thief, was at the point of death; and his relations were unwilling to give it up, as

country, names four species of bears: The Grizzly Bear, or *Ursus ferox* of Zoologists; the Black Bear, or *Ursus Americana* the White Bear. and the Brown Bear.

they wished to bury it in the grave with the deceased. The influence of Neeshnepahkeeook, however, at length prevailed; and they consented to surrender the tomahawk on receiving two strands of beads and a handkerchief from Drewyer, and from each of the chiefs a horse, to be killed at the funeral of their kinsman, according to the custom of the country.

" Soon after their return, Sergeant Ordway and his party, who had been sent to procure fish, and for whose safety we had become extremely anxious, came back from Lewis's River with some roots and seventeen salmon. The distance, however, from which they had been brought was so great, that most of them were nearly spoiled; but such as were still sound were very delicious, the flesh being of a fine rose colour, with a small mixture of yellow, and so fat that they cooked perfectly well without the addition of any oil or grease." * * *

" June 3. Finding that the salmon did not yet appear along the shore, as the Indians had assured us they would, and that all the salmon which they themselves used were obtained from Lewis's River, we began to lose our hopes of subsisting on them. We were too poor, and at too great a distance from Lewis's River to obtain fish from thence; and it was not probable that the river would fall sufficiently for the salmon to reach where we were before it would be necessary for us to leave. Our Indian friends were about sending an express over the mountains to Traveller's Rest, in order to procure intelligence from the Ootlashoots, a band of Flatheads who have wintered on the east side of the mountains; and, as the route was deemed practicable for this express, we also proposed setting out. The Indians, however, dissuaded us from it, as many of the creeks, they said, were still too deep to be forded, the roads very heavy and slippery, and there was no grass yet for our horses; but that in twelve or fourteen days we should not have these obstacles to encounter." * * *

"During the two following days we continued hunting in our own neighbourhood, and by means of these efforts, and trading with the Indians for trifling articles, we succeeded in procuring as much bread and roots, besides other food, as would enable us to subsist while crossing the mountains. The old chief in the mean time gradually recovered the use of his limbs, and our own man was nearly restored to his former health." * * *

The next day they were informed by Neeshne-pahkeeook that his people would not accompany them to the Missouri, but that some of their young men, as they had before promised, should go with them.

CHAPTER XIII.

They join in the Diversions of the Willetpos Indians, a Tribe hitherto unnoticed.—Joy of the Party at the prospect of Returning.—Vegetation of the Rocky Mountains.—Preparations to resume their Journey.—They set out, and arrive at Hungry Creek.—Difficulties that obstructed their Progress.—Compelled to return and wait for a Guide across the Mountains.—Their Distress for want of Provisions.—They resolve to re-turn to the Quamash Flats.—Are at last so fortunate as to procure Indian Guides, with whom they resume their Journey.—Dangers of the Route.—Scarcity of Provisions, and the Perils to which they were exposed, their Course lying along the Ridge of the Mountains. — Description of the warm Springs, where the Party encamp.—Fondness of the Indians for bathing in them.

On the 7th they were engaged in preparing packs and saddles for their journey, having now resolved to start as soon as circumstances would in any way permit.

"June 8. Cut Nose visited us this morning with

ten or twelve warriors, among whom were two belonging to a band of Chopunnish which we had not
before seen, who called themselves Willetpos, and
resided on the south side of Lewis's River. One of
them gave a good horse which he rode in exchange
for one of ours which was in no condition to cross
the mountains, on receiving a tomahawk in addition.
We were also so fortunate as to exchange two
other horses for two that were much better, without giving anything else. After these important
transactions, several foot-races were run between
our men and the Indians: the latter, who are very
active, and fond of these races, proved themselves
very expert, and one of them was as fleet as our
swiftest runners. After the races were over, the
men divided themselves into two parties, and played
at prison bars; an exercise which we were desirous
of encouraging, as several of the party were becoming lazy from inaction. At night these games were
concluded by a dance. One of the Indians told us
that we could not pass the mountains before the
next full moon, or about the first of July; and that,
if we attempted it before that time, the horses would
be three days without food on the top of the mountains. This intelligence was by no means agreeable,
as it excited doubts as to the most proper time for
starting; but, having become very impatient, we
were determined to run all hazards, and leave as
soon as the Indians generally considered the route
practicable, which was about the middle of the present month.

* * * "June 9. Hohastillpilp, who had visited us
the day before, now left us, with other Indians, for
the plains near Lewis's River, where the whole nation were about to assemble. Broken Arm. too, with
all his people, stopped on their way to the general
rendezvous at the same place. Cut Nose, or Neeshnepahkeeook, borrowed a horse, and rode down a
few miles after some young eagles. He soon re-

II.—T

turned with two of the gray kind, nearly grown, which he intended to raise for the sake of the feathers. The young chief who had some time before made us a present of two horses, came with a party of his people and passed the night with us." * * *

The river had now fallen about six feet, which might be regarded as a sure indication that most of the snow had melted on the mountains. They concluded, however, that it would be most prudent still to wait a day or two longer before they finally set out on their journey.

"June 10. After collecting our horses," proceeds the Journal, " which took much time, we set out at eleven o'clock for the Quamash Flats. Our stock was now very abundant, each man being well mounted, with a small load on a second horse, besides several supernumerary ones, in case of accident or want of food. We ascended the river hills, which are very high, and three miles in extent; our course being north 22° east, and then north 15° west for two miles, till we reached Collins's Creek. It was deep and difficult to cross, but we passed without any injury except wetting some of our provisions, and then proceeded due north for five miles to the eastern edge of the Quamash Flats, near where we had first met the Chopunnish in the autumn. We encamped on the bank of a small stream, in a point of woods bordering an extensive level and beautiful prairie, which was intersected by several rivulets, and, as the *quamash* was now in blossom, presented a perfect resemblance to a lake of clear water.

" A party of Chopunnish, who had overtaken us a few miles above, halted for the night with us, and mentioned that they too had come down to hunt in the flats, though we had fears that they expected us to provide for them during their stay.

" The country through which we passed was generally free from stone, extremely fertile, and well supplied with timber, consisting of several species of fir, long-leafed pine, and larch. The undergrowth was chokecherry near the water-courses, and scattered through the country were black alder, a large species of the reed-root now in bloom, a plant resembling the *pawpaw* in its leaf, and bearing a berry with five valves of a deep purple colour. There were also two species of sumach, the purple haw, sevenbark, service-berry, gooseberry, the honeysuckle bearing a white berry, and a species of dwarf pine ten or twelve feet high, which might be confounded with the young pine of the long-leafed species, except that the former bears a cone of a globular form, with small scales, and that its leaves are in fascicles of two, resembling in length and appearance the common pitch pine. We also observed two species of wild rose, both quinquepetalous, both of a damask red colour, and similar in the stem; but one of them was as large as the common red rose of our gardens; its leaf, too, is somewhat larger than that of the other species of wild rose, and the apex, as we saw them last year, was more than three times the size of the common wild rose.

" We saw many sandhill cranes, and some ducks in the marshes near our camp; likewise a great number of burrowing squirrels, some of which we killed, and found them as tender and well-flavoured as our gray squirrels."

The hunters were sent out in different directions the next day, but with very indifferent success. Being determined to start in earnest in the morning, they cut up and dried what meat they had, packed their baggage, and hoppled their horses, to be in readiness at an early hour.

" June 15. The horses," proceeds the Journal, " had strayed to such a distance that we could not collect them without great difficulty; and, as it rained very hard, we waited for it to abate. It soon, however, showed every appearance of a settled rain, and we therefore set out at ten o'clock. We crossed the prairie at the distance of eight miles, where we had sent our hunters, and found two deer which they had hung up for us. Two and a half miles farther we overtook them at Collins's Creek: they had killed a third deer. After dining, we proceeded up the creek about half a mile; then, crossing through a high, broken country for about ten miles, reached an eastern branch of the same creek, near which we encamped in the bottom, after a ride of twenty-two miles. The rains had made the road very slippery, and this, joined to the quantity of fallen timber, rendered our progress slow and laborious. The country through which we passed had a thick growth of long-leafed pine, with some pitch pine, larch, white pine, white cedar or *arbor vitæ* of large size, and a variety of firs. The undergrowth consisted chiefly of reed-root, from six to ten feet in height, with the other species already enumerated. The soil was in general good, and had somewhat of a red cast, like that near the Southwest Mountain in Virginia. We saw in the course of our ride the speckled woodpecker and the bee-martin, and found the nest of a humming-bird which had just begun to lay its eggs.

"June 16. We readily collected our horses, and, having taken breakfast, proceeded at six o'clock up the creek, over handsome meadows of fine grass, and a great abundance of *quamash*. At the distance of two miles we crossed the creek, and ascended a ridge in a direction towards the northeast. Fallen timber still obstructed our way so much, that it was eleven o'clock before we had made seven miles to a small branch of Hungry Creek. In the hollows and on the north side of the hills large quantities of snow still remained, in some places to the depth of two or three feet. Vegetation, too, was proportionably retarded, the dog-tooth violet being just in bloom, and the honeysuckle, whortleberry, and a small species of white maple were but beginning to put forth their leaves. These appearances, in a part of the country comparatively low, were ill omens of the practicability of crossing the mountains. But, being determined to proceed, we halted merely to take a hasty meal while the horses were grazing, and then resumed our march. The route was through thick woods, and over high hills intersected by deep ravines and obstructed by fallen timber. We found much difficulty, also, in following the road, the greater part of it being now covered with snow, which lay in large masses eight or ten feet deep, and would have been wholly impassable had it not been sufficiently firm to bear our horses. Early in the evening we reached Hungry Creek, at the place where Captain Clarke had left a horse for us as we passed in September; and, finding a small glade with some grass, though not enough for our horses, we thought it better to halt for the night, lest by going farther we should find nothing for them to eat. Hungry Creek was small at this place, but deep, and discharged a torrent of water perfectly transparent, and cold as ice. During the fifteen miles of our route this day the principal timber was the pitch pine, the white pine, larch, and fir. The long-leafed pine extends but a small distance on this side of Collins's Creek, and the white cedar does not reach beyond the branch of Hungry Creek on which we dined. In the early part of the day we saw the columbine, the blue bell, and the yellow flowering pea in bloom. There was also on these mountains a great quantity of angelica, stronger to the taste, and more highly scented, than that common in the United States. The smell is very pleasant, and the natives, after drying and cutting it into small pieces, wear it in strings around their necks.

" June 17. The air we found pleasant during the day, but, notwithstanding the shortness of the nights, it became very cold before morning. At an early hour we collected our horses and proceeded down

the creek, which we crossed twice with much difficulty and danger, on account of its depth and rapidity. We avoided two other crossings of the same
kind by passing over a steep and rocky hill. At
the distance of seven miles, the road began to ascend the main ridges which divide the waters of the
Chopunnish and Kooskooskee Rivers. We followed
it up a mountain for about three miles, when we
found ourselves enveloped in snow, from twelve to
fifteen feet in depth, even on the south side, with the
fullest exposure to the sun. Winter now presented
itself to us in all its rigours : the air was keen and
frosty, no vestige of vegetation was to be seen, and
our hands and feet were benumbed with cold. We
halted at the sight of this new difficulty.

" To wait till the snows on the mountains had dissolved so as to enable us to distinguish the road,
would, we knew, defeat our design of returning to
the United States this season. We found, also, that
as the snow bore our horses very well, travelling
was infinitely easier than it had been last fall, when
the rocks and fallen timber so much obstructed our
march. But it would require five days to reach the
fish-wears at the mouth of Colt Creek, even if we
should succeed in following the proper ridges of the
mountains ; and the danger of missing our way was
exceedingly great, as every track was covered with
snow. During these five days, too, we should have
no chance of finding either grass or underwood for
our horses. To proceed, therefore, under such circumstances, would be to hazard our being bewilder-
ed in the mountains, to ensure the loss of our horses,
and, should we even be so fortunate as to escape
with our lives, we might be obliged to abandon all
our papers and collections. It was accordingly decided not to venture any farther ; to deposite here all
the baggage and provisions for which we had no immediate use, and, reserving only subsistence for a
few days, return, while our horses were yet strong,

to some spot where we might live by hunting till a guide could be procured to conduct us across the mountains. Our baggage was placed on scaffolds and carefully covered, as were also the instruments and papers, which we thought it safer to leave than to risk them over the roads and creeks by which we had come. Having completed this operation, we set out at one o'clock, and, retracing our steps, reached Hungry Creek, which we ascended for two miles, and, finding some scanty grass, encamped for the night. The rain fell during the greater part of the evening; and, as this was the first time that we had ever been compelled to make a retrograde movement, we feared that it might depress the spirits of the men; but, though somewhat dejected at the circumstance, the obvious necessity precluded all repining. During the night our horses strayed in search of food to a considerable distance among the thick timber on the hill sides, nor could we collect them till nine o'clock the next morning,

"June 18. Two of them were, however, still missing, and we directed two of the party to remain and look for them. At the same time we despatched Drewyer and Shannon to the Chopunnish, in the plains beyond the Kooskooskee, in order to hasten the arrival of the Indians who it had been promised should accompany us, or, at any rate, to procure a guide to conduct us to Traveller's Rest. For this purpose they took a rifle, as a reward to any one who would engage to go with us, with directions to increase the reward, if necessary, by an offer of two other guns to be given immediately, and ten horses at the Falls of the Missouri : we then resumed our route." * * * They proceeded on to Collins's Creek, where they halted for the night. Although numerous tracks of deer were seen, the hunters did not succeed in killing any.

They remained at their encampment on Collins's Creek the two following days, but, as they had but little success in procuring game, they resolved to return to Quamash Flats. On the 19th, the two men who had been left behind returned, without having been able to find the missing horses.

"June 21. The mortification of being obliged to retrace our steps," continues the Journal, "rendered still more tedious a route everywhere so obstructed by brush and fallen timber that it could not be passed without difficulty, and even danger to our horses. One of these poor creatures wounded himself so badly in jumping over some fallen logs, that he was rendered unfit for use, and sickness had deprived us of the service of another. At the pass of Collins's Creek we met two Indians, who returned with us about half a mile to a spot where we had slept in September, and where we now halted to dine and let our horses graze. These Indians had four supernumerary horses, and were on their way to cross the mountains. They had seen Drewyer and Shannon, who, they said, would not return for two days. We pressed them to remain with us till that time, in order to conduct us over the mountains; to which they consented, and deposited their stores of roots and bread in the bushes at a little distance. After dinner we left three men to hunt till our return, and then proceeded; but we had not gone more than two miles, when the Indians halted in a small prairie, where they promised to remain at least two nights, if we did not come back sooner. We left them, and at about seven in the evening found ourselves at our old encampment on the Flats, and were glad to find that four of the hunters whom we had sent ahead had killed a deer for supper.

"June 22. At daylight all the hunters set out, and, traversing the whole country, were much more successful than we had even hoped, for they brought in eight deer and three bear. Hearing, too, that salmon were now abundant in the Kooskooskee, we despatched a man to our former station above Collins's Creek, for the purpose of purchasing some with a few beads which had been found accidentally in one of our waistcoat pockets. He did not return in the evening, nor had we heard from Drewyer and Shannon, who we began to fear had found much difficulty in engaging a guide ; and we were also apprehensive that the two Indians might set out the next day for the mountains. Early in the morning, therefore,

" June 23, we despatched two hunters to prevail on them, if possible, to remain a day or two longer ; and if they persisted in going on, they were to accompany them, with the three men at Collins's Creek, and mark the route as far as Traveller's Rest, where they were to remain till we joined them by following the same road.

" Our fears for the safety of Drewyer, Shannon and Whitehouse were fortunately relieved by their return in the afternoon. The former brought three Indians, who promised to go with us to the Falls of the Missouri for the compensation of two guns. One of them was the brother of Cut Nose, and the other two had each given us a horse at the house of Broken Arm ; and as they were men of good character, and respectable in the nation, we had the fairest prospect of being well served. We therefore secured our horses near the camp, and at an early hour the next morning,

" June 24, set out on our second attempt to cross the mountains. On reaching Collins's Creek we found only one of our men, who informed us that, a short time before he arrived, the two Indians, tired of waiting, had set out, and the other four men had accompanied them, as they were directed. After halting, we went on to Fish Creek, the branch of Hungry Creek where we had slept on the 19th instant. Here we overtook two of the party who had gone on with the Indians, and who had been fortunate enough to persuade them to wait for us. Du-

II.—U

ring their stay at Collins's Creek they had killed only a single deer, and of this they had been very liberal to the Indians, in order to induce them to remain, so that they were without provisions; and two of them had set out for another branch of Hungry Creek, where we would meet them the next day.

" In the evening, the Indians, to bring fair weather, as they said, for our journey, set fire to the woods. As these consisted chiefly of tall fir-trees, with very numerous dried branches, the blaze was almost instantaneous; and as the flames mounted to the tops of the highest trees, it resembled a splendid display of fireworks. In the morning,

" June 25, one of our guides complained of being sick : a symptom by no means pleasant, as sickness with an Indian is generally the pretext for abandoning an enterprise which he dislikes. He promised, however, to overtake us, and we therefore left him with his two companions, and set out at an early hour. At eleven o'clock we halted for dinner at the branch of Hungry Creek, and here we found our two men, who had killed nothing. Here, too, we were joined, rather unexpectedly, by our guides, who now appeared disposed to be faithful to their engagements. The Indian, indeed, was really sick ; and having no covering except a pair of moccasins and an elkskin dressed without the hair, we supplied him with a buffalo robe.

" In the evening we arrived at Hungry Creek, and halted for the night about a mile and a half below our encampment of the 16th.

" June 26. Having collected our horses and taken breakfast, we set out at six o'clock, pursuing our former route, and at length began to ascend for the second time the ridge of mountains. Near the snowy region we killed two small black pheasants and one of the speckled kind. These birds generally frequent the higher parts of the mountains, where they feed on the leaves of the pine and fir; but both kinds appear to be solitary and silent, as we never heard either of them make any noise; and the Indians told us that they did not drum in flying, nor make a whirring sound with their wings. On reaching the top of the mountain, we found our deposite perfectly safe. The snow in the neighbourhood had melted nearly four feet since the 17th. By measuring it accurately, and comparing it with a mark which we had then made, we found the general depth to have been ten feet ten inches, though in some places still greater; but at this time it was about seven feet. It required two hours to arrange our baggage and prepare a hasty meal, after which the guides urged us to set off, as we had a long ride to make before we should reach a spot where there was grass for our horses. We accordingly mounted, and, following their steps, sometimes crossed abruptly steep hills, and then wound along their sides, near tremendous precipices, where, had our horses slipped, we should have been irrecoverably lost. Our route lay along the ridgy mountains which separate the waters of the Kooskooskee and Chopunnish, and above the heads of all the streams, so that we met no running water. The whole country was completely covered with snow, except occasionally a few square feet of earth at the roots of some trees, round which it had dissolved. We passed our camp of the 18th of September, and late in the evening reached a spot where we encamped, near a good spring of water. It was on the steep side of a mountain, with no wood, and a fair southern aspect, from which the snow seemed to have disappeared for about ten days, and an abundant growth of young grass, like greensward, had sprung up. There was also a species of grass not unlike flag, with a broad succulent leaf, and which is confined to the upper parts of the highest mountains. It is a favourite food with horses, but it was then either covered with snow, or just making its appearance. There is a third plant pe-

culiar to the same regions, a species of whortleberry; and there are also large quantities of a species
of bear-grass, which, though it grows luxuriantly
over all these mountains, and preserves its verdure
during the whole winter, is never eaten by horses.

" In the night there came to our camp a Chopunnish, who had followed us with the view of accompanying us to the Falls of the Missouri. We now
learned that the two young Indians whom we had
met on the 21st, and detained several days, were
merely going on a party of pleasure to the Ootlashoots, or, as they call them, Shallees, a band of
Tushepahs who live on Clarke's River, near Traveller's Rest. Early the next morning,

" June 27, we resumed our journey over the
heights and steep hills of the same great ridge. At
eight miles' distance we reached an eminence where
the Indians had raised a conical mound of stone, six
or eight feet high, on which was fixed a pine pole
about fifteen feet high. Here we halted and smoked
for some time, at the request of the Indians, who
told us that, in passing the mountains with their families, some men are usually sent on foot from this
place to fish at the entrance of Colt Creek, rejoining
the main party at the Ruamash Glade at the head
of the Kooskooskee. From the elevated point where
we now were, we had a commanding view of the
surrounding mountains, which so completely enclosed us, that, although we had once passed them, we
might have almost despaired of ever escaping from
them but for the assistance of the Indians. The
marks on the trees, which had been our chief dependance, were much fewer and more difficult to be
distinguished than we had expected ; but our guides
traversed this trackless region with a kind of in-
stinctive sagacity : they never hesitated, nor were
they ever embarrassed ; and so unerring was their
course, that wherever the snow had disappeared for
even a hundred paces, they found at once the sum-

mer road. With their aid the snow was scarcely a disadvantage; for, although we were often obliged to slide down, the fallen timber and the rocks, which were now covered, had been much more troublesome when we passed in the autumn. The travelling was, indeed, comparatively pleasant, as well as more rapid, the snow being granular and without crust, and sufficiently hard to prevent the horses from sinking more than two or three inches. After the sun had been on it for some hours it became softer than early in the morning, but the horses were almost always able to get a sure foothold.

"After some time we resumed our route, and at the distance of three miles descended a steep mountain, when, crossing two branches of the Chopunnish River just above their forks, we began to mount a second ridge. Along this we proceeded for some time, and at the distance of seven miles reached our camp of the 16th of September. Near this place we crossed three small branches of the Chopunnish, and then ascended a second dividing ridge, along which we continued for nine miles, when it became somewhat lower, and we halted for the night in a position similar to that where we had encamped the preceding evening.

"We had now travelled twenty-eight miles without taking the loads from our horses or giving them anything to eat ; and as the snow where we halted had not entirely melted, there was but little grass. Among other plants we observed great quantities of the white lily, with reflected petals, which were now in bloom, and in the same forwardness as in the plains on the 10th of May. As for ourselves, our stock of meat being entirely gone, we distributed to each mess a pint of bear's oil, which, with some boiled roots, made an agreeable repast. We saw several black-tailed or mule-deer, but could not get a shot at them, and were informed that there were great numbers of elk in the valley, near the fishery

on the Kooskooskee. The Indians also asserted
that on the mountains to our right there were large
numbers of what they call white buffalo, or mountain sheep. Our horses had strayed some distance
in quest of food, and in the morning,

" June 28, when they were brought in, exhibited
rather a gaunt appearance. The Indians promised,
however, that we should reach some good grass by
noon, and we set out after an early breakfast. Our
route lay along the dividing ridge and across a very
deep hollow, till at the distance of six miles we
reached our camp of the 15th of September. A mile
and a half farther we passed a road from the right,
immediately on the dividing ridge, leading to the
fishery. We went on, as we had done during the
former part of the route, over deep snows, when,
having made thirteen miles, we came to the side of
a mountain just above the fishery, which, having no
timber and a southern exposure, the snow had disappeared from it, and there was an abundance of fine
grass. Our horses were very hungry as well as
greatly fatigued, and as there was no other spot
within our reach this evening where we should find
food for them, we determined to encamp, though it
was not yet midday. As there was no water in the
neighbourhood, we melted snow for cooking, and
early in the morning,

" June 29, continued along the ridge we had been
following for several days, till at the end of five miles
it terminated; and now, bidding adieu to the snows
which we had been traversing, we descended to the
main branch of the Kooskooskee. On reaching the
water side we found a deer which had been left for
us by two of our hunters, who had been despatched
at an early hour to the warm springs, and which
proved a very seasonable addition to our food; for,
having neither meat nor oil, we were reduced to a
diet of roots, without salt or any other addition. At
this place (about a mile and a half from the point

where Quamash Creek falls in from the northeast)
the Kooskooskee is about thirty yards wide, and
runs with great velocity over a bed, like those of all
the mountain streams, composed of pebbles. We
forded the river, and ascended for two miles the
steep acclivities of a mountain, and at its summit
found, coming in from the right, the old road which
we had passed on our route in the autumn. It was
now much plainer and more beaten, which the Indians told us was owing to the frequent visits of the
Ootlashoots from the valley of Clarke's River to the
fishery, though there was no appearance of their
having been here this spring. Twelve miles from
our camp we halted to graze our horses on the flats
of the Quamash Creek. These form a handsome
plain of fifty acres in extent, covered with an abundance of *quamash*, and seem to be one of the principal stopping places of the Indians in crossing the
mountains. We saw here several young pheasants,
and killed one of the small black kind, which was the
first we had observed below the region of snow. In
the neighbourhood were also seen the tracks of two
barefoot Indians, which our companions supposed
to be Ootlashoots who had fled in distress from the
Pahkees. Here, too, we discovered that two of our
horses were missing. We sent two men in quest
of them, and then went on seven miles farther to the
warm springs, where we arrived early in the afternoon. The two hunters who had been sent forward
in the morning had collected no game, nor were several others who went out after our arrival more
successful. We therefore had a prospect of continuing our usual diet of roots, when late in the afternoon the men returned with the stray horses and a
deer for supper.

"These warm springs are situated at the foot of
a hill on the north side of Traveller's Rest Creek,
which is ten yards wide at this place. They issue
from the bottoms and through the interstices of a

gray freestone rock, which rises in irregular masses round their lower side. The principal spring, which the Indians have formed into a bath by stopping the run with stones and pebbles, is of about the same temperature as the warmest bath used at the Hot Springs in Virginia. Captain Lewis could with difficulty remain in it nineteen minutes, and was then affected with a profuse perspiration. The two other springs are much hotter, their temperature being equal to that of the warmest of the Hot Springs in Virginia. Our men, as well as the Indians, amused themselves with going into the bath; the latter, according to the universal custom among them, first entering the hot bath, where they remained as long as they could bear the heat, then plunging into the creek, which was now of an icy coldness, and repeating this operation several times, but always ending with the warm bath."

CHAPTER XIV.

The Party, proceeding on their Journey with their Indian Guides, agree to divide, take separate Routes, and meet again at the Mouth of the Yellowstone River.—Captain Lewis, with nine Men, proceeds up the eastern Branch of Clarke's River, and takes leave of the Indian Guides.—Description of that Branch, and Character of the surrounding Country.— The Cokalahishkit River.—They arrive at the Ridge dividing the Missouri from the Columbia River.—Meet with the Buffalo and Brown Bear.—Immense Herds of Buffalo seen on the Borders of Medicine River.—The Party encamp on White Bear Island.—Singular Adventure that befell M'Neil.—Captain Lewis, with three of his Party, proceeds to explore the Source of Maria's River.—Tansy River.—He reaches the dividing Line of these two Streams.—General Character of the surrounding Country.

THE next day they proceeded along Traveller's Rest Creek, and, after making thirty-two miles,

halted for the night on its south side, near where it
enters Clarke's River. In the course of the day
they killed six deer, of which there were great numbers, as well as bighorn and elk, in the neighbourhood.

"July 1. We had now," continues the Journal,
"made one hundred and fifty-six miles from the
Quamash Flats to the mouth of Traveller's Rest
Creek. Here we proposed to separate; and it was
accordingly resolved to remain a day or two, to refresh ourselves and the horses, which had borne the
journey extremely well, and were still in fine order,
though they required a little rest. We had hoped
to meet some of the Ootlashoots at this place, but
no tracks of them were to be seen. Our Indian
companions expressed much anxiety lest they should
have been cut off by the Pahkees during the winter,
and alluded to the tracks of the two barefooted persons as a proof how much they must have been
distressed.

"We now formed the following plan of operations: Captain Lewis, with nine men, was to pursue
the most direct route to the Falls of the Missouri,
where three of his party were to be left, to prepare
carriages for transporting the baggage and canoes
across the portage. With the remaining six he was
to ascend Maria's River, to explore the country, and
ascertain whether any branch of it reached as far
north as the latitude of fifty degrees, after which he
would descend that river to its mouth. The rest of
the party were to accompany Captain Clarke to the
head of Jefferson River, which Sergeant Ordway
and nine men would descend with the canoes and
other articles deposited there. Captain Clarke's
party, which would then be reduced to ten, would
proceed to the Yellowstone at its nearest approach
to the Three Forks of the Missouri, where he would
build canoes, descend that river with seven of his
party, and wait at its mouth till the rest should join
him. Sergeant Pryor, with the two others, would

take the horses by land to the Mandans, and from that nation go to the British posts on the Assiniboin, with a letter to Mr. Henry, to induce him to endeavour to prevail on some of the Sioux chiefs to accompany him to the city of Washington."

Having concluded on these arrangements, they busied themselves with putting their arms in order : the hunters were also sent out, and had good suc cess in killing deer.

"The Indians who had accompanied us," proceeds the narrative, "proposed leaving us here, in order to seek their friends the Ootlashoots ; but we prevailed on them to accompany Captain Lewis a part of his route, so as to show him the shortest road to the Missouri, and in the mean time amused them with conversation, and with running races both on foot and on horseback, in both of which they proved themselves hardy, athletic, and active. To the chief Captain Lewis presented a small medal and a gun, as a reward for having guided us across the mountains; and, in return, the customary civility was observed of exchanging names, by which the former acquired the title of Yomekollick, or White Bearskin Unfolded. The Chopunnish who had overtaken us on the 26th made us a present of an excellent horse for the good advice we had given him, and as a proof, also, of his attachment to the whites, and of his desire to be at peace with the Pahkees. The next morning,

"July 3, all our preparations being completed, we saddled our horses, and the two parties which had been so long companions now separated, with an anxious hope of soon meeting, after each had accomplished its destined purpose.

"The nine men and five Indians who accompanied Captain Lewis proceeded in a direction due north, down the west side of Clarke's River. Half a mile from the camp we forded Traveller's Rest Creek, and two and a half miles farther passed a western branch of the river: one mile beyond this was a small creek on the eastern side, and a mile lower down, the entrance of the eastern branch of the river. This stream is from ninety to one hundred and twenty yards wide, and its waters, which are discharged through two channels, were more turbid than that of the main river. The latter is one hundred and fifty yards in width, and waters an extensive level plain and prairie, the lower parts of which are ornamented with the long-leafed pine and cottonwood, while the tops of the hills are covered with pine, larch, and fir. We proceeded two miles farther, to a place where the Indians advised us to cross; but, having no boats, and wood being scarce, four hours were spent in collecting sufficient timber to make three small rafts, on which, with some difficulty and danger, we passed the river. We then drove our horses into the water, and they swam to the opposite shore; but the Indians crossed on horseback, drawing, at the same time, their baggage alongside of them, in small vessels made of deerskin. The whole party being now reassembled, we proceeded three miles farther, and encamped about sunset at a small creek. The Indians now pointed out to us a road at no great distance, which, they said, would lead up the eastern branch of Clarke's River, to another river called Cokalahishkit; or the *River of the Road to the Buffaloes*, and thence to Medicine River and the Falls of the Missouri. They added, that not far from the dividing ridge of the waters of Clarke's River and the Missouri the roads forked, and, though both led to the Falls, the left-hand route was the best. The road was so well beaten that we could no longer mistake it, and, having now shown us the way, they were anxious to go on in quest of their friends the Shalees; besides which, they feared, by venturing farther with us, that they might encounter the Pahkees, we having in the afternoon seen the fresh track of a horse, which they believed to be that of a Shalee scout. We could not insist on their remaining longer with us; and as they had so kindly conducted us across the mountains, we were desirous of giving them a supply of provisions, and therefore distributed to them the half of three deer, and our hunters were ordered to go out early in the morning in hopes of adding to the stock.

"The horses suffered so dreadfully from the moschetoes, that we were obliged to kindle large fires, and place the poor animals in the midst of the smoke." * * *

"July 4. We smoked a farewell pipe with our estimable Indian companions, who expressed the greatest regret at parting with us, which they felt the more, because of their fears, which they did not conceal, of our being cut off by the Pahkees. We also gave them a shirt, a handkerchief, and a small quantity of ammunition. The meat which they received from us they dried, and left it at this place as a stock for their homeward journey. This circumstance convinced us that there was no route along Clarke's River to the plains on the Columbia so near or so good as that by which we had come; for, although these people meant to go several days' journey down the former river to look for the Shalees, yet they intended returning home by the same pass of the mountains through which they had conducted us. This route is used also by all the nations with whom we became acquainted west of the mountains that are in the habit of visiting the plains of the Missouri; while, on the other side, all the war-paths of the Pahkees, which run into this valley of Clarke's River, concentrate at Traveller's Rest, beyond which these people have never ventured to the west." * * *

After taking leave of their Indian friends, they proceeded up the eastern branch of Clarke's River for ten miles, when they came to the Cokalahishkit, a deep and rapid stream, sixty yards broad, emptying into it; and turning up this stream in a due east course, at the distance of eight miles they encamped for the night.

The road continued to extend along this river most of the following day, during which they came to a considerable stream emptying into it from the north, which they called Werner's Creek; and, after making a distance of twenty-eight miles, they encamped near the entrance of another creek, to which they gave the name of Seaman's Creek. The country through which they passed consisted of plains and prairies.

" July 6. At sunrise," proceeds the Journal, " we continued our course eastward along the river. At seven miles' distance we passed the north fork of the Cokalahishkit, a deep and rapid stream, forty-five yards in width, and, like the main branch itself, somewhat turbid, though the other streams of this country are clear. Seven miles farther the river enters the mountains, and here end the extensive prairies on this side, though they widen in their course towards the southeast, and form an Indian route to Dearborn's River, and thence to the Missouri. From the multitude of knobs irregularly scattered through this country, Captain Lewis called it the Prairie of the Knobs. It abounds in game, as we saw goats, deer, great numbers of the burrowing squirrels, some curlews, bee-martins, woodpeckers, plover, robins, doves, ravens, hawks, ducks, a variety of sparrows, and yesterday observed swans on Werner's Creek. Among the plants we observed the southern wood, and two other species of shrubs, of which we preserved specimens." * * *

" July 7. We proceeded through a beautiful plain," says the Journal, " on the north side of the river, which seemed here to abound in beaver. On the low grounds there was much timber, and the hills were covered chiefly with pitch pine, that of the long-leafed kind having disappeared since we left the Prairie of the Knobs. At the distance of twelve miles we left the river, or rather the creek, and having for four miles crossed two ridges in a direction north 15° east, again struck to the right, proceeding through a narrow bottom covered with low willows and grass, and abundantly supplied with both deer and beaver. After travelling seven miles we reached the foot of a ridge, which we ascended in a direction north 45° east, through a low gap of easy ascent from the westward; and, on descending it, were delighted at discovering that this was the dividing ridge between the waters of the Columbia and those of the Missouri. From this gap Fort Mountain is about twenty miles in a northeastern direction. We now wound through the hills and mountains, passing several rivulets which ran to the right, and at the distance of nine miles from the gap encamped, having made thirty-two miles. We procured some beaver, and this morning saw tracks of buffalo, from which it appears that those animals do sometimes penetrate a short distance among the mountains.

" July 8. At three miles from our camp we reached a stream issuing from the mountains to the southwest. It contains water only for a width of thirty feet, but its bed is more than three times that breadth, and from the appearance of the roots and trees in the neighbouring bottom, its current must sometimes run with great violence: we called it Dearborn's River. Half a mile farther we observed from a height the Shishequaw Mountain, a high, insulated eminence of a conical form, standing several miles in advance of the eastern range of the Rocky Mountains, and then about eight miles from us, and immediately on our road, which was in a northwest direction. But, as our object was to strike Medicine River, and hunt down to its mouth, we determined to leave the road, and therefore proceeded due north, through an open plain, till we reached Shishequaw Creek, a stream about twenty yards wide, with a

considerable quantity of timber on its low grounds.
Here we halted and dined ; and now felt, by the luxury of our food, that we were approaching once more
the plains of the Missouri, so rich in game. We
saw a great number of deer, goats, and wolves, and
some barking squirrels, and for the first time caught
a distant prospect of two buffalo. After dinner we
followed the Shishequaw for six and a half miles, to
its entrance into Medicine River, and along the banks
of this river for eight miles, when we encamped on
a large island. The bottoms continued low, level,
and extensive ; the plains, too, were level; but the
soil of neither was fertile, as it consisted of a light-
coloured earth intermixed with a proportion of gravel : the grass in both was generally about nine inches high. Captain Lewis here shot a large wolf, remarkable for being almost white. We had made
twenty eight miles." * * *

It rained the whole of the next day, and they advanced but eight miles, over extensive bottom lands
tolerably well supplied with the narrow-leafed cottonwood.

" July 10. We set out early, and proceeded through
a country similar to that of yesterday, with wide-
leafed cottonwood occasionally along the borders of
the bottoms, though for the most part the low grounds
were without timber. In the plains were great
quantities of two species of prickly pear, then in
bloom. Gooseberries of the common red kind were
in abundance, and just beginning to ripen, but there
were no currants. The river had now widened to
a hundred yards ; was deep, crowded with islands,
and in many parts rapid. At the distance of seventeen miles the timber disappeared totally from the
bottoms. About this time the wind, which had before blown on our backs, and put the elk on their
guard, shifted round, and we shot three of them and
a brown bear. Captain Lewis halted to skin them,
while two of the men took the pack-horses forward

to seek for a place to encamp. It was nine o'clock before he overtook them, at the distance of seven miles, in the first grove of cottonwood. They had been pursued as they came along by a very large bear, on which they were afraid to fire, lest their horses, being unaccustomed to the report of a gun, might take fright and throw them. This circumstance reminded us of the ferocity of these animals when we were before near this place, and admonished us to be very cautious. We saw vast numbers of buffalo below us, which kept up a dreadful bellowing during the night. With all our exertions we were unable to advance more than twenty-four miles, owing to the miry state of the ground, occasioned by the rain. The next morning, however,

"July 11, was fair, and enlivened by multitudes of birds, which sang delightfully in the clusters of cottonwood. The hunters were sent down Medicine River in pursuit of elk, while Captain Lewis crossed the high plain, in a direction 75° east, to White Bear Island, a distance of eight miles, and here they joined him. They had seen some elk; but in this neighbourhood the buffalo were in such numbers, that on a moderate computation there could not have been fewer than ten thousand within a circuit of two miles. At this season they are heard bellowing in every direction, so as to form an almost continual roar, which at first alarmed our horses, which, being from the west of the mountains, were unaccustomed to the noise and appearance of these animals. Among the smaller game were the brown thrush, pigeons, doves, and a beautiful bird called the buffalo-pecker.

"Immediately on our arrival we began to hunt, and by three in the afternoon had collected a stock of food and hides sufficient for our purpose. We then made two canoes. one in the form of a basin, like those used by the Mandans, the other consisting of two skins, in a form of our own invention. They were completed the next morning.

" July 12 ; but the wind continued so high that it was not till towards night that we could cross the river in them. In the mean time nearly the whole day was consumed in seeking after our horses, which had disappeared during the night; and seven of them were not recovered at dark, Drewyer being still in quest of them." * * *

" July 13. We formed our camp this morning at our old station, near the head of White Bear Island, and immediately set to work in making gear. On opening the *cache*, we found the bearskins entirely destroyed by the water, which in a flood of the river had penetrated to them. All the specimens of plants, too, were unfortunately lost : the chart of the Missouri, however, still remained unhurt, and several articles contained in trunks and boxes had suffered but little injury ; but a vial of laudanum had lost its stopper, and the liquid had run into a drawer of medicines, which it spoiled beyond recovery. The moschetoes were so troublesome that it was impossible even to write without a moscheto bier. The buffalo were leaving us fast, on their way to the southeast.

" July 14. We continued making preparations for transporting our articles, and, as the old deposite was too damp, we secured the trunks on a high scaffold, covered with skins, among the thick brush on a large island : a precaution against the Indians, should they visit us before the main party arrived. The carriage wheels were in good order, and the iron frame of the boat had not suffered materially. The buffalo had now nearly disappeared, leaving behind them a number of large wolves who were prowling about us.

" July 15. To our great joy, Drewyer now returned from his long search after the horses ; for we had concluded from his protracted stay that he had probably met with a bear, and with his usual intrepidity attacked the animal, in which case, if by any accident he had been separated from his horse, his death was

II.—X

almost inevitable. Under this impression, we had resolved to set out in quest of him, when his return relieved us from our apprehensions. He had searched for two days before he discovered that the horses had crossed Dearborn's River, near a spot where there was an Indian encampment, which seemed to have been abandoned about the time the animals were stolen, and around which so much caution had been used, that no trace of a horse was to be seen within the distance of a quarter of a mile. He crossed the river and pursued the track of these Indians westward, till his horse became so much fatigued that he despaired of overtaking them, and then returned. These Indians we supposed to be a party of Tushepaws, who had ventured out of the mountains to hunt buffalo.

"During the day we were engaged in drying meat and dressing skins. At night M'Neal, who had been sent in the morning to examine the *cache* at the lower end of the portage, returned, but had been prevented from reaching that place by a singular adventure. Just as he arrived near Willow Run, he approached a thicket of brush in which was a white bear, which he did not discover till he was within ten feet of him; when his horse started, and, wheeling suddenly round, threw him almost immediately under the animal. M'Neal started up instantly, and, finding the bear raising himself on his hind feet to attack him, struck him on the head with the butt end of his musket. The blow was so violent that it broke the breech of the musket and knocked the bear to the ground; and, before he recovered, M'Neal sprang into a willow-tree which he saw close by, and remained there, while the bear closely guarded the foot of it, till late in the afternoon. He then went off, when M'Neal came down, and, having found his horse, which had strayed to the distance of two miles, returned to camp. These animals are, indeed, terribly ferocious; and it is matter of wonder, that in all our encounters with them we should have had the good fortune to escape unhurt. We were now troubled with another enemy, not quite so dangerous, though even more disagreeable: these were the moschetoes, which swarmed around us in such myriads that we frequently got them into our throats when breathing, and the dog howled with the torture they occasioned. Having now accomplished the object of our stay, Captain Lewis determined to leave Sergeant Gass, with two men and four horses, to assist the party who were expected, in carrying our effects over the portage, while he, with Drewyer, the two Fields, and six horses, proceeded to the sources of Maria's River. Accordingly, early in the morning,

"July 16, he descended in a skin canoe to the lower side of Medicine River, where the horses had previously been sent, and then rode with his party to the fall of forty-seven feet, where he halted for two hours to dine, and took a sketch of the cascade. In the afternoon they proceeded to the Great Falls, near which they slept, under a shelving rock, with a happy exemption from moschetoes. These falls had lost much of their grandeur since they were before seen, the river being now much lower, though they still formed a most sublime spectacle. As we came along we met several white bears, but they did not venture to attack us. There were but few buffalo, however, they having principally passed the river, and directed their course downward. As usual, there were great numbers of goats and antelopes dispersed over the plains, and we saw large flocks of geese, which raise their young about the entrance of Medicine River. We observed here, also, the cuckoo, or, as it is sometimes called, the raincraw, a bird which is not known either among or west of the Rocky Mountains.

"July 17. After taking a second draught of the Falls, Captain Lewis directed his course north 10°

west, with an intention of striking Maria's River at the point to which he had ascended in 1804. The country here spreads into wide level plains, swelling like the ocean, in which the eye is unattracted by the appearance of a single tree or shrub, and which are diversified only by the moving herds of buffalo. The soil consists of a light-coloured earth, intermixed with a large proportion of coarse gravel, without sand, and is by no means as fertile as either the plains on the Columbia, or those lower down the Missouri. When dry it cracks, and is hard and thirsty, while in its wet state it is soft and slimy like soap. The grass is naturally short, and at this time was still more so, from the recent passage of the buffalo." * * *

"The tribes which principally frequent this country are the Minnetarees of Fort de Prairie and the Blackfoot Indians, both of whom are vicious and profligate rovers; and we had, therefore, everything to fear: not only that they might steal our horses, but even our arms and baggage, if they were sufficiently strong."

After proceeding about twenty miles they came to Tansy River, and as they would not be able to reach Maria's River before night, they encamped there.

"July 18. A little before sunrise," proceeds the Journal, "we started on a course north 25° west, which we continued for six miles, when we reached the top of a high plain which divides the waters of Maria and Tansy Rivers; and a mile farther came to a creek of the former, about twenty-five yards wide, though without water except in a few pools in its bed. Down this creek we proceeded for twelve miles, through thick groves of timber on its banks, passing such immense numbers of buffalo that the whole seemed to be but a single herd. Accompanying them were multitudes of wolves, and besides these we saw some antelope and hare. Af-

ter dinner we left this creek, which we called Buffalo Creek, and, crossing the plain for six miles, came
to Maria's River, where we encamped in a grove of
cottonwood on its western side, keeping watch
through the night lest we should be surprised by the
Indians."

The two following days they continued their journey up Maria's River to the distance of forty-eight
miles, seeing great numbers of wild animals of different kinds, though fewer buffalo than before. The
country was spread out in level, beautiful plains,
though the soil, except on the bottoms, was of inferior quality.

CHAPTER XV.

Captain Lewis and his Party arrive at the Forks of Maria's
River.—Alarmed by the Evidence of being in the Neighbourhood of unfriendly Indians, and distressed for Want of Provisions.—The unfavourable Weather compels them to return.
—Interview with the Minnetarees of Fort de Prairie.—Mutual
Consternation.— Resolution of Captain Lewis.— They encamp together for the Night.—Conversation which ensues.-
Conflict occasioned by the Indians attempting to seize the
Rifles and Horses of the Party, in which one of the former is
mortally wounded.—Captain Lewis kills another Indian, and
his narrow Escape.—Having taken four Horses belonging to
the Indians, they hasten to join the Party with Captain Clarke.
—Arriving near the Missouri, they are alarmed by the Sound
of Rifles, which fortunately proves to be from the Party under
Sergeant Ordway.—The two Detachments thus united, leave
their Horses, and descend the Missouri in Canoes.—Continue
their Route down the River to join Captain Clarke.—Vast
Quantities of Game seen on their Passage.—Captain Lewis
accidentally Wounded by one of his own Party.—They at
length join Captain Clarke.

STARTING at sunrise on the 21st, Captain Lewis
and his party, after proceeding eighteen miles, came
to the forks of Maria's River, the largest branch run-

ning south 75° west towards the mountains, and the other north 40° west. They followed the northern branch, believing it would lead them to the most northerly point of the river, and at the distance of thirteen miles encamped under a cliff on its banks.

Ascending this branch for twenty-eight miles on the following day; they were brought within about ten miles of the foot of the Rocky Mountains ; " and being now able to trace distinctly," says the Journal, " that the point at which the river issues from those mountains was to the south of west, we concluded . that we had reached its most northern point; and as we had ceased to believe that any of its branches extend as far north as the fiftieth degree of latitude, we deemed it useless to proceed farther."

They concluded to remain here two days, to take some observations and rest their horses. Being unable to procure either game or fish, they were much distressed for want of provisions ; and their situation was rendered still more unpleasant by certain evidences that the Minnetarees were at no great distance from them. The weather, also, was cold and rainy, preventing their taking any observation, and detaining them beyond the period they had proposed to stop.

They did not start till the 26th, when, proceeding in nearly a southeast direction across the plains, at twelve miles' distance they came to a branch of Maria's River, " which," says the Journal, " we crossed, and continued along its southern side for two miles, where it is joined by another branch of nearly equal size from the southwest, and far more clear than the north branch, which is turbid, though the beds of both are composed of pebbles. We now decided on pursuing this river to its junction with the fork of Maria's River, which we had ascended, and then crossing the country obliquely to Tansy River, to descend that stream to its confluence with Maria's River. We therefore crossed over and de

scended the river, and at one mile below the junction halted to let the horses graze in a fertile bottom,
in which were some Indian lodges that appeared to
have been inhabited during the last winter." * * *

"At the distance of three miles we ascended the
hills close to the river, while Drewyer proceeded
along its valley on the opposite side. But scarcely
had Captain Lewis reached the high plain, when he
saw, about a mile to his left, a collection of about
thirty horses. He immediately halted, and by the
aid of his spyglass discovered that one half of the
horses were saddled, and that on the eminence
above the horses there were several Indians looking down towards the river, probably at Drewyer.
This was a most unwelcome sight. Their probable
numbers rendered any contest with them of doubt-
ful issue, while to attempt to escape would only invite pursuit, and our horses were so bad that we
must certainly be overtaken ; besides which, Drewyer could not yet be aware that the Indians were
near, and if we ran he would most probably be sacrificed. We determined, therefore, to make the best
of our situation, and advanced towards them in a
friendly manner. The flag which we had brought in
case of any such accident was displayed, and we
continued slowly to approach them. Their attention was so entirely directed to Drewyer that they
did not immediately discover us. As soon as they
did perceive us they appeared to be much alarmed,
and ran about in great confusion: some of them
came down the hill and drove their horses within
gunshot of the eminence, to which they then returned, as if to wait our arrival. When we came
within a quarter of a mile, one of them mounted and
rode at full speed to meet us ; but at the distance of
a hundred paces he halted, and Captain Lewis, who
had alighted to receive him, held out his hand and
beckoned to him to approach : he looked at us for
some time, and then, without saying a word, return-

ed to his companions with as much haste as he had advanced. The whole party now descended the hill and rode towards us. As yet we saw only eight, but presumed that there must be more behind them, as there were other horses saddled. We, however, advanced, and Captain Lewis now told his two men that he feared these were the Minnetarees of Fort de Prairie, who, from their infamous character, would in all probability attempt to rob us; but that, being determined to die rather than lose his papers and instruments, he had made up his mind to resist to the last extremity, and advised them to do the same, and to be on the alert should there be any disposition to attack us.

" When the two parties came within a hundred yards of each other, all the Indians except one halted; Captain Lewis therefore ordered his two men to stop while he advanced alone; and, after shaking hands with the Indian, he went on, and did the same with the others in the rear, the foremost Indian at the same time shaking hands with the two men. They all now came up, and, after alighting, the Indians asked to smoke with us. Captain Lewis, who was very anxious for Drewyer's safety, told them that the man who had gone down the river had the pipe, and requested, as they had seen him, that one of them should accompany Fields to bring him back. To this they assented, and Fields went with a young Indian in search of Drewyer. Captain Lewis now asked them by signs if they were the Minnetarees of the north, and was sorry to learn by their answer that his suspicions were too true. He then inquired if there was any chief among them. They pointed out three; but, though he did not believe them, he thought it best to please them, and gave to one a flag, to another a medal, and to a third a handkerchief. They appeared to be well satisfied with these presents, and soon entirely recovered from the agitation into which our first interview had thrown them; for they were, in fact, more alarmed than we were at the first meeting. In turn, however, we became equally satisfied, on seeing that they were not joined by any more companions; for we considered ourselves quite a match for eight Indians, particularly as only two of them had guns, the rest being armed with eye-dogs and bows and arrows.

" As it was growing late, Captain Lewis proposed that they should encamp together near the river; for he was glad to see them, and had a great deal to say to them. They assented; and being soon joined by Drewyer, we proceeded towards the river, and after descending a very steep bluff, two hundred and fifty feet high, encamped in a small bottom. Here the Indians formed a large semicircular tent of dressed buffalo skins, in which the two parties assembled, and by the help of Drewyer the evening was spent in conversation. The Indians informed us that they were a part of a large band, which at present lay encamped on the main branch of Maria's River, near the foot of the Rocky Mountains, and at the distance of a day and a half's journey from this place. Another numerous party were hunting buffalo near the Broken Mountains, from which they would proceed in a few days to the north of Maria's River. With the first of these there was a white man. They added, that from this place to the establishment at which they traded on the Saskashawan was only six days' easy march, that is, such a day's journey as could be made with their women and children; so that we computed the distance at one hundred and sixty miles. There they carry wolfskins and some beaver, and exchange them for guns, ammunition, blankets, spirituous liquors, and other articles of Indian traffic.

" Captain Lewis, in turn, informed them that he had come from a great distance up the large river which runs towards the rising sun, and that he had been as far as the great lake where the sun sets, that he had seen many nations, the greater part of whom were at war with each other, but that by his mediation they had made peace, and all of them had been invited to come and trade with him east of the mountains; that he was now on his way home, but had left his companions at the Falls while he came in search of the Minnetarees, in the hope of inducing them also to live at peace with their neighbours, and to visit the trading-houses which were about to be established at the entrance of Maria's River. They said that they were anxious to be at peace with the Tushepaws, but that those people had lately killed a number of their relations, as they proved by pointing to several of the party who had their hair cut as a mark of mourning. They were equally willing, they added, to come down and trade with us. Captain Lewis therefore proposed that they should send some of their young men to invite all their band to meet us at the mouth of Maria's River, and that the rest of the party should go with us to that place, where he hoped to find his men, offering them, at the same time, ten horses and some tobacco if they would accompany us. To this, however, they made no reply. Finding them very fond of the pipe, Captain Lewis, who was desirous of keeping a vigilant watch during the night, smoked with them until a late hour, and, as soon as they were all asleep, he awoke R. Fields, and ordering him to rouse us all in case any Indian left the camp, as they would probably attempt to steal our horses, he lay down by the side of Drewyer in the tent with all the Indians, while the two Fields were stretched near the fire at the mouth of it.

"July 27. The Indians got up at sunrise and crowded round the fire, near which J. Fields, who was then on watch, had carelessly left his rifle, by the head of his brother, who was still asleep. One of the Indians slipped behind him, and, unperceived, took his brother's and his own rifle, while at the

same time two others seized those of Drewyer and
Captain Lewis. As soon as Fields turned round he
saw the Indian running off with the rifles, and instantly calling his brother, they pursued him for fifty
or sixty yards, and just as they overtook him, in
the scuffle R. Fields stabbed him through the heart
with his knife: he ran about fifteen steps and fell
dead. They now hastened back with their rifles to
the camp. The moment the fellów touched his gun,
Drewyer, who was awake, jumped up and wrested
it from him. The noise awoke Captain Lewis, who
instantly started from the ground, and reached to
seize his gun; but, finding it gone, he drew a pistol
from his belt, and turning about, saw an Indian running off with it. He followed him and ordered him
to lay it down, which he was doing, just as the two
Fields came up and were taking aim to shoot him;
when Captain Lewis ordered them not to fire, as the
Indian did not appear to intend any mischief. He
dropped the gun, and was going off slowly, when
Drewyer came out and asked permission to kill him;
but this Captain Lewis forbade, as he had not attempted to shoot us. But, finding that the Indians
were now endeavouring to drive off all our horses,
he ordered the men to follow the main party who
were chasing the horses up the river, and to fire instantly upon the thieves; while he, without taking
time to run for his shot-pouch, pursued the fellow
who had stolen his gun and another Indian, who
were driving away the horses on the left of the
camp. He pressed them so closely that they left
twelve of their own horses, but continued to drive
off one of ours. At the distance of three hundred
paces they entered a steep niche in the river bluffs,
when Captain Lewis, being too much out of breath
to pursue them any farther, called out, as he had
done several times before, that unless they gave up
the horse he would shoot them. As he raised his
gun one of them jumped behind a rock, and spoke to

the other, who, stopping at the distance of thirty paces, Captain Lewis shot him in the belly.* He fell on his knees and right elbow, but, raising himself a little, fired, and then crawled behind a rock. The shot had nearly proved fatal; for Captain Lewis, who was bareheaded, felt the wind of the ball very distinctly. Not having his shot-pouch, he could not reload his rifle; and, having only a single charge also for his pistol, he thought it most prudent not to attack them farther, and retired slowly to the camp. He was met by Drewyer, who, hearing the report of the guns, had come to his assistance, leaving the Fields to follow the other Indians. Captain Lewis ordered him to call out to them to desist from the pursuit, as we could take the horses of the Indians in place of our own; but they were at too great a distance to hear him. He therefore returned to the camp, and while he was saddling the horses the Fields returned with four of our own, having followed the Indians until two of them swam the river and two others ascended the hills, so that the horses became dispersed.

"We were, on the whole, rather gainers by the contest, for we had taken four of the Indian horses, and lost only one of our own. Besides which, we found in the camp four shields, two bows with quivers, and one of their guns, which we took with us, and also the flag we had presented to them: the medal we left round the neck of the dead man, that they might be informed who we were. The rest of their baggage, except some buffalo meat, we did not disturb; and as there was no time to be lost, we

---

* In consequence of the death of this man at the hands of Captain Lewis, a treacherous and lurking hostility was excited in the breasts of the Blackfeet (and it is presumed still remains), which induced the American Fur Company to establish a strong fort, with a force of sixty men, at the mouth of Maria's River. This band keep about the head-waters of the Missouri, and come down even to the Arkansas, plundering the Flatheads, Nez-Perces, and Shoshonees —*Irving*. .

mounted our horses, and, after ascending the river hills, took our course through the beautiful level plains in a direction a little to the south of east. We had no doubt but we should be immediately pursued by a much larger party, and that, as soon as intelligence was given to the band near the Broken Mountains, they would hasten to the mouth of Maria's River to intercept us. We hoped, however, to be there before them, so as to form a junction with our friends. We therefore pushed our horses as fast as we possibly could (and, fortunately for us, the Indian horses proved very good), the plains being perfectly level, without many stones or prickly pears, and in fine order for travelling after the late rains. At eight miles from our camp we passed a stream forty yards wide, to which, from the occurrence of the morning, we gave the name of Battle River. At three o'clock we reached Rose River, five miles above where we had formerly passed it; and having now come by estimate sixty-three miles, we halted for an hour and a half to refresh our horses, then pursued our journey seventeen miles farther, when, as the night came on, we killed a buffalo, and again stopped for two hours. The sky was now overcast, but as the moon gave light enough to show us the route, we continued along through immense herds of buffalo for twenty miles, and then, almost exhausted with fatigue, halted at two in the morning,

" July 28, to rest ourselves and the horses. At daylight we awoke, sore, and scarcely able to stand; but as our own lives, as well as those of our companions, depended on our pressing forward, we again mounted our horses and set out. The men were desirous of crossing the Missouri at Grog Spring, where Rose River approaches it so nearly that by passing down the southwest side of it we might avoid the country at the junction of the two rivers, across which the enemy would most probably pursue us. But as this circuitous route would consume the whole day, and the Indians might in the mean time attack the canoes at the point, Captain Lewis stated to his party that it was now their duty to risk their lives for their friends and companions; that they should therefore proceed immediately to the point to give them the alarm; and if they had not yet arrived there, they would raft the Missouri, and, after hiding the baggage, ascend the river on foot through the woods till they should meet them. He told them, also, that it was his determination, in case they were attacked in crossing the plains, to tie the bridles of the horses, and stand together till they had either routed their enemies, or sold their lives as dearly as possible. To this they all assented, and we therefore continued our route to the eastward, till at the distance of twelve miles we came near the Missouri, when we heard a noise which seemed like the report of a gun. We therefore quickened our pace for eight miles farther, and, being about five miles from Grog Spring, now heard distinctly the noise of several rifles from the river. We hurried to the bank, and saw with exquisite satisfaction our friends descending the river. They landed to greet us, and after turning our horses loose, we embarked with our baggage, and went down to the spot where we had made a deposite. This, after reconnoitring the adjacent country, we opened; but, unfortunately, the *cache* had caved in, and most of the articles were injured. We took whatever was still worth preserving, and immediately proceeded to the point, where we found our deposites in good order. By a singular good fortune, we were here joined by Sergeant Gass and Willard from the Falls, who had been ordered to come with the horses here to assist in procuring meat for the voyage, as it had been calculated that the canoes would reach this place much sooner than Captain Lewis's party. After a very heavy shower of rain and hail, attended

with violent thunder and lightning, we started from
the point, and giving a final discharge to our horses,
went over to the island where we had left our red
pirogue, which, however, we found much decayed,
and we had no means of repairing her. We therefore took all the iron work out of her, and, proceeding down the river fifteen miles, encamped near
some cottonwood-trees, one of which was of the
narrow-leafed species, and the first of that kind we
had remarked in ascending the river.

"Sergeant Ordway's party, which had left the
mouth of Madison River on the 13th, had descended
in safety to White Bear Island, where he arrived on
the 19th, and, after collecting the baggage, had left
the falls on the 27th in the white pirogue and five canoes, while Sergeant Gass and Willard set out at
the same time by land with the horses, and thus fortunately met together."

They started the next morning, notwithstanding
a violent storm of rain and hail, having first sent
two canoes ahead for the purpose of hunting elk
and buffalo, which were in immense numbers. The
river was high and the current rapid, and they continued their voyage downward for several days, at
the rate, when the weather would permit, of sixty
or seventy miles a day, passing the mouths of the
Muscleshell, Big Dry, Little Dry, and Porcupine Rivers in their descent.

"August 7. Being resolved," proceeds the Journal, "to reach, if possible, the Yellowstone, a distance of eighty-three miles, in the course of the day,
we set out early, and, being favoured by a rapid current and good oarsmen, proceeded with great speed.
In passing Martha's River, we observed that its
mouth was at present a quarter of a mile lower than
it had been last year. Here we perceived the first
appearance of coal-burned hills and pumice-stone,
which seem always to accompany each other. At
this place, also, were the first elms and dwarf ce-

dars, on the bluffs of the river. The ash, too, made its first appearance in a solitary tree at the Ash Rapid, but was seen occasionally scattered through the low grounds at the Elk Rapid, and thence downward, though it was generally small. The whole country on the northeast side, between Martha and Milk Rivers, is a beautiful level plain, with a soil much more fertile than that higher up. The buffalo, elk, and other animals still continued numerous, as were also the bear, who lie in wait at the crossing places, where they seize elk and the weaker cattle, and then stay by the carcass to keep off the wolves till the whole is devoured. At four o'clock we reached the mouth of the Yellowstone, where we found a note from Captain Clarke, informing us of his intention of waiting for us a few miles below. We therefore left a memorandum for two of our huntsmen, who had been sent out, and who, we now supposed, must be behind us, and then pursued our course till night came on, when, not being able to overtake Captain Clarke, we encamped."

The next day they proceeded nearly to the mouth of Whiteearth River without meeting Captain Clarke, and not knowing what to think of it, they landed and remained for two days, during which they employed themselves in caulking and repairing their canoes, and in preparing skins for clothing.

"August 11. Being anxious," continues the narrative, "to reach the Burned Hills by noon, in order to determine their latitude, we went forward with great rapidity, but by the time we reached that place it was twenty minutes too late to take a meridian altitude. Captain Lewis observing on the opposite side of the river a herd of elk on a sand-bar covered with willows, landed with Cruzatte to hunt them. Each of them fired and shot an elk. They then reloaded, and took different routes in pursuit of the game, when, just as Captain Lewis was taking aim at an elk, a ball struck him in the left thigh, about an inch below the hip joint, and missing the bone, passed through the limb, and grazed the other to some depth. It instantly occurred to him that Cruzatte, whose eyesight was not very good, must have shot him in mistake for an elk, as he was dressed in brown leather. He therefore called out that he was wounded, and looked towards the place from which the shot came : seeing nothing, however, he called on Cruzatte by name several times, but received no answer. As, then, his companion was out of hearing, and the shot appeared not to have come from more than forty paces' distance, he now concluded that it must have been fired by an Indian ; and not knowing how many might be concealed in the bushes, he made towards the pirogue, calling out to Cruzatte to retreat, as there were Indians in the willows. As soon as he reached the pirogue, he ordered the men to arms, and stating to them that he had been wounded by the Indians, though he hoped not mortally, bade them follow him to relieve Cruzatte. They instantly followed for a hundred paces, when his wound became so painful, and his thigh stiffened in such a manner, that he could go no farther. He therefore ordered the men to proceed, and if they should be overpowered by numbers, to retreat towards the boats, keeping up a continual fire ; then limping back to the pirogue, he made ready his rifle, pistol, and air-gun, determined to sell his life dearly in case the men should be overcome. In this state of anxiety and suspense he remained for about twenty minutes, when the party returned with Cruzatte, and reported that no Indians were to be seen in the neighbourhood. Cruzatte was now much alarmed, and declared that he had shot at an elk, as he supposed, after Captain Lewis had left him, but disclaimed all idea of having intentionally wounded his officer. There was now no doubt but the shot had come from him ; yet, as it seemed to be perfectly accidental, and he had always conducted himself with propriety, no farther notice

II.—Y

was taken of it.   The wound was dressed, and pat-
ent lint put into the holes.   It bled considerably, but
as the ball had touched no bone or artery, it was
hoped it would not prove fatal.   As it was now rendered impossible for him, however, to take the observations he had proposed, to determine the latitude
of the Burned Hills, which was chiefly desirable from
their being at the most northern point of the Missouri, he declined remaining till the next day, and proceeded on till evening.   As he could not now be removed without great pain, and had a high fever, he
remained on board during the night, and early the
next morning,

"August 12, we proceeded on with as much expedition as possible.   Soon after starting we went on
shore to visit a camp, which we found to be that of
Dickson and Hancock, the two Illinois traders, who
told us that they had seen Captain Clarke the day
before.   While stopping here we were overtaken
by our two hunters, Colter and Collins, who had
been missing since the 3d.   They stated that, after
following us the first day, they concluded we must
be behind, and waited for us several days, until they
became convinced of their mistake, when they came
on as rapidly as they could.   We made some presents
to the two traders, and then proceeded till one
o'clock, when we joined our friends and companions
under Captain Clarke "

CHAPTER XVI.

The Party commanded by Captain Clarke proceed along Clarke's River.—Their sorry Commemoration of the 4th of July.—Instance of Sacajawea's Strength of Memory.—De scription of the River and of the surrounding Country, as the Party proceed.—Horses missing, and supposed to be stolen by the Indians.—They reach Wisdom River.—Extraordinary Heat of a Spring.—Fondness of the Party for Tobacco.—Sergeant Ordway recovers the Horses.—Captain Clarke divides his Party, one detachment to descend the River.—They reach Gallatin and Jefferson Rivers.—Arrive at the Yellowstone River.—Otter and Beaver Rivers.—Indian Fortification. —One of the Party accidentally wounded.—Engaged in building Canoes.—Twenty-four Horses stolen, probably by the Indians.

" July 3. On taking leave of Captain Lewis and the Indians, the division under Captain Clarke, consisting of fifteen men, with fifty horses, set out through the valley of Clarke's River, along the western side of which they rode in a southern direction. This valley is from ten to fifteen miles in width, tolerably level, and partially covered with the longleafed and the pitch pine, with some cottonwood, birch, and sweet willow on the borders of the streams." * * * "After crossing eight different streams of water, four of which were small, they halted at the distance of eighteen miles, on the upper side of a large creek, where they let their horses graze, and after dinner continued their journey in the same direction eighteen miles farther, when they encamped on the north side of a large creek. The valley became more beautiful as they advanced, and was diversified by a number of small open plains, abounding with grass and a variety of sweet-scented plants, and watered by ten streams rushing from

the western mountains with considerable velocity.
These mountains were covered with snow about
one fifth of their way from the top, and some snow
was still to be seen on the high points, and in the
hollows of the mountains to the eastward."

The following day they continued their route up
the valley, which became narrower as they advanced. They were obliged to ford several rapid creeks
on their way, and at the distance of thirty miles encamped on the western branch of Clarke's River.
Crossing the river the next morning, after proceeding one mile they came to its eastern branch, which
they ascended to the foot of the mountain; and, having ascertained that it took its rise in a high, peaked
mountain about twenty miles to the northeast of the
valley, they stopped for the night. "As soon as they
halted," proceeds the narrative, "several men were
despatched in different directions to examine the
road, and from their report it was concluded that the
best path would be one about three miles up the
stream. This was the road travelled by the Ootlashoots, and would certainly shorten the route two
days at least, besides being much better, as they had
been informed by the Indians, than that by which
we had advanced in the fall.

"July 6. The night was very cold, succeeded by
frost in the morning ; and as the horses were much
scattered, the party were not able to set out before
nine o'clock. They then went along the stream for
three miles, and leaving to the right the path by
which they had come in the fall, followed the road
taken by the Ootlashoots, up a gentle ascent to the
dividing mountain which separates the waters of
the middle fork of Clarke's River from those of
Wisdom and Lewis Rivers. On reaching the other side they came to Glade Creek, down which they
proceeded, crossing it frequently into the glades on
each side, where the timber was small, and in many
places destroyed by fire : there were great quantities

of *quamash* then in bloom. Throughout the glades were great numbers of holes made by the whistling or burrowing squirrel ; and they killed a hare of the large mountain species. Along these roads there were also appearances of old buffalo paths, and some old heads of buffaloes ; and as these animals evince wonderful sagacity in the choice of their routes, the coincidence of a buffalo with an Indian track affords the strongest evidence that it is the best. In the afternoon they passed along the hill side, north of the creek, for six miles, when they entered an extensive level plain. Here the Indian tracks scattered so much that they were wholly at a loss which to follow ; but Sacajaweah recognised the plain immediately. She had travelled it often during her childhood, and informed them that it was greatly resorted to by the Shoshonees, who came here for the purpose of gathering *quamash* and of taking beaver, with which the plain abounded ; that Glade Creek was a branch of Wisdom River, and that, on reaching the more elevated part of the plain, they would see a gap in the mountains, on the route to the canoes, and from that gap the high point of a mountain covered with snow. At the distance of a mile they passed over a large creek from the right ; also Fish Creek, coming from a snowy mountain, across which there was a gap. Soon after, on ascending some rising ground, the country spread itself into a beautiful plain, extending north and south about fifteen miles wide and thirty in length, and surrounded on all sides by high points of mountains covered with snow, among which was the gap pointed out by the squaw, bearing south 56° east. . They had not gone two miles from the last creek when they were overtaken by a violent storm of wind, accompanied by a heavy fall of rain, which lasted an hour and a half. Having no shelter, they formed a solid column to protect themselves from the gust, and then went on five miles to a small creek, where, finding some

wood, they encamped for the night, and dried themselves.   Here they observed fresh signs of Indians,
who had been gathering *quamash*. Their distance
was twenty-six miles.   In the morning,

" July 7, their horses were so much scattered, that,
although they sent out hunters to range the country
in every direction for six or eight miles, nine of
them were still missing.   They were the most valuable ones of all, and so much attached to some of
their companions that it was difficult to separate
them in the daytime.   It was therefore concluded
that they must have been stolen by some roving Indians, and, accordingly, a party of five men was left
to continue the pursuit, while the rest went on to
the spot where the canoes had been deposited. They
set out at ten o'clock, and pursued a course south
50° east across the valley, which they found to be
watered by four large creeks, with extensive, low,
miry bottoms, till they reached Wisdom River, along
the northeast side of which they continued, when,
at the distance of sixteen miles, they came to the
three branches.   Near that place they stopped for
dinner at a hot spring situated in the open plain.
The bed of the spring is about fifteen yards in circumference, and composed of loose, hard, gritty
stones, through which the water boils in large quantities.   It is slightly impregnated with sulphur, and
so hot that a piece of meat, about the size of three
fingers, was completely done in twenty-five minutes.
After dinner they proceeded across the eastern
branch and along the north side of the middle branch
for nine miles, when they reached the gap in the
mountains, and took a final leave of this extensive
valley, which they called the Hot-spring Valley. It
is, indeed, a beautiful country : though enclosed by
mountains covered with snow, the soil is exceedingly fertile, and well supplied with esculent plants,
while its numerous creeks furnish immense quantities of beaver.   Another valley less extensive and

more rugged opened itself to their view as they
passed through the gap; but, as they had made twenty-five miles, and the night was advancing, they halted near some fine springs which fall into Willard's
Creek. After a cold night, during which their horses
separated and could not be collected till eight o'clock
in the morning,

" July 8, they crossed the valley along the southwest side of Willard's Creek for twelve miles, when
it entered the mountains, and then, turning S. 20°
E., they came to the Shoshonee Cove after riding
seven miles; thence they proceeded down the west
branch of Jefferson River, and at the distance of
nine miles reached its forks, where we had deposited our merchandise in the month of August. Most
of the men were in the habit of chewing tobacco;
and such was their eagerness to procure it after so
long a privation, that they scarcely waited to take
the saddles from their horses before they ran eager-
ly to the cave, and were delighted at being able to
resume this fascinating indulgence. This, indeed,
was one of the most trying privations they had encountered. Some of the men, whose tomahawks
were so formed as to answer the purpose of pipes,
even broke the handles of these weapons, cut them
into small fragments, and chewed them; the wood
having, by frequent smoking, become strongly impregnated with the taste of that plant. They found
everything safe, though some of the goods were a
little damp, and one of the canoes had a hole in it.
The ride of this day was twenty-seven miles in
length, through a country diversified by low, marshy
grounds, and high, open, stony plains, terminated by
lofty mountains, on the tops and along the northern
sides of which the snow still remained. Over the
whole were scattered great quantities of hyssop, and
the different species of shrubs common to the plains
of the Missouri.

" They had now crossed from Traveller's Rest

Creek to the head of Jefferson's River, which seems to form the best and shortest route over the mountains during almost the whole distance of one hundred and sixty-four miles. It is, in fact, a very excellent road; and by cutting down a few trees it might be rendered a good route for wagons, with the exception of about four miles over one of the mountains, which would require some levelling."

The next day was spent in raising and repairing the canoes, and in the course of it they were joined by Sergeant Ordway with the missing horses.

"July 10. This morning," says the Journal, "a white frost covered the ground, the grass was frozen, and the ice three quarters of an inch thick in a basin of water. The boats were now loaded, and Captain Clarke divided his men into two bands, one to descend the river with the baggage, while he, with the other, should proceed on horseback to the Yellowstone. After breakfast the two parties set out, those on shore skirting the eastern side of Jefferson River, through Service Valley, and over Rattlesnake Mountain, into a beautiful and extensive country, known among the Indians by the name of Hahnahappapelah, or Beaverhead Valley, from the number of those animals found in it, and also from a point of land resembling the head of a beaver. It extends from Rattlesnake Mountain as low as Frazier's Creek, and is about fifty miles in length in a direct line, while its width varies from ten to fifteen miles, being watered in its whole course by the Jefferson, and six different creeks. This valley is open and fertile, and, besides the vast numbers of beaver and otter on its creeks, the bushy low grounds are a favourite resort for deer, while on the higher parts of the valley were seen scattered groups of antelopes, and beyond, on the steep sides of the mountains, many of the bighorn, taking refuge there from the wolves and bears. At the distance of fifteen miles the two parties stopped to dine, when Captain

Clarke, finding that the river became wider and deeper, and that the canoes could advance more rapidly than the horses, determined to proceed himself by water, leaving Sergeant Pryor, with six men, to bring on the horses. They resumed their journey after dinner, and encamped on the eastern side of the river, opposite to the head of Three-thousand-mile Island."

The two following days they continued to descend the river, passing Philanthropy and Wisdom Rivers, and seeing great numbers of beaver as they passed along.

"July 13. Early in the morning," continues the narrative, "they set out, and at noon reached the entrance of Madison River, where Sergeant Pryor had arrived with the horses about an hour before; and, having driven them across Madison and Gallatin Rivers, just below the mouth of the latter the party halted to dine and unload the canoes. Here they again separated; Sergeant Ordway, with nine men, setting out in six canoes to descend the river, while Captain Clarke, with the remaining ten, the wife and child of Chaboneau, and fifty horses, were to proceed by land to the Yellowstone. They set out at five in the afternoon from the forks of the Missouri, in a direction nearly east; but, as many of the horses had sore feet, they were obliged to move slowly, and after going four miles halted for the night on the bank of Gallatin River. This is a beautiful stream, and though rapid, and obstructed by islands near its mouth, is navigable for canoes. On its lower side the land rises gradually to the foot of a mountain, running almost parallel with it; but the country below it and Madison River is a level plain, covered with short grass, the soil being poor, and encumbered with stones and strata of hard white rock along the hill sides. Throughout the whole, game was very abundant. They obtained deer in the low grounds; beaver and otter were seen

II.—Z

in Gallatin River; and elk, wolves, eagles, hawks, crows, and geese were noticed at different points on the route. The plain was intersected by several great roads, leading to a gap in the mountain about twenty miles distant, in a direction E.N.E.; but the Indian woman, who was acquainted with the country, recommended another gap more to the south, through which Captain Clarke determined to proceed."

They started early the next morning, and, pursuing the route recommended by the squaw, came in the afternoon to the three forks of Gallatin River, and in the evening encamped at the entrance of the gap previously mentioned by her.

"July 15. After an early breakfast," says the Journal, "they proceeded through this gap to the heads of the eastern fork of Gallatin River, near which they had encamped the evening before, and at the distance of six miles reached the top of the dividing ridge which separates the waters of the Missouri and the Yellowstone, on descending which ridge they struck one of the streams of the latter river. They followed its course through an open country, with high mountains on each side partially covered with pine, and watered by several streams, - crowded, as usual, with beaver dams. Nine miles from the summit of the ridge they reached the Yellowstone itself, about a mile and a half below where it issues from the Rocky Mountains. It now appeared that the communication between the two rivers was short and easy. The distance from the head of the Missouri at its three forks to this place is forty-eight miles, the greater part of which is through a level plain; while from the forks of the eastern branch of Gallatin River, which is there navigable for small canoes, to this part of the Yellowstone, it is no more than eighteen miles, with an excellent road over a high, dry country, the hills being of inconsiderable height, and easily passable. They halted for three hours to rest their horses, and then pursued the buffalo road along the bank of the river. "Although but just emerging from a high snowy mountain, the Yellowstone is here a bold, rapid, and deep stream, one hundred and twenty yards in width. The bottoms along its course are narrow within the mountains, but widen to the extent of nearly two miles in the valley below, where they are occasionally overflowed, and the soil gives growth to cottonwood, rose-bushes, honeysuckle, rushes, common coarse grass, a species of rye, and various productions found on moist lands. On each side these low grounds are bordered by dry plains of coarse gravel and sand, stretching back to the foot of the mountains, and supplied with a very short grass. The mountains on the east side of the river are rough and rocky, and were still covered with great quantities of snow; while two other high, snowy mountains were seen, one bearing north fifteen or twenty miles, the other nearly east. They had no covering except a few scattered pine, nor, indeed, could they discover any timber fit even for a small canoe." At the distance of nine miles from the mountain they passed a bold, deep stream from the northwest, discharging itself into the Yellowstone, and to which they gave the name of Shields's River.

They continued their course along the river the following day, their horses being unable to travel fast in consequence of the soreness of their feet, and halted in the evening after having made twenty-six miles. On the 17th they passed two large creeks, entering the Yellowstone nearly opposite to each other; the one coming from the northeast they called Otter, and that on the other side Beaver River. " The river," says the Journal, " was now becoming more divided by islands, and a number of small creeks fell into it on both sides. The largest of these was about seven miles from Beaver River, entering on the right : they called it Bratton's River,

from one of the men. The highlands, too, approached more nearly than before; but, although their sides
were partially supplied with pine and cedar, the
growth was too small for canoes. The buffalo were
beginning to be more abundant, and for the first
time on this river they saw a pelican; but deer and
elk were now more scarce than before. In one of
the low bottoms of the river was an Indian fort,
which seemed to have been built during the previous
summer. It.was in the form of a circle, about fifty
feet in diameter, five feet high, and formed of logs
lapped over each other, covered on the outside with
bark set on end. The entrance was guarded by a
work on each side of it facing the river. These intrenchments, the squaw informed us, were frequently made by the Minnetarees and other Indians at war
with the Shoshonees, when pursued by their enemies on horseback."

Gibson, one of the party, was so badly hurt the
following day, by falling on a sharp point of wood,
that he was unable to sit on his horse, and they
were obliged to form a sort of litter for him, so that
he could lie nearly at full length. The wound became so painful, however, after proceeding a short
distance, that he could not bear the motion, and they
left him with two men, while Captain Clarke went
to search for timber large enough to form canoes.
He succeeded in finding some trees of sufficient size
for small canoes, two of which he determined to
construct, and by lashing them together hoped to
make them answer the purpose of conveying the
party down the river, while a few of his men should
conduct the horses to the Mandans. All hands,
therefore, were set busily to work, and they were
employed in this labour for several days. In the
mean time no less than twenty-four of their horses were missing, and they strongly suspected had
been stolen by the Indians, for they were unable to
find them, notwithstanding they made the most diligent search.

" July 23. A piece of a robe and a moccasin," says the Journal, "were discovered this morning not far from the camp. The moccasin was worn out in the sole, and yet wet, and had every appearance of having been left but a few hours before. This was conclusive that the Indians had taken our horses, and were still prowling about for the remainder, which fortunately escaped last night by being in a small prairie surrounded by thick timber. At length Labiche, one of our best trackers, returned from a very wide circuit, and informed Captain Clarke that he had traced the horses bending their course rather down the river towards the open plains, and from their tracks, must have been going very rapidly. All hopes of recovering them were now abandoned. Nor were the Indians the only plunderers around our camp; for in the night the wolves or dogs stole the greater part of the dried meat from the scaffold. The wolves, which constantly attend the buffalo, were here in great numbers, as this seemed to be the commencement of the buffalo country." * * *

"At noon the two canoes were finished. They were twenty-eight feet long, sixteen or eighteen inches deep, and from sixteen to twenty-four inches wide; and, having lashed them together, everything was ready for setting out the next day, Gibson having now recovered. Sergeant Pryor was directed, with Shannon and Windsor, to take the remaining horses to the Mandans, and if he should find that Mr. Henry was on the Assiniboin River, to go thither and deliver him a letter, the object of which was to prevail on the most distinguished chiefs of the Sioux to accompany him to Washington.'

CHAPTER XVII.

Captain Clarke proceeds down the River.—Description of an Indian Lodge.—Sergeant Pryor arrives with the Horses.—Remarkable Rock seen by Captain Clarke, and the Beauty of the Prospect from its Summit.—Yellowstone and Bighorn Rivers compared.—Immense Herds of Buffalo.—Fierceness of the White Bear.—Encamp at the Junction of the Yellowstone and Missouri.—General Outline given of the Yellowstone River.—Sufferings of the Party from the Moschetoes.—Sergeant Pryor arrives, and reports that the Horses were all stolen by the Indians.—In this Emergency they make Canoes of Skins, in which they descend the River over the most difficult Shoals and Rapids.—Unexpectedly meet with two White Men, from whom they procure Intelligence in relation to the Indians formerly visited by the Party.

"July 24. The canoes were loaded, and Sergeant Pryor and his party set out, with orders to proceed down to the entrance of Bighorn River, which was supposed to be at no great distance, where they would be taken in the boats across the Yellowstone. At eight o'clock Captain Clarke embarked, and proceeded on very steadily down the river. which contained a number of islands, some of which were supplied with a growth of small timber. At the distance of a mile from the camp, the river passed along a high bluff for about twenty-three miles, when the bottoms widened on both sides; and twenty-nine miles farther, a stream fell into it from the south, which was supposed to be the Bighorn; but afterward, when the Bighorn was found, the name of Clarke's Fork was given to this stream. It is a bold river, one hundred and fifty yards wide at the entrance, but a short distance above is contracted to a hundred yards. The water is of a light muddy colour, and much colder than that of the Yellowstone, and its general course is southeasterly from the Rocky Mountains. There is a small island situated immediately at its entrance, and this or the adjoining mainland would form a very good position for a fort. The country most frequented by the beaver begins here, and that which lies between this river and the Yellowstone is perhaps the best district for the hunters of that animal. About a mile before reaching this river there was a ripple in the Yellowstone, on passing which the canoes took in some water. The party therefore landed to bale out the boats, and then proceeded six miles farther to a large island, where they halted for the purpose of waiting for Sergeant Pryor. It is a beautiful spot, with a rich soil, covered with wild rye, and a species of grass like the blue grass, and some of another kind, which the Indians wear in plaits round the neck, on account of its fragrance, resembling that of the vanilla. There is also a thin growth of cottonwood. In the centre was a large Indian lodge, which seemed to have been built during the preceding summer. It was in the form of a cone, sixty feet in diameter at the base, composed of twenty poles, each forty-five feet long, and two and a half in circumference, and the whole structure covered with bushes. The interior was curiously ornamented. On the tops of the poles were feathers of eagles, and circular pieces of wood, with sticks across them in the form of a girdle. From the centre was suspended a stuffed buffalo skin; fronting the door was hung a cedar bush; on one side of the lodge, a buffalo's head; and on the other, several pieces of wood were stuck in the ground. From its whole appearance, it was more like a building for holding councils than an ordinary lodge. Sergeant Pryor not having yet arrived, they went on about fifteen and a half miles farther, to a small creek on the right, to which they gave the name of Horse Creek, and just below it overtook him with the horses. He had found it almost impossible, with two men, to drive them on; for, as soon as they discovered a herd of buffalo, the loose horses, having been trained to hunting this animal by the Indians, immediately set off in pursuit, and surrounded the herd with almost as much skill as their riders could have done. At last he was obliged to send one horseman forward, to drive all the buffalo from their route. The horses were here driven across, and Sergeant Pryor started again, with an additional man to his party." As they proceeded, the river deepened and became more navigable; they passed a creek coming from the southeast, which they called Pryor's Creek, and landed in the evening after having made sixty-nine and a half miles.

"July 25. At sunrise they resumed their voyage, and passed a number of small islands and streams, and occasionally high bluffs, composed of a yellow gritty stone. After proceeding a short distance they were overtaken by a storm of rain, with a high southwest wind, which obliged them to land, and form a sort of log hut covered with deerskins. As soon as it ceased they went on; and at about four o'clock, after having made forty-nine miles, Captain Clarke landed to examine a very remarkable rock, situated in an extensive bottom on the right, about two hundred and fifty paces from the shore. It is nearly two hundred paces in circumference, two hundred feet high, and accessible only from the northeast, the other sides consisting of perpendicular cliffs of a light-coloured gritty stone. The soil on the summit is five or six feet deep, of a good quality, and covered with short grass. The Indians have carved the figures of animals and other objects on the sides of the rock, and on the top are raised two piles of stones. From this height the eye ranged over a wide extent of variegated country. On the southwest were the Rocky Mountains covered with snow; there was a low mountain about forty miles distant, in a direction north 55° west; and at the distance of thirty-five miles, the southern extremity of what are called the Little Wolf Mountains. The low grounds of the river extended nearly six miles to the southward, when they rose into plains reaching to the mountains, and were watered by a large creek; while at some distance below, a range of highland, covered with pine, stretched on both sides of the river in a direction north and south. The north side of the river, for some distance, is here surrounded by jutting romantic cliffs, succeeded by rugged hills, beyond which the plains are again open and extensive, and the whole country was enlivened by herds of buffalo, elk, and wolves. After enjoying the prospect from this rock, to which Captain Clarke gave the name of Pompey's Pillar, he descended and continued his route. At the distance of six or seven miles he stopped to secure two bighorns which had been shot from the boat; and while on shore, saw, in the face of the cliff on the left, about twenty feet above the water, a fragment of the rib of a fish, three feet long and nearly three inches round, incrusted in the rock itself, and which, though neither decayed nor petrified, was very rotten. After making fifty-eight miles they reached the entrance of a stream on the right, about twenty-two yards wide, where they encamped.

"July 26. They started early the next morning. The river was now much divided by stony islands and bars, but the current, though swift, was regular, and there were many very handsome islands covered with cottonwood. On the left shore the bottoms were very extensive; the right bank was formed of high cliffs of a whitish gritty stone; and beyond, the country on both sides was diversified with waving plains covered with pine." * * * "At length, after coming sixty-two miles, they landed at the entrance of the Bighorn River; but finding the point between the two composed of soft mud and sand, and liable

to be overflowed, they ascended the Bighorn for
half a mile, then crossed, and formed a camp on its
lower side." * * * "At their junction the two rivers are nearly equal in breadth, extending from two
hundred to two hundred and twenty yards; but the
Yellowstone contains much more water, being ten
or twelve feet deep, while the depth of the Bighorn
varies from five to seven feet. This is the river
which had been described by the Indians as rising in
the Rocky Mountains near the Yellowstone and the
sources of the Platte, and then finding its way
through the Côte Noir and the eastern range of the
Rocky Mountains. In its long course it receives
two large rivers, one from the north and the other
from the south, and being unobstructed by falls, is
navigable in canoes for a great distance, through a
fine, rich, open country, supplied with a great quantity of timber, and inhabited by beaver and numerous species of other animals, among which are those
from which it derives its name of Bighorn. There
are no permanent settlements near it; but the whole
country watered by it is occasionally visited by
roving bands of hunters of the Crow Tribe, by the
Paunch Indians, also a band of Crows, and by the
Castahanas, a small band of the Snake Indians.

"July 27. They again set out very early, and on
leaving the Bighorn, took a last look at the Rocky
Mountains, which had been constantly in view from
the 1st of May. The river now widened to the extent of from four to six hundred yards, was much
divided by islands and sand-bars, and its banks were
generally low and falling in, and resembled those of
the Missouri in many particulars; but its islands
weremore numerous, its waters less muddy, and its
current more rapid." * * * "Throughout the country there were vast numbers of buffalo, which kept
up a continued bellowing. Large herds of elk, also,
were lying on every point, and were so gentle that
they might be approached within twenty paces with-

)ut being alarmed. Several beaver, likewise, were seen in the course of the day. Deer, however, were by no means abundant, and antelopes as well as the bighorns were scarce." They made this day eighty and a half miles, and encamped on a large island in the evening.

"July 28. At daylight the next morning they proceeded down the smooth, gentle current, passing by a number of islands, and several creeks which were now dry. These are, indeed, more like the beds of the dry brooks of the Missouri, merely serving to carry off the vast quantities of water which fall on the plains, and bringing down also a great deal of mud, which contributes to the discoloration of the Yellowstone. The largest of these are, at the distance of six miles, a creek eighty yards in width, coming from the northwest, and called by the Indians Little Wolf River; twenty-nine miles lower, another on the left, seventy yards in width, which they named Table Creek, from several mounds in the plains to the northwest, the tops of which resemble a table; and four miles farther, a stream of more importance, entering behind an island from the south. This last is about one hundred yards in width, with a bold current of muddy water, and is probably the river called by the Indians the Little Bighorn. There is also another stream on the right, twenty-five yards wide, the Indian name of which is Mashaskap. Nearly opposite to this creek they encamped, after making seventy-three miles."

The channel was now from five hundred yards to half a mile in width. They continued to pass the beds of rivers that were then dry; and in the evening of the 29th, after making forty-one miles, they encamped opposite to the entrance of a stream coming from the right, called by the Indians Lazeka, or Tongue River.

"July 30. They set out at an early hour, and after passing, at the distance of twelve miles, the bed of a river one hundred yards wide, but then nearly dry, reached, two miles below it, a succession of bad shoals, extending for six miles, the rock near their termination stretching nearly across the river, with a descent of about three feet. At this place they were obliged to let their canoes down by hand, for fear of their striking on some concealed rock; though, with a perfect knowledge of the shoals, a large canoe might be navigated down with safety. This is the most difficult part of the Yellowstone River, and they called it the Buffalo Shoal, from the circumstance of one of those animals being found there. The neighbouring cliffs on the right are about one hundred feet high, while on the left the country is low, but gradually rises, and at some distance from the shore presents the first appearance of burned hills to be seen on the Yellowstone." Twenty miles beyond they came to a rapid with a channel that was easily navigable on the left, and which they called Bear Rapid. They landed for the night about a mile and a half below the mouth of a stream coming in from the right, one hundred yards in width, to which they gave the name of the Redstone River, having made during the day forty-eight miles.

"July 31. During the whole night," continues the Journal, "the buffalo were hovering about the camp, and excited much alarm lest they should tread on the boats and split them to pieces. They set out, as usual, and at the distance of two miles passed a rapid that was not very formidable, which they called Wolf Rapid. At this place commences a range of highlands. They have no timber, and are composed of earth of different colours, without much rock, but supplied throughout with great quantities of coal or carbonated wood. After passing these hills the country again opens into extensive plains, like those passed the previous day, the river being diversified with islands, and having a great number of wide, but then nearly dry, brooks on either side.

Thus eighteen miles below their camp there was a shallow, muddy stream on the left, one hundred yards wide, and supposed to be that known among the Indians by the name of Saasha, or Little Wolf River; five miles below, on the right, another, forty yards wide and four feet in depth, which, from the steep coal-banks on each side, they called Oakta-roup, or Coal River; and eighteen miles farther, a third, sixty yards in width, to which they gave the name of Gibson's River. Having made sixty-six miles, they stopped for the night; and just as they landed, perceived a white bear, which was larger than any of the party had before seen, devouring a dead buffalo on a sand-bar. Though they fired two balls into him, still he swam to the mainland and walked along the shore. Captain Clarke pursued him; and lodged two more balls in his body; he bled profusely, but still made his escape, as the night prevented them from following him."

The next day, August 1st, they had a strong head wind, which retarded their progress, and their situation was rendered very uncomfortable by continual rain. " The current of the river," proceeds the Journal, " was less rapid, had more soft mud, and was more obstructed by sand-bars, and the rain had greatly increased the quantity of water in the brooks. Buffalo now appeared in vast numbers. A herd happened to be crossing the river ; and such was the multitude of these animals, that for a mile in length, down the river, the herd stretched as thick as they could swim, completely from one side to the other, and the party were obliged to stop for an hour. They consoled themselves for the delay by killing four of them, and then proceeded, till at the distance of forty-five miles they reached an island, below which two other herds of buffalo, as numerous as the first, soon afterward crossed the river.*

* The Indians and hunters frequently destroy these animals in the most wanton manner. " I have seen dozens of buffalo,"

"August 2. The river was now about a mile wide less rapid, and more divided by islands, and bars of sand and mud, than heretofore ; the low grounds, too, were more extensive, and contained a greater quantity of cottonwood, ash, and willows. On the northwest was a low, level plain, and on the southeast some rugged hills, on which we saw, without being able to approach them, some bighorns. Buffalo and elk, as well as their pursuers, the wolves, were in great numbers. On each side of the river there were several dry beds of streams, but the only one of any considerable size was one to which they gave the name of Ibex River, on the right, about thirty yards wide, and sixteen miles from their encampment of the preceding night. The bear, which had given them so much trouble at the head of the Missouri, they found equally fierce here. One of these animals, which was on a sand-bar as the boat passed, raised himself on his hind feet, and after looking at the party for a moment, plunged in and swam towards them ; but, after receiving three balls in the body, he turned and made for the shore. Towards evening they saw another enter the water to swim across ; when Captain Clarke directed the boat towards the shore, and just as the animal landed shot it in the head. It proved to be the largest female they had ever seen, and was so old that its tusks were worn quite smooth. The boats escaped with difficulty between two herds of buffalo that were crossing the river, and came near being again detained by them. Among the elk of this neighbourhood they saw an unusual number of males, while higher up the herds consisted chiefly of females.

says Townsend, " slaughtered merely for the tongues or for practice with the rifle, and I have also lived to see the very perpetrators of these deeds lean and lank with famine, when the meanest and most worthless parts of the poor animals they had so inhumanly slaughtered would have been received and eaten with humble thankfulness."

After making eighty-four miles, they encamped among some ash and elm trees on the right. They might be said rather to have passed the night than slept there, however, for the moschetoes were so troublesome that scarcely any of the party closed their eyes.

"August 3. They set out early in the morning to escape the persecution of the moschetoes. At the distance of two miles they passed Field's Creek, a stream thirty-five yards wide, which enters on the right, immediately above a high bluff which is rapid ly sinking into the river. Here Captain Clarke went ashore in pursuit of some bighorns, but the mosche- toes were so numerous that he was unable to aim with certainty. He therefore returned to the ca- noes ; and, observing a ram of the same species soon after, he sent on shore one of the hunters, who shot it, and it was preserved as a specimen. Eight miles below Field's Creek they reached the junction of the Yellowstone and the Missouri, and landed at the point where they had encamped on the 26th of April the previous year. The canoes were now un- loaded, and the baggage exposed to dry, as many of the articles were wet, and some of them quite spoiled.

" The *Rochejaune*, or Yellowstone River, according to the Indian accounts, has its remote sources in the Rocky Mountains, near the peaks of the Rio del Norte, on the confines of New Mexico, to which country there is a good road for the whole distance along the banks of the Yellowstone. Its western waters are probably connected with those of Lew- is's River, while the eastern branches approach the heads of Clarke's River, of the Bighorn, and the Platte ; so that it waters the middle portion of the Rocky Mountains for several hundred miles, from northwest to southeast. Along its whole course, from the point where Captain Clarke reached it to the Missouri, a distance which he computed at eight hundred and thirty-seven miles, it is large, and nav

igable for pirogues and even batteaux, there being
none of the moving sand-bars which obstruct the
navigation of the Missouri; while there is but one
ledge of rocks, and this is not difficult to pass. Even
its tributary streams, the Bighorn, Clarke's Fork, and
Tongue River, may be ascended in boats for a considerable distance. The banks of the Yellowstone
are low, but bold, and nowhere subject to be overflowed, except for a short distance from the mountains. The predominating colour of its waters is a
yellowish brown; while those of the Missouri, which
have more mud, are of a deep drab colour. The
bed of the former is chiefly composed of loose peb-
ble, which diminish in size, however, in descending
the river, till, after passing the Lazeka, they cease
as the river widens, and mud and sand below this
form the greater part of the bottom. The current
flows with a velocity constantly and equably decreas-
ing in receding from the mountains. From the
mountains to Clarke's Fork it may be estimated at
four and a half miles an hour; thence as low as the
Bighorn, at three and a half; between that and the
Lazeka, at three; from that river to the Wolf Rapid,
at two and three quarter miles; and from thence to
the mouth of the river, at two miles per hour.

"The appearance and character of the country
present nearly similar varieties of fertile, rich, open
lands. Above Clarke's Fork it consists of high
waving plains, bordered by stony hills, partially covered with pine: the middle portion, as low as Buffalo Shoal, contains less timber, and the number of
trees diminishes in proceeding lower down, till,
where the river widens, the country spreads itself
into extensive plains. Like all the branches of the
Missouri which penetrate the Rocky Mountains, the
Yellowstone and its tributary streams within the district of country beyond Clarke's Fork abound in
beaver and otter: a circumstance which strongly
recommends the mouth of the latter river as a ju

dicious position for a trading establishment. To such an establishment at that point, the Shoshonees both from within and westward of the Rocky Mountains would willingly resort, as they would be farther from the Blackfoot Indians and the Minnetarees of Fort de Prairie than in trading with any factories on the Missouri. The same motive of personal safety would probably induce many of the tribes on the Columbia and Lewis Rivers to prefer this place to the mouth of Maria's River, at least for some years; and as the Crow and Paunch Indians, the Castahanas, and the Indians residing south of Clarke's Fork, would also be induced to visit it, this position might be considered as one of the best points for the western fur-trade. The adjacent country, too, possesses a sufficiency of timber, an advantage which is not found anywhere between Clarke's Fork and the Rocky Mountains.*

"August 5. Their camp became absolutely uninhabitable from the multitudes of moschetoes; nor could the men either work in preparing skins for clothing, or hunt in the low timbered grounds; in

* The American Fur Company have for many years had a fort at the mouth of the Yellowstone River, and one. also at the junction of the Teton and the Missouri, in the heart of the buffalo country. In the year 1832, a steamboat in the service of the Company ascended the Missouri from St. Louis to the post at the mouth of the Yellowstone, which was higher than any steamboat had proceeded before. On board this boat, Mr. Catlin, well known as the founder and proprietor of the Indian Gallery, made his first incursion into the Indian country; and at this point, surrounded by different Indian tribes, and in daily intercourse with their chiefs, he commenced his indefatigable labours. In these labours he enthusiastically persevered for several successive years, through the wide regions between the Great Northern Lakes and the Red River, the Rocky Mountains and the Mississippi. It is needless to say, that by his delineation of Indian life and manners, his portraits of the native chiefs, and the rich collections of his museum, he has done more than any other individual towards presenting the living image of a race which is seemingly fast passing away.

II.—A A

short, there was no method of escape but by going on the sand-bars in the river, where, when the wind blew, the insects did not venture." * * * " Captain Clarke therefore determined to remove to some spot that would be free from moschetoes, and afford more game. After writing a note to Captain Lewis, therefore, to inform him of his intention, he stuck it on a pole at the confluence of the two rivers, loaded the canoes at five in the afternoon, and proceeded down the river to the second point, where he encamped on a sand-bar; but here their tormentors appeared to be even more numerous than above. The face of the Indian child was swollen with the bites of these insects, nor could the men procure scarcely any sleep during the night.

" August 5. Finding their situation intolerable where they were, they proceeded farther down. On the way, Captain Clarke went on shore, and ascended a hill in pursuit of a bighorn; but the moschetoes were in such multitudes that he could not keep them from the barrel of his rifle long enough to take aim. At about ten o'clock, however, a light breeze sprung up from the northwest, and in some measure dispersed them. Captain Clarke then landed on a sand-bar, where he intended to wait for Captain Lewis; but, not finding any buffalo in the neighbourhood, he proceeded on again in the afternoon, and after killing a large white bear, encamped under a high bluff, exposed to a light breeze from the southwest, which drove away the moschetoes."

The next day they continued to descend, and encamped on a sand-bar below the mouth of White-earth River; and on the 7th, after proceeding till six in the evening, they again landed on a sand-bar for the night.

" August 8. In the morning they were here joined by Sergeant Pryor, accompanied by Shannon, Hall, and Windsor, but without the horses. They stated that, the second day after leaving the party, they halted to let the horses graze near the bed of a large creek which contained no running water, but that, soon after, a shower of rain fell, and the creek swelled so suddenly that several horses which had strayed across it while dry could return only by swimming. They formed their camp at this place, but were astonished the next morning at not being able to find a single one of their horses. They immediately examined the neighbourhood, and soon discovering the track of the Indians who had stolen the horses, they pursued them for five miles, when they came to the place where the fugitives divided into two parties. They now followed the largest party five miles farther, when, losing all hopes of overtaking them, they returned to the camp, and packing the baggage on their backs, pursued a northeast course towards the Yellowstone. The following night a wolf bit Sergeant Pryor through the hand as he lay asleep, and made an attempt to seize Windsor, when Shannon got sight of him, and shot him. They passed over an open, broken country, and having reached the Yellowstone near Pompey's Pillar, they determined to descend it, and for this purpose made two skin canoes, such as they had seen among the Mandans and the Ricaras. They are constructed in the following manner: two sticks of about an inch and a quarter in diameter are tied together so as to form a round hoop, which serves for the gunwale, while a second hoop for the bottom is made in the same way, both being secured by sticks of the same size extended from the hoops, and fastened to them and to each other by thongs. Over this frame the skin is drawn closely and tied with thongs, so as to form a perfect basin of about seven feet in diameter and sixteen inches in depth, strengthened by sixteen ribs or cross-sticks, and capable of carrying six or eight men with their burdens. Being unacquainted with the river, they thought it most prudent to divide their guns and ammunition, so that in case of accident all might not be lost, and for this purpose built two of these canoes. In these frail vessels they embarked, and were not a little surprised at the perfect safety with which they passed over the most difficult shoals and rapids, without taking in any water, even in the highest winds.

"On reaching the confluence of the Yellowstone and Missouri, Sergeant Pryor took down the note from the pole, supposing that Captain Lewis had already passed; and now learning where the party were, he pressed on with his skin canoes to join them.

"The day was spent in hunting, in order to procure skins to trade with the Mandans; for, having now neither horses nor merchandise, their only resource to obtain corn and beans was to lay in a stock of skins, which those Indians greatly admire."

The next day they continued their route down the river till late in the evening, and encamped on the southeast side, where they remained until the 11th. "In the low grounds of the river," continues the Journal, "Captain Clarke found a species of cherry which he had never seen before, and which seems peculiar to this small district of country, though even here it is not very abundant. The men also dug up quantities of a large and very insipid root, called by the Indians *hankee*, and by the *engagés* the white apple. It is used by them in a dry, pounded state, to mix with their soup; but our men boiled it and ate it with meat. In descending the river the day before, the squaw brought in a large, well-flavoured gooseberry, of a rich crimson colour; and also a deep purple berry, being a species of currant common along this river as low as the Mandans, and called by the *engagés* the Indian currant.

"August 11. They set out early in the morning, and at about ten o'clock landed on a sand-bar for the

purpose of taking breakfast and drying their meat.
At noon they started again, and after proceeding
about two miles, observed a canoe near the shore.
They immediately landed, and were no less surprised than gratified at discovering two men by the
names of Dickson and Hancock, who had come from
the Illinois on a hunting excursion up the Yellowstone. They had left the Illinois in the summer of
1804, and spent the last winter with the Tetons, in
company with a Mr. Ceautoin, who came there as a
trader, and whom they had robbed, or, in other
words, taken all his merchandise and given him a
few robes in exchange. These men had met the
boat we had despatched from Fort Mandan, on board
of which they were told there was a Ricara chief on
his way to Washington, and also a party of Yank-
ton chiefs, accompanying Mr. Durion on a visit of
the same kind. We were sorry to learn that the
Mandans and Minnetarees were at war with the
Ricaras, and had killed two of them. The Assiniboins, too, were at war with the Mandans. They
had, in consequence, prohibited the Northwest Company from trading to the Missouri, and even killed
two of their traders near Mouse River, and were now
lying in wait for Mr. M'Kenzie of that Company,
who had been for a long time among the Minnetarees. These appearances were rather unfavourable
to the project of carrying some of the chiefs to the
United States; but we still hoped that by effecting a
peace between the Mandans, Minnetarees, and Ricaras, the views of our government might still be
accomplished.

"After leaving these trappers, Captain Clarke
went on and encamped nearly opposite to the entrance of Goatpen Creek, where the party were again
assailed by their old enemies the moschetoes."

CHAPTER XVIII.

Captain Clarke and his Party are overtaken by the Detachment under Captain Lewis, and they all descend the Missouri together.—They revisit the Minnetaree Indians, and hold a Council with that Nation, as well as the Mahahas.—Captain Clarke endeavours to persuade their Chiefs to accompany him to the United States, which they decline on Account of their Fears of the Sioux in their Passage down the River.—Colter, one of the Party, requests and obtains Liberty to remain among the Indians, for the Purpose of hunting Beaver.—Friendly Deportment of the Mandans.—Council held by Captain Clarke with the Chiefs of the different Villages.—The Chief named Big White, with his Wife and Son, agrees to accompany the Party to the United States.—He takes an affecting Farewell of his Nation.—Chaboneau, with his Wife, declines going to the United States, and they are left among the Indians.—The Party at length proceed on their Route.—They arrive among the Ricaras.—Character of the Chayennes, their Dress, Habits, &c.—Captain Clarke offers a Medal to the Chief of this Nation, which he at first refuses, believing it to be Medicine, but which he is afterward prevailed on to accept.—The Ricaras decline permitting one of their Number to accompany Captain Clarke to the United States, preferring to wait the Return of their Chief who had already gone.—The Party proceed rapidly down the River.—Prepare to defend themselves against the Tetons.—Incredible Number of Buffalo seen near White River.—They meet with the Tetons, and decline their Invitations to Land.—Intrepidity of Captain Clarke.

" August 12. The party continued slowly to descend the river. One of the skin canoes had by accident a small hole made in it, and they halted for the purpose of covering it with a piece of elkskin, and also to wait for two of the party who were behind. While there, about noon they were overjoyed at seeing the boats of the other party heave in sight; but this feeling was changed into alarm on perceiving them reach the shore without Captain

Lewis, who had been wounded, they were informed, the day before, and was then lying in the pirogue.

"After giving to his wound all the attention in our power," proceeds the narrative, "we remained here for some time, during which we were overtaken by our two men, accompanied by Dickson and Hancock, who wished to go with us as far as the Mandans. The party being now happily reunited, we left the two skin canoes, and at about three o'clock all embarked on board the boats. The wind was, however, very high from the southwest, accompanied with rain, so that we did not proceed far before we halted for the night on a sand-bar. Captain Lewis's wound was now sore and somewhat painful. The next day,

"August 13, we set out by sunrise, and with a strong breeze from the northwest proceeded on rapidly. At eight o'clock we passed the mouth of the Little Missouri. Some Indians were seen at a distance below in a skin canoe, and were probably some of the Minnetarees on their return from a hunting excursion, as we passed one of their camps on the southwest side, where they had left a canoe. Two other Indians were seen far off on one of the hills, and we therefore expected soon to meet with our old acquaintances the Mandans. At sunset we arrived at the entrance of Miry River, and encamped on the northeast side, having come by the aid of the wind and our oars a distance of eighty-six miles. The air was cool, and the moschetoes now ceased to trouble us as they had done.

"August 14. We again set out at sunrise, and at length approached the grand village of the Minnetarees, where the natives had collected to view us as we passed. We fired the blunderbuss several times by way of salute, and soon after landed near the village of the Mahahas or Shoe Indians, and were received by a crowd of people, who came to welcome us on our return. Among these were the principal chief of the Mahahas, and the chief of the Little Minnetarce village, both of whom expressed great pleasure at seeing us again; but the latter wept most bitterly. On inquiring the cause, it appeared that his tears were excited by the sight of us reminding him of his son, who had been lately killed by the Blackfoot Indians. After remaining there a few minutes, we crossed to the Mandan village of the Black Cat, where all the inhabitants seemed very much gratified at seeing us. We immediately sent Chaboneau with an invitation for the Minnetarees to visit us, and despatched Drewyer to the village of the Mandans, to bring Jesseaume as an interpreter. Captain Clarke, in the mean time, walked up to the village of Black Cat, and smoked and ate with that chief. This village had been rebuilt since our departure, and was now much smaller; a quarrel having arisen among its inhabitants, in consequence of which a number of families had removed to the opposite side of the river.

"On the arrival of Jesseaume, Captain Clarke addressed the chiefs. He spoke to them new, he said, in the same language he had done before; and repeated his invitation to them to accompany him to the United States, to hear in person the counsels of their great father, who could at all times punish his enemies. In reply, Black Cat declared that he wished to visit the United States, and to see his great father, but was afraid of the Sioux, who, had killed several of the Mandans since our departure, and who were now on the river below, and would intercept him if he attempted to pass. Captain Clarke endeavoured to quiet his apprehensions by assuring him that he would not suffer the Sioux to injure any one of our red children who should accompany us, and that they should return loaded with presents, and protected at the expense of the United States. The council was then broken up; after which we crossed and formed our camp on the oth..

er side of the river, where we should be sheltered from the rain. Soon after, the chief of the Mahahas informed us, that if we would send to his village we should have some corn. Three men were therefore despatched, and returned soon after loaded with as much as they could carry. They were soon followed by the chief and his wife, to whom we presented a few needles and other articles suitable for a woman.

"In a short time Borgne, the great chief of all the Minnetarees, came down, attended by several other chiefs, to whom, after smoking a pipe, Captain Clarke made a speech, renewing his assurances of friendship, and the invitation to accompany us to Washington. In reply, Borgne began by declaring that he much desired to visit his great father, but that the Sioux would certainly kill any of the Mandans who should attempt to go down the river: they were bad people, and would not listen to any advice. When he saw us last, we had told him that we would make peace with all the nations below, yet the Sioux had since killed eight of his tribe, and stolen a number of their horses. The Ricaras, too, had stolen their horses, and in the contest his people had killed two of them. Yet, in spite of these things, he had always his ears open to our counsels, and had actually made a peace with the Chayennes and the Indians of the Rocky Mountains. He concluded by saying that, however much disposed they might be to visit the United States, the fear of the Sioux would prevent them from going with us. The council was then concluded, and soon afterward an invitation to visit him was received from Black Cat, who, on Captain Clarke's arrival at his village, presented him with a dozen bushels of corn, which he said was a large proportion of what his people possessed ; and, after smoking a pipe, declared that his tribe were too apprehensive of the Sioux for any of them to venture with us. Captain Clarke then spoke to the chiefs and warriors of the village: he told them of his anxiety that some of them should see their great father, and hear his good words, and receive his gifts, and requested them to fix on some confidential chief who might accompany us. To this they made the same objections as before, till at length a young man offered to go, and the warriors all assented to it. But the character of this man was known to be bad, and one of the party with Captain Clarke informed him that at that moment he had in his possession a knife which he had stolen. Captain Clarke thereupon told the chief of the theft, and demanded the knife to be given up. This was done, with but a poor apology for having it in his possession; and Captain Clarke then reproached the chiefs for wishing to send such a fellow to see and hear so distinguished a person as their great father. They all hung down their heads for some time, till Black Cat at length apologized by saying that the danger was such that they were afraid to send any one of their chiefs, as they should consider his loss almost inevitable. Captain Clarke remained some time with them, smoking, and relating various particulars of his journey; and then left them to visit the second chief of the Mandans, or Black Crow, who had expressed some disposition to accompany us. He seemed well inclined to the journey, but was unwilling to decide till he had called a council of his people, which he intended to do in the afternoon. On returning to the camp, Captain Clarke found the chief of the Mahahas, and also the chief of the Little Minnetaree village, who had brought a present of corn on their mules, of which they have several, and which they procure from the Crow Indians, who either buy or steal them on the frontiers of the Spanish settlements. A great number of the Indians visited us, either for the purpose of renewing their acquaintance, or of exchanging robes and other articles for the skins brought by the party.

" In the evening Colter applied to us for permission to join the two trappers who had accompanied us, and who now proposed an expedition up the river, in which they were to find traps and to give him a share of the profits. The offer was a very advantageous one; and as he had always performed his duty, and his services could be dispensed with, we consented to his going upon condition that none of the rest were to ask or expect a similar indulgence. To this they all cheerfully assented, saying that they wished Colter every success, and would not apply for liberty to separate before we reached St. Louis. We therefore supplied him, as did his comrades also, with powder and lead, and a variety of articles which might be useful to him, and he left us the next day. The example of this man shows how easily men may be weaned from the habits of civilized life to the ruder, though scarcely less fascinating, manners of the woods. This hunter had now been absent for many years from the frontiers, and might naturally be presumed to have some anxiety, or at least curiosity, to return to his friends and his country; yet, just at the moment when he was approaching the frontiers, he was tempted by a hunting scheme to give up all those delightful prospects, and to go back without the least reluctance to the solitude of the wilds.

" In the evening, Chaboneau, who had been mingling with the Indians, and learned what had taken place during our absence, informed us that, as soon as we had left the Minnetarees, they sent out a war party against the Shoshonees, whom they had attacked and routed, though in the engagement they lost two men, one of whom was the son of the chief of the Little Minnetaree village. Another war party also went against the Ricaras, two of whom they had killed. A misunderstanding had likewise taken place between the Mandans and Minnetarees, in consequence of a dispute about a woman, which had nearly occasioned a war; but at length a pipe was presented by the Minnetarees, and a reconciliation took place.

"August 16. The Mandans had offered to give us some corn, and on sending this morning we found a greater quantity collected for our use than all our canoes would contain. We therefore thanked the chief, and took only six loads. At ten o'clock the chiefs of the different villages came down to smoke with us, and we embraced this opportunity to endeavour to engage Borgne in our interest by the present of our swivel, which was no longer of any use, as it could not be discharged from our largest pirogue. It was now loaded, and the chiefs having been formed in a circle round it, Captain Clarke addressed them with great ceremony. He said that he had listened with much attention to what had yesterday been declared by Borgne, whom he believed to be sincere, and then reproached them with their disregard of our counsels, and their wars with the Shoshonees and Ricaras. Little Cherry, the old Minnetaree chief, answered that they had long stayed at home and listened to our advice, but that at last they went to war against the Sioux because they had stolen their horses and killed their companions; and that, in an expedition against that people, they had met the Ricaras, who were on their way to strike them, when a battle ensued. But in future, he said, they would attend to our words and live in peace. Borgne, too, added, that his ears would always be open to the words of his good father, and shut against bad counsel. Captain Clarke then presented to him the swivel, which he told him had announced the words of his great father to all the nations we had seen; and which, whenever it was fired, should recall those which we had now delivered. The gun was then discharged, and Borgne had it conveyed in great pomp to his village, when the council was adjourned.

" In the afternoon Captain Clarke walked up to the village of Little Crow, taking a flag which he intended to present to him, but was surprised on being told by him that he had given up all intention of accompanying us, refusing at the same time the flag. He found that this change was occasioned by a jealousy between him and the principal chief, Big White : by the interference of Jesseaume, however, the two chiefs were reconciled, and it was agreed that Big White himself should accompany us, with his wife and son.

" August 17. The principal chiefs of the Minnetarees now came down to bid us farewell, as none of them could be prevailed on to go with us. This circumstance induced our interpreter, Chaboneau, to remain here with his wife and child, as he could no longer be of use to us, and, although we offered to take him with us to the United States, he declined, saying that there he had no acquaintance, and no chance of making a livelihood, and preferred remaining among the Indians. This man had been very serviceable to us, and his wife was particularly useful among the Shoshonees : indeed, she had borne with a patience truly admirable the fatigues of so long a route, encumbered with the charge of an infant, who was then only nineteen months old. We therefore paid him his wages, amounting to five hundred dollars and thirty-three cents, including the price of a horse and a lodge purchased of him, and soon afterward dropped down to the village of Big White, attended on shore by all the Indian chiefs, who had come to take leave of him. We found him surrounded by his friends, who sat in a circle smoking, while the women were crying. He immediately sent his wife and son, with their baggage, on board, accompanied by the interpreter and his wife, and two children ; and then, after distributing among his friends some powder and ball which we had given him, and smoking a pipe, he went with us to the river side.

The whole village crowded about us, and many of the people wept aloud at the departure of their chief. "As Captain Clarke was shaking hands with the principal chiefs of the different villages, they requested that he would sit with them a moment longer. Being willing to gratify them, he stopped and ordered a pipe, when, after smoking it, they informed him that they had not believed all that we told them at the time they first saw us; but having now found that our words were all true, they would carefully remember them, and follow our advice; and that he might tell their great father that the young men should remain at home, and not make war on any people except in their own defence. They requested him to tell the Ricaras to come and visit them, which they might do without fear, as they meant that nation no harm, but, on the contrary, were desirous of peace with them. On the Sioux, however, they could place, they said, no dependance, and must kill them whenever they sent war parties against their country. Captain Clarke replied that we had never insisted on their not defending themselves, but only requested that they would not strike those whom we had taken by the hand; that we would apprize the Ricaras of their friendly intentions; and that, although we had not seen the Sioux with whom they were at war, we should relate their conduct to their great father, who would take measures for effecting a general peace among all his red children.

"Borgne now requested that we would take good care of the chief, who would report whatever their great father should say; and the council then breaking up, we took leave with a salute from a gun, and proceeded. On reaching Fort Mandan we found a few pickets standing on the river side, but all the houses except one had been accidentally burned. At the distance of eighteen miles we reached the old Ricara village, and encamped on the southwest side, the wind being too violent, and the waves too high, to permit our going any farther.

"August 18. The same cause prevented us from setting out before eight o'clock in the morning. Soon after we had embarked, an Indian came running down to the beach, and appeared very anxious to speak to us. We therefore went ashore, and found it was the brother of Big White, who was encamped at no great distance, and hearing of our departure, had come to take leave of the chief. Big White gave his brother a pair of leggins, and they separated in the most affectionate manner: we then continued our voyage, though the wind and waves were still high. The Indian chief seemed quite satisfied with his treatment, and during the day employed himself in pointing out the ancient monuments of the Mandans, or in relating their traditions. At length, after making forty miles, we encamped on the northeast side, opposite to an old Mandan village, and below the mouth of Chesshetah River.

"August 19. The wind was so violent that we were not able to proceed until four in the afternoon, and in the mean time the hunters had killed four elk and twelve deer. We then went on for ten miles, and came to a sand-bar. The wind and rain continued through the night, and during the whole of the next day,

"August 20, the waves were so high that one man was constantly occupied in bailing the boats. At noon we passed Cannonball River, and at three in the afternoon the mouth of Wardepon River, which bounds the country claimed by the Sioux; and after proceeding eighty-one miles, landed for the night on a sand-bar. The plains were beginning to change their appearance, the grass assuming a yellowish colour. We this day saw great numbers of wolves, and some buffalo and elk, though these were by no means as abundant as on the Yellowstone.

"Since we passed in 1804, a very obvious change

had taken place in the course and appearance of the Missouri. In places where, at that time, there were sand-bars, the current of the river now passed, and where the channel was then, there were, in turn, banks of sand. Sand-bars, then naked, were now covered with willows several feet high; the entrances of some of the creeks and rivers had been changed by the quantity of mud thrown into them; and in some of the bottoms there were layers of mud eight inches in depth.

" August 21. We rose after a night of broken rest, having been much annoyed by moschetoes, and after putting our arms in order, to be prepared for any attack, continued our course. We soon met three traders, two of whom had wintered with us among the Mandans in 1804, and who were now on their way thither. They were out of powder and lead, and we supplied them with both. They informed us that seven hundred Sioux had passed the Ricara towns on their way to attack the Mandans and Minnetarees, leaving their women and children encamped near the Big Bend of the Missouri; but that the Ricaras had all remained at home, declining to take any part in the war. They also told us that the Pawnee or Ricara chief who had gone to the United States the spring before, died on his return near the Sioux River.

" We then left them, and soon afterward arrived opposite to the upper Ricara villages. We saluted them with the discharge of four guns, which they answered in the same manner; and on our landing we were met by the greater part of the inhabitants of each village, and also by a band of the Chayennes, who were encamped on a hill in the neighbourhood.

" As soon as Captain Clarke stepped on shore, he was greeted by the two chiefs to whom we had given medals in our former visit; and as they and the rest appeared much rejoiced at our return, and desirous of hearing from the Mandans, he sat down

on the bank, while the Ricaras and Chayennes formed a circle round him ; and, after smoking, he inform-
.d them, as he had already done the Minnetarees, of
the various tribes we had visited, and of our anxiety
to promote peace among our red brethren. He then
expressed his regret at their having attacked the
Mandans, who had listened to our counsels, and had
sent on a chief to smoke with them, and to assure
them that they might now hunt in the plains, and
visit the Mandan villages in safety, and he concluded by inviting some of the chiefs to accompany us
to Washington. The man whom we had acknowledged as the principal chief when we ascended the
river, now presented another, who, he said, was a
greater chief than himself; and to him, therefore
he had surrendered the flag and medal with which
we had honoured him. This chief, who had been
absent at our former visit, was a man of thirty-five
years of age, stout and good-looking, and called by
the Indians Gray Eyes.

"He now made a very animated reply. He declared that the Ricaras were willing to follow the
counsels we had given them ; but that a few of their
bad young men would not live in peace, but had
joined the Sioux, and thus embroiled them with the
Mandans. These young men had, however, been
driven out of the villages ; and as the Ricaras
were now separated from the Sioux, who were a
bad people, and the cause of all their misfortunes,
they desired to be at peace with the Mandans,
and would receive them with kindness and friendship. Several of the chiefs, he said, were desirous
of visiting their great father ; but as the chief who
had gone to the United States the last summer had
not returned, and they had some fears for his safety
on account of the Sioux, they did not wish to leave
home until they had heard from him. As to himself, he should continue with his nation, to see that
they followed our advice.

II.—B b

" The sun being very hot, the chief of the Chayennes invited us to his lodge, which was at no great
distance from the river. We followed him, and
found a very large lodge, made of twenty buffalo
skins, surrounded by eighteen or twenty others of
nearly equal size. The rest of the nation were expected the next day, and would make the number
of from one hundred and thirty to one hundred and
fifty lodges, containing from three hundred and fifty
to four hundred men, at which the men of the nation
might be computed. These Chayennes are a fine-
looking people, of large stature, with straight limbs,
and high cheek-bones and noses, and of a complexion
similar to that of the Ricaras. Their ears are cut at
the lower part, but few wear ornaments in them.
Their hair is generally cut over the eyebrows, and
small ornaments hang from it down the cheeks, the
remainder being either twisted with horse or buffalo
hair, and divided over each shoulder, or else flowing
loosely behind. Their decorations consist chiefly
of blue beads, shells, red paint, brass rings, bears'
claws, and strips of otter skins, of which last they,
as well as the Ricaras, are very fond. The women,
however, are coarse in their features, with wide
mouths, and ugly. Their dress consists of a habit
reaching to the mid-leg, made of two equal pieces of
leather, sewed from the bottom, with armholes, and
with a flap hanging nearly half way down the body
both before and behind. On these are burned various figures by means of an ignited stick, and they
are adorned with beads, shells, and elk's tusks, which
all the Indians greatly prize. The other ornaments
are blue beads in the ears, but the hair is left plain,
and flows down the back. The summer dress of
the men is a simple buffalo robe, a cloth round the
waist, moccasins, and occasionally leggins. Living
remote from the whites, they are shy and cautious,
but are peaceably disposed, and profess to make war
against no people except the Sioux, with whom they .

have been engaged in contests from time immemorial. In their excursions they are accompanied by their dogs and horses, of which they have a great number ; the former serving to carry almost all their light baggage.

"After smoking for some time, Captain Clarke gave a small medal to the Chayenne chief, explaining at the same time the meaning of it. He seemed alarmed at the present, and sending for a robe and a quantity of buffalo meat, he gave them to Captain Clarke, requesting him to take back the medal, as he knew that all white people were *medicine*, and he was afraid of everything which they might give to the Indians. Captain Clarke again explained his object in giving the medal, which, he said, was the medicine his great father had directed him to deliver to all their chiefs who should listen to his word and follow his counsels ; and that, as he had done so, it had been given him as a proof that we believe him sincere. He now appeared satisfied, and receiving the medal, gave in return double the quantity of buffalo meat he had offered before. He seemed now quite reconciled to the whites, and requested that some traders might be sent among his people, who lived, he said, in a country full of beaver, but did not understand the best modes of catching them, and, farthermore, were deterred from it by having no market for them when caught. Captain Clarke promised that they should soon be supplied with goods, and taught the best mode of catching beaver.

" Big White, chief of the Mandans, now addressed them at some length, explaining the pacific intentions of his nation ; and the Chayenne observed that both the Ricaras and Mandans seemed to be in fault ; but at the end of the council the Mandan chief was treated with much civility, and the greatest harmony prevailed between them. The great chief informed us, however, that none of the Ricaras could be prevailed on to accompany us till the return of the other chief; and that the Chayennes were a wild people, and afraid to go. He invited Captain Clarke to his house, and gave him two carrots of tobacco, two beaver skins, and a trencher of boiled corn and beans. It is the custom of the nations on the Missouri to offer to all white men food and refreshment when they first enter their tents.

" Captain Clarke now returned to the boats, where he found the chief of the lower village, who had cut off part of his hair, and disfigured himself in such a manner that we did not recognise him until he explained that he was in mourning for his nephew, who had been killed by the Sioux. He proceeded with us to the village on the island, where we were met by all the inhabitants. The second chief, on seeing the Mandan, began to speak to him in a loud and threatening tone, till Captain Clarke declared that the Mandans had listened to our councils, and that, if any injury was attempted to be done to the chief, we should defend him to the utmost extremity. He then invited the chief to his lodge, and after a very ceremonious smoking, assured Captain Clarke that he was as safe as at his home, for the Ricaras, as well as the Mandans, had opened their ears to our councils. This was repeated by the great chief; and the Mandan and Ricara chiefs now smoked and conversed with great apparent harmony, after which we returned to our boats. The whole distance made this day was twenty-nine miles.

" August 22. It rained the whole night, so that we all rose in the morning quite wet, and were about proceeding, when Captain Clarke received from the chiefs a request to visit them. They made to him several speeches, in which they observed that they must decline going with us, as their countryman had not yet returned; and that, although all their troubles came from the Sioux, yet, as they had more horses than they wanted, and were in want of guns and powder, they should be obliged to trade with them once more for those articles, after which they would break off all connexion with them. He then returned to the boats, and after taking leave of the natives, who seemed to regret our departure, and firing a salute of two guns, we proceeded on our way. We made only seventeen miles this day, being obliged to land near Wetarboo River to dry our baggage; besides which, the sand-bars were very numerous, as the river became wider below the Ricara villages. Captain Lewis was now so far recovered that he was able to walk a little for the first time. While here we noticed that the Mandans, as well as the Minnetarees and Ricaras, keep their horses in the same lodges with themselves."

During the two following days they made a distance of eighty-three miles, and in the morning of the 24th encamped at the gorge of the Lookout Bend.

"August 25. Before daylight," continues the Journal, "we sent five of the men ahead to hunt on Pawnee Island, and followed them soon after. At eight o'clock we reached the entrance of the Chayenne, where we remained till noon to take a meridian observation. At three o'clock we passed the old Pawnee village, near which we had met the Tetons in 1804, and encamped in a large bottom on the northeast side, a little below the mouth of No-timber Creek. Just above our camp the Ricaras had formerly a large village on each side of the river, and there were still to be seen the remains of five villages on the southwest side below the Chayenne, and one on Lahoocat's Island, all of which had been destroyed by the Sioux. The weather was clear and calm, but by the help of our oars we made forty-eight miles." * * *

"August 26. We set out early, and at nine o'clock reached the entrance of Teton River, below which were a raft and a skin canoe, which made us suspect that the Tetons were in the neighbourhood.

Our arms, therefore, were put in order, and every preparation was made to revenge the slightest insult from those people, who required, we knew, to be treated with rigour. We went on, however, without seeing any of them, though we were obliged to land near Smoke Creek, and remained there for two hours to stop a leak in the pirogue. Here we saw great quantities of plums and grapes, but they were not yet ripe. At five o'clock we passed Louisville's Fort, on Cedar Island, twelve miles below which we encamped, having made sixty miles by using our oars, with the wind ahead during the greater part of the day."

Setting out before sunrise the next morning, at the distance of a few miles they landed on a sandbar near Taylor's River. "Near this place," says the Journal, "we observed the first signs of the wild turkey, and not long after landed in the Big Bend, and killed a fine fat elk. Towards night we heard the bellowing of the buffalo bulls on the lower island of the Big Bend; and following the direction of this agreeable sound, we killed some of the cows, and encamped on the island, forty-five miles from our camp of the previous night.

" August 28. We started at an early hour, having first despatched some hunters ahead, with orders to join us at our old camp a little above Corvus Creek, where we intended to remain one day, for the purpose of procuring the skins and skeletons of some animals, such as the mule-deer, the antelope, the barking squirrel, the magpie, &c., which we were desirous of taking with us. After rowing thirty-five miles, we landed at twelve o'clock, and formed our camp in a high bottom, thinly timbered, and covered with grass. Soon after our arrival the squaws and several of the men went to the bushes near the river, and brought a great quantity of large, well-flavoured plums, of three different species.

" The hunters returned in the afternoon without

having been able to procure any of the game we wished except the barking squirrel, though they killed four common deer, and had seen large herds of buffalo, of which they brought in two."

Setting out at ten o'clock the next morning, at a short distance they passed the mouth of White River, the water of which was nearly of the colour of milk. As they were much occupied with hunting, they made but twenty miles. "The buffalo," says the Journal, "were now so numerous, that from an eminence we discovered more than we had ever seen before at one time; and though it was impossible accurately to calculate their number, they darkened the whole plain, and could not have been, we were convinced, less than twenty thousand. With regard to game in general, we have observed that wild animals are usually found in the greatest numbers in the country lying between two nations at war.

"August 30. We set out at the usual time, but after going some distance were obliged to stop two hours for one of our hunters. During this time we made an excursion to a large orchard of delicious plums, where we were so fortunate as to kill two buck elks. We then proceeded down the river, and were about landing at the place where we had agreed to meet all the hunters, when several persons appeared on the high hills to the northeast, and by the help of our spyglass we distinguished them to be Indians. We landed on the southwest side of the river, and immediately after saw on a height opposite to us about twenty men, one of whom, from his blanket greatcoat and a handkerchief round his head, we took for a Frenchman. At the same time, about eighty or ninety Indians, armed with guns and bows and arrows, came out of a wood some distance below them, and fired a salute, which we returned. From their hostile appearance we were apprehensive that they might be Tetons; but as, from the country through which they were passing, it was possible they might be Yanktons, Pawnees, or Mahas, we did not know in what way to receive them. In order, however, to ascertain who they were without risk to the party, Captain Clarke crossed, with three persons who could speak different Indian languages, to a sand-bar near the opposite side, for the purpose of conversing with them. Eight young men soon met him on the sand-bar, but none of them could understand either the Pawnee or Maha interpreter. They were then addressed in the Sioux language, and answered that they were Tetons, of the band headed by the Black Baffalo, Tahtackasabah. It was the same band which had attempted to stop us in 1804; and being now less anxious about offending this mischievous tribe, Captain Clarke told them that they had been deaf to our counsels, had ill treated us two years ago, and had abused all the whites who had since visited them. He believed them, he added, to be bad people, and they must return, therefore, to their companions, for if they crossed over to our camp we would put them all to death. They asked for some corn, which Captain Clarke refused them : they then requested permission to come and visit us, but he ordered them back. He then returned, and our arms were all made ready in case of an attack. But when these Indians reached their comrades, and informed their chiefs of our determination, they all set off for their own camp : some of them, however, halted on a rising ground, and abused us with their tongues very copiously, threatening to kill us if we came across. We took no notice of this for some time, as three of our hunters were absent, and we were afraid the Indians might meet them; but as soon as they joined us we embarked, and, to see what the Indians would attempt, steered near their side of the river. At this the party on the hill seemed not a little agitated : some of them set off for their camp, others walked about, and one man came towards the boats and invited us to land. As he approached, we recognised him to be the same who had accompanied us for two days in 1804, and was considered a friend of the whites. Unwilling, however, to have any intercourse with these people, we declined his invitation, upon which he returned to the hill, and struck the earth three times with his gun, a great oath among the Indians, who consider swearing by the earth as one of the most solemn forms of imprecation. At the distance of six miles we stopped on a bleak sand-bar, where we thought ourselves secure from any attack during the night, and also safe from the moschetoes. We had made but twenty-two miles, but in the course of the day had killed a mule-deer, an animal we were very anxious to obtain. About eleven in the evening the wind shifted to the northwest, and it began to rain, accompanied by thunder and lightning, after which the wind changed to the southwest, and blew with such violence that we were obliged to hold fast the canoes, for fear of their being driven from the sand-bar: still, the cables of two of them broke, and two others were blown quite across the river; nor was it till two o'clock that the whole party were reassembled, waiting in the rain for daylight."

CHAPTER XIX.

The Party return in Safety to St. Louis.

" August 31. We examined our arms, and proceeded with the wind in our favour. For some time we saw different Indians on the hills, but at length lost sight of them. In passing the Dome, and the first village of barking squirrels, we stopped and killed

II.—C c

two fox squirrels, an animal we had not seen on the
river higher than this place; and at night we encamped on the northeast side, after making a distance of seventy miles. We had seen no game for
some time past on the river, but in the evening the
moschetoes were not slow to discover us.

"September 1. We set out early, but were shortly
compelled to land, and wait for half an hour, till a
thick fog dispersed. At nine o'clock we passed the
mouth of the Quicurre, which presented the same
appearance as when we ascended, the water being
rapid and of a milky-white colour. Two miles below, several Indians ran down to the bank and beckoned us to land; but as they appeared to be Tetons,
and of a war party, we paid no attention to them,
except to inquire to what tribe they belonged: our
Sioux interpreter, however, did not understand much
of their language, and they probably mistook his
question. As one of our canoes was behind, we
were afraid of its being attacked; we therefore landed on an open, commanding situation, out of view
of the Indians, to wait for it. We had not been in
this position fifteen minutes, when we heard several
guns, which we immediately concluded were fired
at the men in the canoe; and being determined to
protect them against any number of Indians, Captain
Clarke, with fifteen men, ran up the river, while Captain Lewis hobbled up the bank, and formed the rest
of the party in such a manner as would best enable
them to protect the boats. On turning a point of
the river, however, Captain Clarke was agreeably
surprised at seeing the Indians still in the place
where we had left them, and our canoe at the distance of a mile. He now went on to a sand-bar, and,
the Indians crossing over to him, he gave them his
hand, when they informed him that they had been
amusing themselves with shooting at an old keg we
had thrown into the river as it was floating down.
We now found them to be part of a band of eighty

lodges of Yanktons on Plum Creek, and therefore invited them down to our camp. After smoking several pipes, we told them that we had mistaken them for Tetons, and had intended putting every one of them to death if they had fired at our canoe; but finding them Yanktons, who were good men, we were glad to take them by the hand as faithful children, who had opened their ears to our counsels. They saluted the Mandan with great cordiality, and one of them said that their ears had indeed been open, and that they had followed our advice since we gave a medal to their great chief, and should continue to do so. We now tied a piece of riband to the hair of each Indian, and gave them some corn. We also made a present of a pair of leggins to the principal chief, when we took our leave of them, having been previously overtaken by our canoe. At two o'clock we landed to hunt on Bonhomme Island, but obtained a single elk only. The bottom on the north side is very rich, and was so thickly overgrown with pea-vines and grass, interwoven with grape-vines, that some of the party who attempted to hunt there were obliged to leave it and ascend the plain, where they found the grass nearly as high as their heads. These plains are much more fertile below than above the Quicurre, and the whole country was now very beautiful. After making fifty-two miles against a head wind, we landed for the night on a sand-bar opposite to Calumet Bluff, where we had encamped on the 1st of September, 1804, and where our flagstaff was still standing. We suffered very much from the moschetoes till the wind became so high as to blow them away.

"September 2. At eight o'clock we passed the mouth of the Jacques River, but soon after were compelled to land, in consequence of the high wind from the northeast, and to remain till sunset, after which we went on to a sand-bar twenty-two miles from our camp of the previous evening. While we were on shore we killed three buffaloes and four prairie-fowl, which were the first of the latter we had seen in descending. Two turkeys were also killed, and were very much admired by our Indians, who had never seen that bird before." * * *

" September 3. Towards daylight we started again, and at eleven o'clock we passed the Redstone. The river was crowded with sand-bars, which were now very differently situated from what they had been when we ascended; but, notwithstanding these and the head wind, we had made sixty miles towards night, when, seeing two boats and several men on the shore, we landed, and found a Mr. James Airs, a partner of a house at Prairie de Chien, who had come from Mackinaw by the way of St. Louis, with a license to trade among the Sioux for one year. He had started two canoes loaded with merchandise, but lost many of his most valuable articles in a squall some time before. After so long an absence, the sight of any one who could give us information of our country was peculiarly delightful, and much of the night was spent in making inquiries as to what had occurred since we had left. We found Mr. Airs a very friendly and liberal gentleman, and when we proposed to him to purchase a small quantity of tobacco, to be paid for at St. Louis, he very readily furnished every man of the party with as much as he could use during the rest of the voyage, and insisted also on our receiving a barrel of flour. This last was very acceptable, though we had still a little flour, which we had deposited at the mouth of Maria's River. We could give in return only about six bushels of corn, which was all that we could spare The next morning,

" September 4, we left Mr. Airs at about eight o'clock, and after passing the Big Sioux River, stopped at noon near Floyd's Bluff. On ascending the hill we found that the grave of Floyd had been opened, and was now half uncovered. We filled it up, and then continued down to our old camp near the Maha village, where all our baggage, which had been wet by the rain in the night, was exposed to dry. There was no game on the river except wild geese and pelicans. Near Floyd's grave were some flourishing black-walnut trees, the first we had seen on our return. At night we heard the report of several guns in a direction towards the Maha village, and supposed it to be a signal for the arrival of some trader. But not meeting any one when we set out the next morning,

"September 5, we concluded that the firing was merely to announce the return of the Mahas to their village, this being the season at which they come home from buffalo hunting, to take care of their corn, beans, and pumpkins. The river was now more crooked, the current more rapid, and crowded with snags and sawyers, while the bottoms on both sides were well supplied with timber. At three o'clock we passed Bluestone Bluff, where the river leaves the highlands and meanders through a low, rich bottom, and encamped for the night after making seventy-three miles.

"September 6. The wind continued ahead, but the moschetoes were so tormenting that to remain was more unpleasant than to proceed, however slowly, and we therefore started. Near the Little Sioux River we met a trading-boat belonging to Mr. Augustus Chateau, of St. Louis, with several men on their way to trade with the Yanktons at the Jacques River. We obtained from them a gallon of whiskey, and gave each of the party a dram, which was the first spirituous liquor any of them had tasted since the 4th of July, 1805."

During this and the following day they made a distance of seventy-four miles, encamping, as usual, on sand-bars for the night, to avoid the moschetoes, though even here they were greatly tormented by them.

"September 8. We set out early," continues the Journal, "and stopped for a short time at Council Bluffs to examine the situation of the place, when we were confirmed in our belief that it would be a very eligible spot for a trading establishment. Being anxious to reach the Platte, we plied our oars so well that by night we had made seventy-eight miles, and landed at our old White Catfish encampment, twelve miles above that river. We could not but here remark the wonderful evaporation from the Missouri, which does not appear to contain more water, nor is its channel wider than at one thousand miles nearer its source, though within the intervening distance it receives about twenty rivers, some of them of considerable width, and a great number of creeks. This evaporation seemed, in fact, to be greater now than when we ascended the river; for we were obliged to replenish the inkstand every day with fresh ink, nine tenths of which must have escaped by evaporation.

"September 9. By eight o'clock we passed the mouth of the Platte, which river was lower than when we saw it before, and its waters were almost clear, though its channel was turbulent, as usual. The sand-bars, however, which then obstructed the Missouri were now washed away, and nothing of them was to be seen except a few remains. Below the Platte the current of the Missouri became evidently more rapid, and the obstructions from fallen timber increased. The river bottoms are here extensive, rich, and covered with tall, large timber, which is still more abundant in the hollows of the ravines, where may be seen oak, ash, and elm, interspersed with some walnut and hickory. The moschetoes, though still numerous, seemed to have lost some of their vigour. As we advanced the difference of climate was very perceptible, the air being more sultry than we had experienced it for a long time before. and the nights were so warm that a thin blanket was now sufficient, although a few days before two had been no more than comfortable. Late in the afternoon we encamped opposite to the Bald-pated Prairie, after having come a distance of seventy-three miles.

"September 10. We again set out early, and the wind being moderate, though still ahead, we proceeded sixty-five miles, to a sand-bar a short distance above the Grand Nemaha. In the course of the day we met a trader, with three men, on his way to the Pawnee Loups, or Wolf Pawnees, on the Platte. Soon after another boat passed us with seven men from St. Louis, bound to the Mahas. With both of these parties we had some conversation, but our anxiety to go on would not suffer us to remain long with them. The Indians, particularly the squaws and children, had become weary with the length of the route, and we were impatient to reach our country and our friends. We saw on the shore deer, raccoons, and turkeys.

"September 11. A high wind from the northwest detained us till after sunrise, when we started, but proceeded slowly, since, from the river being now rapid and narrow, as well as more crowded with sand-bars and timber than above, much caution was necessary in avoiding these obstacles, especially as the water was low. The Nemaha seemed less wide than when we saw it before, and Wolf River had scarcely any water. In the afternoon we halted above the Nadowa to hunt, and killed two deer, after which we went on to a small island forty miles from our last encampment. Here we were no longer annoyed by the moschetoes, which did not seem to frequent this part of the river; and, after having been persecuted by these insects the whole distance from the Falls, it was a most agreeable release. Their noise was very agreeably exchanged for that of the common wolves, which were howling in different directions, and of the prairie wolves.

whose barking resembles precisely that of a cur
dog.

"September 12. After a thick fog and a heavy dew,
we set out by sunrise, and at the distance of seven
miles passed two pirogues, one of them bound to the
Platte for the purpose of trading with the Pawnees,
the other on a trapping expedition to the neighbourhood of the Mahas. Soon after we met the trading
party under Mr. M'Clellan; and with them was Mr.
Gravelines, the interpreter whom we had sent with
a Ricara chief to the United States. The chief had
unfortunately died at Washington, and Gravelines
was now on his way to the Ricaras with a speech
from the president, and the presents which had been
made to the deceased. He had also directions to in-
struct the Ricaras in agriculture. He was accompanied on his mission by old Mr. Durion, our former
interpreter, for the purpose of employing his influence to secure a safe passage for the Ricara presents
through the country of the Sioux, and also to engage some of the Sioux chiefs, not exceeding six, to
visit Washington. Both of them were instructed to
inquire particularly after the fate of our party, no
intelligence having been received from us for a long
time. We authorized Mr. Durion to invite ten or
twelve of the Sioux chiefs to accompany him, particularly the Yanktons, whom we had found well
disposed towards our country. The afternoon being
wet, we determined to remain with Mr. M'Clellan
during the night; and sending five hunters ahead,
spent the evening in inquiries respecting what had
transpired in the United States since we left.

"September 13. By eight o'clock in the morning
we overtook the hunters, but they had killed nothing.
The wind being now too high to proceed safely
through the timber that was stuck in every part of
the channel, we landed and sent the small canoes
ahead to hunt. Towards evening we overtook them,
and encamped, having been able to advance only

eighteen miles. The weather was very warm, and the rushes in the bottoms were so thick and high that we could scarcely hunt; still, we were so fortunate as to obtain four deer and a turkey, which, with the hooting owl, and the common buzzard, crow, and hawk, were the only game we saw. Among the timber was the cottonwood, sycamore, ash, mulberry, papaw, walnut, hickory, prickly ash, and several species of elm, interspersed with great quantities of grape-vines, and three kinds of pea.

"September 14. We resumed our journey, and this being the part of the river to which the Kanzas resort for the purpose of robbing the boats of the traders, we held ourselves in readiness to fire upon any Indians who should offer us the slightest indignity, as we no longer needed their friendship, and had found that a tone of firmness and decision was the best possible method of making a proper impression upon these freebooters. We did not, however, encounter any of them, but just below the old Kanzas village met three trading boats from St. Louis, on their way to the Yanktons and Mahas. After leaving them we saw a number of deer, of which we killed five, and landed on an island fifty-three miles from our last encampment.

"September 15. A strong breeze ahead prevented us from proceeding more than forty-nine miles, to the neighbourhood of Hay Cabin Creek. The Kanzas was very low at this time. About a mile beyond it we landed to examine the situation of a high hill, which has many advantages for a trading house or fort; while on the shore we gathered great quantities of papaw, and shot an elk. The low grounds were now delightful, and the whole country exhibited a rich appearance; but the weather was oppressively warm, and descending as rapidly as we did from a cool, open country, situated in the latitude of from 46° to 49°, in which we had been for nearly two years, to the wooded plains in 38° and 39°, the heat would have been almost insufferable but for the winds constantly blowing from the south and southeast.

"September 16. We set out at an early hour, but the weather soon became so warm that the men rowed but little. In the course of the day we met two trading parties on their way to the Pawnees and Mahas, and after making fifty-two miles, landed on an island, and remained there till the next morning.

"September 17. We started early, and passed in safety the island of the Little Osage village. This place is considered by the navigators of the Missouri as the most dangerous part of it, the whole stream being compressed, for two miles, within a narrow channel crowded with timber, into which the violence of the current is constantly washing the banks. At the distance of thirty miles we met a Captain M'Clellan, lately of the United States army, with whom we encamped. He informed us that the general opinion in the United States was that we were lost, the latest accounts of us being from the Mandan village. Captain M'Clellan was on his way to attempt to open a new trade with the Indians. His plan was to establish himself on the Platte, and after trading with the Pawnees and Ottoes, to prevail on some of their chiefs to accompany him to Santa Fé, where he hoped to obtain permission to exchange his merchandise for gold and silver, which were there abundant. If this should be granted, he would transport his goods on mules and horses from the Platte to some part of Louisiana, convenient to the Spanish settlements, where he would be met by the traders from New Mexico.

"September 18. We parted with Captain M'Clellan, and within a few miles passed the mouth of Grand River, below which we overtook the hunters who had been sent forward the day before. They had not been able to kill anything, nor did we see any game except ·one bear and three turkeys, so that our whole stock of provisions was reduced to one biscuit for each person; but as there was an abundance of papaw, the men were perfectly contented. The current of the river was more gentle than when we had ascended, the water being lower, though it was still rapid in places where it was confined. We continued to pass through a very fine country for fifty-two miles, when we encamped nearly opposite to Mine River. The next morning, " September 19, we worked our oars all day, without taking time to hunt, or even landing, except once to gather papaws; and at eight o'clock reached the entrance of the Osage River, a distance of seventy-two miles. Several of the party had been for a day or two attacked with soreness of the eyes, the eyeball being very much swelled, and the lid appearing as if burned by the sun, and being extremely painful, particularly when exposed to the light. Three of the men were so much affected by it as to be unable to row. We therefore turned one of the boats adrift, and distributing the men among the others, we set out a little before daybreak,

" September 20. The Osage was at this time low, and discharged but a very small quantity of water. Near the mouth of the Gasconade, where we arrived at noon, we met five Frenchmen on their way to the Great Osage village. As we were rapidly moving along, we saw on the banks some cows feeding, when the whole party almost involuntarily raised a shout of joy on perceiving this image of civilization and domestic life.

" Soon after, we reached the little French village of La Charette, which we saluted with a discharge of four guns, and three hearty cheers. We then landed, and were received with kindness by the inhabitants, as well as some traders from Canada, who were going to traffic with the Osages and Ottoes. They were all equally surprised and pleased at our arrival, for they had long since abandoned all hopes of ever seeing us again.

"These Canadians have boats prepared for the navigation of the Missouri, which seem better calculated for the purpose than those of any other form. They are in the shape of bateaux, about thirty feet long and eight wide; the bow and stern pointed, the bottom flat, and being propelled by six oars only: their chief advantage is their width and flatness, which saves them from the danger of rolling sands.

"Having come forty-eight miles, and the weather threatening to be bad, we remained at La Charette till the next morning,

"September 21, when we proceeded, and as several new settlements had been made during our absence, we were refreshed with the sight of men and cattle along the banks. We also passed twelve canoes of the Kickapoo Indians going on a hunting excursion. At length, after proceeding forty-eight miles, we saluted with heartfelt satisfaction the village of St. Charles, and on landing were treated with the greatest hospitality and kindness by all the inhabitants of the place. Their civility detained us till ten o'clock the next morning,

"September 22, when the rain having ceased, we set out for Coldwater Creek, about three miles from the mouth of the Missouri, where we found a cantonment of United States troops, with whom we passed the day; and then,

"September 23, descended to the Mississippi, and round to St. Louis; at which place we arrived at twelve o'clock; and having fired a salute, went on shore, where we received a most hearty and hospitable welcome from the whole village."

APPENDIX.

FARTHER ENUMERATION AND DESCRIPTION OF THE
QUADRUPEDS, BIRDS, FISHES, AND PLANTS NOTICED
DURING THE EXPEDITION.

The quadrupeds of the country extending from the
Rocky Mountains to the Pacific may be conveniently divided into domestic and wild animals. The first class em-
braces the horse and dog only.

The horse is confined principally to the nations inhabiting the great plains of the Columbia, lying between the
fortieth and fiftieth degrees of north latitude, and extending from the Rocky Mountains to a range of mountains
which pass the Columbia near the Great Falls, between
the one hundred and sixteenth and the one hundred and
twenty-first degrees of west latitude. The Shoshonees,
Chopunnish, Sokulks, Echeloots, Eneeshurs, and Chilluckittequaws, all enjoy the benefit of that docile, generous,
and noble animal ; and all of them, except the last three,
possess immense numbers.

They appear to be of an excellent race ; are lofty, ele-
gantly formed, active, and hardy ; and many of them appear like fine English coursers. Some of them are pied,
with large spots of white irregularly distributed, and intermixed with a dark-brown bay : the greater part, however, are of a uniform colour, marked with stars and white
feet, and in fleetness and bottom, as well as in form and
colour, resemble the best blooded horses of Virginia. The
natives suffer them to run at large in the plains, the grass
of which affords them their only subsistence, their masters taking no trouble to lay in a winter's store for them ;
and, if they are not overworked, they will even at this
season fatten on the dry herbage. These plains are rarely moistened by rain, and the grass is consequently short
and thin The natives, excepting those of the Rocky ·

Mountains, appear to take no pains in selecting the male horses for breed, and, indeed, those of that class appear much the most indifferent. The soil and climate of th's country appear to be perfectly well adapted to the nature of the animal, which is said to be found wild in many parts. The several tribes of Shoshonees, who reside towards Mexico, on the waters of the Multnomah River, and partic ularly one of them, called Shaboboah, have also a great number of mules, which they prize more highly than horses. * * *

The dog is unusually small, about the size of an ordinary cur. He is usually parti-coloured, black, white, brown, and brindle being the colours most predominant: the head is long, the nose pointed, the eyes are small, and the ears erect and pointed, like those of the wolf. The hair is short and smooth, excepting on the tail, where it is long and straight, like that of the ordinary cur-dog. The natives never eat the flesh of this animal, and he appears to be in no other way serviceable to them than in hunting the elk.

The second division comprehends the brown, white, or grizzly bear, the black bear, the common red deer, the black-tailed fallow deer, the mule deer, the elk, the large brown wolf, the small wolf of the plains, the large wolf of the plains, the tiger-cat, the common red fox, the silver fox, the fisher or black fox, the large red fox of the plains, the kit-fox or small fox of the plains, the antelope, the sheep, the beaver, the common otter, the sea-otter, the mink, the seal, the raccoon, the large gray squirrel, the small gray squirrel, the small brown squirrel, the ground squirrel, the *blaireau*, the rat, the mouse, the mole, the panther, the hare, the rabbit, and the polecat or skunk.

The brown, white, or grizzly bear, which seem all to be of the same family, with an accidental variation of colour only, inhabit the timbered parts of the Rocky Mountains. They are rarely found on the western side, and are more commonly below those mountains, in the plains, or on their borders, amid copses of brush and underwood, and near the water courses.* * * *

The black bear differs in no respect from those common

* See Journal, i., 189, 195, 198, 200, 227, 240 ; ii., 225, 235, 261, 299.

to the United States. It chiefly inhabits the timbered parts of the Rocky Mountains and the borders of the great plains on the Columbia. * * *

The common red deer inhabits the Rocky Mountains in the neighbourhood of the Chopunnish, also about the Columbia, and down that river as low as where the tide-water commences. It does not appear to differ essentially from those of the United States, being the same in shape, size, and appearance. The tail, however, is of an unusual length, far exceeding that of the common deer : Captain Lewis measured one, and found it to be seventeen inches long.

The black-tailed fallow deer is peculiar to the Pacific coast, and is a distinct species, partaking equally of the qualities of the mule and common deer. Its ears are longer, and its winter coat is darker than that of the common deer. The receptacle of the eye is more conspicuous, its legs are shorter, and its body thicker and larger. The tail is of the same length with that of the common deer, the hair on the under part white, and on its sides and top of a deep jetty black : its hams, in form and colour, are like those of the mule deer, which it likewise resembles in its gait. The black-tailed deer never runs at full speed, but bounds with all its feet from the ground at the same time, like the mule deer. It sometimes inhabits the woodlands, but more often the prairies and open grounds. It is generally of a size larger than the common deer, and less than the mule deer. * * *

The mule deer inhabits the coast of the Pacific, the plains of the Missouri, and the borders of the Kooskooskee River, in the neighbourhood of the Rocky Mountains. * * * The qualities of this animal have been already noticed.

The elk is of the same species as those found in the greater part of North America. It is common to every part of this country, as well the timbered lands as the plains, but is much more abundant in the former than in the latter.* * * *

Of wolves, there are the large brown wolf and the wolf of the plains, of which last there are two kinds, the large and the small. The large brown wolf inhabits the woody

* Journal, ii., 108.

countries on the borders of the Pacific, and the mountains on either side of the Columbia between the Great Falls and Rapids, and resembles in all points those of the United States.*

The large and small wolves of the plains are principally found in the open country, and in the woodlands on its borders. They resemble, both in appearance and habits, those of the plains of the Missouri.† * * *

The tiger-cat inhabits the borders of the plains and the woody regions in the neighbourhood of the Pacific. This animal is a size larger than the wild-cat of our country,' and much the same in form, agility, and ferocity. The colour of the back, neck, and sides is a reddish brown, irregularly variegated with small spots of dark brown. The tail is about two inches long, and nearly white, except the extremity, which is black; it terminates abruptly, as if it had been amputated. The belly is white, beautifully variegated with small black spots; the legs are of the same colour with the sides; the back is marked transversely with black stripes; the ears are black on the outer side, covered with fine short hair except at the upper point, which is furnished with a pencil of hair, fine, straight, and black, and three fourths of an inch in length. The hair of this animal is longer and finer than that of the wild-cat of the United States; and the skin of the animal is in great demand among the natives, as they form their robes of it.

Of foxes we saw several species. The large red fox of the plains, and the kit-fox, or small red fox of the plains, are the same on the Columbia as those on the banks of the Missouri. They are found almost exclusively in the open plains, or on the tops of brush within the level country. * * *

The black fox, or, as it is called in the neighbourhood of Detroit, the fisher, is found in the woody country bordering on the coast of the Pacific. How it should have acquired this appellation it is difficult to imagine, as it certainly does not live upon fish. These animals are exceedingly strong and active, and admirably expert in climbing, which they perform with the greatest ease, and bound from tree to tree in pursuit of the squirrel or raccoon, their most usual prey. Their colour is of a jetty black, except-

* Journal, i., 195.　　　† Journal : 194.

ıng a small white spot upon.the breast : the body is long, and the legs short, resembling those of the common turnspit dog. The tail is remarkably long, and does not differ in other particulars from that of the ordinary fox.

The silver fox is an animal very rare, even in the country it inhabits. We saw only the skins of this animal in the possession of the natives of the woody country below the Falls of the Columbia, which induced us to believe that it is confined to that country. From the skin, it appeared to be of about the size of the large red fox of the plains, resembling that animal in form, and particularly in the dimensions of the tail. Its legs Captain Lewis conjectured to be somewhat larger. It has a long, deep, lead-coloured fur, intermixed with long hairs, either of a black or white colour at the lower part, and invariably white at the top, forming a most beautiful silver gray. Captain Lewis thought this the most beautiful of the species, excepting one which he saw on the Missouri, near the Natural Falls.

The antelope inhabits the great plains of the Columbia, and resembles those found on the banks of the Missouri, and, indeed, in every part of the untimbered country, but it is by no means as abundant on the west as on the east side of the Rocky Mountains. * * *

The sheep is found in many places, but mostly in the timbered parts of the Rocky Mountains. It lives in greater numbers on the chain of mountains forming the commencement of the woody country on the coast, and passing the Columbia between the Falls and Rapids. We saw only the skins of this animal (which the natives dress with the wool on), and the blankets which they manufacture from the wool. The animal appears to be of about the size of our common sheep, and of a white colour ; the wool being fine on many parts of the body, but not equal in length to that of the domestic sheep. On the back, and particularly on the top of the head, the wool is intermixed with a considerable quantity of long straight hairs. From the Indian accounts, this animal has erect, pointed horns ; but one of our engagés informed us that he had seen it in the Black Hills, and that its horns were lunated, like those of the common sheep.* * * *

* Journal, i., 146 ; ii., 179

II.—D D

The beaver of these countries is large and fat, its flesh very palatable, and we considered it quite a luxury. On the 7th of January, 1806, our hunter found a beaver in his traps, from which he prepared a bait for taking others. This bait will entice the animal as far as he can smell it, which may be fairly stated at a mile, as its sense of smell is very acute. To form this bait, the castor or bark-stone (so called from its having the smell of tanners' bark) is first gently pressed from the bladder-like bag which contains it into a vial of four ounces with a large mouth : five or six of these stones are thus taken, and there must be added to them a nutmeg, a dozen or fifteen cloves, and thirty grains of cinnamon, finely pulverized and stirred together, with as much ardent spirits as will reduce the whole to the consistency of mustard. The bottle must be then carefully corked, as the compound soon loses its efficacy if exposed to the open air. The scent becomes much stronger in four or five days, and, provided proper precau tion is taken, the compound will retain its virtue for months Any strong aromatic spices will answer, as their only object is to give variety and pungency to the scent of the bark-stone. * * * The female beaver has young once in a year only, sometimes two and sometimes four at a birth, and this is usually in the latter end of May and the beginning of June, at which time she is said to drive the male from the lodge, as he would otherwise destroy her progeny. * * *

The common otter does not differ from those inhabiting other parts of America.

The sea-otter resides only on the seacoast or in the neighbourhood of salt-water. When fully grown it at tains the size of a large mastiff dog. The ears are not an inch in length, thick, pointed, fleshy, and covered with short hair. The tail is about ten inches long, thick at the point of insertion, and partially covered with a deep fur on the upper side. The legs are very short, and covered with fur and the feet, which have five toes each, are broad, large and webbed, and covered with short hair. The body of the animal is long, and of the same thickness throughout and from the extremity of the tail to the nose measures about five feet. The colour is a uniform dark brown and when the animal is in good order and in season, it is per fectly black. This animal is unrivalled for the beauty, richness, and softness of its fur, the inner part of it, when opened, being lighter than the surface in its natural position ; and there are some black, shining hairs intermixed with it which are rather longer, and add much to its beauty. The fur in some of this species presents a lighter colour, sometimes brown, about the ears, nose, and eyes. Their young are often seen of a cream-coloured white about the nose, eyes, and forehead, which are always much lighter than the other parts, and the fur of these is much inferior to that of the full-grown animal.

The mink inhabits the woody country bordering on the seacoast, and does not differ in any point from those of the United States.

The seal is found on the coast of the Pacific in great numbers, and as far up the Columbia as the Great Falls, none having been discovered beyond them. * * *

The raccoon inhabits the woody districts bordering on the coast in considerable numbers, and is caught by the natives with snares or pitfalls ; but they hold its skin in little or no estimation, and very seldom make it into robes.

Of squirrels we saw several species.

The large gray squirrel appears to inhabit a narrow tract of country, well covered with white-oak timber, situated on the upper side of the mountains, just below the Falls of the Columbia ; nor is it found except in tracts where there is this kind of timber, never appearing in districts where pine is most abundant. This animal is much superior in size to the common gray squirrel, resembling in form, colour, and size the fox-squirrel of the Atlantic States. The tail exceeds the whole length of the body and head : the eyes are dark ; the whiskers long and black ; the back, sides of the head and tail, and outward part of the legs, are all of a blue-coloured gray ; and the breast, belly, and inner part of the body are of a pure white. The hair is short, like that of the fox-squirrel, though much finer, and intermixed with a portion of fur. The natives hold the skin of this animal in high estimation, and use it in making their robes. It subsists on acorns and filberts, the last growing in great abundance in the oak country.

The small gray squirrel is common to every part of the Rocky Mountains where timber abounds. It differs from the dark brown squirrel in colour only. The back, sides, neck, head, tail, and outer part of the legs are of a brown-ish lead-coloured gray; the tail is slightly tinged with a dark reddish colour near the extremity of some of the hairs; the throat, breast, belly, and inner part of the legs are of the colour of tanners' ooze, and there is a narrow strip of black, commencing behind each shoulder, and entering longitudinally for about three inches, between the colours of the sides and belly. Its habits are precisely those of the dark brown squirrel, and, like the latter, it is extremely nimble and active.

There is another species of squirrel, evidently distinct, which we denominated the burrowing squirrel. It inhabits the plains of the Columbia, and somewhat resembles those found on the Missouri. Its length is about one foot five inches, of which the tail makes two and a half inches only: the neck and legs are short, as are also the ears, which are obtusely pointed, and lie close to the head, the aperture being larger than is generally found among burrowing animals. The eyes are of a moderate size, the pupil being black, and the iris of a dark sooty brown: the whiskers are full, long, and black; the teeth, and, indeed, the whole contour of the animal, resemble those of the squirrel. Each foot has five toes, the two inner ones of the fore feet being remarkably short, and armed with blunt nails, while the remaining toes on these feet are long, black, slightly curved, and sharply pointed. The hair of the tail is thick on the sides only, which gives it a flat appearance, and a long, oval form; the tips of the hair forming the outer edges of the tail being white, the other extremity of a fox red; the under part of the tail being of an iron-gray colour, and the upper part of a reddish brown. The lower part of the jaws, and the under part of the neck, legs, and feet, from the body and belly downward, are of a light brick red; the nose and eyes of a darker shade of the same colour; and the upper part of the head, neck and body, of a curious brown gray, with a slight tinge of brick red: the longer hairs of these parts are of a reddish white colour at their extremities, and falling together, give the animal a speckled appearance. These animals west of the mountains, like those on the Missouri, form large communities, occupying sometimes with their burrows two hundred acres of land : these burrows are separate, and each contains, perhaps, ten or twelve inhabitants. There is a little mound in front of the hole, formed of the earth thrown out of the burrow, and frequently there are three or four of these holes, forming one burrow, around the base of the little mounds. Some of these mounds, which are about two feet in height and four in diameter, are occupied as watch-towers by the inhabitants. The animals, one or more, are irregularly distributed over the tract thus occupied, at the distance of from ten to forty yards; and when any one approaches, they set up a shrill whistling sound, somewhat resembling *tweet, tweet, tweet,* which is the signal for their companions to take the alarm, and retreat within their intrenchments. They feed on the roots of grass, &c.

The small brown squirrel is a beautiful little animal, about the size and form of the red squirrel of the eastern Atlantic States and along the western lakes. The tail is as long as the body and neck, and in shape like that of the red squirrel. The eyes are black, the whiskers long and black, but not abundant; the back, sides, head, neck, and outer part of the legs are of a reddish brown ; the throat, breast, belly, and inner part of the legs of a pale red ; the tail is of a mixture of black and fox-coloured red, in which the black predominates in the middle, and the other on the edges and extremity. The hair of the body is about an inch and a half long, and so fine and soft that it has the appearance of fur ; that of the tail is coarser, and double the length. This animal feeds chiefly on the seeds of different species of pine, and is always found in the pine country.

The ground squirrel we found in every part of the country, and it differs in no respect from those of the United States.

There is still another species, called by Captain Lewis the barking squirrel, found in the plains of the Missouri. This animal commonly weighs about three pounds : its colour is a uniform bright brick red and gray, the former predominating ; and the under side of the neck and belly are lighter than the other parts of the body. The legs are short, and the breast and shoulders wide ; the head is stout and muscular, terminates more bluntly, and is wider and flatter than that of the common squirrel; the ears are short, and appear as though they had been cropped; the jaw is furnished with a pouch to contain his food, but it is not so large as that of the common squirrel; the nose is armed with whiskers on each side, and a few long hairs are inserted on each jaw and directly over the eyes; the eye is small and black; and each foot has five toes, the two outer ones being much shorter than those in the centre. The two inner toes of the fore feet are long and sharp, and well adapted to digging and scratching. From the extremity of the nose to the end of the tail, this animal measures about one foot five inches, of which the tail makes four inches. Notwithstanding the clumsiness of its form, it is remarkably active, and digs in the ground with great rapidity. These animals reside in little subterraneous villages like the burrowing squirrel; and although six or eight usually live together, they have but one entrance to their domicil. Their holes are of great depth, and Captain Lewis once followed one to the depth of ten feet without reaching its termination: they will occupy in this manner several hundred acres of ground. When they are at rest their position is generally erect on their hinder feet and rump; and they sit in this way seemingly with much confidence, barking at any intruder that may approach with a fretful and harmless intrepidity. The noise they make resembles that of the little pet-dog, the yelps being in quick and angry succession, attended by rapid and convulsive motions, as if they were determined to sally forth in defence of their freehold. They feed on the grass of their village, beyond the limits of which they never venture to pass. As soon as the frost commences they shut themselves up in their holes, and continue there till the spring opens. The flesh of this animal is not unpleasant.

Sewellel is the name given by the natives to a small animal found in the timbered country on the Pacific coast, though it is most abundant in the neighbourhood of the Great Falls and Rapids of the Columbia.

The natives make great use of the skins of this animal for robes, dressing them with the fur on, and sewing them together with the sinews of the elk or deer. When dressed, the skin is from fourteen to eighteen inches long, and

from seven to nine in width ; and the natives always separate the tail from it when they make it into robes. This
animal climbs trees and burrows in the ground precisely
like a squirrel. Its ears are short, thin, and pointed, and
covered with a fine short hair of a uniform reddish brown :
the bottom or base of the long hairs, which exceed the fur
but little in length, as well as the fur itself, are of a dark
colour next to the skin for two thirds of the length of the
animal ; the fur and hair are very fine, short, thick-set, and
silky ; the ends of both being of a reddish brown, that colour predominating generally in the appearance of the animal. Although Captain Lewis offered a considerable reward to the Indians for one of these animals, he could
never procure one alive.

The *blaireau*, so called by the French engagés, appears
to be of the civet species, and much resembles the common
badger. These animals inhabit the open plains of the Columbia, in some places those of the Missouri, and are occasionally found in the woods : they burrow in hard ground
with surprising ease and dexterity, and will cover themselves in a very few moments. They have five long nails
on each foot ; those on the fore feet being much the longest, and one on each hind foot being double, as with the
beaver. They weigh from fourteen to eighteen pounds.
The body is long in proportion to its thickness ; the fore
legs are remarkably large and muscular, formed like those
of the turnspit dog, and, as well as the hind legs, are short.
They are broad across the shoulders and breast ; the neck
is short, the mouth wide, and furnished with sharp, straight
teeth both above and below, with four sharp, straight, pointed tusks, two in the upper and two in the lower jaw. The
eyes are black and small ; the whiskers placed in four
points on each side near the nose, and on the jaws near
the opening of the mouth ; the ears short and wide, appearing as if a part had been cut off. The tail is about
four inches in length, the hair on it being longest at the
point of its junction with the body, and growing shorter
till it ends in an acute point. The hair on the body is much
longer on the sides and rump than on any other part,
which gives to the animal an apparent flatness, particularly when it rests upon its belly. The hair is upward of

three inches in length, being longest on the rump, where it extends so far towards the point of the tail that it conceals the shape of the hinder part of the body, giving to it the appearance of a right-angled triangle, the point of the tail forming an acute angle : the small quantity of coarse fur intermixed with the hair is of a reddish pale yellow.

The rat inhabiting the Rocky Mountains, like those on the borders of the Missouri in the neighbourhood of the mountains, is distinguished by having a tail covered with hair like the other parts of the body. * * * The ordinary house rat we found on the banks of the Missouri as far up as the woody country extends ; and the rat first mentioned Captain Lewis found in Georgia, and also in Madison's Cave in Virginia.*

The mice which we saw are precisely the same with those in the United States ; nor does the mole differ in any respect from the species so common there.

The panther is found in the great plains on the Columbia, on the western side of the Rocky Mountains, and on the coast of the Pacific. It is the same animal so well known on the Atlantic coast, and which is most commonly found on the frontiers or in the unsettled parts of the country. * * *

The hare west of the Rocky Mountains inhabits the great plains of the Columbia ; and to the east of those mountains, the plains on the Missouri. It weighs from seven to eleven pounds. The eye is large and prominent, the pupil being of a deep sea-green, and occupying one third of its diameter ; and the iris is of a bright yellowish and silver colour. The ears are placed far back, very near each other, and the animal can dilate and throw them forward, or contract or lay them upon its back, with surprising ease and quickness. The head, neck, back, shoulders, thighs, and outer part of the legs are of a lead colour ; the sides, as they approach the belly, become gradually more white ; the belly, breast, and inner part of the legs and thighs are white, with a light shade of lead colour ; the tail is round and bluntly pointed, covered with white, soft, fine fur, not quite so long as on the other parts of the

* See Journal, i., 244.

body; and the body is covered with a deep, fine, soft, close fur. The colours here described are those which the animal assumes from the middle of April to the middle of November, being the rest of the year of a pure white, except the black and reddish brown of the ears, which never change. A few reddish brown spots are sometimes intermixed with the white, in February, on the head and the upper part of the neck and shoulders. The body of the animal is smaller and longer in proportion to its height than that of the rabbit. When it runs, it carries its tail straight behind: it bounds with surprising agility; is extremely fleet, and never burrows or takes shelter in the ground when pursued. Its teeth are like those of the rabbit, as is also its upper lip, which is divided as high as the nose. Its food is grass and herbs, and in winter it feeds much on the bark of several aromatic herbs growing on the plains. Captain Lewis measured the leaps of this animal, and found them generally from eighteen to twenty-one feet: they are generally found separate, and are never seen to associate in greater numbers than two or three.

The rabbit here is the same as those of our own country, and it is found both on the prairies and woodlands, but is not very abundant.

The polecat is also found in every part of this country. It is very abundant in some parts on the Columbia, particularly in the neighbourhood of the Great Falls and Narrows of that river, where it lives in the cliffs, and feeds on the offal of the Indian fishing establishments. It is of the same species as those found in other parts of North America.

Of the birds which we saw between the Rocky Mountains and the Pacific, we will first mention the grouse or prairie-hen. This bird frequents the great plains of the Columbia, and does not differ from those of the upper portion of the Missouri. Its tail is pointed, the feathers in the centre being much longer than those on the sides. This species differs essentially in the formation of its plumage from those of the Illinois, the tails of the latter being composed of feathers of an equal length. In the winter season it is booted to the first joint of the toes, which are curiously bordered on their lower edges with narrow, hard scales, placed very close to each other, and extending horizontally about an eighth of an inch on each side, adding much to the broadness of the feet: a provision which bounteous Nature has furnished them for passing with more ease over the snows ; and, what is very remarkable, in the summer season these scales drop off. This bird has four toes on each foot, and its colour is a mixture of dark brown, reddish and yellowish brown, and white, confusedly blended. In this assemblage of colours, the reddish brown predominates on the upper parts of the body, wings, and tail, and the white on the belly, and the lower parts of the breast and tail. These birds associate in large flocks in autumn and winter, and even in summer are seen in companies of five or six. They feed on grass, insects, the leaves of various shrubs in the plains, and on the seeds of several species of speth and wild rye, which grow in the richer soils. In winter their food consists of the buds of the willow and cottonwood, and different berries.

The cock of the plains is found in great abundance from the mouth of the southeast fork of the Columbia to that of Clarke's River. Its size is about two and three quarter inches less than that of our ordinary turkey. The beak is large, short, curved and convex, the upper chap exceeding the lower : the nostrils are large, the back is black, and the colour of the rest of the body of a uniform mixture of dark brown, and a reddish and yellowish brown, with some small black specks. In this mixture the dark brown predominates, and has a slight cast of the dove-colour : the wider side of the large feathers of the wings are dark brown, without any other shade. The tail is composed of nineteen feathers, that in the centre being the longest, and the other nine on each side of it gradually diminishing. When folded, the tail comes to a very sharp point, and appears long compared with the body. In the act of flying, the tail appears like that of the wild pigeon, but the motion of the wings closely resembles that of the pheasant and grouse. This bird has four toes on each foot, of which the hindmost is the shortest, and the leg is covered with feathers about half way from the joint to the foot. When its wings are expanded there are wide openings between the feathers, the plumage being too narrow to fill up the space ; and the wings are short compared with those of the grouse o pheasant. The habits of the bird resemble those of the grouse, excepting that it feeds on the leaf and buds of the pulpy-leafed thorn. Captain Lewis did not remember to have seen it but in the neighbourhood of a shrub which they also sometimes feed on, the prickly pear. The gizzard is large, much less compressed and muscular than in most birds, and perfectly resembles a craw. When the bird flies it utters a cackling sound, not unlike that of the dunghill fowl. Its flesh is dark, and only tolerable in point of flavour, being less palatable than that of the pheasant or grouse. The feathers about the head are pointed, stiff, and short, and fine and stiff about the ears ; at the base of the beak there are several hairs. This bird is invaria bly found in the plains.

Of pheasants we observed the large black and white pheasant, the small speckled pheasant, and the small brown pheasant.

The large black and white pheasant differs but little from that of the United States, the brown being rather brighter, with a more reddish tint. This bird has eighteen feathers in the tail, about six inches in length. He is booted to the toes, and the two tufts of long black feathers on each side of the neck are no less observable than in the male of this species inhabiting the United States. The feathers on the body are of a dark brown, tipped with white and black, the black predominating, while the white are irregularly intermixed with the black and dark brown in every part, though in greater proportion about the neck, breast, and belly ; and this mixture makes the bird resemble that kind of dunghill fowl which the housewives of our country call Domminicker. On the breast of some the white predominates. The tufts on the neck leave a space about two and a half inches long and one wide, where no feathers grow, though it is concealed by the plumage on the higher and under parts of the neck ; this space enables them to contract or dilate the feathers on the neck with more ease. The eye is dark, the beak black, curved, and somewhat pointed, the upper chap exceeding the under one ; and a narrow vermillion stripe runs along above each eye, not protuberant, but uneven, with a number of minute rounded dots. The bird feeds on wild fruits, par-ticularly the berry of the *sacacommis*, and inhabits exclu sively the portion of the Rocky Mountains watered by the Columbia.

The small speckled pheasant is found in the same district as the foregoing, and differs from it only in size and colour. It is but half the size of the black and white pheasant, associates in much larger flocks, and is very gentle; the black in its colour is more predominant, and the dark brown feathers are less frequent; the mixture of white is also more general on every part. This bird is smaller than our pheasant, and the body more round; the flesh both of this and the last-named species is dark, and, with our means of cooking, was not well flavoured.

The small brown pheasant inhabits the same country, and is of the same size and shape as the speckled pheasant, which he resembles also in his habits. The stripe above the eye in this species is scarcely perceptible, and is found, when closely examined, to be of a yellow or orange colour instead of vermillion, as in the other species. The colour of the bird is a uniform mixture of dark yellowish brown, with a slight sprinkling of brownish white on the breast and belly, and under the tail; and in its whole appearance it much resembles the common quail. It is booted to the toes, and its flesh is preferable to that of the two preceding.

The buzzard is, we believe, the largest bird of North America. One taken by our hunters, and not in good condition, weighed twenty-five pounds. Between the extremities of the wings he measured nine feet two inches; from the extremity of the beak to the toe, three feet nine and a half inches; and from the hip to the toe, two feet. The circumference of the head was nine and three quarter inches; that of the neck, seven and a half inches; and that of the body, two feet three inches. The diameter of the eye was four and a half tenths of an inch; the iris is of a pale scarlet red, and the pupil of a deep sea-green. The head and part of the neck are without feathers; the tail is composed of twelve feathers of equal length, each being about fourteen inches; the thigh is covered with feathers as low as the knee, and the legs are naked, and not entirely smooth. The toes are four in number, three forward, and that in the centre much the largest; the fourth is short, inserted near the inner part of the three others, and rather

projecting forward; the top or upper part of the toes is imbricated with broad scales lying transversely, and the nails
are black, short, and bluntly pointed. The under side of
the wing is covered with white down and feathers; a
white stripe of about two inches in width marks the outer
part of the wing, embracing the lower points of the plumage, and covering the joint; and the remainder is of a
deep black. The skin of the beak and head to the joining
of the neck is of a pale orange colour, and the other part
destitute of plumage is of a light flesh colour. It is not
known that this bird preys upon living animals : we have
seen him feeding on the remains of the whale and other
fish thrown upon the coast. He was not seen by any of
the party until we had descended below the Great Falls of
the Columbia, and he is believed to be of the vulture
genus, although he lacks some of the characteristics, particularly the hair on the neck and the plumage on the
legs.

The robin is an inhabitant of the Rocky Mountains.
The beak of this bird is smooth, black, and convex; the
upper chap exceeds the other in length, and a few small
black hairs garnish the sides of its base. The eye is of a
uniform deep sea-green colour ; the legs, feet, and talons
are white, the longest claw, including the talon, being of
the same length as the leg : these are slightly imbricated,
curved, and sharply pointed. The crown, from the beak.
back to the neck, embracing more than half the circumference of the neck, and the back and tail, are all of a bluish dark brown; the two outer feathers of the tail being
dashed with white near their tips, though imperceptible when
the tail is folded. A fine black forms the ground of the
wings ; two stripes of the same colour pass on either side
of the head, from the base of the beak to the upper edge of
the eye ; and a third stripe of the same extends from the
sides of the neck to the tips of the wings, across the crop,
in the form of a gorget. The throat, neck, breast, and
belly are of a fine brick red, tinged with yellow, a narrow
stripe of which colour commences just above the centre
of each eye, extending backward to the neck till it comes
in contact with the black stripe before mentioned, to
which it answers as a border. The first and second
ranges of feathers covering the joint of the wing next to

the body are beautifully tipped with brick red, as is also each large feather of the wing on the short side of its plumage. This beautiful little bird feeds on berries. It inhabits exclusively the woody country : we never heard its note, which might be owing to the coldness of the season.

The crow and raven are exactly the same in appearance and note as those on the Atlantic, except that they are much smaller on the Columbia.

Neither do the hawks of the Pacific coast differ from those of the United States. * * * With the crows and ravens, they are common to every part of the country, their nests being found in the high cliffs along the whole course of the Columbia and its southeastern branches.

The large blackbird is the same as those of our country, and is found everywhere west of the mountains.

The large hooting owl we saw only on the Kooskooskee, near the Rocky Mountains. It is the same in form and size as the owl of the United States, though its colours, particularly the reddish brown, appear deeper and brighter.

The turtle-dove and the robin (except the Columbian robin already described) do not differ from those of the United States, and are found both in the plains and in the common broken country.

The magpie most generally inhabits the open country, and resembles those of the Missouri.

The large woodpecker or laycock, the lark woodpecker and the common small white woodpecker with a red head are found only in the timbered lands, and differ in no respect from birds of the same species in the United States.

The lark, which frequents the plains only, and is not unlike what is called in Virginia the old-field lark, is the same with those seen on the Missouri.

The fly-catcher is of two species.

The body of the first is small, of a reddish brown colour, with some fine black specks ; the tail and neck are short, and the beak is pointed. This is of the same species as that which remains all the winter in Virginia, where it is sometimes called the wren. It is the smallest bird we saw except the humming-bird.

The back, head, neck, wing, and tail of the second species are of a yellowish brown ; the breast and belly yellowish white. The tail is short like that of the wren, but the bird itself is a size smaller than the wren : the beak is straight, pointed, convex, rather large at the base, and the chaps are of equal length. Both these species are found exclusively in the woody country.

The blue-crested and the small white-crested corvus are confined to the pine country, as well on the Rocky Mountains as along the Pacific coast.

The snipe of the marshes and the common sand-snipe, the bat, and the white woodpecker, are of the same species as those in the United States.* * *

The black woodpecker is found in most parts of the Rocky Mountains, and in the western and southwestern mountains. It is about the size of the lark woodpecker or turtle-dove, though his wings are longer than those of either of these. The beak is an inch in length, black, curved at the base, and sharply pointed, with the chaps of equal length ; and around its base, including the eye and a small part of the throat, there is a fine crimson red. The neck, as low down as the crop in front, is of an iron gray ; the belly and breast present a curious mixture of white and blood-red, which has much the appearance of paint, the red predominating ; the top of the head, the back and sides, and the upper surface of the wings and tail, appear of a glossy green in a certain exposure to the light, and the under side of the wings and tail is of a sooty black. The tail has ten feathers, sharply pointed, those in the centre being the longest, or about two and a half inches in length. The tongue is barbed and pointed, and of an elastic, cartilaginous substance ; the eye is rather large, the pupil black, and the iris of a dark yellowish brown. The movements of this bird when flying, and also its notes, resemble those of the small red-headed woodpecker common in the United States. The pointed tail renders it essential service in retaining its resting position against the perpendicular sides of trees. The legs and feet are black, and covered with wide imbricated scales ; and it has four toes on each foot, two extending back and two forward, the nails of which are much curved, pointed, and very sharp. It feeds on bugs and other insects.

The calumet eagle is sometimes found on the western side of the Rocky Mountains, as Captain Lewis was informed by the natives, in whose possession he saw their plumage. They are of the same species as those on the Missouri, and are the most beautiful of all the eagles in America. The colours are black and white, richly variegated. The tail feathers (so highly prized by the Indians) are twelve in number, of unequal length, and white to within two inches of their extremities, where they suddenly change to a jetty black. The wings have a large circular white spot in the middle, which is only visible when they are extended; and the body is variously marked with black and white. In form they resemble the bald eagle, but are rather smaller, and fly with much greater rapidity. This bird is feared by all his carnivorous competitors, which, on his approach, instantly abandon the carcass on which they had been feeding. The female breeds in the most inaccessible parts of the mountains, where she makes her summer residence, and descends to the plains only in the fall and winter seasons. The natives are constantly on the watch for them at these seasons, and so highly is their plumage prized by the Mandans, the Minnetarees, and the Ricaras, that for the tail feathers of two of these birds they will give a good horse or gun; and among the Great and Little Osages, and the nations inhabiting countries where the bird is more rarely seen, the price is even double this. With these feathers the Indians decorate the stems of their sacred pipes or calumets, whence the name of calumet given to the bird is derived. The Ricaras often domesticate this bird for the purpose of obtaining its plumage. The natives also fasten these feathers in their hair, decorate their war caps or bonnets with them, and attach them to the manes and tails of their favourite horses.

As we were near the coast only during the winter, many of the aquatic birds may have retired from the cold, and been lost to our observation. We saw, however, the large blue and brown heron; the fish-hawk; the blue-crested fisher; several species of gulls; the cormorant; two species of loons; brant of two kinds; geese; swan, and several species of ducks.

The large blue and brown herons, or cranes, as they are usually termed, are found on the Columbia below tidewater, and differ in no respect from the same species in the United States. The same remark will apply to the fish-hawk and the blue-crested or king fisher, both of which are found everywhere on the Columbia and its tributary waters.

Of gulls we noticed four species on the coast and river. all common to the United States.

The cormorant is, properly speaking, a large black duck that feeds on fish ; and Captain Lewis could perceive no difference between this bird there and those frequenting the Potomac and other rivers on the Atlantic coast.

Of loon there were two species, the first, or speckled loon, being found on all the rivers west of the mountains, and of the same size, colour, and form as those of the Atlantic coast.

The second species we saw at the Falls of Columbia, and from thence downward to the ocean. This bird is not more than half the size of the other : its neck is long, slender, and white ; the plumage on the body, and on the top of the head and neck, is of a dun or ash colour ; the breast and belly are white ; the beak is like that of the speckled loon ; and, like it, it cannot fly, but flutters along on the surface of the water, or dives when pursued.

The brant are of three kinds : the white, the brown, and the pied.

The white brant are very common on the shores of the Pacific, where they remain in vast numbers during the winter ; and, like the swan-geese, feed on the grass, roots, and seeds which grow in the marshes.*   *   *

The brown brant are nearly of the same colour, size, and form as the white, only that their wings are considerably longer and more pointed. The plumage on the upper part of the body, neck, head, and tail resembles in colour that of the Canadian goose, though somewhat darker, from some dark feathers being irregularly scattered throughout ; neither have they the same white on the neck and sides of the head as the goose, nor is the neck darker than the body ; though, like the goose, they have some white feathers on the rump at the insertion of the tail. The beak is dark, as are also the legs and feet, with a greenish cast ; the breast and belly are of a lighter colour than the back, and are also irregularly spotted with dark brown and black feathers, which give it a pied appearance ; the flesh

* For description, see Journal, i., 194,

II.—E ᴇ

is darker and better than that of the goose. * * * There is no difference between this bird and the brant so common on the lakes, the Ohio, and the Mississippi.

The pied brant weighs about eight and a half pounds, differing from the ordinary pied brant in its wings, which are neither so long nor so pointed. * * * Its note is also much like that of the common pied brant, from which, in fact, it is not to be distinguished at a distance, although it is certainly of a distinct species. * * *

Of geese there are two kinds, the large and small. The large goose is like our ordinary wild or Canadian goose: the small is rather less than the brant, which it resembles in the head and neck, which are larger in proportion than those of the goose ; the beak is likewise thicker and shorter, and its note is similar to that of the tame goose. In all other points it resembles the larger kind, with which it so frequently associates that it was some time before we discovered it to be a distinct species.*

There are also two kinds of swan, the large and the small. The large swan is the same as that in the Atlantic States : the small differs from it only in size and in note, it being about one fourth less, and its note entirely different. The note, which is as loud as that of the large species, begins with a kind of whistling sound, terminating in a round, full tone, loudest at the end, whence it might be denominated the whistling-swan. Its habits, colour, and contour appear to be precisely like those of the larger kind. This bird was first found below the Great Narrows of the Columbia, near the Chilluckittequaw nation : they were very abundant about the coast, and remained there all the winter, being five times as numerous as those of the large species.

Of ducks there are many kinds : the duckinmallard, the canvass-back duck, the red-headed fishing duck, the black and white duck, the little brown duck, the black duck, two species of divers, and the blue-winged teal.

The duckinmallard, or common large duck, resembles the domestic duck, is very abundant, and found on every part of the Columbia below the mountains. * * *

The canvass-back duck is a most beautiful bird, and, as

is well known, very delicious to the palate. It is found in considerable numbers at the mouth of the Columbia. It is of the same species as those in the Delaware, Susquehannah, and Potomac, and of equally fine flavour. * * *

The red-headed fishing-duck is common to every part of the river, and was the only duck we saw on the waters of the Columbia within the Rocky Mountains. It is the same in every respect as those on the Atlantic coast.

The black and white duck is small, and of a size larger than the teal. The male is beautifully variegated with black and white ; the white occupying the breast and back, the tail, the feathers of the wings, and two tufts of feathers which cover the upper part of the wings when folded, and likewise the neck and head : the female is the largest. This is believed to be of the same species as the duck common on the Atlantic coast, called the butter-box. The beak is wide and short, and, as well as the legs, of a dark colour : its flesh is extremely well flavoured. * * *

The black duck found on the Columbia is the same as Captain Lewis noticed on many parts of the Ohio and Mississippi Rivers ; and the divers and the blue-winged teal resemble in all respects those of the United States.

The fish we saw on the coast and in the Columbia were the whale, porpoise, skait, flounder, salmon, red char, two species of salmon trout, mountain or speckled trout, bottlenose, anchovy, and sturgeon.

The whale is sometimes pursued and taken with the harpoon by the Indians, but is much more frequently killed by running against the rocks in violent storms, and thrown on shore by the wind and tide. * * *

The porpoise, skait, and flounder are the same as those found on the Atlantic coast.

The common salmon and red char are inhabitants both of the sea and rivers. The former are usually the largest, and weigh from five to fifteen pounds. They are found in all the rivers and little creeks on the western side of the continent, and the natives are greatly indebted to them for their subsistence. The body of the fish is from two and a half to three feet long, proportionably broad, and covered with imbricated scales of a moderate size : the eye is large, the iris of a silvery colour, and the pupil black ; the rostrum or nose extends beyond the under jaw, and both jaws are armed with a single series of long teeth, which are subulate and inflected near the extremities of the jaws, where they are also more closely arranged ; they have also some sharp teeth of smaller size, and sharp points on the tongue, which is thick and fleshy. The fins of the back are two : the first is placed nearer the head than the ventral fins, and has several rays ; while the second is far back, near the tail, and has no rays. The flesh of this fish, when in order, is of a deep flesh-coloured red, and of every shade from that to an orange yellow, but when very meagre it is almost white. The roe is in high estimation among the natives, who dry it in the sun, and preserve it for a great length of time. * * *

The red char is rather broader in proportion to its length than the common salmon. The scales are also imbricated, but rather larger ; the rostrum extends far beyond the under jaw, and the teeth are neither so large nor numerous as those of the salmon. Some of these fish are almost entirely red on the belly and sides ; others are much whiter than the salmon, and none of them are variegated with dark spots, though in regard to their flesh, roe, and every particular with regard to form, they are like that fish.

Of salmon trout we observed two kinds, differing only in colour. They are seldom more than two feet in length, and are much narrower in proportion to their length than the salmon or red char. The jaws are nearly of the same length, and are furnished with a single series of subulate, straight teeth, neither as long nor as large as those of the salmon. The mouth is wide, and on the tongue there are also some teeth : the fins are placed much like those of the salmon. At the Great Falls we found this fish of a silvery white colour on the belly and sides, and of a bluish light brown on the back and head. The other kind is of a dark colour on its back, and its sides and belly are yellow, with transverse stripes of dark brown ; a little red being sometimes intermixed with these colours on the belly and sides towards the head. The eye, flesh, and roe are like those of the salmon.

The white species found below the Falls were in excellent order when the salmon were entirely out of season, and not fit for use : they associate with the red char in little rivulets and creeks. This fish is about two feet eight

inches in length, and weighs about ten pounds : the eye is
moderately large, the pupil black, with a small admixture
of yellow, and the iris of a silvery white, a little tinged
near its border with a yellowish brown. The fins are
small in proportion to the size of the fish, and are bony,
though not pointed, except the tail and back fins, which
are slightly so. The prime back fin and the ventral ones
contain each ten rays ; those of the gills, thirteen ; that of
the tail, twelve ; and the small fin placed near and above
the tail has no bony rays, but is a tough, flexible substance,
covered with a smooth skin. It is thicker in proportion to
its width than the salmon : the tongue is thick and firm,
armed on each border with small subulate teeth in a single
series, and the teeth and the mouth are as before described:
Neither this fish nor the salmon are caught with the hook,
nor do we know on what they feed.

The mountain or speckled trout is found in the waters
of the Columbia within the mountains. It is the same as
those in the upper part of the Missouri, but is not so abundant : we never saw this fish below the mountains.

The bottlenose is the same as that seen in the Missouri,
and is found exclusively within the mountains.

The anchovy, called by the natives *olthen*, is so delicate
a fish that it soon becomes tainted unless pickled or
smoked. The Indians run a small stick through the gills,
and either hang them up to dry in the smoke of their
lodges, or kindle small fires under them for this purpose. * * *

Of shellfish we observed the clam, the periwinkle, the
common muscle, the cockle, and a species with a circular
flat shell. The clam of the Pacific coast is very small ;
the shell consisting of two valves opening with hinges, and
being smooth, thin, of an oval form like that of the common
muscle, and of a sky-blue colour. It is about one and a
half inches in length, and hangs in clusters to the moss of
the rocks : the natives sometimes cat them. The periwinkle, both of the river and the ocean, is similar to
those found in the same situation on the Atlantic coast.
The common muscle of the river is the same as that
in the rivers on the Atlantic : the cockle is small, and
also closely resembles that in the Atlantic. There is
likewise an animal inhabiting a shell that is perfectly cir-

cular, about three inches in diameter, thin and entire on the margin, convex and smooth on the upper side, plain on the under part, and covered with a number of minute capillary fibres, by means of which it attaches itself to the sides of the rocks. The shell is thin, and consists of one valve, with a small circular valve in the centre of the under shell : the animal is soft and boneless.

The pellucid jelly-like substance, called the sea-nettle, is found in great abundance along the strand of the Pacific, where it is thrown up by the waves and tide.

There are two species of fuci thrown up in this manner. The first species consists, at one extremity, of a large vesicle or hollow vessel, which will contain from one to two gallons : it is of a conic shape, the base of which forms the extreme end, and is convex and globular, having in its centre some short, broad, angular fibres. Its substance is of about the consistence of the rind of a citron melon, and three fourths of an inch thick ; the rind being smooth from the small extremity of the cone... A long, hollow, cylindrical, and regularly tapering tube extends to twenty or thirty feet, and terminates in a number of branches, which are flat, half an inch in width, and rough, particularly on the edges, where they are furnished with a number of little ovate vesicles or bags of the size of a pigeon's egg. This plant seems calculated to float at each extremity, while the little end of the tube, from whence the branches proceed, lies deepest in the water. The other species, seen on the coast towards the Killamucks, resembles a large pumpkin : it is solid, and its specific gravity greater than the water, though sometimes thrown on shore by the waves. It is of a yellowish brown colour, the rind smooth, and its consistence harder than that of the pumpkin, but easily cut with a knife : there are some dark brown fibres, rather harder than any other part, which pass longitudinally through the pulp or fleshy substance which forms the interior of this marine production.

The reptiles we saw in the country west of the Rocky Mountains are the rattlesnake,* the gartersnake, the lizard, and the snail.

The gartersnake appears to belong to the same family

* See Journal, i., 202.

as the common gartersnake of the Atlantic coast, and, like that snake, it has no poisonous qualities. It has one hundred and sixty scuti on the abdomen, and seventy on the tail : those on the abdomen near the head and jaws, as high as the eye, are of a bluish white, and as they recede from the head they become of a dark brown. The field of the back and sides is black : a narrow stripe of light yellow runs along the centre of the back ; and on each side of this stripe there is a range of small, tranverse, oblong spots, of a pale brick red, diminishing as they recede from the head, and disappearing at the commencement of the tail. The pupil of the eye is black, with a narrow ring of white bordering on its edge, and the remainder of the iris is of a dark yellowish brown.

The horned lizard, called, and for what reason we could never learn, the prairie buffalo, is a native of the country west of the mountains, as well as on the Missouri : it is of the same size, and much the same in appearance, as the black lizard.*

The vegetable productions of the country on the Columbia, furnishing a large proportion of the food of the natives, are the roots of a species of thistle, the fern, rush, liquorice, and a small cylindrical root resembling in flavour and consistency the sweet potato.

The thistle, called by the natives *shanataque*, grows in a deep, rich, dry loam, with a considerable mixture of sand. The stem is simple, ascending, cylindric, and hispid, and rises to the height of three or four feet. The cauline leaf is simple, crenate, and oblong, rather more obtuse at its apex than at its insertion, decurrent, and its position declining, while its margin is armed with prickles, and its disk hairy. The flower was dry and mutilated when we saw it, but the pericarp seemed to be much like that of the common thistle. The root-leaves, which still possessed their verdure, and were about half grown, were of a pale green colour. The root, which is the only part used, is from nine to fifteen inches long, about the size of a man's thumb, perpendicular, fusiform, and with from two to four radicles ; the rind being of a brown colour, and somewhat rough. When first taken from the earth it is

* For further account. see Journal, ii., 230.

white, and nearly as crisp as a carrot, and in this state is sometimes eaten without any preparation. But when pre pared by the same process as that used for the *pashecɩ quamash,* which is the most usual and the best method, it becomes black, and is much improved in flavour. Its taste is exactly like that of sugar, and it is the sweetest vege· table eaten by the Indians. After being baked in the kiln, it is eaten either simply or with train oil; sometimes pounded fine and mixed with cold water, until it is reduced to the consistence of *sagamity,* or Indian mush, which last was the most agreeable to our palates.

Three species of fern grew in the neighbourhood of our winter encampment at the mouth of the Columbia, but the root of only one is eaten. It is very abundant in those parts of the open lands and prairies which have a deep, loose, rich, black loam, without any sand, where it attains the height of four or five feet, and is a beautiful plant, of a fine green colour in summer. The stem, which is smooth, cylindric, and slightly grooved on one side, rises erectly for about half its height, when it divides into two branches, or, rather, long footstalks, which put forth in pairs from one side only, and near the edges of the groove, declining backward from the grooved side. These footstalks them· selves are likewise grooved and cylindric; and as they gradually taper towards the extremities, put forth others of a smaller size, which are alternate, and have forty or fifty alternate, pinnate, horizontal, and sessile leaves. The leaves are multipartite for half the length of their footstalk, when they assume the tongue-like form altogether; being also revolute, with the upper disk smooth, and the lower resembling cotton. The top is annual, and was therefore dead when we saw it, but it produces neither flower nor fruit. The root is perennial, and grows horizontally, sometimes a little diverging or obliquely descending, and frequently dividing itself as it extends, and shooting up a number of stems. It lies about four inches under the surface of the earth, is of a cylindrical form, with few or no radicles, and varies from the size of a goose-quill to that of a man's finger. The bark is black, thin, brittle, and rather rough, and easily separates in flakes from the part which is eaten, being divided in the centre into two parts by a strong, flat, white ligament, like a piece of thin tape;

on each side of which is a white substance, resembling, after the root is roasted, both in appearance and flavour, the dough of wheat. It has a pungency, however, which was disagreeable to us, though the natives eat it voraciously, and it seems to be very nutritious.

The rush is most commonly used by the Killamucks and other Indians along the seacoast, on the sands of which it grows in greatest abundance. From each root a single stem rises erectly to the height of three or four feet, somewhat thicker than a large quill, hollow and jointed : about twenty or thirty long, lineal, stellate, or radiate and horizontal leaves surround the stem at each joint, about half an inch above which its stem is sheathed like the sandrush. When green it resembles that plant also in appearance, as well as in having a rough stem. It is not branching, nor does it bear, as far as we could discover, either flower or seed. At the bottom of this stem, which is annual, is a strong radicle, about an inch long, descending perpendicularly to the root ; while just above the junction of this radicle with the stem, the latter is surrounded, in the form of a wheel, with six or nine other radicles descending obliquely. The root attached to the perpendicular radicle is a perennial solid bulb, about an inch long, and of the thickness of a man's thumb, of an ovate form, depressed on one or two of its sides, and covered with a thin, smooth, black rind : the pulp is white, brittle, and easily masticated. It is commonly roasted, though sometimes eaten raw, but in both states is rather an insipid root.

The liquorice of this country does not differ from that common in the United States. It here delights in a deep, loose, sandy soil, and grows very large and abundantly. It is prepared by being roasted in the embers, and pounded slightly with a small stick, in order to separate from it the strong ligament in its centre, which is thrown away, and the rest is eaten. Prepared in this way it has an agreeable flavour, not unlike that of the sweet potato.* The root of the cattail, or cooper's flag, is likewise eaten by the Indians ; and also a small, dry, tuberous root, two inches in length, and about the thickness of the finger : this is eaten raw, and is crisp, milky, and of an agreeable flavour.

* See Journal, ii., 115.

Besides the small cylindrical root mentioned above, there is another of the same form and appearance, which is usually boiled, and eaten with train oil. Its taste, however, is disagreeably bitter.

But the most valuable of all the Indian roots is the *wappatoo*, or the bulb of the common sagittifolia, or arrowhead. It does not grow near the mouth of the Columbia, but is found in great abundance in the marshy grounds of that beautiful valley, which extends from near the Quicksand River seventy miles westward, and is a principal article of trade between the inhabitants of that valley and those of the seacoast.

This shrub rises to the height of four or five feet, the stem being simple and much branched. The bark is of a reddish dark brown, being on the main stem somewhat rough, while on the boughs it is smooth : the leaf is obtuse at the apex, and acute and angular at the insertion of the pedicle ; three fourths of an inch in length, and three eighths in width, smooth, and of a paler green than evergreens generally are. The fruit is a small deep purple berry, of a pleasant flavour ; the natives eat the berry when ripe, but seldom collect it in quantities to dry for winter use.*

The native fruits and berries in most general use among the Indians are the *shallun*, the *solmc*, the cranberry, a berry like the black haw, the scarlet berry of the plant called *sacacommis*, and a purple berry like the whortleberry.

The *shallun* is an evergreen plant, abounding near the mouth of the Columbia, and its leaves are the favourite food of the elk. It is of a thick growth, rising cylindrically to the height of three, and sometimes five feet, and varying from the size of a goose-quill to that of a man's thumb. The stem is simple, branching, reclining, and partially flexuose, with a bark which, on the older part, is of a reddish brown colour, while the younger branches are red where exposed to the sun, and green elsewhere. The leaf is three fourths of an inch in length, two and a half in breadth, and of an oval form ; the upper disk being of a glossy deep green, and the under of a pale green. The fruit is a deep purple berry about the size of a common.

* See Journal ii., 85, 171.

black cherry, oval, and rather bluntly pointed : the pericarp is divided into five acute angular points, and envelops a soft pulp containing a great number of small brown
seeds.

The *solme* is a small pale red berry, the production of a
plant resembling in size and shape that which produces
the fruit called in the United States Solomon's seal-berry,
the berry being attached to the stem in the same manner.
It is of a globular form, containing a soft pulp which envelops four seeds about the size of the seed of the common
small grape. It grows among the woodland moss, and is,
to all appearance, an annual plant.

The cranberry is of the low, viny kind, and grows in
marshes or bogs : it is precisely the same as the cranberry
of the United States.

The fruit which, though rather larger, resembles in
shape the black haw, is a light brown berry, the product of
a tree resembling in size, shape, and appearance that
which in the United States is called the wild crab-apple.
The leaf, too, is precisely the same, as is also the bark both
in texture and colour. The berries grow in clumps of from
three to eighteen or twenty, at the end of the small branches, each berry being supported by a separate stem : the
berry is ovate, and its lower end slightly concave. The
wood of this tree is excessively hard, and the natives
make wedges of it to split their boards and firewood, and to
hollow out their canoes. Our party likewise made use of
it for wedges and axe-handles. The fruit is exceedingly
acid, and resembles in flavour the wild crab. The pericarp contains a soft, pulpy substance, divided into four
cells, each containing a single seed ; and its outer coat
consists of a thin and smooth, though firm and tough pellicle.

The plant called *sacacommis* by the Canadian traders
derives its name from the clerks of the trading companies
being generally very fond of smoking its leaves, which
they carry about them in a small bag. It grows generally
in open pine districts or on their borders. We found it in
the prairies bordering on the Rocky Mountains, and in the
more open woodlands. It is indiscriminately the growth
of a very rich and very poor soil, and is found in the same
abundance in both. The natives on the western side of

the Rocky Mountains are very fond of this berry, althc .,h
to us it was a very tasteless and insipid fruit. The s.r.ib
is an evergreen, and retains its verdure in the same per-
fection the whole year round. However inclement the
climate, the root puts forth a great number of stems, which
separate near the surface of the ground, each stem being
from the size of a small quill to that of a man's finger.
The stems are much branched, the branches forming an
acute angle with them, and are more properly procumbent than creeping, although both the stems and branches
sometimes put forth radicles, which strike obliquely into
the ground. These radicles, however, are by no means
general, or equal in their distances from each other, nor
do they appear calculated to furnish nutriment to the
plant. The bark is formed of several layers of a smooth,
thin, brittle, and reddish substance, easily separated from
the stem. The leaves, with respect to their position, are
scattered, yet closely arranged, particularly near the ex
tremities of the twigs : they are about three fourths of an
inch in length, oval, obtusely pointed, of a deep green,
slightly grooved, and the footstalk is of proportionable
length. The berry is attached in an irregular manner to
the small boughs among the leaves, and is always supported by a separate, small, short peduncle : the insertion produces a slight concavity in the berry, while its opposite
end is slightly convex. The outer coat of the pericarp is
a thin, firm, tough pellicle, while the inner coat consists
of a dry, mealy powder, of a yellowish white colour, en-
veloping from four to six large, light brown seeds. The
colour of the fruit is a fine scarlet, and the natives eat it
without any preparation. It ripens in September, and remains on the bushes all the winter, unaffected by the frost.
These berries are sometimes gathered and hung in the
lodges in bags, where they are dried without farther
trouble.

The deep purple berry, like the whortleberry, terminates
bluntly, and has a cap or cover at the end. The berries
are attached separately to the sides of the boughs by a
short stem hanging underneath, and they often grow very
near each other on the same bough : they separate very
easily from the stem ; the leaves adhere closely. The
shrub is an evergreen, and rises to the height of six or

eight feet, growing sometimes on high lands, but more frequently on low marshy grounds. It is about ten inches in circumference, divides into many irregular branches, and seldom more than one stem springs from the same root, though they associate very thickly : the bark is somewhat rough, and of a reddish brown colour, and the wood is very hard. The leaves are alternate, and attached by a short footstalk to the horizontal sides of the boughs : their form is a long oval, rather more acute towards the apex than at the point of insertion ; their margin slightly serrate, the sides collapsing, thick, firm, smooth, and glossy ; the under surface being of a pale or whitish green, and the upper of a fine deep green. This beautiful shrub retains its verdure throughout the year, and is more peculiarly beautiful in winter. The natives sometimes eat the berries without preparation, sometimes they dry them in the sun, and at others in their sweating-kilns. They very frequently pound them, and bake them in large loaves weighing from ten to fifteen pounds ; the bread keeping very well for one season, an l retaining its juices better by this mode of preparation than any other. This bread is broken and stirred in cold water until it acquires the consistency of soup, when it is eaten.

Trees of a large growth are very abundant, the whole neighbourhood of the Pacific coast being well supplied with excellent timber. The predominating wood is the fir, of which we saw several species. There is one singular circumstance attending all the pine of this country, which is, that when consumed it yields not the slightest particle of ashes. The first species grows to an immense size, and is very commonly twenty-seven feet in circumference six feet from the ground, rising to the height of two hundred and thirty feet, and one hundred and twenty of that height without a limb. We often found them thirty-six feet in circumference. One of our party measured one, and found it to be forty-two feet in circumference at a point above the reach of an ordinary man. This trunk for the distance of two hundred feet was destitute of limbs : the tree, too, was perfectly sound, and, at a moderate calculation, its height might be estimated at three hundred feet. The timber is straight-grained throughout, and rives better than any other species : the bark scales off in flakes irregularly round, and is of a reddish brown colour, particularly the younger growth; the trunk is simple, branching, and not very proliferous. The leaf is acerose, one tenth of an inch in width, and three fourths in length, firm, stiff, and acuminate: it is triangular, a little declining, and thickly scattered on all sides of the bough, and springs from small triangular pedestals of soft, spongy, elastic bark at the junction of the boughs. The bud-scales continue to encircle their respective twigs for several years: Captain Lewis counted as many as four years' growths beyond the scales. This tree yields but little resin, and we were never able to discover any cone, although we felled several of the trees.

The second is a much more common species, and constitutes at least one half of the timber near the mouth of the Columbia. It seems to resemble the spruce, rises from one hundred and sixty to one hundred and eighty feet, and is from four to six feet in diameter, straight, round, and regularly tapering. The bark is thin, of a dark colour, and much divided by small longitudinal interstices: that of the boughs and of young trees is somewhat smooth, but less so than that of the balsam fir. The wood is white, very soft, but difficult to rive: the trunk is a simple, branching, diffuse stem, not so proliferous as the pines and firs usually are. It puts forth buds from the sides of the small boughs as well as from their extremities, and the stem terminates, like the cedar, in a slender pointed top. The leaves are petiolate, their footstalks being short, acerose, and rather more than half a line in width, while the leaves themselves are very unequal in length, the longest seldom exceeding one inch, while others, intermixed on every part of the bough, are not more than a quarter of an inch. The leaf has a small longitudinal channel on the upper disk, which is of a deep glossy green, while the under disk is of a whitish green: the wood yields but little resin. The cone is not longer than the end of a man's thumb; it is soft, flexible, of an ovate form, and produced at the ends of the small twigs.

The third species resembles in all points the Canadian balsam fir: it grows from two and a half to four feet in diameter, and rises to the height of eighty or a hundred feet. The stem is simple, branching, and proliferous: its leaves are sessile, acerose, one eighth of an inch in length, and one sixteenth in breadth, thickly scattered on the twigs, and adhering to the under sides only ; gibbous, a little declining, obtusely pointed, soft, and flexible. The upper disk is marked longitudinally with a slight channel of a deep glossy green ; the under one is of a pale green, and not glossy. This tree affords considerable quantities of a fine aromatic balsam, resembling the balsam of Canada in taste and appearance. The small pistils, when filled, rise like a blister on the trunk and branches. The bark that envelops these pistils is soft, and easily punctured. The general appearance of the bark is dark, and smooth, but less so than that of the white pine of our country. The wood is white and soft.

The fourth species in size resembles the second. The stem is simple, branching, ascending, and proliferous : the bark is of a reddish dark brown, thicker than that of the third species, and divided by longitudinal interstices, not so large as in the second species. The leaves are placed like those of the balsam fir, but are only two thirds as wide, and of little more than half their length, nor is the upper disk as green and glossy. The wood yields no balsam, and but little resin ; it is white and tough, although rather porous.

The fifth species is also of about the same size as the second, and has a trunk simple, branching, and proliferous. The bark is thin, of a dark brown colour, divided longitudinally by interstices, and scales off in thin rolling flakes : it yields but little balsam. Two thirds of the diameter of the trunk in the centre presents a reddish white, and the remainder is white, porous, and tough. The twigs are much longer and more slender than in either of the other species : the leaves are acerose, one twentieth of an inch in width, and one inch in length ; sessile, inserted on all sides of the bough, straight, and obliquely pointing towards the extremities. The upper disk has a small longitudinal channel, is of a deep green, and not so glossy as in the balsam fir. The under disk is of a pale green.

We have seen a species of this fir on low marshy grounds, resembling in all points the foregoing, except that it branches more diffusely. This tree is generally about thirty feet in height and two in diameter. The diffuseness of

its branches may result from its open situation, as it seldom grows in the neighbourhood of other trees. The cone
is two and a half inches in length, and three and three
quarters round in its greatest circumference. It tapers
regularly to a point, and is formed of imbricated scales, of
a bluntly-rounded form. A thin leaf is inserted in the pith
of the cone, which overlays the centre of, and extends half
an inch beyond, the point of each scale.

The sixth species does not differ from what is called the
white pine in Virginia, except in the unusual length of its
cone, which is sometimes sixteen or eighteen inches long,
and about four in circumference. It grows on the north
side of the Columbia, near the ocean.

The seventh and last species is found in low grounds,
and in places frequently overflowed by the tide, seldom rising higher than thirty-five feet, and not being more than
from two and a half to four feet in diameter. The stem
is simple, branching, and proliferous ; and the bark resembles that of the first species, though more rugged. The
leaves are acerose, two tenths of an inch in width, and
three fourths in length, firm, stiff, and a little acuminated :
they end in short, pointed tendrils, gibbous, and thickly
scattered on all sides of the branch, though adhering only
to the three under sides : those inserted beneath incline
sidewise, with upward points, presenting the leaf in the
shape of a scythe ; while the others are pointing upward,
sessile, and, like those of the first species, grow from small
triangular pedestals of a spongy, soft, and elastic bark.
The under disk is of a deep glossy green, the upper of a
pale whitish green. The boughs retain leaves of six years'
growth : the bud scales resemble those of the first species.
The cone is of an ovate figure, three and a half inches in
length, and three in circumference, thickest in the middle,
tapering, and terminating in two obtuse points : it is composed of small, flexible scales, imbricated, and of a reddish
brown colour. Each scale covers two small seeds, and is
itself covered in the centre by a small, thin, inferior scale,
acutely pointed : these scales proceed from the sides of
the boughs as well as from their extremities. This tree
was nowhere to be seen above the Wappatoo.

The stem of the black alder arrives to a great size. It
is simple, branching, and diffuse : the bark is smooth, of a

light colour, with white spreading spots, resembling those of the beech ; and the leaf, fructification, &c., resemble precisely those of the common alder of our country. They grow separately from different roots, and not in clusters, like those of the United States. The black alder does not cast its leaf until the 1st of December. It is sometimes found growing to the height of sixty or seventy feet, and from two to four feet in diameter.

There is a tree growing along the Columbia, below the entrance of Cataract River, which, when divested of its foliage, much resembles the ash. The trunk is simple, branching, and diffuse ; the leaf petiolate, plain, divided by four deep lines, similar to that of the palm, and considerably lobate ; the lobes terminating in from three to five angular points, and their margins being indented with irregular and somewhat circular incisures. The petiole is cylindrical, smooth, and seven inches long, and the leaf itself eight inches in length, and twelve in breadth. This tree is frequently three feet in diameter, and rises from forty to fifty feet : its fruit is a winged seed, somewhat resembling that of the maple.

In the same part of the country there is a tree resembling the white maple, though much smaller, and seldom of more than six or seven inches in diameter. These trees grow in clusters, from fifteen to twenty feet in height, from the same bed of roots, spreading and leaning outward. The twigs are long and slender ; the stem is simple and branching ; the bark resembles in colour that of the white maple : the leaf is petiolate, plain, scattered, nearly circular, with acute angular incisures round the margin, of an inch in length, and from six to eight in number ; the acute angular points being crenate, three inches in length and four in width. The petiole is cylindric, smooth, and an inch and a quarter in length : the fruit was not seen.

. The undergrowth consists of the honeysuckle, the alder, the seven bark, or, as it is called in the United States, nine bark, the whortleberry, a shrub like the quillwood, a plant resembling the mountain-holly, the green brier, and the fern.

The honeysuckle common in the United States we found about the mouth of the Columbia, having first discovered it on the waters of the Kooskooskee, near the country of the Chopunnish, and afterward below the Grand Rapids.

II.—F f

An alder resembling that of our country we found also in great abundance in the woodlands on the west side of the Rocky Mountains. It differs, however, in the colour of its berry, which is of a pale sky blue, whereas that of the United States is of a deep purple.

The seven bark, which is the same as the nine bark of the United States, is also common here.

There is a species of whortleberry here, found on the highlands from the Columbia Valley to the seacoast, rising to the height of six or eight feet, branching and diffuse. The stem is cylindrical, and of a dark brown colour; the collateral branches being green, smooth, and square, and putting forth a number of alternate branches of the same colour from the two horizontal sides only. The fruit is a small deep purple berry, held in much esteem by the natives. The leaf is of a pale green, three fourths of an inch in length, and three eighths in width; oval, and terminating more acutely at the apex than at the insertion of the footstalk; the base nearly entire, and but slightly serrate: the footstalks are short; their relative position being alternate, two-rowed, and proceeding from the horizontal sides of the boughs only.

There are two species of shrubs, which were first seen at the Grand Rapids of the Columbia, and afterward elsewhere, growing in rich dry grounds, usually in the neighbourhood of some watercourse. The roots are creeping and cylindrical: the stem of the first species is from a foot to eighteen inches in height, and about as large as an ordinary goosequill; simple, unbranched, and erect. Its leaves are cauline, compound, and spreading; the leaflets being jointed, oppositely pinnate, three paired, terminating in one footstalk, widest at the base, and tapering to an acuminate point. They are an inch and a quarter in their greatest width, and three inches and a quarter in length; each point of the margin being armed with a subulate thorn, of which there are from thirteen to seventeen in number. They are veined, glossy, carinate, and wrinkled, their points tending obliquely towards the common footstalk.

The stem of the second species is procumbent, about the size of that of the first species, jointed and unbranched. Its leaves are cauline, compound, and oppositely pinnate ; the rib being from fourteen to sixteen inches in length, cylindric, and smooth. The leaflets are two inches and a half long, one inch wide, and of the greatest breadth half an inch from the base, which they regularly surround, and taper from it to an acute apex, usually terminated by a small subulate thorn. They are jointed and oppositely pinnate, consisting of six pairs, and terminating in one ; sessile, serrate, and ending in a small subulate point, of which there are from twenty-five to twenty-seven in all. They are smooth, plain, of a deep green, and all obliquely tending towards the footstalk, and retain their colour through the winter.

The green brier grows most abundantly in rich dry lands in the vicinity of water-courses, but is also found in small quantities in pine lands at a distance from water. In the former situation the stem is frequently of the size of a man's finger, and rises perpendicularly four or five feet ; it then descends in an arch, becoming procumbent, or resting on some neighbouring plant : it is simple, un-branched, and cylindric ; and in the last-mentioned situation it grows much smaller, and is usually procumbent. The stem is armed with sharp, forked briers ; the leaf is peti-olate, ternate, and resembles in shape and appearance that of the purple raspberry, so common in the Atlantic States. The fruit is a berry resembling in all respects the black-berry ; and it is eaten when ripe by the natives, who hold it in much esteem, although they do not dry it for winter consumption. This shrub was first discovered at the en-trance of Quicksand River ; and it grows so abundantly in the fertile valley of the Columbia and on the islands, that the country is almost impenetrable. It retains its verdure until late in the summer.

Besides the fern already described as furnishing a nutri-tious root, there are two other plants of the same species, which may be divided into the large and the small. The large fern rises three or four feet : the stem is a common footstalk, proceeding immediately from the radix, some-what flat, about the size of a man's arm, covered with in-numerable black, coarse, capillary radicles, issuing from every part of its surface ; and a single root sends forth from twenty to forty of these footstalks, bending out ward from the common centre. The ribs are cylindric, their whole length being marked longitudinally with a groove on the upper side ; and on either side of this groove, a little below its edge, the leaflets are inserted. These are shortly petiolate for about two thirds the length of the middle rib, commencing from the bottom, and from thence to the extremity are sessile : the rib is terminated by a single undivided lanceolate leaflet from two to four inches in length, having a small acute angular projection oblique-ly cut at the base. The upper surface is smooth, and of a deep green ; the under of a pale green, and covered with a brown protuberance of a woolly appearance, particularly near the central fibre. The leaflets are alternately pinnate, and in number from one hundred and ten to one hundred and forty : they are shortest at the two extremities of the common footstalk, largest in the centre, gradually length-ening, and diminishing as they succeed each other.

The small fern likewise rises in common footstalks from the radix, from four to eight in number, and from four to eight inches in length. The central rib is marked with a slight longitudinal groove throughout its whole length : the leaflets are oppositely pinnate for about one third of the length of the footstalk from the bottom, and thence alter-nately pinnate. The footstalk terminates in a simple undi-vided lanceolate leaflet, which is oblong, obtuse, convex, entire, and has its upper disk marked with a slight longitu-dinal groove : near the upper extremity these leaflets are decursively pinnate, as are all those of the large fern. Both these species remain green through the winter.

ENUMERATION OF INDIAN NATIONS,

AND

THEIR PLACES OF GENERAL RESIDENCE.

1. THE Shoshonee nation—residing in the spring and summer on the west fork of Lewis's River, a branch of the Columbia, and in the fall and winter on the Missouri : sixty lodges, eight hundred souls.

2. The Ootlashoot tribe of the Tushepah nation—residing in the spring and summer on Clarke's River, within the Rocky Mountains, and in the fall and winter on the Missouri and its tributary waters : thirty-three lodges, four hundred souls.

3. The Chopunnish nation—residing on the Kooskooskee River below the Forks, and on Colter's Creek, and sometimes passing over to the Missouri : thirty-three lodges, two thousand souls.

4. The Pelloatpallah band of the Chopunnish—residing on the Kooskooskee above the forks, and on the small streams which fall into that river west of the Rocky Mountains and the Chopunnish River, and sometimes passing over to the Missouri : thirty-three lodges, sixteen hundred souls.

5. The Kimooenim band of the Chopunnish—residing on Lewis's River, above the entrance of the Kooskooskee, as high up that river as the Forks : thirty-three lodges, eight hundred souls.

6. The Yeletpo band of the Chopunnish—residing along the southwest mountains, on a small river which falls into Lewis's River above the entrance of the Kooskooskee, which they call Weaucum : thirty-three lodges, two hundred and fifty souls.

7. The Willewah band of the Chopunnish—residing on

a river of the same name, which discharges itself int'
Lewis's River on the southwest side, below the Forks c·
that river : thirty-three lodges, five hundred souls.

8. The Soyennom band of the Chopunnish—residing o⊀
the north side of the east fork of Lewis's River, from it
junction to the Rocky Mountains, and on Lamaltar Creek
thirty-three lodges, four hundred souls.

9. The Chopunnish of Lewis's River — residing below
the entrance of the Kooskooskee, on either side of that rivei
to its junction with the Columbia : forty lodges, two thousand three hundred souls.

10. The Sokulk nation—residing on the Columbia above
the entrance of Lewis's River, as high up as the entrance
of Clarke's River : one hundred and twenty lodges, two
thousand four hundred souls.

11. The Chimnahpums—residing on the northwest side
of the Columbia, both above and below the entrance of
Lewis's River, and on the Tapteal River, which falls into
the Columbia fifteen miles above Lewis's River : forty two
lodges, one thousand eight hundred and sixty souls.

12. The Wollawollah nation—residing on both sides of
the Columbia, from the entrance of Lewis's River as low
as the Muscleshell Rapid, and in winter passing over to
the Tapteal River : forty-six lodges, one thousand six hundred souls.

13. The Pishquitpah nation—residing at the Muscleshell
Rapid, and on the north side of the Columbia to the commencement of the high country ; wintering on the borders
of the Tapteal River : seventy-one lodges, two thousand
six hundred souls.

14. The Wahowpum nation — residing on the north
branch of the Columbia, in different bands, from the Pishquitpahs as low as the River Lepage, and wintering on the
banks of Tapteal and Cataract Rivers : thirty-three lodges,
seven hundred souls.

15. The Eneeshur nation—residing at the upper part of
the Great Narrows of the Columbia on either side : forty-
one lodges, twelve hundred souls.

16. The Echeloot nation—also residing at the upper
part of the Great Narrows of the Columbia, on the north
side of which is the great mart for all the courtry : twen
ty-one lodges, one thousand souls.

17. The Chilluckittequaw nation—residing next below the Narrows, and extending down on the north side of the Columbia to the River Labiche: thirty-two lodges, fourteen hundred souls.

18. The Smackshop band of the Chilluckittequaws—residing on the Columbia River, on each side of the entrance of the Labiche, to the neighbourhood of the Grand Rapids of that river: twenty-four lodges, eight hundred souls.

19. The Shahala nation—residing at the Grand Rapids of the Columbia, and extending down in different villages as low as the Multnomah River, consisting of the following tribes: viz., the Yehhuhs, above the Rapids; the Clahclellahs, below the Rapids; the Wahclellahs, below all the rapids; and the Neerchokioos (one house, one hundred lodges), on the south side, a few miles above the Multnomah River: altogether, sixty-two houses, two thousand eight hundred souls.

The Wappatoo Indians, viz.:

20. The Nechacokee tribe—residing on the south side of the Columbia, a few miles below Quicksand River, and opposite Diamond Island: one lodge, one hundred souls.

The Shoto tribe—residing on the north side of the Columbia, back of a pond, and nearly opposite to the entrance of the Multnomah River: eight lodges, four hundred and sixty souls.

The Multnomah tribe—residing on Wappatoo Island, at the mouth of the Multnomah, the remains of a large nation: six lodges, eight hundred souls.

The Clahnahquah tribe of the Multnomahs—residing on Wappatoo Island, below the Multnomahs: four lodges, one hundred and thirty souls.

The Nemalquinner tribe of the Multnomahs—residing on the northeast side of the Multnomah River, three miles above its mouth: four lodges, two hundred souls.

The Cathlacomatups, a tribe of the Multnomahs—residing on the south side of Wappatoo Island, at a bend of the Multnomah: three lodges, one hundred and seventy souls.

The Cathlanahquiahs, a tribe of the Multnomahs—residing on the southwest side of Wappatoo Island: six lodges, four hundred souls.

The Clackstar nation—residing on a small river which discharges itself on the southwest side of Wappatoo Island: twenty-eight lodges, one thousand two hundred souls.

The Claninnatas—residing on the southwest side of Wappatoo Island: five lodges, two hundred souls.

The Cathlacumups—residing on the main shore, southwest of Wappatoo Island: six lodges, four hundred and fifty souls.

The Clannahminamuns—residing on the southwest side of Wappatoo Island: twelve lodges, two hundred and eighty souls.

The Quathlapotle nation — residing on the southwest side of the Columbia, above the entrance of Towahnahiook River, opposite the lower point of Wappatoo Island: fourteen lodges, nine hundred souls.

The Cathlamahs—residing on a creek which falls into the Columbia on the north side, at the lower part of the Columbian Valley: ten lodges, two hundred souls.

21. The Skilloot nation—residing in different villages on both sides of the Columbia, from the lower part of the Columbian Valley to Sturgeon Island, and on either side of the Coweliske River: fifty lodges, two thousand five hundred souls.

The Hullooetells also reside on the Coweliske.

22. The Wahkiacums—residing on the north side of the Columbia, opposite to the Marshy Islands: eleven lodges, two hundred souls.

23. The Cathlamahs—residing on the south side of the Columbia, opposite to the Sea Islands: nine lodges, three hundred souls.

24. The Chinnooks—residing on the north side of the Columbia, at the entrance of and on the Chinnook River: twenty-eight lodges, four hundred souls.

25. The Clatsop nation—residing on the south side of the Columbia, and a few miles along the southeast coast, on both sides of Point Adams: fourteen lodges, two hundred souls.

26. The Killamuck nation—residing from the Clatsops of the coast along the southeast coast for many miles: fifty lodges, one thousand souls. .

Nations speaking the Killamuck Language, concerning which we obtained the following information from the Indians.

27. The Lucktons — residing on the seacoast to the southwest of the Killamucks : twenty souls.

The Kahuncles—residing on the seacoast southwest of the Lucktons : four hundred souls.

The Lukawis—residing on the seacoast to the south-southeast : a large town, eight hundred souls.

The Youikcones—residing on the seacoast to the south-southeast : large houses, seven hundred souls.

The Necketoos—residing on the seacoast to the south-southeast : a large town, seven hundred souls.

The Ulseahs—residing on the seacoast to the south southeast : a small town, one hundred and fifty souls.

The Youitts—residing on the seacoast to the south-southeast : a small town, one hundred and fifty souls.

The Sheastuckles—residing on the seacoast to the south-east of the Lucktons : a large town, nine hundred souls.

The Killawats—residing on the seacoast to the south-east of the Lucktons : a large town, five hundred souls.

28. The Cookkoo-oose nation—residing on the seacoast to the south of the Killawats : one thousand five hundred souls.

The Sahlalah nation—residing on the seacoast to the south of the Killawats : fifteen hundred souls.

The Luckaso nation — residing on the same, to the south : twelve hundred souls.

The Hannakalal nation—residing on the same, to the south : six hundred souls.

Indians along the Coast to the Northwest.

29. The Killaxthocles—residing on the seacoast from the Chinnooks to the north-northwest : eight lodges, one hundred souls.

The Chiltz nation—residing from the Killaxthocles to the north-northwest : thirty-eight lodges, seven hundred souls.

The Clamoitomish—residing from the Chiltz to the north-northwest : twelve lodges, two hundred and sixty souls.

The Potoashees—residing on the coast northwestward of the Clamoitomish : ten lodges, two hundred souls.

The Pailsh tribe—residing northwest of the Potoashees · ten lodges, two hundred souls.

The Quinults—residing northwest of the Pailsh : sixty lodges, one thousand souls.

The Quieetsos — residing northwest of the Quinults: eighteen lodges, two hundred and fifty souls.

The Chillates — residing northwest of the Quieetsos, along the coast : eight lodges, one hundred and fifty souls.

The Calasthocles—residing northwest of the Chillates, along the same coast : ten lodges, two hundred souls.

The Quinnechant nation—residing on the seacoast and a creek, north and northwest of the Calasthocles : two thousand souls.

30. The Clarkamus nation—residing on a large river of the same name, which heads in Mount Jefferson, and dis-charges itself into the Multnomah forty miles up that river on its northeast side : this nation has several villages on either side, and numbers eighteen hundred souls.

31. The Cushooks—residing on the northeast bank of the Multnomah, immediately below the Falls of that river, and about sixty miles above its entrance into the Colum-bia : six hundred and fifty souls.

32. The Charcowah nation—residing on the southwest bank of the Multnomah, immediately above the Falls : two hundred souls.

33. The Callahpoewah nation—inhabiting the country on both sides of the Multnomah, above the Charcowahs for a great extent : two thousand souls.

34. The Shoshonees, or Snake Indians—residing in the fall and winter on the Multnomah River, southward of the Southwest Mountains, and in spring and summer near the heads of the Towahnahiooks, Lepage, Yaumalolam, and Wollawollah Rivers, and especially at the Falls of the Towahnahiooks, for the purpose of fishing : three thousand souls.

35. The Shoshonees on the Multnomah and its tributary waters—their particular places of residence we could not ascertain from the Indians on the Columbia : six thousand souls.

36. The Shobarboobeer band of Shoshonees—residing

on the southwest side of the Multnomah, high up that river : one thousand six hundred souls.

37. The Shoshonees residing on the south fork of Lewis's River, and on the Nemo, Walshlemo, Shallette, Shushpellanimmo, Shecomshink, Timmoonumlarwas, and Copcoppakark Rivers, branches of the south fork of Lewis's River : three thousand souls.

We saw Parts of the following Tribes at the Long Narrows:

38. The Skaddal nation—residing on Cataract River, twenty-five miles north of the Big Narrows : two hundred souls.

The Squannaroos—residing on Cataract River below the Skaddals : one hundred and twenty souls.

The Shallattoos—residing on Cataract River above the Skaddals : one hundred souls.

The Shanwappoms—residing at the heads of the Cataract and Tapteal Rivers : four hundred souls.

39. The Cutsahnim nation—residing on both sides of the Columbia, above the Sokulks, on the northern branches of the Tapteal River, and also on the Wahnaschee : sixty lodges, one thousand two hundred souls.

The Lahanna nation—residing on both sides of the Columbia, above the entrance of Clarke's River : one hundred and twenty lodges, two thousand souls.

The Coospellar nation—residing on a river which falls into the Columbia to the north of Clarke's River : thirty lodges, one thousand six hundred souls.

The Wheelpoo nation—residing on both sides of Clarke's River, from the entrance of the Lastaw to the Great Falls of the first-named river : one hundred and thirty lodges, two thousand five hundred souls.

The Hihighenimmo nation—residing from the entrance of the Lastaw into Clarke's River, on both sides of the former as high as the Forks : forty-five lodges, one thousand three hundred souls.

The Lartielo nation—residing at the Falls of the Lastaw River, below the Great Wayton Lake, on both sides of the river : thirty lodges, six hundred souls.

The Skeetsomish nation—residing on a small river of the same name, which discharges itself into the Lastaw below the Falls, around the Wayton Lake, and on two islands in that lake : twelve lodges, two thousand souls.

The Micksucksealton tribe of the Tushepahs — residing on Clarke's River, above the Great Falls of that river, in the Rocky Mountains : twenty-five lodges, three hundred souls.

The Hohilpos, a tribe of the Tushepahs—residing on Clarke's River above the Micksucksealtons, in the Rocky Mountains : twenty-five lodges, three hundred souls.

The Tushepah nation—residing on a north fork of Clarke's River in spring and summer, and in the fall and winter on the Missouri, the Ootlashoots being a band of this nation : thirty-five lodges, four hundred and thirty souls.

Estimated number of Indians west of the Rocky Mountains, 80,000.*

* Of the tribes occupying the upper part of the Oregon Territory, Mr. Parker numbers the Shoshonees at 10,000 ; the Nez-Percés, 2500 ; the Cayuses, 2000 ; the Wollawollahs, 500 ; the Paloos.'s, along the Pavilion River, 300 ; the Spokains, northeast of the Palooses, 800 ; the *Cœur d'Alène* Indians, 700 ; the Flatheads, to the east and southeast, 800 ; the Pondecas, north of Clarke's River, and on a lake of the name of the tribe, 2200 ; the Cootanies, along M'Gillivray's River, 1000 ; the Canices, north of the Cootanies, 4000 ; the Lake Indians on the Arrow Lakes, 500 , Kettle Falls' Indians, 560 ; the Sinpaivelish, 1000 ; the Okinagans, at the west and northwest, 1050 : of other tribes, wanting the active and manly spirit which he ascribes to the above named, this traveller does not give the numbers. The whole number of those enumerated he estimates at about 32,000, without including the Falls and La Dalle Indians, and other tribes north and south of the Falls, which would, he thinks, more than double that number.

A SUMMARY STATEMENT

OF THE

RIVERS, CREEKS, AND MOST REMARKABLE PLACES,

THEIR DISTANCES FROM EACH OTHER AND FROM THE MISSISSIPPI, UP
THE MISSOURI, ACROSS THE ROCKY MOUNTAINS, AND DOWN THE CO-
LUMBIA TO THE PACIFIC OCEAN, AS DETERMINED BY CAPTAINS
LEWIS AND CLARKE.

	Total Distance.
To the Village of St. Charles	21 : 21
" Osage-Woman's River . . .	20 : 41
" Charette's Village and Creek . .	27 : 68
' Shepherd's Creek	15 : 83
' Gasconade River	17 : 100
' Muddy River	15 : 115
" Grand Osage River	18 : 133
" Murrow Creek	5 : 138
" Cedar Island and Creek . . .	7 : 145
" Leadmine Hill	9 : 154
" Manitou Creek	8 : 162
" Split-Rock Creek	8 : 170
" Saline or Salt River	3 : 173
" Manitou River	9 : 182
" Good-Woman's River	9 : 191
" Mine River	9 : 200
" Arrow Prairie	6 : 206
" Two Charleton Rivers	14 : 220
" Ancient village of the Missouri nation, near which place Fort Orleans stood	16 : 236
" Grand River	4 : 240
" Snake Creek	6 : 246
" Ancient village of the Little Osages .	10 : 256
" Tiger's Island and Creek . . .	20 : 276
" Hubert's Island and Creek . . .	12 : 288

		Total Distance.
To the Fire-Prairie Creek	12 :	300
" Fort Point	6 :	306
" Hay-Cabin Creek	6 :	312
" Coal Bank	9 :	321
" Bluewater River	10 :	331
" Kanzas River	9 :	340
" Little Platte River	9 :	349
" First old Kanzas village . . .	28 :	377
" Independence Creek, a mile below the second old Kanzas village . . .	28 :	405
" St. Michael's Prairie	25 :	430
" Nodawa River	20 :	450
" Wolf or *Loup* River	14 :	464
" Big Nemaha River	16 :	480
" Tarkio Creek	3 :	483
" Neeshnabatona River	25 :	508
" Little Nemaha River	8 :	516
" Baldpated Prairie, the Neeshnabatona, within 150 yards of the Missouri .	23 :	539
" Weeping-water Creek	29 :	568
" River Platte, or Shoal River . .	32 :	600
" Butterfly or *Papillon* Creek . . .	3 :	603
" Moscheto Creek	7 :	610
" Ancient village of the Ottoes . .	11 :	621
" Ancient Ayaways' village, below a bluff, on the northeast side . . .	6 :	627
" Bowyer's River	11 :	638
" Council Bluffs (establishment) . .	12 :	650
" Soldier's River	39 :	689
" Eaneahwaudepon, or Little Sioux River	44 :	733
" Waucarde, or Bad-Spirit Creek . .	55 :	788
" Around a bend of the river to the northeast, the gorge of which is only 974 yards	21 :	809
" Island three miles northeast of the Maha village	27 :	836
" Floyd's Bluff and River . . .	14 :	850
" Big Sioux River	3 :	853
" Commencement of the Copperas, Cobalt, Pyrites, and Alum Bluffs . . .	27 :	880
" Hot or Burning Bluffs	30 :	910
" Whitestone River	8 :	918

			Total Distance.
To the *Petit-Arc*, an old Mahá village at the mouth of Littlebow Creek	.	.	20 : 938
" Jacques, or James's River	.	.	12 : 950
" Calumet Bluff (mineral)	.	.	10 : 960
" Ancient fortification, Goodman's Island			16 : 976
" Plum Creek	.	.	10 : 986
" Whitepoint Creek	.	.	8 : 994
" Quicurre	.	.	6 : 1000
" Poncar River and village	.	.	10 : 1010
" Dome and village of the burrowing squirrels	.	.	20 : 1030
" Island of cedars	.	.	45 : 1075
" White River	.	.	55 : 1130
" Three Rivers of the Sioux Pass	.	.	22 : 1152
" Island at the commencement of the Big Bend	.	.	20 : 1172
" Upper part of the Big Bend, the gorge of which is 1¾ miles	.	.	30 : 1202
" Tylor's River	.	.	6 : 1208
" Loisel's Fort on Cedar Island	.	.	18 : 1226
" Teton River	.	.	37 : 1263
" The upper one of five old Ricara villages, reduced by the Sioux and abandoned	.	.	42 : 1305
" Chayenne River	.	.	5 : 1310
" An old Ricara village on Lahoocat's Island	.	.	47 : 1357
" Sarwarkarna River	.	.	40 : 1397
" Wetarhoo River	.	.	25 : 1422
" The first Ricara village on an island	.		4 : 1426
" Second Ricara three villages	.	.	4 : 1430
" Stone-Idol Creek	.	.	18 : 1448
" Warreconne River	.	.	40 : 1488
" Cannonball River	.	.	12 : 1500
" Chesschetar River, near six old Mandan villages	.	.	40 : 1540
" Old Ricara and Mandan villages	.		40 : 1580
" Fort Mandan (wintering post of 1804)			20 : 1600
" Mandan villages on either side	.	.	4 : 1604
" Knife River, on which, and near its mouth, are the two Minnetaree and Maha villages	.	.	2 : 1606

		Total Distance.
To the Island	11 :	1617
" Miry River	16 :	1633
" Island in the Little Basin . . .	28 :	1661
" Little Missouri River	29 :	1690
" Wild Onion Creek	12 :	1702
" Goose-Egg Lake	9 :	1711
" Chaboneau's Creek	16 :	1727
" Goatpen Creek	16 :	1743
" Hall's Strand, Lake, and Creek . .	47 :	1790
" Whiteearth River	50 :	1840
" *Rochejaune*, or Yellowstone River .	40 :	1880
" Martha's River	60 :	1940
" Porcupine River	50 :	1990
" Little Dry Creek	40 :	2030
" Big Dry Creek	9 :	2039
" Little Dry River	6 :	2045
" Gulf in the Island Bend . . .	32 :	2077
" Milk River	13 :	2090
" Big Dry River	25 :	2115
" Werner's Run	9 :	2124
" Pine Creek	36 :	2160
" Gibson's River	17 :	2177
" Brown Bear-defeated Creek .	12 :	2189
" Bratton's River	24 :	2213
" Burned-lodge Creek	6 :	2219
" Wiser's Creek	14 :	2233
" Muscleshell River	37 :	2270
" Grouse Creek	30 :	2300
" North Mountain Creek . . .	36 :	2336
" South Mountain Creek . . .	18 :	2354
" Ibex Island	15 :	2369
" Goodrich's Island	9 :	2378
" Windsor's Creek	7 :	2385
" Elk Rapid (swift water) . . .	15 :	2400
" Thomson's Creek	27 :	2427
" Judith's River	12 :	2439
" Ash's Rapid (swift water) . . .	4 :	2443
" Slaughter River	11 :	2454
" Stonewall Creek, above the Natural Walls	26 :	2480
" Maria's River	41 :	2521
" Snow River , ' . . .	19 :	2540

Total
Distance.

To Shields's River . . . . . 28 : 2568
To the foot of the entrance of Portage River,
    five miles below the Great Falls . 7 : 2575

   Leaving the Missouri below the Falls, and passing by
land to the navigable waters of the Columbia River,

To the entrance of Medicine River . . 18 : 2593
" Fort Mountain, passing through the
    plain between Medicine River and
    the Missouri, near the Missouri . 15 : 2608
" Rocky Mountains, to a gap on the ridge
    which divides the waters of the Mis-
    souri from those of the Columbia,
    passing the north part of a mount-
    ain, and crossing Dearborn's River 35 : 2643
" Fork of Cohahlarishkit River from the
    north, passing four creeks from the
    north . . . . . . 40 : 2683
" Seaman's Creek from the north . . 7 : 2690
" Werner's Creek from the north . . 10 : 2700
" East fork of Clarke's River, at the en-
    trance of the Cohahlarishkit . . 30 : 2730
" Clarke's River, below the Forks . 12 : 2742
" Traveller's Rest Creek, on the west
    side of Clarke's River, about the
    Forks . . . . . . 5 : 2747
" Forks of Traveller's Rest Creek, at a
    road on the right . . . . 18 : 2765
" Hot Springs on the Creek . . . 13 : 2778
" Quamash Glades, passing the head of
    the Creek to a branch of Kooskoos-
    kee River . . . . . 7 : 2785
" North branch of the Kooskooskee, at a
    road leading off to the right . . 7 : 2792
" Junction of the roads on the top of a
    snowy mountain, the left-hand road
    passing by a fishery . . . 10 : 2802
" To Hungry Creek from the right, pass-
    ing along a dividing mountain cover-
    ed with deep snow except at two pla-

II.—G g

	Total Distance.
ces, which were open, with a southern exposure, at 8 and 36 miles	54 : 2856
To a glade on Hungry Creek	6 : 2862
" a glade on a small branch of the same	8 : 2870
" a glade on Fish Creek	9 : 2879
" Collins's Creek	13 : 2892
" Quamash Flats	11 : 2903
To the Kooskooskee, or Flathead River, in a pine country	12 : 2915

Thus, from the Missouri, across the Rocky Mountains, to the navigable waters of the Columbia, is three hundred and forty miles, two hundred of which is over a good road, and one hundred and forty over rugged mountains, sixty miles of which we found covered with snow from two to eight feet deep in the last of June.

To the entrance of Rockdam Creek	8 : 2923
" Chopunnish River	5 : 2928
" Colter's Creek	37 : 2965
" Lewis's River, at the entrance of the Kooskooskee	23 : 2988
" Sweathouse village and Run	7 : 2995
" Pilot's village	11 : 3006
" Kimooenim Creek	48 : 3054
" Drewyer's River, below the Narrows of Lewis's River	5 : 3059
" Cave Rapid	28 : 3087
" Basin Rapid (bad)	34 : 3121
" Discharge Rapid (bad)	14 : 3135
" Columbia, at the mouth of Lewis's River, from the east	7 : 3142
" Wollawollah River, at eleven large mat lodges of that nation	16 : 3158
" Muscleshell Rapid (bad), at thirty-three mat lodges of the Wollawollahs	25 : 3183
" Pelican Rapid, at forty-eight lodges of the Pishquitpah nation	22 · 3205
" Twenty-one lodges of the Wahowpum nation, residing on three islands at the commencement of the high country	18 · 3223

		Total Distance.
To the eight lodges of the Wahowpums at Short Rapid	27 :	3250
" Rocky Rapid, nine lodges of the same nation	13 :	3263
" Lepage River (bad rapid) . . .	9 :	3272
" Twenty-seven lodges of the Eneeshur nation at Fishstack Rapid . .	10 :	3282
" Towahnahiook River . . .	8 :	3290
" Great Falls of the Columbia of 57 feet 8 inches, near which were forty mat lodges of the Eneeshur nation . .	4 :	3294
" Short Narrows, 45 yards wide . .	2 :	3296
" Skilloot village of twenty-one large wooden houses at the Long Narrows, from 50 to 100 yards wide . .	4 :	3300
" Chilluckittequaw village of eight large wooden houses	5 :	3305
" Cataract River, a few miles below a village of seven houses, and immediately above one of eleven houses of the Chilluckittequaw nation .	19 :	3324
" Sepulchre Rock, opposite to a village of the Chilluckittequaws . . .	4 :	3328
" Labiche River, opposite to twenty-six houses of the Smackshop nation, houses scattered on the north side .	9 :	3337
" Little Lake Creek, three houses of the Smackshops	10 :	3347
" Cruzatte's River	12 :	3359
" Grand Rapid, just below the village of the Yehhuh tribe of the Shahala nation, occupying fourteen wooden houses	6 :	3365
" Clahclellah village of the Shahala nation, near the foot of the Rapids, seven houses	6 :	3371
" Wahclellah village of the Shahala nation, twenty-three houses, just below the entrance of Beacon Rock Creek	6 :	3377

At this point Tide-water commences.

To the Phoca Rock in the river, sixty feet above water	11 :	3388

Total
Distance.

To the Quicksand River   .   .   .   .   9 : 3397
"   Seal River .   . . . . .   3 : 3400
"   Neechaokee village, opposite to Dia-
      mond Island .   . . . .   4 : 3404
"   Shahala village of twenty-five tempo-
      rary houses .   . . . .   12 : 3416
"   Multnomah River   .   .   .   .   14 : 3430
"   Multnomah village   .   .   .   .   6 : 3436
"   Quathlapotle village .   . . .   8 : 3444
"   Towahnahiooks River   .   .   .   1 : 3445
"   Cathlahaw Creek and village   . .   10 : 3555
"   Lower extremity of Elallah, or Deer
      Island .   . . . . .   6 : 3461
"   Coweliske River, about the entrance
      (up this river the Skilloot nation re-
      side) .   . . . . .   13 : 3474
"   Fanny's Island .   . . . .   18 : 3492
"   Sea Otter Island   .   .   .   .   10 : 3502
"   Upper village of the Wahkiacum nation   6 : 3508
"   Cathlamah village of nine large wood-
      en houses, south of Seal Islands   .   14 : 3522
"   Point William, opposite Shallow Bay .   10 : 3532
"   Point Meriwether, above Meriwether
      Bay .   . . . . .   9 : 3541
"   Clatsop village below Meriwether Bay,
      and seven miles northwest of Fort
      Clatsop .   . . . .   8 : 3549
"   Point Adams, at the entrance of the
      Columbia into the Pacific Ocean, in
      latitude 46° 15′ north, and longitude
      124° 57′ west from Greenwich   .   6 : 3555

Fort Clatsop is situated on the west side of, and three
miles up the Netul River from Meriwether Bay, and seven
miles east from the nearest part of the seacoast : here we
passed the winter of 1805–6.

The length of our route in going out, by the way of the
Missouri to its head, was 3096 miles : thence by land, following Lewis's River over to Clarke's River, and down
that river to the entrance of Traveller's Rest Creek, where
all the different roads meet, and thence across the rugged

part of the Rocky Mountains to the navigable waters of the Columbia, was 398 miles: thence down the river to the Pacific Ocean, making the total distance 4134 miles. On our return in 1806, we came from Traveller's Rest Creek directly to the Falls of the Missouri, which shortens the distance about 579 miles, and is a much better route, reducing the distance from the Mississippi to the Pacific Ocean to 3545 miles, 2575 miles of which distance is up the Missouri to the Falls of that river.

THE END.

www.ingramcontent.com/pod-product-compliance
Lightning Source LLC
Chambersburg PA
CBHW022258280326
41932CB00010B/898